The Routledge Doctoral Supervisor's Companion

D1246262

Accompanying *The Routledge Doctoral Student's Companion*, this book examines what it means to be a doctoral student in education and the social sciences, providing a guide for those supervising students. Exploring the key role and pedagogical challenges that face supervisors in students' personal development, the contributors outline the research capabilities that are essential for confidence, quality and success in doctorate-level research. Providing guidance about helpful resources and methodological support, the chapters:

- frame important questions within the history of debates
- act as a road map through international literatures
- make suggestions for good practice
- raise important questions and provide answers to key pedagogical issues
- provide advice on enabling students' scholarly careers and identities.

Although there is no one solution to ideal supervision, this wide-ranging text offers resources that will help supervisors develop their own personal approach to supervision. Ideal for all supervisors whether assisting part-time or full-time students, it is also highly suitable for helping academics to support international students who confront Western doctoral traditions and academic cultures, helping both supervisor and student to understand why things are as they are.

Melanie Walker is Professor of Higher Education at the University of Nottingham, and is also Extraordinary Professor at the University of the Western Cape, South Africa.

Pat Thomson is Professor of Education at the University of Nottingham, and an Adjunct Professor at the University of South Australia and a Visiting Professor at Deakin University, Victoria, Australia.

The Routledge Doctoral Supervisor's Companion

Supporting Effective Research in Education and the Social Sciences

Edited by
Melanie Walker and Pat Thomson

Routledge
Taylor & Francis Group

LONDON AND NEW YORK

BOWLING GREEN STATE
UNIVERSITY LIBRARIES

This first edition published 2010
by Routledge
2 Park Square, Milton Park, Abingdon, Oxon, OX14 4RN

Simultaneously published in the USA and Canada
by Routledge
270 Madison Avenue, New York, NY 10016

Routledge is an imprint of the Taylor & Francis Group, an informa business

© 2010 Melanie Walker and Pat Thomson for selection and editorial material. Individual chapters, the contributors.

Typeset in Bembo by
Taylor & Francis Books
Printed and bound in Great Britain by
TJ International Ltd, Padstow, Cornwall

All rights reserved. No part of this book may be reprinted or reproduced or utilised in any form or by any electronic, mechanical, or other means, now known or hereafter invented, including photocopying and recording, or in any information storage or retrieval system, without permission in writing from the publishers.

British Library Cataloguing in Publication Data
A catalogue record for this book is available from the British Library

Library of Congress Cataloging in Publication Data
The Routledge doctoral supervisor's companion : supporting effective research in education and the social sciences / edited by Melanie Walker and Pat Thomson. – 1st ed.
    p. cm.
Includes bibliographical references.
1. Education–Study and teaching (Graduate)–Handbooks, manuals, etc. 2. Education–Research–Handbooks, manuals, etc. 3. Social sciences–Study and teaching (Graduate)–Handbooks, manuals, etc. 4. Social sciences–Research–Handbooks, manuals, etc. 5. Doctoral students–Handbooks, manuals, etc. I. Walker, Melanie. II. Thomson, Pat, 1948- III. Title: Doctoral supervisor's companion.
    LB2372.E3R683 2010
    370.7'2–dc22
                    2009045976

ISBN10: 0-415-48413-8 (hbk)
ISBN10: 0-415-48414-6 (pbk)
ISBN10: 0-203-85176-5 (ebk)

ISBN13: 978-0-415-48413-8 (hbk)
ISBN13: 978-0-415-48414-5 (pbk)
ISBN13: 978-0-203-85176-0 (ebk)

Contents

List of figures

List of tables

Notes on contributors

Aitchison, Claire PhD is a Senior Lecturer (Postgraduate Literacies) at the University of Western Sydney, Australia. Her research interests are doctoral writing and pedagogies for doctoral education. Recent publications include *Publishing Pedagogies for the Doctorate and Beyond* with B. Kamler and A. Lee (Routledge, 2010) and 'Research Writing Groups' in *Writing Qualitative Research on Practice* (J. Higgs, D. Horsfall and S. Grace, Eds, Sense, 2009).

Bloch, Marianne PhD is Professor in the Department of Curriculum and Instruction at the University of Wisconsin-Madison, with joint appointment in the Department of Gender and Women's Studies. She coordinates the Global Studies, Teaching and the Curriculum masters in C&I at UW–Madison. Recent research and teaching have focused on early education/child care policy, and poststructural, postcolonial and feminist studies of education. Recent books include *Governing children, families, and education: Restructuring the welfare state* (Palgrave, 2003), *Women and Education in Sub-Saharan Africa* (Lynn Reinner, 1998).

David, Miriam PhD is Professor of Sociology of Education and was interim Director of the Teaching and Learning Research Programme at the Institute of Education, University of London. Her research interests include feminist methodologies, diversity, equity and inclusion in postcompulsory and higher education. Her most recent publications include *Improving Learning by Widening Participation in Higher Education* (Routledge, 2009) and editing a special issue of *Higher Education Policy* (March 2009), with L. Morley on 'Celebrations and Challenges: Gender and Higher Education'.

Dixon, Kerryn PhD is a Lecturer in the Applied English Language Department in the School of Education at the University of the Witwatersrand, Johannesburg, South Africa. She has a PhD from the University of the Witwatersrand and is particularly interested in the application of Foucault in educational contexts. Her teaching and research are in the area of critical and early childhood literacy, language policy, world Englishness and research methodology.

Evans, Terry PhD is a Professor of Education at Deakin University, Geelong, Australia. He has supervised many doctoral candidates and also researched, published and taught doctoral education. He has edited, with C. Denholm, three books on doctorates, the latest is *Beyond Doctorates Downunder: maximising the impact of your Australian or New Zealand doctorate* (ACER, 2009).

Golde, Chris PhD is the Associate Vice Provost for Graduate Education at Stanford University, California, USA. Her scholarly interests include the doctoral student experience, disciplinary differences in graduate education, and improving graduate programs. Her recent publications include the books *Envisioning the Future of Doctoral Education* (2006) and *The Formation of Scholars* (2008).

Goode, Jackie PhD is a Senior Research Associate in the Social Sciences Department at Loughborough University. Her education publications include 'Telling tales out of school: connecting the prose and the passion in the learning and teaching of English' (*Qualitative Inquiry*, 2007), 'Empowering or disempowering the international PhD student?: constructions of the dependent and independent learner' (*British Journal of Sociology of Education*, 2007) and '"Managing" Disability: early experiences of university students with disabilities' (*Disability and Society*, 2007).

Gough, Noel PhD is Foundation Professor of Outdoor and Environmental Education and Associate Dean (Academic) in the Faculty of Education, La Trobe University, Victoria, Australia. His research interests include refining poststructuralist methodologies in education, with particular reference to curriculum inquiry, environmental education, and science education.

Grant, Barbara PhD is a Senior Lecturer at The University of Auckland. Her research interests are postgraduate supervision, academic identities and academic development. Her most recent publications include articles on supervision in *London Review of Education* and *Arts and Humanities in Higher Education* and a practical book *Academic Writing Retreats: A facilitator's guide* (HERDSA Guide, 2008)

Harland, Tony PhD is Associate Professor of Higher Education at the University of Otago, New Zealand. His research is founded on a critique of the practices and values of a university education. The questions that concern him are: what ideas are valued in a university education, how are such values informed, and how might they change in the future?

Hughes, Michael PhD is a Senior Research Fellow with the Curtin Sustainable Tourism Centre at Curtin University, Western Australia. Michael's research interests currently revolve around communication and natural and cultural heritage values, and associated beliefs, attitudes and perceptions.

Janks, Hilary PhD is a Professor in the School of Education at the University of the Witwatersrand, Johannesburg, South Africa. Her teaching and research are in the areas of language education in multilingual classrooms, language policy, critical literacy and postgraduate pedagogy. Her work is committed to a search for equity and social justice in contexts of poverty.

Lee, Alison is Professor of Education and Director of the Centre for Research in Learning and Change at the University of Technology, Sydney. She has researched and published in doctoral education, with a focus on supervision, writing and professional doctorates. Her most recent publications in this area include *Changing Practices of Doctoral Education* (with D. Boud, Routledge, 2009) and *Publishing Pedagogies for the Doctorate and Beyond* (with C. Aitchison and B. Kamler, Routledge, 2010).

Leonard, Diana PhD is Emeritus Professor at the Institute of Education University of London and a Visiting Professor at the University of Sussex. Her research interests include gender and education, the history of feminism, and the sociology of postgraduate studies. Her recent publications include *A Women's Guide to Doctoral Studies* (Open University Press, 2001) and with M. Rab 'The inter-relationship of employment, marriage and higher education for Pakistani students in the UK', in Unterhalter, E. and Carpentier, V. (Eds), *Whose interests are we serving? Global inequalities and higher education* (Palgrave, in press).

Manathunga, Catharine PhD is a Senior Lecturer in Higher Education at The University of Queensland, Australia. Her research interests include doctoral education, doctoral supervision pedagogies and the history of teaching and learning in universities. Her most recent publications include 'Research as an intercultural contact zone'. *Discourse: studies in the cultural politics of education.* 30(2): 165–77, and *Making a place: an oral history of academic development in Australia*, which was co-edited with A. Lee and P. Kandlbinder (HERDSA, 2008).

McLeod, Julie PhD is Associate Professor in the Melbourne Graduate School of Education, University of Melbourne. Her research interests encompass youth studies, feminism, inequality and education, and qualitative methodologies. Recent publications include *Researching Social Change: Qualitative Approaches* (with R. Thomson, Sage, 2009) and *Troubling Gender and Education* (edited with J. Dillabough and M. Mills, RoutledgeFalmer).

Middleton, Sue PhD is a Professor in the School of Education, University of Waikato. Combining documentary analysis with life-history narrative methods, her research projects have focused on educational and wider social theories as 'lived' in everyday educational settings. The social history of academic research, especially in the discipline of 'Education' is a particular interest. Sue has researched the experiences and perspectives of doctoral graduates in Education and recently, as part of a team, the supervision of Maori doctoral students.

Moore, Sue PhD is an Associate Professor in Environmental Policy at Murdoch University, Western Australia. Her research focuses on the social aspects of natural resource management.

Morrison-Saunders, Angus PhD is Senior Lecturer in Environmental Assessment at Murdoch University, Western Australia. His research interests focus on the application of environmental impact assessment to achieve sustainable outcomes.

Newsome, David PhD is an Associate Professor in nature based tourism at Murdoch University, Western Australia. His research interests also include geo-tourism and wildlife tourism.

Rizvi, Fazal PhD is Professor of Education in the Department of Educational Policy Studies, University of Illinois. He is also Adjunct Professor at Deakin University, Australia and a Professorial Fellow at the Faculty of Education, University of Melbourne, Australia. His research interests focus on the areas of global studies in education, comparative and international education, internationalisation of higher education, cultural globalisation and education policy, postcolonial theories of identity, representation and education, global inequalities and educational policy and international student mobility.

Robinson-Pant, Anna PhD is Director of the Centre for Applied Research in Education, University of East Anglia. Before coming to UEA, she was based for around 10 years in Nepal as a teacher trainer, educational planner and researcher with various development agencies. Her experiences with participatory action-orientated methodologies and cross-cultural learning in a development context have contributed directly to her UK-focused research – including projects with international students at UEA on their experiences of doctoral supervision. She was awarded the BMW Group Award for Intercultural Learning (Theory Category) 2007 for her research in this area.

Seddon, Terri PhD is Professor of Education at Monash University. She researches in the field of education (life-long learning), focusing particularly on policies and politics of educational work. Her most recent book is *Learning and Work and the Politics of Working Life: Global transformations and collective identities in teaching, nursing and social work* (with L. Henriksson and B. Niemeyer, Routledge, 2009).

Starfield, Sue PhD is Director, the Learning Centre, and Associate Professor, School of Education at the University of New South Wales. She is co-author of *Thesis and Dissertation Writing in a Second Language: A Handbook for Supervisors* (Routledge, 2007). She is currently working on a project examining practice-based doctoral theses in the visual and performing arts. She is co-editor of the journal *English for Specific Purposes*.

Thomson, Pat PhD is Professor of Education in the School of Education, The University of Nottingham and an Editor of the *Educational Action Research Journal*. A former headteacher, her current research focuses on the arts and creativity in school and community change, headteachers' work, and doctoral education. Her recent publications include *Helping doctoral students write: pedagogies for supervision* (with B. Kamler, Routledge, 2006), *Doing visual research with children and young people* (Routledge, 2008) and *School leadership-heads on the block?* (Routledge, 2009).

Trigwell, Keith PhD is Professor of Higher Education at The University of Sydney, Australia. He was formerly Reader in Higher Education at the University of Oxford where he conducted research into the student experience of learning. His research interests also include scholarship of teaching and learning and research–teaching relations.

Unterhalter, Elaine PhD is Professor of Education and International Development, Institute of Education, University of London with research interests in gender, education, and development. Recent books include *Gender, Schooling and Global Social Justice* (RoutledgeFalmer, 2007), and *Towards gender equality. South Africa Schools during* *the HIV and Aids epidemic* (University KwaZulu Natal Press, 2009 with R. Morrell, D. Epstein, D. Bhana and R. Moletsane).

Walker, Melanie PhD is Professor of Higher Education in the School of Education, The University of Nottingham and Extraordinary Professor at the University of the Western Cape, South Africa. Her research explores the normative purposes of higher education and its potential contribution to more equal societies under contemporary policy and economic conditions, and to poverty reduction. She is former Director of Postgraduate Students and current Director of Research. She co-edits the *Journal of Human Development and Capabilities*. Her recent publications include *Amartya Sen's Capability Approach and Social Justice in Education* (with E. Unterhalter, Palgrave, 2007), and *Higher education pedagogies* (Open University Press, 2006).

Watts, Jacqueline PhD is Senior Lecturer in the Health & Social Care Faculty at the Open University, UK. Her research interests include postgraduate research education, gender and the professions, social context of death and dying. Her work has been published in leading journals such as *Work, Employment and Society*; *Qualitative Research*; *Illness, Crisis and Loss*; *European Journal of Palliative Care*; *Feminism and Psychology*; *Teaching in Higher Education*; and *Open Learning*.

Using this book

Volume 2 is not a duplicate of Volume 1. Our intention in compiling these texts was to produce two complementary volumes. We imagine that many supervisors/advisers and doctoral researchers will not only want to read the text specifically designed for them, but will also find resources that are useful in the other text. We hope that both supervisors/advisers and doctoral researchers will in fact draw selectively on both volumes and find resources that they want to work on together. We are confident that scholars who are responsible for doctoral education courses and supervisor training programmes will select materials from each volume. In each of these cases we see chapters being used as conversation starters, frames and/or guides, rather than recipes or answers.

Volume 2, Part 1

The first half of this volume reframes supervision as pedagogical practice(s). We understand that the concept of pedagogy/ies reads differently in different locations and disciplinary traditions. However, we see it as a preferable notion to that of supervision, which, in managerial times has an unfortunate resonance with technical processes of surveillance and audit. It is also preferable in our view to the terminology of teaching and learning, which omits substantive questions of knowledge and context altogether in favour of a strongly process orientation.

We understand pedagogy to refer to both theories and practices of knowledge production. We believe that the term pedagogy/ies includes questions of what kinds of knowledge are to be produced, their disciplinary boundaries, traditions and conventions. But it also covers teaching/learning (both formal and informal), as well as how learning is to be demonstrated and assessed. In the context of higher education, doctoral pedagogies are enacted in the conversations between supervisors/advisors and students, and in the numerous interactions about texts, particularly research schedules and tools, drafts and the final thesis texts itself. Supervisors differ in their approaches to pedagogical practice and have various preferences for the kind and amount of writing for instance that is undertaken, the way in which feedback is given, and the kinds of interventions that they make. However, what happens between supervisors and doctoral researchers is strongly framed by disciplinary and institutional conventions, as well as higher education policies and broader geographically and historically situated scholarly traditions.

Although there are enormous differences in the ways in which supervision and pedagogy/ies can be discussed and debated, we are confident in saying that there is still far too little public conversation and scholarship. Supervision in particular is highly privatised, and something that largely happens behind closed doors between consenting adults. Whereas contemporary managerial practices seek to prise open our office doors to count, monitor and regulate what goes on in supervision/advising, our intention here is to present a series of chapters that create a space for collegial conversations, as well as conversations with the doctoral researchers whom we educate. We do not endorse supervision pedagogies as individualised and secretive pastimes, but want instead to promote more open and generative dialogue about what it means to supervise/advise.

The challenges in supervision pedagogies

This volume is specifically designed to raise questions about pedagogy and about the kinds of challenges faced by supervisors. Like any other pedagogical process, supervising doctoral students generates both pleasures and challenges, all the more in contemporary higher education, given the context of globalisation, internationalisation and different modes of doctoral study and diversity in doctoral students, further complicated by the changing nature of higher education, the changing environment for doctoral study and students' own differing purposes for their research (Chapter 1). There are more students, more diverse students, with more diverse aims and plans; increasingly not all doctoral graduates will choose professional lives in the university as might have been the pedagogical assumption in the past.

So what are some of these challenges? The basic challenges must still be to enable a student to successfully complete his or her dissertation in a reasonable amount of time; to foster a productive and enriching pedagogical relationship in which the student grows in confidence and discernment into his or her scholarly and critical identity; and, the supervisor reflexively improves his or her own pedagogical approach, pedagogical repertoire and professional judgement through working with different kinds of students. These are intense and delicate relationships so that, like other pedagogies, doctoral pedagogy demands practitioners who are open to peer learning (and listening to students talk about their learning) and pedagogical dialogue and discussion, a particular challenge in the light of the rather disabling privatised tradition we noted above. Yet there is a huge amount to be learned from each other, and when given the opportunity to find out about the good practices of colleagues, supervisors, we find, respond with interest and enthusiasm. Such peer exchange helps us to make judgements about the quality of our own work and to counter the emphasis on a managerial tickbox compliance culture, increasingly infecting doctoral level study.

The diversity of students, we think, poses particular challenges and tremendous pleasures. For example, many supervisors work with part-time students who are usually mature mid-career professionals well established in a particular field. These students not only have to balance doctoral study, work and personal commitments, but also have to contend with forming a new identity as doctoral scholar in which they are, at least in the early stages, cast in the role of novice learner and student in contrast to their professional standing. The length of part-time doctoral study means that the unexpected can and usually does crop up for many students, so that the process of supporting but also enabling part-time students to manage their doctoral research and progress demands considerable pedagogical skill and enabling relationships.

Most universities also now find themselves with increasing numbers of doctoral students from other countries, many of whom will conduct their doctoral research in a second language. Both student and supervisor need to come to terms with cross-cultural issues in working together respectfully, as well as different approaches to academic writing and knowledge, while also genuinely valuing the richness that international students bring to the research environment in a particular department. Supervisors need to develop and expand their own cross-cultural capabilities, and try to understand how the academic world and this new place looks to their students, what Martha Nussbaum calls having a 'narrative imagination'.

Perhaps the greatest challenge – and the greatest reward – is that there is no one right way to supervise, and each individual student presents new challenges across some or all of the stages of doctoral study, with the pedagogical relationship having to be adapted and tailored to the particular biography, experiences, and abilities of each new student. Although supervision experience helps in developing good pedagogy, it by no means guarantees success. There is always more to learn and to talk about with each other in enabling the production of worthwhile research, responsibly open to the challenges facing us in the world today, research that asks significant questions and produces valuable knowledge.

Part 1

Introduction

Why *The Doctoral Companions?*

M. Walker and P. Thomson

The Doctoral Companions are designed for doctoral researchers and their supervisors/advisers to read separately and together. The two volumes are neither advice books nor commentaries on the experiences of doctoral research and supervision. Their purpose is to provide complementary and situating commentary about doctoral research and to map key debates that work in and around the burgeoning research methods and doctoral literatures.

Indeed, there are an ever-expanding number of books available to support doctoral research – doing it-guides, toolkits and advice books, methods books, research and evidence-informed policy and practice and how-to-get published. There are countless methodology and methods texts. There is a growing literature on the changing nature of the doctorate, on the doctorate in different parts of the world, on the doctorate and the knowledge economy, on supervision, student experiences and the viva. However, this extensive literature is difficult for doctoral researchers and their supervisors to navigate and will thus not necessarily take students forward in their own doctoral projects. Supervisors are often unaware that their students are consulting advice books and, due to the existence of postgraduate methods training courses, may assume that students understand the nature of the enterprise in which they are involved. Their own intensifying work load also militates against supervisors taking time away from the details of specific supervision projects to engage in more general conversations about the doctorate and the processes of doctoral researchers becoming scholars. Students therefore may well end up confused, with the result that they may follow unproductive methodological and philosophical explorations. Alternatively, they may simply feel inadequate when apparently straightforward advice fails to do the trick. Holbrook and Johnston (1999) explain that such books are unhelpfully decontextualised and fail to acknowledge the messiness of real lives, not amenable to easy control or resolution. They write that, 'Tears and tantrums, frustrations, phobias and personal agendas are missing, so are the supervisors who do have the correct answer or students with unmanageable problems' (1999: 7). Our goal is to support doctoral researchers and their supervisors to interrogate the many catalogues of texts now available for doctoral purchase.

The widely read and highly successful books (Cham 2008a; 2008b; 2008c) and the comic strip titled 'Piled Higher and Deeper' (PhD), developed by graduate student Jorge

Cham, offer a humorous take on the life of a graduate student inhabiting a 'world of grant deadlines, employment worries, political correctness and other sources of relentless angst' (Marcus 2009: 1). The most common response to Cham's comic books and the lectures he gives at universities in the USA on the graduate experience is, he says, about students' sense of alienation and isolation so that doctoral students, 'feel like they're the only ones having these difficulties with their advisers or their funding agencies, that they're lost or they don't really know what they're doing with their lives ... they see that there are other people out there like them' (Marcus 2009: 2). Cham's books develop comic characters who resonate with readers and take on a life of their own, characters such as 'Mike Slackenerny' and 'Cecilia'. Of academics Cham says, that while being a graduate student is hard going, 'being a professor is even worse' (Marcus 2009: 2). His website is replete with comments from doctoral students at different stages of their endeavour from around the globe (see www.phdcomics.com), suggesting that he has managed to capture, in ways that advice books often do not, the everyday experience of doctoral research.

The reason Cham's cartoons resonate so strongly with doctoral researchers is, we think, because he addresses one of their key challenges. 'Getting' the doctorate is always much more than simply completing the research – in reality it is about becoming and being a scholar. Being scholarly and becoming a scholar are tasks integral to becoming part of, and belonging to, an academic community. Doing a quality doctorate in contemporary times requires more than the technical skills required of a research process; it involves coming to see oneself as a researcher and taking on a confident and articulate researcher identity. This book, therefore, has an integrating theme of exploring how identity and knowledge formation happen together. Producing 'an original contribution to knowledge' is also to construct oneself as a scholar. These two volumes address a set of interlocking and overlapping big questions that run through the practice of knowledge/ identity work.

We take the view that becoming a researcher involves engaging with a range of ideas and issues mediated through a particular research project. We believe that our texts will enable students and their supervisors to navigate their way through the vast library of doctoral and research books by bringing together questions that are generally scattered through a range of texts. For example, discussions about the importance of public intellectual work rarely sit alongside questions of getting started on a research project, or discussions about how to choose a research method together with a conversation about the power relationships embedded in scholarship. Yet, in today's internationalised higher education systems and globalised societies, *not* to bring these things together is to create myopic and unnecessarily parochial and partial understandings of the institutionalised enterprise of knowledge production.

Moreover, these are not yet more books on competing paradigms, how to do a piece of doctoral work from beginning to end, a view of the doctorate that comprises 'tips and tricks', approaches to 'writing up' a thesis, or a set of researcher biographies. Rather, *The Doctoral Companions* place at their centre the interwoven questions of what it means to be a doctoral student in the social sciences, and what is involved in becoming and being a researcher. They further ask what 'capabilities' through research are key to confidence, quality and success. We also provide pragmatic and practical thinking about progressing research/scholarly career and identity.

The rationale behind the two volumes is not simply that the concerns of doctoral researchers and their supervisors are both shared and different, rather we hope to promote dialogue. However important it is that students establish and join peer communities amongst whom they exchange and circulate the nascent knowledge they are producing and the joys and tribulations that accompany this process, it is in the inter-relationship of student and supervisors that young scholars are produced as confident and successful researchers, or where confidence is as easily diminished. The books, therefore, address the sorts of questions that need to be taken up by developing researchers and which can fruitfully be discussed with supervisors. We suspect from our conversations with doctoral researchers at our own institution, at national and international conferences, and from a variety of reports and research articles, that doctoral candidates want more than conversations about their substantive research. They also want focused 'insider' discussion about 'the rules of the game', what it means to be a scholar, and the purposes and practices of higher education. Much of what appears in the doctoral companions is directed to this end. Authors do not seek to provide answers, but rather to raise issues, which can then be pursued further.

The organisation of *The Doctoral Companions*

Briefly, now, something about the design of each Volume. We have organised both books into large sections, each addressing a key theme associated with becoming and being a doctoral scholar. Volume 1 addresses doctoral students and Volume 2 their supervisors. There is some deliberate repetition of material across the two volumes but we also envisage supervisors finding much of interest in Volume 1, and students locating material of interest in Volume 2.

We begin both volumes by outlining the current global and national policy climate for doctoral education and explain the rapid rise up higher education policy agendas of doctoral students. In Volume 1, Part 2, we take up the theme of becoming a doctoral student and some of the issues students are likely to confront early in their journeys. In Part 3, we address a range of issues around coming to terms with research practice. Chapter authors take up issues and questions; they do not try to address the practical detail of doing a research project but offer ways into thinking about what it means to do and be a doctoral student. We then address the question that sits at the heart of the doctorate but is often rather vaguely explained, that of making a contribution to knowledge (although see Yates 2004). Quite what does it mean to make an original contribution? Do different kinds of knowledge count? Who are the students and does their knowledge count at all? We then draw together these interlocking and overlapping themes in our concluding chapter. After the introductory section in Volume 2, we focus on supervision pedagogies, creating productive doctoral education cultures, making contributions to scholarly knowledge and then draw these together in our conclusion. In Volume 2 we also summarise and link as appropriate back to Volume 1.

The brief we gave to the chapter authors was broad and open. We invited specific contributions, sent everybody the outline for both volumes and then trusted authors to decide how they might take up the specifics of their own contribution. We think they have all risen magnificently to this challenge. In many cases there are references to further helpful work by authors, which can be followed up; while their references provide further access to additional helpful resources.

We want to emphasise that these books are not necessarily linear in their workings. Each chapter in and of itself offers a challenge and an invitation to doctoral readers to reflect on their own learning to become and to be, and to provide also resources to support and reflect on this becoming. We imagine readers moving backwards and forwards across the big themes, revisiting early themes and engaging later themes even at an early stage of their studies. We hope that readers will continue to draw on the resources of the book in ways that support their own individually staged doctoral development.

Our understandings, ambitions and acknowledgements

We embarked on this extensive editorial project because of our commitments to the value and process of high quality in doctoral education. We understand the doctorate as a relational and pedagogical project of student/supervisor development and identity formation, grounded in the shared project of addressing significant questions and making knowledge under specific contextual and policy conditions. This sounds serious but we also believe that the doctoral experience ought to be about excitement, engagement and achievement. We know it is also often one of remaking identities, of considerable intellectual challenge, and of emotional bumps and bruises.

Doctoral education and the experience of doing a doctorate ought, we think, to be a period when students develop knowledge, 'capabilities' (Sen 1999) and relationship resources for continuing their 'life-long' professional journeys, including new and unpredictable doctoral study challenges. Experiences of doctoral education – positive and life-enhancing, or narrowing horizons and self-belief – will, we believe, shape life-long learner identities. As supervisors, we hope for the former rather than the latter, while recognising that each doctoral venture is biographical, complicated and partly unpredictable. As with any pedagogy or educational process, we cannot pin down the one right way – and nor would we want to – but we can develop knowledge resources that help us work towards better practices produced in the interstices of the student, her thesis, her university context, and our supervision interlaced across all three.

Our interests in putting together this extensive edited collection as researchers and doctoral supervisors and examiners ourselves, with personal experience of doctoral education in three different countries and an international network of supervisor colleagues, is the growing significance of doctoral education as a site of practice in universities internationally. The shift in attention to doctoral education over the last 15 years or so has been remarkable: from a kind of cottage industry involving individual students and supervisors with disciplinary expertise, to a deepening focus for policy, research and publications of diverse kinds. Under contemporary conditions of the knowledge economy and the need for professional credentials beyond the masters level, doctorates in education are of increased importance and professional value to practitioners in a variety of professional settings. More and more people are doing doctorates, not only because new forms of work require higher knowledge production capabilities developed through research, but also because of credential inflation. Students are looking to make an economic and educational investment in their own workplace careers; the doctorate is no longer only about becoming a career academic in a university.

We take education in its broadest sense as our field of concern and we hope that the two volumes will be of broad interest in the social sciences. But we think it is not surprising that so much of the work on doctoral education emanates from scholars who see education and pedagogy as the subject of research. We have been informed by a variety of research into doctoral education – for example, signature pedagogies in doctoral education (Golde 2007); a rich and growing field of research on doctoral writing pedagogies from early work by Connell (1985) to recent studies (Bendix Petersen 2007; Kamler and Thomson 2006; Kamler and Thomson 2008; Paltridge and Starfield 2007); supervision practices and pedagogies (Brew and Peseta 2008; Boucher and Smith 2006; Delamont *et al.* 1997; Denholm and Evans 2007; Hasrati 2005; Grant 2003; Green 2005; Holligan 2005; Lamm 2004; Lee 2008; Li and Searle 2007; Manathunga 2005a; 2005b; Murphy *et al.* 2007; Neumann 2005; Sambrook *et al.* 2008); emerging attention to more collective models of supervision and collaborative knowledge sharing environments (Malfroy 2005; Parker 2009); pedagogies of doctoral publishing (Lee and Kamler 2008; Kamler 2008); professional doctorates (Brennan 1998; Evans 1997; Scott *et al.* 2004; Maxwell *et al.* 2008; Wellington and Sikes 2006); supervising professional doctorates (Health 2006); doctoral student development (Gardner 2008); managerialism and supervision processes (Cribb and Gewirtz 2006); and doctoral education and future academic faculty development and recruitment (Ehrenberg and Kuh 2008).

It is particularly noteworthy that this research literature has been generated primarily in the last five years, and although there is much of value to supervisors, it is an expansive terrain to negotiate in busy academic lives. We hope, therefore, in these two volumes to signpost key debates and findings from this emergent corpus of research.

We not only owe an intellectual debt to the community of doctoral education researchers, but we also have had considerable practical assistance in putting *The Doctoral Companions* together and to bed. Producing two edited volumes of this size has been greatly helped by the sterling secretarial support we have had from Uta Feinstein, who developed an effective system to keep track of the large number of contributors and has been the central point of contact for authors. She was also instrumental in the last stages of getting the texts ready for the publishers. Helen Hearn and Tham Nguyen, doctoral students in the School of Education, efficiently undertook some of the early copy-editing support. Martina Daykin also provided secretarial support. We are very grateful for the help we have received from all four of them, and for the support of the School of Education for this project. We must also thank Philip Mudd, our commissioning editor at Routledge, who first raised the possibility of the books with us, who provided feedback on our evolving idea to sharpen our thinking on focus, structure and organisation of the two volumes, and who has been encouraging throughout. Finally, our long-suffering partners, Randy Barber and Ian Phimister, have inevitably lived this project with us and there is little doubt that our efforts here depended on their support. Our dogs, too, have played their part in providing welcome unconditional regard!

In conclusion, we must also thank the following authors and publishers for permission to reprint chapters that have previously appeared elsewhere, although most have been revised and updated for this publication:

(1) Terry Evans 'Supervising part time candidates'. Adapted from T. Evans (2007) 'Effective supervision of part-time candidates'. In Denholm, C. and Evans, T. D. (Eds) *Supervising Doctorates Downunder: keys to effective supervision in Australia and New Zealand*. Melbourne, ACER Press. Revised and reprinted with permission from ACER.

(2) Noel Gough 'The truth is not out there: becoming "undetective" in social and educational inquiry; Crime fiction and social inquiry: intertextual continuities'. Adapted from N. Gough (2002) 'Fictions for representing and generating semiotic consciousness: the crime story and educational inquiry'. *International Journal of*

5

Applied Semiotics, 3(2): 59–76. Revised and reprinted with permission from Atwood publishing, www.atwoodpublishing.com

(3) Barbara Grant 'Negotiating the layered relations of supervision'. Adapted from B Grant (2003) 'Mapping the Pleasures and Risks of Supervision'. *Discourse* 24(2): 175–90. Revised and reprinted with permission from Taylor & Francis.

(4) Elaine Unterhalter 'Global social justice, critical policy, and doctoral pedagogical spaces'. Adapted from E. Unterhalter (2009) 'Global justice or other people's problems? Computer gaming and critical reflection in an international classroom'. *London Review of Education*, 7(1): 41–53. Revised and reprinted with permission from Taylor & Francis.

(5) Jacqueline Watts 'Supervising part-time doctoral students. Issues and Challenges'. Adapted from J. H. Watts (2008) *Challenges of supervising part-time students: towards student-centred practice*, *Teaching Higher Education*, 13(3), 369–73.

References

Bendix Petersen, E. (2007) Negotiating academicity: postgraduate research supervision as category boundary work, *Studies in Higher Education*, 32(4): 475–88

Boucher, C. and Smith, A. (2006) Up close and personal: reflections on our experience of supervising research candidates who are using personal reflective techniques, *Reflective Practice*, 5(3): 345–56.

Brennan, M. (1998), Struggles over the definition and practice of the Educational Doctorate in Australia, *Australian Educational Researcher* 25(1): 71–89.

Brew, A. and Peseta, T. (2008). Supervision development and recognition in a reflexive space. In Boud, D. and Lee, A. (eds). Changing Practices of Doctoral Education. New York and London: Routledge, 126–39.

Cham, J. (2008a) *Piled Higher and Deeper*. Los Angeles, CA: Piled Higher and Deeper LLC.

——(2008b) *Life is Tough and Then You Graduate*. Los Angeles, CA: Piled Higher and Deeper LLC.

——(2008c) *Scooped! the Third Piled Higher and Deeper*. Los Angeles, CA: Piled Higher and Deeper LLC.

Connell, R.W. (1985) How to Supervise a PhD, *Vestes*, 2: 38 (Available at www.ph.unimelb.edu.au/pgss/2520/node33.html. Accessed 5 January 2008.)

Cribb, A. and Gewirtz, S. (2006) Doctoral student supervision in a managerial climate, *International Studies in Sociology of Education*, 16 (3): 223–36.

Delamont, S., Atkinson, P. and Parry, O. (1997) *Supervising the PhD*. Buckingham: SRHE/Open University Press.

Denholm, C. and Evans, T. (Eds) (2007) *Supervising Doctorates Downunder*. Camberwell, ACER Press.

Ehrenberg, R. G. and Kuh, C. V. (Eds) (2008) *Doctoral Education and the Faculty of the Future*. Ithaca, NY: Cornell University Press.

Evans, T. (1997) Flexible doctoral research: emerging issues in professional doctorate programs, *Studies in Continuing Education*, 19(2): 174–82.

Gardner, S. (2008) *The Development of Doctoral Students: Phases of challenge and support: ASHE Higher Education Report, 34*. San Francisco, CA: Jossey Bass

Golde, C. M. (2007) Signature pedagogies in doctoral education: Are they adaptable for the preparation of education researchers? *Educational Researcher*, 36(6): 344–51.

Grant, B. (2003) Mapping the pleasures and risks of supervision, *Discourse*, 24(2): 175–90.

Green, B. (2005) Unfinished business: subjectivity and supervision, *Higher Education Research and Development*, 24(2): 151–63.

Hasrati, M. (2005) Legitimate peripheral participation and supervising PhD students, *Studies in Higher Education*, 30(5): 557–70.

Health, L. (2006) Supervision of professional doctorates: education doctorates in English universities, *Higher Education Review*, 38(2): 21–41.

Holbrook, A. and Johnston, S. (Eds) (1999) *Supervision of postgraduate research in education*. Coldsteam: AARE.

Holligan, C. (2005) Fact and fiction: a case history of doctoral supervision, *Educational Research*, 47(3); 267–78.

Kamler, B. (2008) Rethinking doctoral publication practices: writing from and beyond the thesis, *Studies in Higher Education*, 33(3); 283–94.

Kamler, B. and Thomson, P. (2004) Driven to abstraction: doctoral supervision and Writing pedagogies, *Teaching in Higher Education*, 9(2); 195–210.

——(2006) *Helping doctoral students write. Pedagogies for supervision*. London: Routledge.

——(2008) The failure of dissertation advice books: Toward alternative pedagogies for doctoral writing. *Educational Researcher*, 37(8), 507–14.

Lamm, R. (2004) *Nurture or challenge in research higher degree supervision*. Paper presented at the annual conference of the Australian Association for Research in Education, Melbourne 28 November to 2 December 2004.

Lee, A. and Kamler, B. (2008) Bringing pedagogy to doctoral publishing, *Teaching in Higher Education*, 13(5): 511.

Lee, A. (2008) How are doctoral students supervised? Concepts of doctoral research supervision, *Studies in Higher Education*, 33(3); 267–81.

Li, S. and Searle, C. (2007) Managing criticism in PhD supervision: a qualitative case study, *Studies in Higher Education*, 32(4): 511–26.

Malfroy, J. (2005) Doctoral supervision, workplace research and changing pedagogic practices, *Higher Education Research and Development*, 24(2): 165–78.

Manathunga, C. (2005a) The development of research supervision: 'turning the light on a private space', *International Journal for Academic Development*, 10(1): 17–30.

——(2005b) Early warning signs in postgraduate research education: a different approach to ensure timely completions, *Teaching in Higher Education*, 10(2): 219–33.

Marcus, G. (2009) Comic-strip hero, *THE*, 12 February 2009 (Available at www.timeshighereducation. co.uk/story.asp?sectioncode=26&storycode=405321. Accessed 9 July 2009.)

Maxwell, T.W., Hickey, C. and Evans, T. (Eds) (2008) *Working doctorates: the impact of Professional Doctorates in the workplace and professions*. Revised papers from the fifth Professional Doctorates conference, Deakin University.

Murphy, N., Bain, J. D. and Conrad, L. (2007) Orientations to research higher degree supervision, *Higher Education*, 53(2): 209–34.

Neumann, R. (2005) Doctoral differences: professional doctorates and PhD compared, *Journal of Higher Education Policy and Management*, 27(2): 173–88.

Paltridge, B. and Starfield, S. (2007) *Thesis and dissertation writing in a second language*. London: Routledge.

Parker, R. (2009) A learning community approach to doctoral education in the social sciences, *Teaching in Higher Education*, 14 (1): 43–59.

Sambrook, S., Stewart, J. and Roberts, C. (2008) Doctoral supervision … a view from above, below and the middle! *Journal of Further and Higher Education*, 32(1): 71–84.

Scott, D., Brown, A., Lunt, I. and Thorne, L. (2004) *Professional doctorates: Integrating academic and professional knowledge*. Maidenhead: SRHE/Open University Press.

Sen, A. (1999) *Development as freedom*. Oxford: Oxford University Press.

Wellington and Sikes (2006) 'A doctorate in a tight compartment': Why do students choose a professional doctorate and what impact does it have on their personal and professional lives? *Studies in Higher Education*, 31 (6): 723–34.

Yates, L. (2004) *What does Good Education Research look like?* Maidenhead: Open University Press.

1

Doctoral education in context

The changing nature of the doctorate and doctoral students

P. Thomson and M. Walker

In June 1996, *The Times Higher Education Supplement* (A. Thomson 1996) reported on a discussion paper called 'Quality and Standards of Postgraduate Research Degrees', produced by the United Kingdom Council for Graduate Education (UKCGE). The article suggested that the postgraduate research sector needed urgent review to secure better quality monitoring, and commented that funding councils had focused little attention on doctoral education because they were more concerned with undergraduate and masters courses. According to the UKCGE report, there was now an urgent need for discussion and clarification of the issues concerning postgraduate research, not least because of a 'dramatic' increase in postgraduates doing research, (A. Thomson 1996). Illustrative figures from the Higher Education Funding Council for England showed a 310 per cent increase in postgraduate research (masters and doctoral) between 1979 and 1994, (HEFCE 1996). The report argued for the need to establish effective postgraduate quality assurance policies and procedures, and monitoring and enhancement mechanisms to reassure 'stakeholders', including students.

Earlier that same year the *THES* had published an article by Davies (1996) on 'What is the role of a PhD supervisor?' pointing to the variation in the quality of support students received, and anticipating the debates that were to accelerate over the next decade. Davies reported the, 'by no means exceptional' experiences, of one PhD student whose relationship had broken down with his supervisor, pointing to the problematic power relations inherent in the relationship. As a result this student did not expect to complete his doctorate, saying:

> I was taken on as a research assistant without meeting (him), and when I arrived it turned out he didn't have a PhD and hadn't supervised before. ... There has been a breakdown in our relationship. But my funding depends on my supervisor – he's an expert in the area – and the institution doesn't really have anyone to replace him. I'm an outsider and he is an insider – anything I say carries no weight. I do have a second supervisor, but she doesn't have the time to see me. There have been four postgraduates in the past two years in my department, and I'm the only one left. Maybe if I'm lucky I'll get an MPhil here, but I don't have any control over my funding, and I'll need a reference from this institution if I look for a job.
>
> Davies 1996: 1

In the same article, Davies (1996) quotes Tricia Skuse, who was then finishing a psychology PhD; she observed that a wide range of different supervisory problems exist because:

> [O]ne of the fundamental problems with PhDs in Britain is that nothing's standardized. I have friends who start their PhD, see a supervisor a few times and then they're left to fend for themselves. In other universities supervisors will go with you and help you set up your fieldwork, or help you do your analysis and give you a training in research skills.
>
> Davies 1996: 1

The 1996 Chairman's Foreword to the Harris Report on postgraduate education (HEFCE 1996: 1) highlighted 'the central importance of high quality postgraduate education to the creation of the ever more highly skilled workforce which is necessary if the United Kingdom is to flourish in an increasingly complex and competitive world', but also 'the benefits which education at this level, now delivered in a multiplicity of ways, brings to individuals and, through them, to society as a whole'. In the next decade, there was a flurry of policy activity in the UK. By 2006, in the wake of the Harris Report (HEFCE 1996), the HEPI Report (2004) on higher education supply and demand, and the development of UKGCE and the Quality Assurance Agency (QAA) standards for doctoral education, the field and arena of doctoral education had changed considerably, driven at least in part by the fact that postgraduates were by then increasingly seen as the best source for future university income (Leonard *et al.* 2006; Park 2007).

Nor have these developments been confined to the UK. In Australia, in 1996 Australian universities awarded just fewer than 3,000 PhDs across all subjects. By 2006 the total number was more than 5,500, an 85 per cent increase (Western and Lawson 2008: 1; and see Evans in Chapter 5). This expansion was accompanied by intense interest in the process of supervision, with Australian researchers arguably leading the field in investigating the many facets of research supervision in education at a time when there was little empirical research taking place elsewhere. Notably, a pioneering collection edited by Holbrook and Johnston (1999: 6) explored the process and culture of research supervision within the field of education in Australian universities in order to render both less opaque and hence open to improvement. The editors observed that manuals of procedures and lists of suggestions do not successfully address cultures of doctoral education and supervision because getting a PhD involves more than 'generating a product or perfecting a set of skills'. They pointed instead to the significance of acquiring an academic identity, of belonging to a research culture, and of the work–life pressures that practical self-help books do not address.

In the USA, 52,600 doctorates were awarded in 2004–5, a 14 per cent increase on the figure of 1997–8 (Western and Lawson 2008: 1), while around 1.7 million graduate students study at USA universities alone (Marcus 2009). Not surprisingly, given these figures, the Carnegie Foundation for the Advancement of University Teaching established an *Initiative on the Doctorate* and commissioned essays edited by Golde and G. Walker (2006) on envisaging its future, including in education (Berliner 2006; Richardson 2006). With a focus on doctoral students as the future 'stewards of the disciplines', the essays express a deep concern with the goals and purposes of doctoral education, and especially with the development of a doctoral scholar as 'someone who will creatively generate new knowledge, critically conserve valuable and useful ideas, and responsibly transform those understandings through writing, teaching, and application' (Golde, 2006: 5).

In others parts of Europe, doctoral education is similarly expanding and transforming. Considerable changes have taken place over the last decade as doctoral training and education has come under scrutiny as an object of interest to policy makers in the face of global competition for talented 'knowledge worker' doctoral students (Bleiklie and Hostaker 2004; Bitusikova 2009; Kehm 2007; Leonard *et al.* 2006; Szkudlarek in Volume 1). In 1999, The Bologna Declaration announced the creation of a European Higher Education Area, followed in 2000 by the Lisbon Strategy to create a European Research and Innovation Area. The intention is to produce around 700,000 doctoral researchers in Europe (Park 2007), and to make Europe the most competitive global knowledge economy (Kehm 2007). As with developments elsewhere, the European doctorate is no longer viewed only as a research degree but also as a qualification for other professional fields. In general, there is agreement that high-quality research training and an expanded supply of qualified researchers are both important 'in achieving the vision of a globally competitive Europe of knowledge' (Kehm 2007: 314). Doctoral education in Europe is seen to now require more direction and structure and not to be solely driven by intellectual curiosity. Rather, new knowledge is a strategic resource and economic factor. The effect, according to Kehm (2007), is that knowledge becomes another commodity and its shape acquires a more instrumental approach.

Not surprisingly, policy makers in Europe have begun to be keenly interested in the state of research training and universities have been requested to develop institutional strategies for it. In addition, research training is deemed so important a resource that it is no longer to be left in the hands of professors and departments but has become an object of policy making and has moved to the institutional, and national, even supra-national level (Kehm 2007: 314). Academics are to be monitored by outside 'agents who have motives, purposes and goals that are not purely academic' (Kehm 2007: 316). Kehm (2007) highlights a key tension running through higher education and from which doctoral education is not immune. She puts the problem in this way: 'If a utilitarian concept of relevance becomes so strong that it determines academic notions of quality or excellence and the idea of curiosity-driven research, then we could all end up poorer than we were before' (Kehm 2007: 316).

Diversity of doctoral programmes

Accompanying this accelerating interest in doctoral education, the traditional doctorate in social sciences and education is changing and evolving. In the past it generally involved a period of research by the lone student, supported by a supervisor, culminating in a thesis of around 80,000–100,000 words; this text is required above all to make an original contribution to knowledge (Yates 2004). The PhD is recognised as the standard entry qualification for an academic career (although in the past this was not always the case), but also as an important qualification for other professional fields, such as school leadership, educational development roles in higher education, and professional fields such as health and social care. Nowadays, this traditional doctorate model survives, although the student, especially if studying full-time, is likely to participate in a research culture of projects, seminars and conferences, and typically to have more than one supervisor. Unlike in the past, extended time periods for completion are discouraged, and indeed in the UK there is strong pressure for students to complete a full time doctorate in three to four years and six to eight years for a part-time student. In the USA the PhD period of study is typically longer at around five or six years for full-time students, and requires two initial years of course work as well as a thesis (Reisz 2008). But these are increasingly more focused and time-bound studies, rather than life-long projects that may have stretched over 10, 11 or more years, as universities bring in rules to limit the period for which a student may be registered for a doctorate.

New forms of doctoral education have also expanded over the last two decades with the professional doctorate growing in popularity, notwithstanding contested views over the value of something described as a 'professional' doctorate (Gill 2009). The thrust of professional doctorates is both to encourage research which contributes to professional practice, but also to open up doctoral education to a wider group of career professionals and a different demographic (Gill 2009). Burgess, founder of UKCGE, explains that the professional doctorate 'opens up opportunities for higher education to talk with professional people who are interested in intellectual problems that arise from their work experience, and that seems to me to be appropriate' (quoted in Gill 2009: 32). Others are less certain about the claim of professional doctorates to have parity of esteem with the PhD, given the lack of standardisation and lack of clarity over what a taught doctorate is (Gill 2009), even though it might also be argued that it is not entirely obvious what a PhD is, nor that it might not always be fit for diverse purposes. It is, however, certainly the case, that over the last 20 years, the part-time professional doctorate has become widespread in education in the UK and Australia especially (Brennan 1998; Collinson 2005; Costley and Armsby 2007; Evans Chapter 5; Health 2006; Neumann 2007; Sarros *et al.* 2005; Stephenson 2006; Wellington and Sikes 2006; Taysum 2007a; Taysum 2007b), while already being more established in the USA and Canada. Such professional doctorates are generally comprised of two years of taught coursework and two to four years towards a dissertation, the latter study typically being shorter, more applied and practice-focused than the usual PhD thesis. For most universities the balance of taught and research elements is over 50 per cent for the research, and most often two-thirds for the research part. Certainly, in the UK this is required for the degree to qualify for research funding.

In addition, there are other routes to a PhD. There is a PhD by publication based on the submission of peer-reviewed papers, usually accompanied by an overview linking the papers (and see Goode Chapter 3). The new route PhD available in a number of UK universities may contain significant taught elements, usually over one year at masters level, which is examined and must be passed before the student proceeds to doctoral research and thesis, which is usually of the standard length. In other cases, the research project is present from the beginning and runs alongside any taught course in year one (Johnston and Murray 2004; Park 2005; Park 2007 and see www.newroutephd.ac.uk/). There are also practice-based PhDs, with a project report and an exegesis, portfolio and artefact dissertations, and even experiments with group research projects.

Doctoral study can now be face to face, or at a distance using electronic communication technologies or a blend of both of these (e.g. Butcher and Sieminiski 2006; Crossouard 2008; Sussex 2008). Furthermore, the marketisation of higher education means that doctoral researchers can now enrol in universities far away from their home location, and thus may find themselves part of a culturally rich student body, although universities themselves may do little to encourage cross-cultural dialogue and exchange.

More diverse doctoral researchers

Not only is the field of doctoral study far more diverse than it has been in the past, but it also attracts more diverse students with a wide range of reasons for choosing doctoral study, and increasingly it is the focus of academic research. The typical first class honours graduate proceeding directly to doctoral study has arguably never been the norm for education, nursing and social work. In these areas there is no obviously typical doctoral student and ages may range from 24 to 74, in a range of professions, and include white and black candidates, candidates of different ethnicities and religions, men and women, able-bodied and disabled and middle and working class applicants and international students studying away from their home countries (see, for example, Castellanos *et al.* 2006; Chapman and Pyvis 2006; Gillies and Lucey 2007; Green and Scott 2003; Goode 2007; Leonard 2001; McClure 2005; Mastekaasa 2005; Tubin and Lapidot 2008). In the UK, fear of taking on debt appears to deter many working class students from continuing on to doctoral studies (Rodgers 2006).

Increasingly, not all doctoral graduates will choose professional lives in a university. A recent report published by VITAE (2009) for the UK on first destinations of doctoral graduates by subject for 2003–7 indicates the high value employers place on specialised and doctoral-level generic skills. But, significantly for our concern here, only 35 per cent of the total number of doctoral graduates went into a research role across all sectors, only 25 per cent were employed as research staff in higher education, and 14 per cent as lecturers in higher education. Looking more specifically at social science, 42 per cent of the doctoral graduates had studied part-time to 34 per cent went into higher education lecturing and 18 per cent into research roles in higher education (VITAE 2009: 42ff.). All this is to underline that the social science and education doctoral candidate is almost as likely to be studying part-time as full-time, whereas only a minority will enter teaching and research positions in higher education. Many will have come to doctoral studies as professionals in other fields wanting to systematise their professional knowledge, or research policy formation and implementation in their professional fields, or enquire into changing and improving practices in their own contexts. In education, for example, doctoral students include head teachers, teachers in schools, policy researchers, academic administrators, nurse educators, not-for-profit and third-sector professionals, and so on. For the most part, they will continue in this work during their studies and return to it afterwards. They are, in effect, knowledge workers in diverse professional fields.

The diversity of doctoral candidates has implications for doctoral student experiences, given that students differently located will have differing opportunities, as Sen (1999) would say, to 'convert' their particular resources into capabilities to be and become doctoral graduates (see Walker Chapter 2). Diversity produces new obligations for institutions and thus for doctoral supervisors. Thus, for example, a disabled doctoral student may need more or different support from an able-bodied student; a working class student may need more or different support from that of a middle class student, and so on. Supervisors now need to be attentive to and aware of such differences amongst students, and students themselves also need to attend to and be sensitive to diversity in their own peer engagements so that they develop what Nussbaum (1997) describes as a 'narrative imagination', that is the capability to imagine the lives of others and to respond positively.

Doctoral education in globalised times

Golde (2006) points to the changing and changed circumstances of doctoral programmes in the USA, not least shaped by globalisation and the globalisation of knowledge, which is effectively borderless in an age of sophisticated information technologies. Under these globalised conditions, doctoral education offers tremendous opportunities to imaginatively contribute to knowledge, to critically systematise valuable ideas and transform and generate organised knowledge and understanding both through doctoral scholarship and dissemination (Golde and G. Walker 2006). This is, Golde and G. Walker (2006) argue, much more than a technical activity of skills acquisition; as an educational endeavour it is suffused with moral and ethical dimensions that turn on what kind of doctoral education and doctoral scholars are needed by a democratic knowledge society. As G. Walker (2006) writes:

> Today's PhDs have extraordinary new opportunities to lead efforts to extend human knowledge. They already enjoy new possibilities for educating the next generation of scholars and citizens and for doing so in a wide spectrum of institutional settings. They are also called upon to provide expert opinion in a dizzying array of high-profile public areas. They have a special opportunity and responsibility to inform the public about their disciplines and, ultimately, to shape the public's attitudes about the importance of their fields and the attendant habits of mind of an informed, engaged and ethical scholar.
>
> G. Walker 2006: 427

However, such optimism is insufficient to take account of how developments in the nature and type of doctorates, the increasing numbers of doctoral candidates and shifts in the importance of doctoral students for policy makers are located in and produced by the macro-discourses that surround globalisation and the idea of knowledge economies.

It is not coincidental that the increase in the numbers of doctoral students has accelerated in the last 15 to 20 years, nor that they have risen significantly up the agenda of most universities as graduate schools and other institutional structures have been put in place to offer training support and to encourage dynamic 'communities of practice' (Lave and Wenger 1998). As global economies are reorganised around knowledge and information as key resources, a view in part produced by scholarship about globalisation, this in turn shapes and reshapes education (Carnoy and Rhoten 2002). Knowledge and skills are now understood as crucial for comparative economic advantage. Although definitions are contested (see Peters 2004), that offered by the OECD (1996: 7) is still helpful when it describes a knowledge-based economy as 'economies which are directly based on the production, distribution and use of knowledge and information'.

The effect is that higher education 'has become the new starship in the policy fleet for governments around the world' (Peters and Besley 2006a: 83). Internationally and nationally, the task of higher education is directed to the creation of intellectual capacity and the construction of knowledge and skills for participation in an increasingly knowledge-based world economy. Castells (2004) argues that if knowledge is the 'electricity' of the new international economies, then higher education institutions are the power sources on which a new development process must rely. New theories of economic growth have conferred on education, on knowledge production and the knowledge society (having replaced the older industrial model) a central role as an essential engine of development (Peters 2004; Peters and Besley 2006; OECD 1996; Coyle and Quah 2002; Stiglitz 1999). But for Nobel Laureate Joseph Stiglitz (1999), knowledge is a global public good; it is not finite in the way that commodities like coal and iron are and indeed, in and through its use, increases and disperses. Knowledge when used does not become used-up but can be increased through sharing and further development, so that 'knowledge once discovered and made public operates expansively to defy the law of scarcity' (Peters and Besley 2006: 799).

Not surprisingly, in turn, doctoral education and what purposes it promotes and serves have also been affected by this globalised turn. It must be understood in the context of the tensions between ethical and critical citizenship and human well being, and a focus on economic development and economic life, as Kehm (2007) alludes to in her concern for the possible directions of doctoral education. Kwiek (2003: 81) neatly sums up the shifts that surround, permeate and influence higher education, and for our purposes here doctoral education, when he writes that higher education 'is asked to adapt to new societal needs, to be more responsive to the world around it, to be more market-, performance-, and student oriented, to be more cost-effective, accountable to its stakeholders, as well as competitive with other providers'.

But the effects of globalisation go further than a utilitarian press for employability and labour market responsive knowledge and skills and the commodification of knowledge. National higher education institutions around the world face declining investment of public funds, and thus there is pressure to diversify institutional sources of income, accompanied by managerial forms of governance, performative and risk avoidance cultures and quality assurance regimes (Kwiek 2003; Peters 2004; Stromquist 2002). International graduate students are sought after for various reasons, but undoubtedly those include the fees premium they command in balancing university budgets.

In recent decades it seems that university education policy (if not academic professionals) has been much more concerned with science and technology and with economic applications of knowledge. The idea of higher education as a public good, enriching both the individual and all of society, has arguably been overtaken by a rhetoric of business models and market relations, together with an audit and accounting regulatory culture. Higher education is, as a result, increasingly regarded as a private commodity rather than a public good. Pessimists assert the decline or erasure of critical learning in the 'ruins' (Readings 1996) of the university, 'except as the rear-guard protests of an exhausted faculty and a fragment of the largely demobilized student body' (Aronowitz and Giroux 2000: 338).

However, such developments are not uncontested and the pages of *Times Higher Education* in the UK feature regular responses to, and critiques of, the 'human capital' direction (where the value of educated persons and their knowledge is solely the economic contribution). Giroux and Myriades (2001), for example, offer a robust critique of corporate university cultures and the spread of commercial values in higher education where 'social visions are dismissed as hopelessly out of date' (Giroux 2001: 3). In her book on contemporary life in British universities, Evans (2004) suggests in her title *Killing Thinking* the death of universities under current regimes of funding, regulation and accountability. Evans (2004) concludes that universities are in fact unlikely to collapse, but she also suggests that they may 'empty of creative engagement and creativity, as new generations, having experienced the deadly possibilities of the bureaucratized university, refuse to consider further involvement with that world and take their energies and talents elsewhere' (Evans 2004: 152). Those 'taking their talents elsewhere' will, of course, include prospective doctoral students.

That education should equip graduates with the knowledge and skills to participate in the economy is, unsurprisingly, the aspect that most concerns governments. But the problem arises when the meaningfulness of economic opportunities is not debated, and when goals such as intellectual development, equal democratic citizenship and broader social goods are overlooked. Moreover, what Kenway *et al.* (2006) characterise as an

15

older 'gift economy' is rendered fragile by this commodification of knowledge. They argue that an economy cannot simply be defined as a system of exchange. It can also be defined as 'the regulated circulation of values' (Frow 1997: 115 in Kenway *et al.* 2006: 2). It is safe to assume that this includes educational values and versions of the ideal doctoral graduate. The cultural competitive thrust of doctoral education may be inimical to the older gift economy of 'knowledge as a non-rival good' (Frow 1997: 65), as shared and circulated, holding 'an obligation to return to the community what one has taken, with interest' (Frow 1997: 72).

For higher education policy makers, it seems that 'serving the economy has become their raison d'être' (Holford 2008: 25). For many higher education policy makers what is valued and promoted is 'acquisitive learning' (Brown 2003) of economic man or woman rather than the 'inquisitive learning' (Brown 2003: 160) of citizen man or woman. Parker (2007: 124), in considering what the humanities have to offer in Europe, warns against 'instrumental assumptions that need to be resisted'. Rather, she emphasises the significance of multi-voiced and complex narratives, of rhythms counter to those of the digital age, and the importance of offering disputed knowledge and allowing learning to thrive in a 'supercomplex' world (Barnett 2000).

Policy and the 'skills' agenda

Peters and Besley (2006) helpfully develop the concept of 'knowledge cultures' as a response to neoliberal interpretations of the knowledge economy and education, and provide resources for thinking about the purposes and processes of doctoral education. They describe knowledge cultures as involving 'the cultural preconditions that must be established before economies and societies based on knowledge can operate successfully as genuine democratic cultures' (Peters and Besley 2006: 803). Such knowledge cultures are based on 'shared practices' and 'culturally preferred ways of doing things'. In other words, they ask for thinking about the cultural conditions that enable knowledge to be created, produced and disseminated, and by implication, the cultural arrangements that constrain or cramp such knowledge production. They suggest that such cultural conditions include, 'trust, reciprocal rights and responsibilities between different knowledge partners ... The term has the advantage of helping to focus on learning' (Peters and Besley 2006: 803). A focus on knowledge practices and social relations directs us potentially to a richer version of the knowledge economy, they suggest, more focused on public knowledge cultures, less on the neoliberal and bending more towards social democratic interpretations and practices.

Their argument, in turn, points to the broader purposes of doctoral education as developing educated persons for whom 'living life meaningfully' (Higgs 2006: 838) involves more than knowledge and skills but rather personal transformation and change and 'a continual becoming'. In his explication of this educated person, Higgs (2006) suggests that education includes 'the outcome of human agency as a matter of personal engagement'. Intersubjective human experiences require social engagement and social relationships in which students are afforded spaces to struggle 'to give form and character and meaning to the experiences of his or her own unique existence ... to develop their own voice ... to become autonomous persons ... [with a] critical disposition in relation to themselves, others and the world ... [and] whose empowered practice will be directed at a better life for all' (Higgs 2006: 839–40). Thus, doctoral education and the knowledge culture in which it is embedded are rather richer and more expansive than the production only of skills and human capital (see Walker, Chapter 2).

As we outlined earlier, the current focus on doctoral research skills is an element of or response to the dominant human capital and knowledge economy agenda, rather than the notion of becoming and being 'an educated person'. Gilbert (2004) notes a significant shift in doctoral education to reflect a changing emphasis on the PhD – from having one outcome, the thesis; it now foregrounds the actual process of producing the thesis. This has involved a significant shift from an emphasis on a scholarship model to a training model, Gilbert (2004) argues, but we argue that this shift also changes the quality of doctoral students' experiences of undertaking and succeeding in doctoral education by producing critical and innovative work.

We exemplify this argument and the shift by examining events in the UK. From the Harris Report (HEFCE 1996) on, there have been moves in the UK to systematise doctoral education so that what may be expected of students enrolling for a PhD is spelled out clearly, with requirements that doctoral study meets observable and measurable standards. The Harris Report introduced the idea of a Code of Practice for formal adoption by institutions. Such a code, the Report recommended, would require institutions to have in place appropriate facilities and supervisory arrangements.

There may indeed have been serious material concerns about doctoral education that warranted intervention – Coate and Leonard (2002) note the view of the UK Research Councils that the PhD not only lacked the rigour to prepare early career scholars, but it was also not an appropriate professional development for those not choosing academic careers. The issue is not whether there were problems in the PhD, but rather how they were understood and acted on, generating in this case a concern for skills development outcomes understood in the context of a specific view of the inevitability of a particular kind of knowledge economy (Gilbert 2004). Gilbert (2004) generates a number of questions to focus any evaluation of the doctoral training curriculum, including asking how doctoral education meets the needs both of students, and 'other interested parties' (Gilbert 2004: 307). Reisz (2008), however, argues that more discipline and rigour in the PhD process is desirable to counter extended completion dates or hopelessly vague or unrealistic proposals. But, he asks how this is to be done without 'dumbing down', given the growing pressure in the UK for timely doctoral completion rates.

Although agreed a few years earlier, the QAA D (doctoral) level descriptors were published in 2008, after consultations with the sector. The QAA had translated these early recommendations into a set of doctoral standards, which remained unchanged. According to the QAA (2008), doctoral degrees are awarded to students who have demonstrated:

- The creation and interpretation of new knowledge, through original research or other advanced scholarship, of a quality to satisfy peer-review, extend the forefront of the discipline and merit publication.
- A systematic acquisition and understanding of a substantial body of knowledge, which is at the forefront of an academic discipline or area of professional practice.
- The general ability to conceptualise, design and implement a project for the generation of new knowledge, applications or understanding at the forefront of the discipline, and to adjust the project design in the light of unforeseen problems.
- A detailed understanding of applicable techniques for research and advanced academic enquiry.

17

- The QAA goes further to describe specific qualities and 'transferable skills' that the holder of a doctorate might be expected to have – being able to 'make informed judgments on complex issues in specialist fields', being 'able to communicate their ideas and conclusions clearly and effectively', being equipped to continue with research at an advanced level, and embodying qualities and transferable skills 'necessary for employment requiring the exercise of personal responsibility and largely autonomous initiative in complex and unpredictable situations, in professional or equivalent environments'.

Perhaps not surprisingly, critics and supporters of a skills agenda abound. Advocates of a Code of Practice for postgraduate education have included Tim Brown, at the time general secretary of the National Postgraduate Committee, who argued that a code of practice for doctoral education 'will end cronyism in departments. Students will at last be clear about what they can expect in the way of support from their university' (quoted in Sanders 2004: 1). Howard Green, onetime Chair of UKCGE, similarly welcomed a Code saying it would 'raise standards and will be something universities can work with – although some will find it challenging' (Sanders 2004: 1).

There are also critiques. We focus here on (admittedly selective) approaches to the issues of codes of practice, doctoral standards and transferable skills that capture key elements of the oppositional debate. The first is from Rowland (2006), a keen critic of technicist versions of skills, including narrowly instrumental understandings of critical thinking skills (see also Papestephanou and Angeli 2007).

Rowland (2006) opens his critique of the research training agenda by citing a University College, London PhD student as saying of his studies: 'I am currently working on my PhD and am learning a variety of new skills such as self-discipline, time management and developing my own initiative' (Rowland 2006: 45). Rowland's concern is that an undue emphasis on the development of skills to meet the economic growth needs of any society 'may undermine the critical purpose of academic work' (Rowland 2006: 45) and of the university's role to 'provide a critical service to society'. Rowland (2006) characterises the tension as that 'between the intellectual, theoretical and critical purposes of higher education on the one hand and the economic, practical and service purposes on the other exemplified in the skills agenda' (Rowland 2006: 45). Exploring the 2001 statement of the Research Council UK's joint statement of research skills training requirements for doctoral students, he notes that the lists of skills outlined emphasise performance and demonstration so that, for example, the ability to summarise is not sought, but rather the ability to demonstrate this ability. Rowland asks why, if the PhD thesis is itself a demonstration of knowledge and understanding, is any further performance needed? This approach, he argues, shifts the emphasis on the PhD as being judged in its contribution to knowledge (or 'truth') and recasts it in terms of performance. Put another way, there is a move from research knowledge to the person of the knower, the researcher. Increasingly, therefore, PhD students need to market themselves to diverse employers, and to demonstrate that they have generic, core advanced and transferable skills. All this, Rowland says, is to erode a fundamental element of higher education, the nurture of 'criticality' (Barnett 1997).

Turning to a more specific pedagogical issue, critical thinking is arguably the core capability that higher education claims to develop in all its students. Papestephanou and Angeli (2007) point to two different discourses that shape critical thinking. On the one hand, there is the skills paradigm (found in discourses and practices of key skills, generic skills, transferable skills, and some versions of graduate attributes) embedded in what Habermas (1987) would style as purposive rationality, technicism and instrumentality. This, they argue, is 'relevant to the roles of the customer and consumer of services and goods, and not to the active participant in the possible transformation of the public sphere' (Papestephanou and Angeli 2007: 609). Under neoliberalism, they suggest, the dominant policy and the pedagogical vocabulary emphasise skills, performativity and outcomes and purposive rationality (instrumental and strategic), which in turn domesticate critique. The idea, they say, is to optimise outcomes, in the case of higher education, human capital outcomes but these are not open to critique. Thus, they write, 'the skills perspective identifies uncritically with the criteriology of the sociopolitical system since it focuses so much on successful performance' (Papestephanou and Angeli 2007: 605–6).

By contrast to this instrumental approach, becoming and being critical and producing 'critical' knowledge means seeing that current policy agendas are subject to contested interpretations. Doctoral students even if embedded in training agendas need to think, with support from their supervisors, about this agenda and how it positions them. They need time and space to consider where their own research is located on a criticality spectrum, ranging from narrow to expansive, from thin to thick, with deep incommensurabilities across this range. If not simply being trained, the question to ask is: How am I critical? And what kind of critical am I?

Different approaches to the doctorate

We have suggested that we understand doctoral education as a process of identity formation. This involves crossing a kind of borderland, transforming an identity as an experienced, highly skilled professional to one of researcher. We have certainly heard our own full-time doctoral students in particular remark on not underestimating the difficulties of suddenly no longer being a valued and respected professional in becoming 'just a student'. What one might have been very good at and very secure about in one's own practice is suddenly of rather less significance. For part-time students the disruptions may work differently, in that students remain grounded in the workplace but are required to scrutinise it in new and often discomforting ways. Yet these disruptions, while difficult, are also productive of the new critically reflexive identity.

We offer two different but related ways of rethinking the work of doctoral education.

1. From professional to researcher-as-professional

In a recent account, Andrews and Edwards (2008: 4) trace their own doctoral trajectory and their 'invention' of themselves as researchers. In both cases they chose to study for an EdD because of the attraction of collaborative, cohort study. Of their doctoral experience they write that: 'It was tempting at first to think of oneself as a deficit model (particularly "not a statistician") but, gradually, we began to move forward with more confidence'. As researchers they became more critical about their own workplace assumptions, but also less uncritically compliant and more creative and confident in taking risks 'rather than settling for the false security that all ticks have been marked against a list of competencies' (Andrews and Edwards 2008: 5). In becoming researchers they found themselves to be more rather than less professional as educators, rediscovering an *educational* identity so that,

[W]e feel able to step back, to theorize to engage with reflexivity rather than letting it leave us baffled and frustrated. … it has given us greater insight into ourselves as professionals and our ability to articulate what it means to be a professional in postmodernity. It has also given us the courage to stand by the values in education that we feel are important and also to understand how we came to those values.

Andrews and Edwards 2008: 7

Thus, we suggest, the notion of professionalism as involving continuous learning can hold both ends/identities together, albeit in tension.

'Professionalising' doctoral education

The notions of being professional and professionalism are taken up from a slightly different angle by Barnacle and Dall'Alba (2008), who consider the 'professionalising' of the research degree curriculum and the specialised and hence 'professional' knowledge that characterises a doctorate. They ask whether the current concern with generic and transferable skills training might enable a re-engagement with the knowledge that arises through practice (in this case the practice of doctoral education), 'despite the techno-rationality that is evident within the way such skills are often conceived?' (Barnacle and Dall'Alba 2008: 3). They suggest that this goes to the matter of the value of a research degree and how doctoral graduates might contribute to the workplace and society. Increasingly, as we have explained, this contribution is being formed by the demand for knowledge workers with disciplinary knowledge as only one component of the doctoral award. Added to this is a range of skills and dispositions necessary for undertaking such knowledge work and contributing to innovation so that doctoral graduates are able to translate their research skills into economic, social and cultural returns, which are both of private and public benefit. Yet, as they explain, a focus on research training can mean technical skilling, 'rather than the craft or artistry of research required for genuine skilful performance' (Barnacle and Dall'Alba 2008: 5), which is also nevertheless an alternative possible response.

Barnacle and Dall'Alba (2008) concur with those who argue that the artistry of professional practice 'involves a matter of "feel" and judgment, of knowing when to act, of being able to frame problematic situations and fashion new approaches, rather than just applying established routines' (Barnacle and Dall'Alba 2008: 5). But the other side of a focus on 'artistry' is the danger, they suggest, of an over reliance on tacit knowledge, which reinforces individualistic approaches to research practice and supervisory relationship not being open to scrutiny. They summarise the case as one of enhancing the process of doctoral research by identifying and promoting relevant skills on the one hand; or the reverse effect on the other:

If we are seeking graduates with the ability to work creatively and contribute to innovation, are generic skills really what are required? Skilful practice and know-how arise within the specificity of particular disciplinary, social and technological practices. If as a society, we want to benefit from the research knowledge and skills of higher degree research graduates, then we need approaches to research education that are neither reductive nor instrumental. An instrumental, reductive view of generic capabilities is necessarily detrimental to efforts to address skilful research practice.

Barnacle and Dall'Alba 2008: 6

They go even further than this. They acknowledge that it is 'reasonable' to expect research education as a preparation for contributions to social, cultural and economic development (broadly, self, others and society, see Booth *et al.* 2009); they raise questions about the feasibility or desirability of assuming any specific match with employment. To do so, they suggest, may ironically produce *less* rather than more skilful graduates.

If, following Barnacle and Dall'Alba (2008), doctoral education can be understood as professional preparation, as much as research preparation, then we need understandings of professionalism that are educational rather than economic. We also need to be aware of both the crisis and promise of professionalism in contemporary society (Sullivan 2005). As Barnacle and Dall'Alba (2008) suggest, we cannot take for granted that the 'professionalising' of the research curriculum will generate rich understandings of doctoral education as intellectual, technical and moral, having a responsibility for influencing public values and public goods, and 'connections to professionalism as a public value' (Sullivan 2005: 11). In our view, doctoral education is both a private benefit to students, and also a public good in which new and original knowledge and contributions are shared publicly, and professional claims are extended beyond the purely cognitive or technical.

In its own way a skills and training agenda opens up these questions, as Barnacle and Dall'Alba (2008) suggest, and makes available an important debate about doctoral education. The issue is what discourse of professionalism underpins such debates and the extent to which such a discourse is thick or thin. However, opening the debate opens space to assert an approach to doctoral education as embedded in 'thick' professionalism, which includes seeing one's work 'as part of a larger collective project' shaping personal identities and requiring 'considerable individual discernment and capacity for initiative and judgment' (Sullivan 2005: 15). Sullivan argues that a thick discourse of professionalism might address the problems generated by economic development, but also 'takes us beyond the simplistic idea that a market framework can solve the most important issues of social and political life', including 'what constitutes good work, for the society, and for the individual' (Sullivan 2005: 18).

Framed in this way, doctoral education poses significant and exciting challenges for students and their supervisors, and for and to universities. We are challenged to consider what 'good work' means in current times – and to ask how we blend the normative and the technical (skills and training), frame our concern with doctoral standards as concern for 'developing in [doctoral] students the capacity and disposition to perform in accordance with the best standards of a field in a way that serves the larger society' (Sullivan 2005: 30), and strengthening the connections between professionalism and democratic public life. We agree and suggest that doctoral education ought to be suffused with the practical technical competence necessary to do research well, but also be oriented to civic and social purposes and significant questions.

Doctoral education understood as 'thick' professionalism might then be seen as 'a life project' (Sullivan 2005: 22), a source of personal growth and professional renewal for those who undertake and successfully complete doctorates of different kinds, but also 'lived within a larger life' (Haworth, 1977 quoted in Sullivan 2005: 22), having civic, ethical and public leadership 'capability' (Sen 1999) dimensions.

2. Life-long learning

Debates about the purposes, practices and outcomes of contemporary doctoral education in higher education institutions can also be productively situated in the context of life-long learning and life-long education (Aspin 2007). Taking this as a starting point means that the doctoral degree ought to be a preparation for learning beyond the award itself and this in turn has implications for what is offered and what is learnt through undertaking doctoral study.

The agendas of life-long learning and doctoral education are remarkably similar. Thus, the European Cologne Charter *Aims and Ambitions for Lifelong Learning,* states that, 'Economies and societies are increasingly knowledge-based. Education and [research] skills are indispensable to achieving economic success, civic responsibility and social cohesion' (quoted in Aspin 2007: 22). Like research training, the term life-long learning is contested but generally used approvingly, a good and worthwhile enterprise (Aspin 2007). After exploring various contested understandings and definitions of life-long learning, Aspin (2007) offers a metaphor for life-long learning, which seems deeply applicable also to the process of doctoral education as a process and contribution to each person's life-long education. Aspin (2007) likens life-long learning to a process of coming to comprehend and review:

> [T]he theories with which we are working, to compare them with other theoretical efforts and productions of others faced with similar problems, to subject them to positive criticism, and to attempt to improve them and make them fit for their educational purpose; which is both efficient and excellent and to the good of individuals and societies.
>
> Aspin 2007: 32

According to Aspin (2007), we go on learning in this way, adopting a pragmatic 'evolutionary epistemology' (Bernstein 1983 in Aspin, 2007: 33) to make our own theories, 'meet for application, modification, and repair at every stage of our intellectual journey'. Such a view of life-long learning goes beyond economic purposes to increase, says Aspin (2007), the emancipation and participation of all citizens.

Increasingly, doctoral graduates face discontinuities and 'risk' (Beck 1992) through the life course and these intellectual journeys through which they must make their way. In the context of such uncertainties, a navigational reflexivity is central to doctoral education as a process of life-long learning that involves more than simply passively acquiring generic research skills and qualifications, but rather a form of learning, which is, 'more consonant with the needs of civic participation and of agents capable of autonomously generating change for themselves' (Edwards *et al.* 2002: 527). Having the kind of reflexivity that enables both self and social questioning develops our agency to shape contexts and conditions. Thus, Edwards *et al.* (2002) suggest that learning of this kind involves:

> [T]he transformation of understanding, identity and agency. ... involving a developing awareness which results in growing understanding of customary practice, leading to reflexive social and self-questioning and the transformation of 'habitus'. It is the development of reflexivity, the capacity to develop critical awareness of the assumptions that underlie practices, especially the meta-cognitive, interpretive

schema that constitute worlds, which we see as central to an adequate theory of lifelong learning … the capacity to develop and sustain reflexivity.

Edwards *et al.* 2002: 532–33

Such reflexivity and dispositions are learnt in the context of actual practices, activities and learning relationships, including those of doctoral education, and in situated socio-cultural, institutional and historical contexts. Crucially, knowledge is the key to a *critical* reflexivity.

Life-long learning, and indeed doctoral education, is multi-dimensional, embracing economic opportunities, individual development and social goods, rather than a more impoverished neoliberal agenda of education as a private good (see, for example, Rizvi 2007). Although there may be 'no turning back' (Rizvi 2007: 129) from the shifts, which have in turn influenced doctoral education, it is possible to 'imagine and work with' and create alternative traditions that embrace 'an open dialogue about the new requirements of education' (Rizvi 2007: 129), and promote educated citizens and educated publics (Barr and Griffiths 2007).

Given the world in which doctoral graduates live and work and our human futures, we need to retain knowledge at the centre of doctoral education as has been its traditional role, but also pay attention to being in the world (Barnett 2000). This leads us to ask not only what the knowledge outcomes of doctoral education are, but also what kind of human being are we hoping a doctorate might form through a rich mix of knowledge, skills and dispositions (see Walker, Chapter 2).

References

Andrews, D. and Edwards, C. (2008) Consciousness in transition: the experience of doctoral study. In B. Cunningham (Ed.). *Exploring Professionalism*. London: Institute of Education.

Aronowitz, S. and Giroux, H. (2000) The corporate university and the politics of education, *The Educational Forum*, 64: 332–39.

Aspin, D. N. (2007) Introduction. In D. N. Aspin (Ed.). *Philosophical Perspectives on Lifelong Learning*. Dordrecht: Springer.

Barnacle, R. and Dall'Alba, G. (2008) *Professionalising the Research Higher Degrees Curriculum?* Paper presented at the Australian Association for Research in Education annual conference, Brisbane.

Barnett, R. (1997) *Higher Education: A Critical Business*. Buckingham: SRHE/Open University Press.

——(2000) *Realizing the University in an Age of Supercomplexity*. Buckingham: SRHE/Open University Press.

Barr, J. and Griffiths, M. (2007) The Nature of Knowledge and Lifelong Learning. In D. N. Aspin (Ed.). *Philosophical Perspectives on Lifelong Learning*. Dordrecht: Springer.

Beck, U. (1992) *Risk Society: Towards a New Modernity*. London: Sage.

Berliner, D. (2006) Towards a Future as Rich as Our Past. In C. M. Golde and G. E. Walker (Eds). *Envisioning the Future of Doctoral Education*. San Francisco, CA: Jossey Bass.

Bitusikova, A. (2009) Reforming Doctoral Education in Europe, *Academe Online*. (Available at www.aaup.org/AAUP/pubsres/academe/2009/JF/Feat/bitu.htm PF=1 Accessed 11 February 2009).

Bleiklie, I. and Hostaker, R. (2004) Modernizing research training – education and science policy between profession, discipline and academic institution, *Higher Education Policy*, 17(2): 221–36.

Booth, A., McLean, M. and Walker, M. (2009) Self, others and society: A case study of university integrative learning, *Studies in Higher Education*, 34(8).

Brennan, M. (1998) Struggles over the definition and practice of the Educational Doctorate in Australia, *Australian Educational Researcher*, 25(1): 71–89.

Brown, P. (2003) The Opportunity Trap: education and employment in a global economy, *European Educational Research Journal*, 2(1): 141–79

Butcher, J. and Sieminiski, S. (2006) The challenge of a distance learning professional doctorate in education, *Open Learning*, 21(1): 59–69.

Carnoy, M. and Rhoten, D. (2002) What Does Globalization Mean for Educational Change? A Comparative Approach, *Comparative Education Review*, 46(1): 1–9.

Castells, M. (2004) *Universities and Cities in a World of Global Networks*, Sir Robert Birley Lecture, City University, London, 17 March 2004.

Castellanos, J., Gloria, A. M. and Kamimura, M. (Eds) (2006) *The Latina/o Pathway to the PhD: Abriendo carninos*. Sterling: Stylus Publishing.

Chapman, A. and Pyvis, D. (2006) Dilemmas in the formation of student identity in offshore higher education: a case study in Hong Kong, *Educational Review*, 58(3): 291–302.

Coate, K. and Leonard, D. (2002) The structure of research training in England, *Australian Educational Researcher*, 29(3): 19–42.

Collinson, J. A. (2005) Artistry and analysis: student experiences of UK practice-based doctorates in art and design, *International Journal of Qualitative Studies in Education*, 18(6): 713–28.

Costley C. and Armsby, P. (2007) Research influences on a professional doctorate, *Research in Post-Compulsory Education*, (12)3: 343–57

Coyle, D. and Quah, D. (2002) *Getting the measure of the new economy*. London: The Work Foundation.

Crossouard, B. (2008) Developing alternative models of doctoral supervision with online formative assessment, *Studies in Continuing Education*, 30(1): 51–67.

Davies, J. (1996) Dangers of no liaisons, *Times Higher Education*. Online. (Available at www.timeshigher education.co.uk/storyasp?setioncode=26&storycode=924534 Accessed 6 March 2009).

Edwards, R. Ranson, S. and Strain, M. (2002) Reflexivity: towards a theory of lifelong learning, *International Journal of Lifelong Education*, 21(6): 525–36.

Evans, M. (2004) *Killing Thinking: The Death of the Universities*. London: Continuum Felton 2002.

Frow, J. (1997) *Time and Commodity Culture*. Oxford: Clarendon Press.

Gilbert, R. (2004) A framework for evaluating the doctoral curriculum, *Assessment and Evaluation in Higher Education*, 29(3): 299–309.

Gill, J. (2009) Professional Doctorates, *Times Higher Education*, 26 February 2009: 30–35.

Gillies, V. and Lucey, H. (Eds) (2007) *Power, Knowledge and the Academy*. Hampshire: Palgrave MacMillan.

Giroux, H. (2001) Commodification of Higher Education. In H. Giroux and K. Myrsiades (Eds). *Beyond the Corporate University*. Lanham, MD: Rowman and Littlefield Publishers.

Giroux, H. A. and Myriades, K. (Eds) (2001) *Beyond the Corporate University*. Lanham, MD: Rowman and Littlefield.

Golde, C. E. (2006) Preparing Stewards of the Discipline. In C. M. Golde and G. E. Walker (Eds). *Envisioning the Future of Doctoral Education*. San Francisco, CA: Jossey Bass.

Golde, C. M and Walker, G. E. (Eds) (2006) *Envisioning the Future of Doctoral Education*. San Francisco, CA: Jossey Bass.

Goode, J. (2007) Empowering or disempowering the international PhD student? Constructions of the dependent and independent learner, *British Journal of Sociology of Education*, 28(5): 589–604.

Green, A. and Scott, L. V. (Eds) (2003) *Journey to the PhD How to Navigate the Process as African Americans*. Sterling: Stylus Publishing.

Habermas, J. (1987). *The theory of communicative action. Volume 2. Lifeworld and system*. Trans. T. McCarthy. Boston, MA: Beacon Press.

Haworth, L. (1977) *Decadence and Objectivity*. Toronto: University of Toronto Press.

Health, L. (2006) Supervision of professional doctorates: education doctorates in English universities, *Higher Education Review*, 38(2): 21–41.

HEFCE (1996) *Review of Postgraduate Education*, Bristol: HEFCE. Online. (Available at www.hefce.ac. uk/pubs/hefce/1996/m14_96.htm Accessed 9 July 2009).

HEPI (2004) *Higher Education Supply and Demand to 2010 – an Update*. Oxford: Higher Education Policy Institute.

Higgs, P. (2006) Higher Education is more than just about the economy, *South African Journal of Higher Education*, 20(6): 838–42.

Holbrook, A. and Johnston, S. (Eds) (1999) *Supervision of Postgraduate Research in Education*. Coldsteam: AARE.

Holford, J. (2008) There is a wider purposes for universities than 'serving the economy', *The Times Higher*, 13 November 2008: 24–5.

Johnston, B. and Murray, R. (2004) New routes to the PhD: cause for concern? *Higher Education Quarterly*, 58(1): 31–42.

Kehm, B. (2007) Quo Vadis Doctoral Education? New European Approaches in the Context of Global Changes, *European Journal of Education*, 42(3): 307–19.

Kenway, J., Bullen, E., Fahey, J. and Robb, S. (2006) *Haunting the Knowledge Economy*. London and New York: Routledge.

Kwiek, M. (2003) The State, the Market and Higher Education, Challenges for the New Century. In M. Kwiek (Ed.) *The University, Globalization and Central Europe*. Frankfurt and New York: Peter Lang.

Lave, J. and Wenger, E. (1998). *Communities of Practice: Learning, Meaning, and Identity*. Cambridge: Cambridge University Press.

Leonard, D. (2001) *A Woman's Guide to Doctoral Studies*. Buckingham: Open University Press.

Leonard, D., Metcalfe, J., Becker, R. and Evans, J. (2006) *Review of literature on the impact of working context and support on the postgraduate research student learning experience*. York: Higher Education Academy.

Marcus, J. (2009) Comic Strip Hero, *Times Higher Education*, 12 February 2009.

Mastekaasa, A. (2005) Gender differences in educational attainment: the case of doctoral degrees in Norway, *British Journal of Sociology of Education*, 26(3): 375–94.

McClure, J. W. (2005) Preparing a laboratory-based thesis: Chinese international research students' experience of supervision, *Teaching in Higher Education*, 10(1): 3–16.

Neumann, R. (2007) Policy and practice in doctoral education, *Studies in Higher Education*, 32(4): 459–74.

Nussbaum, M. (1997) *Cultivating Humanity. A Classical Defence of Reform in Liberal Education*. Cambridge, MA: Harvard University Press.

OECD (1996) *The Knowledge-Based Economy*. Paris: OECD.

Papestephanou, M. and Angeli, C. (2007) Critical Thinking Beyond Skill, *Educational Philosophy and Theory*, 39(6): 604–21.

Park, C. (2005) New variant PhD: the changing nature of the doctorate in the UK, *Journal of Higher Education Policy and Management*, 27(2): 189–207.

——(2007) *Redefining the Doctorate*. York: Higher Education Academy.

Parker, J. (2007) Future Priorities of the Humanities in Europe: What Have the Humanities to Offer? *Arts and Humanities in Higher Education*, 6(1): 123–7.

Pearson, M. (1996) Professionalizing PhD Education to enhance the quality of the student experience, *Higher Education*, 32: 303–20

Peters, M. (2004) Higher Education, Globalization and the Knowledge Economy. In M. Walker and J. Nixon (Eds). *Reclaiming Universities from a Runaway World*. Maidenhead: SRHE/Open University Press.

Peters, M. and Besley, A. C. (2006) 'Public Knowledge Cultures', *South African Journal of Higher Education*, 20(6): 792–806.

Peters, M. and Besley, A. C. (2006a) *Building Knowledge Cultures*. Lanham: Rowman and Littlefield.

QAA (2008) *The Framework for higher education qualifications in England, Wales and Northern Ireland*. Online. (Available www.qaa.ac.uk/academicinfrastructure/fheq/ewnio8/ Accessed 18 March 2009).

Readings, B. (1996) *The University in Ruins*. Cambridge, MA: Harvard University Press.

Reisz, M. (2008) 'Doctor, doctor, quick, quick', *Times Higher Education*, 4 December 2008: 32–35.

Richardson, V. (2006) Stewards of a Field, Stewards of an Enterprise. The Doctorate in Education. In C. M. Golde and G. E. Walker (Eds). *Envisioning the Future of Doctoral Education*. San Francisco, CA: Jossey Bass.

Rizvi, F. (2007) Lifelong Learning: Beyond Neo-Liberal Imaginary. In D. N. Aspin (Ed.). *Philosophical Perspectives on Lifelong Learning*. Dordrecht: Springer.

25

Rodgers, M. (2006) Poor less likely to study for PhD, *Times Higher Education*. Online. (Available www.timeshighereducationco.uk/story.asp?sectioncode=26&storycode-204651 Accessed 6 March 2009).

Rowland, S. (2006) *The Enquiring University*. Maidenhead: SRHE/Open University Press.

Sanders, C. (2004) QAA targets PhD 'cronyism', *Times Higher Education*. Online. (Available www.timeshighereducation.co.uk/story.asp?sectioncode=26&storycode=183734 Accessed on 6 March 2009).

Sarros, J. C., Willis, R. J. and Palmer, G. (2005) The nature and purpose of the DBA: a case for clarity and quality control, *Education + Training*, 47(1): 40–52.

Sen, A. (1999) *Development as Freedom*. Oxford: Oxford University Press.

Stephenson, J. (2006) Managing their own programme: a case study of the first graduates of a new kind of doctorate in professional practice, *Studies in Continuing Education*, 28(1): 17–32.

Stiglitz, J. (1999) Knowledge as a global public good. In I. Kaul, I. Grunberg and M. A. Stern (Eds). *Global Public Goods: international cooperation in the 21st century*. Oxford: Clarendon Press.

Stromquist, N. (2002) *Education in a Globalized World. The Connectivity of Economic Power, Technology and Knowledge*. Lanham, MD: Rowman and Littlefield Publishers.

Sullivan, W. M. (2005) *Work and Integrity: The Crisis and Promise of Professionalism in America*. 2nd edn. Sanford, CA: Jossey-Bass.

Sussex, R. (2008) Technological options in supervising remote research students, *Higher Education*, 55 (1): 121–37.

Taysum, A. (2007a) The distinctiveness of the EdD within the university tradition, *Journal of Higher Educational Administration and History*, 39(2): 323–34.

Taysum, A. (2007b) The distinctiveness of the EdD in Producing and Transforming Knowledge, *Journal of Higher Educational Administration and History*, 39(3): 285–96.

Thomson, A. (1996) Doctoral research in standards limbo, Times Higher Education Supplement. Online. (Available at www.timeshighereducation.co.uk/storyasp?sectioncode=26%storycode=94108 Accessed 9 July 2009).

Tubin, D. and Lapidot, O. (2008) Construction of 'glocal' (global—local) identity among Israeli graduate students in the USA, *Higher Education*, 55(2): 203–17.

VITAE (2009) *What do researchers do? First destinations of doctoral graduates by subject*. Online. (Available at voate.ac.uk/CMS/files/upload/Vitae-WDRD-by-subject-Jun-09.pdf Accessed 5 July 2009).

Walker, G. E. (2006) The Questions in the Back of the Book. In C. M. Golde and G. E. Walker (Eds). *Envisioning the Future of Doctoral Education*. San Francisco, CA: Jossey Bass.

Wellington and Sikes (2006) 'A Doctorate in a Tight Compartment': Why Do Students Choose a Professional Doctorate and What Impact Does It Have on Their Personal and Professional Lives? *Studies in Higher Education*, 31(6): 723–34.

Western, M. and Lawson, A. (2008) *Doctorates ailing on the world stage*, The Australian. Online. (Available at www.theaustralian.news.com.au/story/0,25197,23319781–27702,00.html Accessed 8 March 2008).

Yates, L. (2006) *What does Good Education Research look like?* Maidenhead: Open University Press.

Part 2

Supervision as pedagogy/ies

Supervision as pedagogies

2

Doctoral education as 'capability' formation

M. Walker

This chapter makes the argument that the processes of doctoral students becoming researching professionals and of life-long learning, outlined in Chapter 1, fundamentally requires that they are provided with genuine opportunities to form the 'capabilities' and 'achievable functionings' (Sen 1992; 1999), which, on the one hand, they have reason to value as researching professionals, and on the other, are capabilities which their doctoral supervisors see as valuable. The chapter first outlines normative goals for higher education, including doctoral education, and then introduces key ideas from the capability approach indicating what might appear to be a surprising relevance to postgraduate researchers. It locates doctoral education as a process of human development in which doctoral scholars individually and as members of doctoral communities participate in an educational environment 'in which they can develop their full potential and lead productive, creative lives in accord with their needs and interests' (UNDP 2006, quoted in Taylor 2008: xxiv). The goal of human development is to have the freedom to exercise genuine choices (freedoms described by Sen as capabilities), and to participate in equal decision making that affects each person's life. In practice, exercising such agency to realise the capabilities formed through doctoral education may be constrained both by prior advantage or disadvantage (Burchardt 2009) and by social and economic arrangements. But for my purposes the point is to underline our responsibility as educators to work with our students to form capabilities that enable their genuine choices, albeit influenced by wider conditions, which we and they may have less power to change.

The normative purposes of higher education in universities internationally

Education is inescapably normative; it requires us to consider the worthwhile human qualities we want education to form and the kind of world we hope for through graduates' contributions to society. It is, therefore, 'difficult to conceive of educational interventions disconnected from some hope for social improvement' (Bridges 2008: 467). More specifically, universities have as their core functions research, teaching, professional education and diverse forms of public engagement. This technically describes their main activities, but gives us little for thinking about a full and rich education for personal and social development. Yet we do not, any of us, live in the best of possible worlds, and higher education ought to be engaged in leading and responding to the complex human understanding and judgements demanded by what Habermas (1989) describes as the 'moral urgencies' of our age in Europe and the wider world. Moreover, at the time of writing, the global economic crisis continues to have effects on people's lives and on diminishing graduate employment opportunities.

The focus on human capital outcomes and market policy drivers in higher education over several decades (see Chapter 1) has neither equipped us to avoid such an outcome, nor has it removed continuing inequalities at the heart of societies. Some might, of course, advocate that we need policy that is even more narrowly focused on human capital growth. Yet there is no evidence to show that human capital as education policy can predict or prevent economic crises. On the other hand, that doctoral education should equip graduates with the knowledge and generic research skills to participate in the knowledge economy is unsurprisingly the aspect that most concerns governments (see Chapter 1). But human capital cannot, as Robeyns (2006) explains, account for any non-economic goods from education. Moreover, human capital policies seem nowhere near to solving resurgent conflicts based on contested identities, cultures and religions, or human greed and cruelty. Paolo Blasi puts the case well when he writes that:

> [T]he challenge of the European society today is to go beyond 'the knowledge society, and to evolve into what could be called 'the wisdom society'. Knowledge is conscious use of information; 'wisdom' means choosing one's behaviour on the basis of knowledge and shared values, in order to enhance the well-being of all, and the awareness that personal actions have social consequences.
>
> Blasi, quoted in Marga 2008: 117

In a recent plenary address, Brighouse (2007) made the important question explicit. We need, he argued, a new normative account of higher education, one which asks 'Whose interests is higher education serving?', and of course for my purposes, whose interests are promoted through doctoral pedagogical arrangements. Even more than this, we ought in higher education, as in life, to be asking how do we as human beings try to live well, and flowing from this, what kind of persons are being formed in and through doctoral education in our universities?

My concern is specifically with what this means for the humanistic and cultural goals of universities, and particularly pedagogical processes and the acquisition and critical knowledge and values formation by doctoral scholars. Although accepting that the contemporary emphasis on instrumental ends has the effect of shrinking concerns with Habermas's (1987) 'human lifeworld' of personality, culture and society – we ought to expect in universities to see efforts to educate doctoral citizens with self and ethical awareness for engagement with social and civic responsibilities (Booth *et al.* 2009). Practically, the goal is for doctoral education to contribute to individual and social well being through pedagogical arrangements that form human capabilities (Sen 1992; 1999), oriented to praxis outcomes that integrate academic knowledge (acquired through doctoral research) and 'practical knowledge reflected in how one lives as a citizen and human being. ... informed by *phronesis* or practical wisdom' (Bridges *et al.* 2008: 10). We might also argue that doctoral education ought to cultivate in doctoral scholars a 'research imagination' (Kenway and Fahey 2009: 8), which is 'audacious' (p. 19) and global in its moral reach and perspective (and see Unterhalter, Chapter 16).

The formation of human capabilities

The chapter draws on the work of economist Amartya Sen (1992; 1999; 2008) and philosopher Martha Nussbaum (2000; 2006), who have developed the capability approach, taking it in slightly different directions, to offer a rich and innovative framework for evaluating and developing education. Their ideas are only introduced here, but a burgeoning literature on capabilities and social science, and education philosophical and practical applications can now be found and the ideas pursued further for those who wish to do so (see Walker and Unterhalter 2007 for education, the *Journal of Human Development and Capabilities* for emerging work, and Robeyns 2005 for an excellent introductory overview). The opportunity exists for research into doctoral capabilities, using Sen and Nussbaum to conceptualise opportunities and outcomes in doctoral scholarship and learning for diverse students.

Sen's concern has been to find a way to evaluate human well being and interpersonal comparisons of quality of life. In arguing for political, cultural and social aspirations and well being as integral to indicators of expansive human development, he has elaborated the capability approach, producing a critique of approaches to thinking about well being in welfare economics and political philosophy. First, Sen is critical of measures of quality of life based on commodities (e.g. food, shelter) and gross national income. The difficulty for Sen is that gross national income and average income do not tell us how much access to this wealth each person has in the society or within their family. Some may have a great deal more than the average and others considerably less. For example, because we work in a rich country such as the UK, this does not tell us very much about the circumstances of our doctoral students and which of them may, for example, be struggling financially in ways that negatively impact on their research. Second, Sen is also critical of the evaluation of quality of life based on individual utility – expressed subjective preferences or satisfactions – in relation to standard of living. He argues that this can be misleading in that a person may express satisfaction with their situation (e.g. inadequate doctoral supervision) because that is what they have come to accept, or they are not aware that supervision can and should be different so they do not argue for an improvement. If a doctoral student drops out and says that really she is no longer interested in research at this level – it is no longer her subjective preference – we cannot assume that this is a freely chosen position. Sen explains that to assume that a preference equals someone's unconstrained choice rather than the effect of social conditions on their preference formation is problematic, and has large implications for how disadvantage is understood.

Third, Sen addresses ideas on justice from moral philosophy, especially the influential work of John Rawls (1971) and his focus on the holding of 'primary goods', which include income, basic liberties and self-respect. For Sen the problem with primary goods is that it does not take into account that people will differ in their ability to convert primary goods into freedoms. He argues that the capability approach gives a better account of the freedoms actually enjoyed by different people than can be obtained from merely looking at their holding of social primary goods. For example, a disabled doctoral student might struggle to convert her bundle of primary goods into education freedoms compared to an able-bodied person in collecting data, accessing library stacks, or physically writing her dissertation. A female doctoral student might find herself margin-alised in informal gender-based networking among male students and their professors, even though all students have the same formal rights to contact time with a supervisor. A doctoral student who does not speak English as first language studying in the English language and in a UK cultural environment will have differential opportunities to con-vert her bundle of resources into achievable doctoral functionings than that of a home student (see Goode Chapter 3; and Starfield Chapter 11). The first student may need additional language support; the second student may need to learn how to work in a multi-cultural community of doctoral students.

The important point Sen makes is that human diversity is central to the capability approach, not an add-on, or something to only be considered at some (vague) later stage. Diversity should not be seen as something to be considered only after the needs of able-bodied, or male, or middle class students have been agreed. In the arena of doctoral education his approach, therefore, asks us to look seriously at diversity among our stu-dents and to consider how this diversity shapes students' ability to 'convert' resources into opportunities and functionings.

Sen has, therefore, developed an approach to 'equality of what' by looking at the space between commodities and preferences to develop the idea of the evaluative space of capabilities. In evaluating, for example, the quality of doctoral education, we would focus on the formation of students' capabilities, both those identified of value by students but also those we as supervisors and universities deem valuable (see Walker and Unter-halter 2007 for the debate on who gets to choose capabilities in education). Following Sen, capabilities are not simply generic research 'skills' (see Chapter 1), but rather com-prise the real and effective freedoms people have to do and be what they value being and doing, for example taking part in discussions with peers and academics, reading critically, writing well and confidently, having an ethical disposition, being treated with respect, having one's culture acknowledged, and so on. Capability refers to combinations of achievable functionings (choices and outcomes) of each person, and from which she can choose one collection to lead her own good life. For example, one of Goode's inter-national students (Goode 2007: 599) explains: 'I achieve a different kind of life I never thought I could achieve'. Individual well being depends on having the underlying opportunity freedoms or capabilities (in the case of Goode's student, to be able to cope with mental loneliness, for example). Capabilities are always multi-dimensional, and we would therefore look not at a singular measure of advantage but at a capability set, which gives us information on the various functioning vectors that are within reach of each person to undertake the actions and activities in which they want to engage, and be whom they want to be (Sen 1992; and see Robeyns 2003).

Table 2.1 shows an example of one capability, among others, for a student, let's call her Hannah Brown.

Our evaluation of e/quality in doctoral education must take account of both freedom in opportunities and observed choices (the achievable functionings noted above), and this will vary for different students. Accessing research and doctoral networks may be easier for some students than others, even where all students are equally competent in the stage they have reached of their doctoral studies. Thus, we would ask evaluative questions based in this case on the achieved functioning of choosing to network. Or we might observe a regrettable outcome where two doctoral students both withdraw from their studies halfway through. In the one case the student withdrew because she had been offered a managerial position, which she had long wanted, and her doctoral studies could

Table 2.1 Capability and functioning

Capability	to be confident about her academic work
Achievable functionings (from which Hannah can choose one or more, given that she has the underlying capability to be confident about her academic work)	present a paper at seminar in her School present a paper at an international conference draft an academic article and send to a journal contribute to a social networking site of postgraduate students in her field put forward and defend her ideas, data and conceptualisation in discussions with peers and her professor argue for practical change based on her research (for example, assessment practices) disagree with her supervisors write a short 'oped' piece for the University newsletter make formal and informal contacts with established academics researching in her field participate in a peer doctoral reading group support a less confident student

be resumed at a later stage. For the other student the stress of juggling childcare, money and study led her to give up on her studies, her confidence sufficiently dented that she is unlikely to try again. In both cases the outcome (regrettable) is the same. But the opportunities that lie beneath both students' decisions are very different. We could pose the same questions of each student who graduates – has each had the opportunity to form the capabilities they have reason to value? The achievable functioning of gaining the doctorate will not wholly answer our question.

As doctoral educators, capabilities would require that we and our universities pay attention to the diversity of our students (men and women, middle and working class, home and international, race and ethnicity, religion and able-bodiedness) so that each student has equal opportunity through the design of doctoral education arrangements to participate and succeed 'as an equal among others' (Terzi 2008: 184).

In advocating the importance of expanding people's capabilities for achievable functionings to be and to do in ways that they each value being and doing, Sen includes both instrumental and intrinsic ends so that education ought not to be only for something else (like a job, or higher earnings). In the capability approach a human capital basis for education is useful but limited. Sen (2003) does not reject human capital outright; indeed he sees synergies in so far as human capital and the capability approach are both concerned with the role, agency and abilities of human beings. Doctoral students make considerable investments of time and money and it is quite reasonable that some or many might expect or hope that this investment in their own human capital will lead to a different job or a promotion. Thus, Jane one of the EdD students in Wellington and Sikes's (2006: 730) study explained that the EdD 'was definitely a positive fact in my getting my present job as Director of Education', while Simon commented that, 'I recently changed jobs – that fact that I was doing the EdD, influenced the panel and was instrumental in my appointment'. Nonetheless, for Sen education is not just for human capital and economic productivity, but has intrinsic value for individuals (a love of knowledge, for example, for its own sake) and social value for communities (for example, in subjecting education polices to informed and democratic scrutiny). Jane, for example, also talks about having had to 'use parts of my brain that I never knew existed! It really stretched me and I have loved it', as well as the 'instant and continuing support network' from her cohort, which is 'a great help and confidence booster' and the valued support of 'friends, family and the [EdD] team' (Wellington and Sikes 2006: 730, 732). Finally, Catherine explains that she enjoyed the EdD even though, 'it cost me financially, emotionally and physically – but I feel it gave me the opportunity to re-evaluate my teaching, consider my development in a new light and to become a truly reflective practitioner' (Wellington and Sikes 2006: 733). From these short extracts we can begin to suggest that multi-dimensional valued doctoral capabilities include: to have economic opportunities, to have the support of others, to be able to think critically, to be a reflective practitioner and to be confident.

Martha Nussbaum (2000) has further developed the idea of 'capabilities', deepening the philosophical basis of Sen's approach. In her view, 'Education is a key to all human capabilities' (2006: 322); it enables us to develop and deepen other capabilities. In higher education she advocates an education that develops each person's capacity 'to be fully human' (2002: 290). Following Seneca, says Nussbaum, this means someone who is: 'self-aware, self-governing, and capable of recognizing and respecting the humanity of all our fellow human beings, no matter where they are born, no matter what social class they inhabit, no matter what their gender or ethnic origin' (Nussbaum 2002: 290). Nussbaum defends a Socratic view of education, which places the examined life at its centre, Aristotle's notion of reflective citizenship, and the Stoic view of education as that which frees us from habit and custom to function with sensitivity and awareness in the world. Therefore, she advocates three core capabilities for the 'cultivation of humanity': critical self-examination, the ideal of the world citizen, and the development of the narrative imagination. She (Nussbaum 2000) has also developed and defends a list of ten central universal human capabilities, unlike Sen (2004) who argues that capabilities should be agreed through processes of public reasoning and scrutiny. For our purposes here, the point is to underscore the multi-dimensionality of capabilities and achievable functionings, rather than selecting some uni-dimensional measure for evaluation (e.g. human capital).

Quality doctoral education would involve expanding students' freedoms through 'the removal of various types of unfreedoms that leave people with little choice and little opportunity of exercising their reasoned agency' (Sen 1999: xii). In their narrative of their own doctoral education, Andrews and Edwards (2008, and see Chapter 1) exemplify what a doctoral education can do in enabling people to become researching professionals and life-long learners. Completing a doctorate has enabled them to scrutinise the 'unfreedoms' they felt as common sense, but without the critical awareness to know what was wrong with the performative measures that suffused their professional lives as teachers. In recounting their experiences of undertaking an EdD in England, they explain how they 'invented' themselves as researchers and gained professional insights to make the familiar new and newly critical. The EdD, they write, 'has given us the confidence to continue taking [educational] risks' (p. 6); to interrogate language about education, to develop reflexivity through the process of learning how to undertake insider research into professional practice and to author original knowledge. They have become 'avid lifelong learners' (p. 8) and acquired courage to stand by their educational values. They write that doing a doctorate 'has given us the personal and professional development to allow us to reclaim our identity as education professionals' (p. 8). It has also expanded their economic opportunities, with both moving out of teaching in post-compulsory (post-16) education into higher education, but not with enhanced salaries. We might say doctoral education has been intrinsically and instrumentally valuable, expanding their capabilities to be and to do in ways they value being and doing.

A rich doctoral education cannot then be one that focuses only on human capital and the 'usefulness' of human beings to the exclusion of valuable non-economic ends and more expansive understandings of what is valuable in human lives and for human flourishing.

Obligations to others

But capabilities would also require something of those who have the advantage of doctoral education in societies where not everyone, or even a majority, has this opportunity. Especially in professional fields like education, capabilities direct us to consider obligations to others because, argues Sen (2008: 336), capability 'is a kind of power' and a 'central concept in human obligation' to use that power for social betterment. In becoming certain kinds of people through doctoral education – being knowledgeable, being confident, being able to reason critically, being reflexive choosers – we also take on social obligations and responsibility 'to bring about the changes that would enhance human development in the world' (Sen 2008: 335). Sen proposes that 'if someone has the power to make a change that he or she can see will reduce injustice in the world, then there is a strong social argument for doing just that' (p. 335).

Although at first sight this may appear to leave obligation up to the individual only, to be about altruism and even paternalism, it is rather a deeply social as well as a pragmatic approach. Having and owing obligations to others arises out of our view of ourselves not as isolated individuals but as members of communities, as selves-in-society. At one level we make individual moral decisions (and individual acts are important in themselves), but we also make these decisions as social beings in social collectives so that our acts bind us to others and form and reform the institutions and structures that might guarantee equality (or at the very least improvements in society that make people's lives go better) beyond our individual actions. Sen's principle of justice requires each of us to take and have responsibility for our actions-with-others and contribute to making the world go better, not displacing this responsibility to apparently impenetrable and impervious structures, which remove individual obligations to act for the common good. For example, doctoral graduates might choose roles as public intellectuals of different kinds as one way to realise such obligations to others (see Conclusions, Volume 1). They might advocate for changes in teaching and learning beyond human capital. They might share their work with colleagues to help in more critical approaches to the impact of policy on professional lives. They might simply become and be better professionals, acting to improve the lives of those whom they serve.

Conclusion

The issue for doctoral education would be to ask how it might look if we approached it through the lens of capability expansion and rich life-long learning rather than more narrowly through training and skills, and what we gain or lose as doctoral students and supervisors if we do the latter rather than the former. As doctoral graduates, students gain individually, but they are also bearers of the public good through the knowledge they have acquired. With this needs to go a critical spirit and democratic values as integral to gaining knowledge so that we not only acquire knowledge to be social scientists, but that we also form a moral perspective on how to exercise that knowledge to improve lives in society. We know that education systems are part of their societies and those changes in higher education need to be connected to changes in social systems. But this is not to say that higher education cannot be a vital part of helping to bring about transformation in individuals and groups in ways that can improve societies and well being. At the very least there is still a debate to be had, even in the face of market ideology, about the normative purposes and outcomes of doctoral education in universities. A specific challenge might be to develop a method to promote capability dimensions through participatory methods, and then use this to monitor actual, not just philosophical, justice in education.

References

Andrews, D. and Edwards, C. (2008) Consciousness in transition: the experience of doctoral study. In B. Cunningham (Ed.). *Exploring Professionalism.* London: Institute of Education.

Booth, A., McLean, M. and Walker, M. (2009) Self, others and society: A case study of university integrative learning, *Studies in Higher Education,* 34(8).

Bridges, D. (2008) Educationalization: On the Appropriateness of Asking Educational Institutions To Solve Social And Economic problems, *Educational Theory,* 58(4): 461–74.

Bridges, D., Smeyers, P. and Smith, R. (2008) Educational Research and the Practical Judgment of Policy Makers, *Journal of Philosophy of Education,* 42(1): 5–14.

Brighouse, H. (2007) The globalization of higher education and a professional ethics for academics', plenary lecture presented at the conference 'Learning Together-Reshaping higher education in a global age, London, 22–24 July 2007.

Burchardt, T. (2009) Agency Goals, Adaptation and Capability Sets, *Journal of Human Development and Capabilities,* 10(1): 3–20.

Goode, J. (2007) Empowering or disempowering the international PhD student? Constructions of the dependent and independent learner, *British Journal of Sociology of Education,* 28(5): 589–604.

Habermas, J. (1987) *The theory of communicative action, volume 2. Lifeworld and system.* Trans. T. McCarthy. Boston, MA: Beacon Press.

——(1989) The idea of the university: learning processes. In J. Habermas (Ed.). *The new conservatism.* Trans. S. Weber Nicholson. Cambridge: Polity Press.

Kenway, J. and Fahey, J. (Eds) (2009) *Globalizing The Research Imagination.* London and New York: Routledge

Marga, A. (2008) Multiculturalism, Interculturality and Leadership. In GUNI (Eds). *Higher Education in the World.* New York: Palgrave MacMillan.

Nussbaum, M. (2000) *Women and Human Development.* Cambridge: Cambridge University Press.

——(2002) Education For Citizenship In An Era Of Global Connection, *Studies in Philosophy and Education,* 21: 289–303.

——(2006) Education and democratic citizenship: capabilities and quality education, *Journal of Human Development,* 7(3): 385–96.

Rawls, J. (1971) *A Theory of Justice.* Oxford: Oxford University Press.

Robeyns, I. (2003) Sen's Capability Approach and Gender Inequality: Selecting Relevant Capabilities, *Feminist Economics,* 9(2–3): 61–91.

——(2005) The Capability Approach. A Theoretical Survey, *Journal of Human Development,* 6(2): 93–117.

——(2006) Three models of education: rights, capabilities and human capital, *Theory and Research in Education* 4(1): 69–84.

Sen, A. (1992) *Inequality Re-examined.* Oxford: Oxford University Press.

——(1999) *Development as Freedom.* New York: Alfred A. Knopf.

——(2003) Human capital and human capability. In S. Fukudo-Parr and A. K. Kumar (Eds) *Readings in Human Development*. New Delhi, Oxford and New York: Oxford University Press.

——(2004) Capabilities, Lists and Public Reason: Continuing the Conversation, *Feminist Economics*, 10(3): 77–80.

——(2008) The Idea of Justice, *Journal of Human Development*, 9(3): 329–42.

Taylor, P. (2008) Introduction. In GUNI *Higher Education in the World*. New York: Palgrave MacMillan.

Terzi, L. (2008) *Justice and Equality in Education. A Capability Perspective on Disability and Special Educational Needs*. London: Continuum.

Walker, M. and Unterhalter, E. (Eds) (2007) *Amartya Sen's capability Approach and Social Justice in Education*. New York: Palgrave MacMillan.

Wellington, J. and Sikes, P. (2006) 'A doctorate in a tight compartment': why do students choose a professional doctorate and what impact does it have on their personal and professional lives?, *Studies in Higher Education*, 31(6): 723–34.

3

'Perhaps I should be more proactive in changing my own supervisions'?

Student agency in 'doing supervision'

J. Goode

What does 'doing supervision' entail? This chapter begins by explaining the choice of the term 'doing' in this context. It continues with a brief review of how supervision has been theorised, primarily from the supervisor perspective (studies that may, therefore, be seen as concerned with 'doing supervisor' as opposed to the focus of this chapter, which, if it didn't retain some connotations of 'being done to', we might more accurately think of as 'doing supervisee'). The review is placed in the context of a changing landscape of doctoral studies, determined by wider economic and institutional forces, and characterised by tensions between 'artistic' and 'rational' models of doctoral study. The chapter goes on to illustrate the implications for practice of contemporary models of doctoral study by drawing on a fairly limited number of empirical studies of doctoral supervision that do incorporate the student experience, including a project employing peer observation and videoing of supervision meetings. And although recognising the inherent power differentials within the supervisory relationship, as well as the ways in which personal responsibility for learning can act as a form of governmentality, it concludes by highlighting the possibilities for and importance of student agency in 'doing supervision'.

A practice approach

The choice of the word 'doing' in the title of this chapter is significant. In empirical sociology, cultural studies and anthropology, we can identify Garfinkel's (1984 [1967]) ethnomethodology, Butler's (1990) 'performative' gender studies, and Latour's (1991) science studies as 'practice theories' or 'theories of social practice', that might be grouped together as members of what Reckwitz (2002) calls the 'praxeological family of theories' (2002: 244). A concrete example is West and Zimmerman's (1987) influential paper on 'Doing Gender', which conceptualised gender as 'a routine accomplishment embedded in everyday interaction'. Being a gendered person in society thus involves 'interactional work'. 'Doing supervision' similarly involves routinised interactions, which are a kind of 'work' (in addition to the academic work that forms the subject of the interactions). I am going to suggest that a specific kind of interactional work – 'management work' – is key to 'doing supervision' successfully. For the doctoral student, it is perhaps more familiar to

talk of 'having' supervision, or of 'being supervised', both of which have passive connotations at odds not only with a higher education ethos that emphasises self-direction or
self-determination in learning, but with the 'practice' approach in which West and
Zimmerman's work is located. The model of 'management work' being suggested here is
not a bureaucratic one, but is intended to signal a far more agentic approach to undertaking
certain practices that might constitute 'doing supervision'.

Gherardi (in press) outlines three identifiable strands within a practice approach:
workplace studies (e.g. Heath and Luff 2000; Heath and Button 2003; Goode and
Greatbatch 2005) anchored in an ethnographic and ethnomethodological framework,
which seek to determine how the verbal, visual and material take shape through practice
(especially discursive practices) during the production and co-ordination of interaction;
technological studies, which build on Giddens' (1984) structuration theory (e.g. Orlikowski 2000); and Gherardi's (2001) privileging of a *process* conception of practising, as
knowing-in-practice, which conceptualises knowledge not as a product but as a situated
and semiotic activity mediated by a variety of artefacts and institutions. Within a work-
space, she explains, a stabilised way of doing things becomes a practice when it is institutionalised and made normatively accountable, both for its practitioners and for those
who view it from the outside:

> When practices are read 'from the outside' … inquiry concentrates on their reg-
> ularity, on the pattern which organizes activities, and on the more or less shared
> understanding that allows their repetition. The recursiveness of practices is the
> element which enables both practitioners and researchers to recognize a practice as
> a practice, that is, a way of doing sustained by canons of good practice (a normative
> accountability) and beautiful practice (an aesthetic accountability). Therefore a
> practice is such when it is socially recognized as an institutionalized doing.
>
> Gherardi 2001

Theorising supervision

One of the problems with applying this to 'doing supervision' is that there has to date
been little empirical research on the kinds of practices that constitute doctoral supervision. Although classroom practice has long been opened up to observation and assessment, doctoral supervision has remained a 'black box', a privatised space, but it has been
the subject of a growing body of theoretical conceptualisations. Much of this has been
from the perspective of supervisors, however. Some look at supervisory styles (Acker
et al. 1994; Hockey 1996; Deuchar 2008); some offer supervisors 'guides to success'
(Delamont *et al.* 1997; Cryer 1997); some focus on supervisor training and development
(Pearson and Brew 2002; Manathunga 2005); and others offer models of supervisor–
student relationships (Styles and Radloff 2001; Wisker *et al.* 2003; Mackinnon 2004;
Grant 2005). There is also recognition of the gendered and 'raced' elements of autonomy
and dependency (Johnson *et al.* 2000; Boud and Lee 2005; Goode 2007), which them-
selves need to be interrogated and set within a wider political context of governmentality
(Holligan 2005).

Another strand within the scholarship of higher education focuses specifically on
supervision as a form of pedagogy, applying models of adult (Haggis 2002), peer (Boud
and Lee 2005), workplace (Hasrati 2005; Paré and Le Maistre 2006) and life-long

39

(Watson 2000) learning, as well as studies that examine specific aspects of the pedagogy that may or may not take place within supervision, such as writing pedagogies (Cargill 2004; Kamler and Thomson 2004; Norton *et al.* 2005); and doctoral examination (Burnham 1994; Hartley and Jory 2000; Morley *et al.* 2002; Mullins and Kiley 2002; Tinkler and Jackson 2004). Finally, there are studies of specific groups of doctoral students, such as those with disabilities (Premia 2004); and international doctoral students (Todd 1997; Cadman 2000; Broekmann and Pendlebury 2002; Coates 2004; Goode 2007). Such studies offer important theoretical tools with which doctoral students may reflect upon and analyse their own experiences of supervision.

Doctoral study in transition

Another problem for mapping the practices that constitute supervision, however, and for analysing what *it* is 'doing' and what *students* are doing when they are 'doing it', is that we are trying to capture a moving target. Against a background of increasing competition in recruitment of doctoral students from India, China and the USA, high fee levels in the UK, and claims that 'for some time this single-purpose qualification has no longer fitted the expectations of students and employers' (CRAC 2002), there has been a call to launch a national debate on the UK doctorate (Park 2007), and what it is for. Key drivers of change in this area include a new emphasis on skills and training; concerns about completion rates and quality of supervision; issues of compliance with the quality assessments; greater supervisor responsibility for their own training and for the career development and skills training of their students; an accent on the provision of a lively and productive 'research environment' in which students draw upon a variety of resources and networks beyond supervisors themselves; questions about examination practices; and the introduction of national benchmarking. In the longer term, the nature and future of the UK PhD is also likely to be influenced by a number of key European initiatives such as the Bologna and Lisbon agendas, and the European Charter for Researchers and Code of Conduct for the Recruitment of Researchers.

Other evidence suggests that supervisory practice has not caught up with the sheer variety of types of doctoral degree (Bourner *et al.* 2001; Lunt 2002; Heath 2006; Stephenson 2006; Winter *et al.* 2000; Hockey 2003; Powell 2004), and the doctoral student population itself is also changing. Furthermore, existing conceptualisations of what the PhD is for, how it should be supervised, and what outcomes it should produce are predominantly predicated on a model that constructs the doctoral student as young, full-time, and without primary domestic responsibilities. This does not fit the demographic profile of the doctoral student population, however, increasing numbers of which are not 'young researchers' but mature men and women (Leonard and Metcalfe 2006).

Thrills and skills

Regardless of the variety of doctorates and of students, the demands for higher degrees to equip graduates for a competitive global economy have led to a somewhat polarised debate about the nature of the doctoral curriculum and its implications for supervision. There are widely articulated tensions between those who emphasise 'product' (a thesis of adequate quality; evidence of research competence; an original contribution to the literature; a labour market credential; an 'oven-ready' researcher with the skills needed by the economy), and those that emphasise 'process' (an intellectual journey; socialisation into a disciplinary habitus; a process of 'becoming' someone new; the beginning of a longer process of researcher career development; one element of a broader agenda of 'life-long learning'). The 'product' that looms large in the students' imaginings may well remain the doctoral thesis, but this is no longer sufficient. The powerful discourse of 'employability' that requires that doctoral graduates are turned out with a set of 'trans-ferable' skills that can be used within and beyond an academic setting has been read as indicating a fundamental change in the mode of regulation in society associated with the social control of expertise and the position and role of professional groups. For Ball (1990), the notion of 'competency' underlying the skills debate is an influential 'moral technology', which represents a move from a cultural to a technical mode of control over expertise, and from a professional to a technical model for the role and status of the practitioner.

From this perspective, initiatives arising out of the UK 'Roberts Review' (2002), which require doctoral students to be given training in the acquisition of 'generic' as well as 'research' skills, have been seen to represent such a decontextualising. These reductive procedures, it is claimed, 'construct partial, disembedded representations of the complex social interactions of work and elsewhere … and stand in opposition to cultural practices of "everyday life" and to the "lay" understandings and constructions of meaning active there' (Jones and Moore 1993: 388–89). Furthermore, the notion of generic skills is seen on the one hand to risk failing to acknowledge the skills many part-time and highly skilled professionals who undertake doctoral study bring with them (Leonard and Metcalfe 2006), and on the other to lead to variations in practice in relation to the accreditation of prior learning (see Lunt 2002).

What is being threatened here, for some critics, are what we might think of as the inherent 'thrills' of doctoral study – the political, social and aesthetic elements of the research process. What is losing out to the technical rationality that underpins the skills/training model, are what Leonard refers to as the 'messy and confusing political issues of human concern' within the research process, that constitute the necessary conditions for the social construction of both genuinely original knowledge, and a transformed researcher identity. This is where thrills are to be had! Rather than the acquisition of disembedded skills, the vital element in doctoral research is that of learning to exercise disciplinary judgement, of 'acquiring the academic equivalent of good taste'. And supervisors have a key role to play in supporting students on this 'voyage of guided personal intellectual exploration' (Leonard 2000:186–87). So how does all this play out in practice?

The student experience of supervision

There are, in fact, relatively few studies that directly tap into the doctoral student experience, and those that do arise predominantly from feedback as part of formal eva-luation exercises (e.g. Cadman 2000), or from 'accounts', such as the reflexive auto-ethnography of Thornborrow et al. (2006). 'Accounts' may also take the form of the oral sharing of experiences, for example, between doctoral students at different stages in the process. In a graduate school session that I observed on doctoral supervision, new stu-dents' questions were answered not only by an experienced supervisor but by a recent 'postdoc'. The latter explained that he had used his supervisors differently throughout the life of the PhD. The first year had involved receiving guidance on doing a literature search; the second, practical issues around operationalising chosen methods; and the third was largely a matter of 'tying it all together'. Students asked about the 'quantity' of supervision – did he feel he'd got a 'fair deal'? Yes, he did, but that had in part been due to the fact that he gave his supervisors a fair deal by always preparing for supervision sessions. In terms of time available to him, this had varied throughout the life of the PhD. In his first year, sessions had been difficult to organise, and happened every two to three months; in the second year, he had one per week with an individual supervisor, which worked well in forcing him to 'push on'; by the third year, they were every two to three weeks, depending on supervisors' availability – and they took place in locations as various as on trains, planes and at 'Quick-Fit'! 'I basically followed them around Europe', he commented. He had also started writing from very early on. At first, only one of his supervisors looked at what he'd written. As English was his second language, the supervisor commented on his use of English, and gave general help with his academic writing style, but not to the extent of proofreading. Towards the end of his PhD, he was getting feedback that was general rather than detailed – by this stage, the PhD was 'his', and he felt able to accept or reject their suggestions. He advised negotiating with supervisors from the start how to run the sessions, and how to time them. 'It's best to get things very organised even if you then have to be flexible', he commented. His advice echoed that of the supervisor: 'Be proactive/interactive, not just passive/reactive'. He also gave advice in relation to the politics of assessment. He had got into an email discussion with an author of whose work he was critical. Initially, he thought it would make for some very interesting and productive dialogue in a viva if he had him as his 'external'. On reflection, he decided that this was perhaps a little too naïve and high risk. Maybe the most important thing in relation to this choice, he suggested, is to know who *not* to choose.

Personal accounts from those who have 'made it' can be useful, therefore. But as Delamont *et al.* note,

> [T]here is ... a continuing lack of observational data on the actual conduct of the most private supervisory relationships. The data that are available, and that have been reported in recent years, consist almost exclusively of accounts, collected under the auspices of qualitative interview studies.
>
> Delamont *et al.* 2000: 134

Observational studies are needed to uncover what actually happens in supervisory meetings, and to build an evidence base for understanding what 'doing supervision' means in practice.

Sarah Li and Clive Seale, who have written about various aspects of their own experiences of supervisee and supervisor, respectively (2007a; 2007b; 2008), using transcripts of their recorded sessions as well as contemporaneous written records, written comments on drafts of submitted work, progress reports, email correspondence and a research diary, identified just three other studies involving analysis of audio-taped supervisor–student dialogues (McMichael 1992; Wisker *et al.* 2003; Cargill 2000). Cargill's study, based on transcripts of interactions with international students, uses conversation analysis to analyse the interactions between two supervisor–student pairs in agricultural science. She concludes that the students seemed reluctant to *take up turns in talk* with their supervisors, unless given very clear signals that they were expected to do so. Neither did they intervene in the flow of the talk to address issues of miscommunication or non-understanding, despite having participated in a programme designed to make clear Australian supervisors' expectations that postgraduate students will exhibit initiative and independence and should not be unduly deferential. She accounts for this in terms of a conflict between taking steps to communicate clearly, and remaining within the model of student role the students saw as appropriate for them. This is at odds with a finding from my own research with international doctoral students and supervisors, however (Goode 2007), in which an 'international' supervisor reinterpreted the perceptions her UK colleagues held of international students. She saw the commonly remarked upon displays of deference in supervision being treated as 'attributes', and felt this denied both the agency of the student, and the reciprocal nature of the more hierarchical Chinese supervisor–student relationship, within which there is an understanding that the student will be well 'looked after' and that the supervisor will behave in an 'ethical' way in fulfilling his/her obligations. She saw what UK supervisors tend to attribute to cultural traits as requiring a more sociological explanation:

> I regard this as a sociological process – we need to understand more about how students, from their point of view, survive the system – rather than see [supervision] as a purely intellectual exercise.
>
> Goode 2007: 596

She interpreted the way students initially respond within the supervisory relationship, and to their studies, as a set of social practices rather than as a matter of intellectual capacity – as taking time to learn 'how things are done around here' – and she went on to refute an inherent inability to challenge authority by citing how students at Beijing and Qinghua had challenged various visiting Heads of State. Indeed, Li and Seale (ibid.) interpret Li's own non-uptake of turns in talk with Seale (reproduced in Li and Seale 2007a) as passive resistance to the imputed criticism being delivered, which Seale then has actively to manage with the use of a 'repair' strategy. At other points of disagreement, Seale abandons the debate but offers an opportunity to return to it later. Li comments on how crushing she initially found Seale's criticism, but how she was able to 'resurface', in part due to his 'gentleness' and 'sensitive delivery of criticism' (p. 521). And although she acknowledges the gendered nature of power that can operate in supervisory interactions, she also exercised power on occasions, through 'rebuttals', thereby demonstrating the agency that is often missing from characterisations of doctoral students in accounts coming from supervisor perspectives. A further finding of my research with international doctoral students was due to the fact that there was a longitudinal element to the study. Interviews were repeated over an 18-month period, and the development and use of many of the generic skills identified by Roberts was evident over this time, even though, in interviews, participants did not use a 'skills' vocabulary. This suggests that 'situated learning' and disciplinary socialisation on the one hand, and the acquisition of generic skills on the other, need not be mutually exclusive.

Two other studies that draw on observations/recordings are based on more than just one or two cases. Paré *et al.* (in press) focus particularly on how doctoral writing is talked about and constructed in supervision meetings, whereas the previously unreported study I conducted, as part of a 'Roberts-funded' initiative designed to improve doctoral supervision meetings, used peer observation of all aspects of such meetings. Both were interested in similar questions: What do people talk about during supervisory meetings? What topics and issues come up? What advice is given/taken? What strategies are considered/deployed? What relationships are formed/enacted? What roles are played? What seems to work? What doesn't? What are participants thinking when they come to these meetings? What do they think/do after the meetings?

Paré and his colleagues, who focus on the writing of the dissertation, show how talk using spatial and design metaphors was aimed at helping students organise and sequence their dissertations, whereas rhetorical justifications for the inclusion of certain information, or sometimes blunt truths about who to choose or avoid as examiners, were designed to help students place their work within larger debates taking place in their field. In the last case, we can see once more how this kind of interaction will not only develop the intellectual and organisational skills of the student, but also constitutes 'doing socialisation into a disciplinary habitus'.

The methodology of the peer observation project I conducted involved recruiting participants at all stages of their studies, across seven different schools, to observe and/or be observed; supporting them in negotiating access to a supervision session with their supervisors; and briefing observers (using video recordings of actual supervision meetings, made as part of the project) on how to conduct and record (in written notes) an observation, and on how to engage in and write up a two-stage postobservation reflection exercise. The first stage of this was to act as a 'sounding board' for their peer to reflect on the effectiveness of the supervision meeting and on their own contribution to it; and the second stage was to write a brief report on what they felt they had learned from being an observer, that they might apply to their own future practice as a 'supervisee'. Finally, participants were invited to focus groups to share their experiences.

In terms of content, observers reported:

- Funding issues (for example, in relation to the PhD itself and to conference attendance).
- Discussion of methods/methodological issues (such as the use of theoretical models; the development of research question; the location of the study; sampling; time period for and methods of data collection, including questionnaires, surveys, experiments, and vignettes; ethical issues, such as getting ethical approval and researcher safety).
- Discussion of 'artefacts' produced by the student (such as a literature review, or part of a sample chapter, with associated issues such as the standard required for doctoral work and the notion of originality).
- Writing (ethics applications, conference papers and abstracts, articles, portfolios – but also the issue of *starting* to write the thesis, and the standard of written English being used).
- Staging post/assessments (end of year report, upgrading, the viva).
- The wider 'research environment' (including opportunities for teaching, conference attendance and networking opportunities, graduate school courses on offer and attended).

Process issues covered: degrees of formality or informality; the use of humour; degree of eye contact between participants at different times; displays of anxiety by the student; agenda-setting (formal and informal), its control, and how and when this shifted; roles and levels of interaction between co-supervisors; indicators of status (between co-supervisors and between supervisors and mature students); points of disagreement/conflict (between student and supervisor, and between co-supervisors) and how these were managed; and external interruptions and how these were handled.

Actions/interventions undertaken by students included: sending in advance questions/ issues for discussion; bringing a written agenda; controlling/handing over control of agenda; asking questions (for information and for advice, e.g. on data analysis); responding to questions; expressing concerns about work; explaining their work; reflecting on work done; making decisions/plans in relation to future work; justifying decisions; recording the meeting (on the 'official' form, in own notes, and in one case audio-recording); giving an update on progress; agreeing to suggestions; disagreeing with suggestions; expressing a difficulty; defending stance taken; asking for specific feedback; summarising feedback to clarify understanding; airing fears about conference attendance; sharing disappointment/loss of confidence resulting from rejection of journal article; expressing views on training courses; refocusing discussion according to own priority; monitoring time; calling meeting to a close when own agenda completed.

In their postsupervision reflections (which took place straight after the meeting), students who had been observed revealed a variety of things that they had found both helpful and unhelpful. An example of the former was 'being able to communicate comfortably in a safe environment that doesn't make me feel foolish', an experience the student felt served to boost her confidence in her own abilities. Others were in relation to students feeling that supervisors were familiar with and understood what they were doing, the stage they were at, and the progress they had made, in one case including confronting them on an acknowledged weakness and offering advice on how to overcome it; and in relation to the clarity of discussions, with appreciation expressed of direct guidance given (which was distinguished from being given the 'right answer'), and of supervisors being explicit rather than obfuscating. What was clearly not appreciated were occasions when supervisors took phone calls or allowed callers to the office during the session, and when supervisors had clearly not read work sent in advance. One student who had sent work two weeks earlier commented to his peer, 'If supervisors do not read the documentation sent to them prior to the meeting, a lot of time is spent re-discussing what was said in previous meetings, halting ... progression ... as they can't remember what was previously discussed and decided.' A third set of comments related to co-supervisors and how to manage them, with one student explaining that one of her supervisors used to dominate meetings by doing all the talking, but that she had now learnt how to stop him.

In some cases the observers' comments on what *they* had learnt reflected the comments made to them by those they had observed, especially if they either chimed or contrasted markedly with their own experiences, as with these comments:

I felt really disappointed for the student ... I felt that the supervisor did not commit enough energy to the student's research ... the student had clearly worked to meet a deadline with writing and yet the supervisor had not met their deadline to review the work. This is not something I have experienced in my own research, and I am glad, as I would find this very de-motivating.

Am struck by both supervisors taking notes, and looking like they remember this discussion.

The majority of comments, however, were related to observers reflecting, in the light of what they had seen and heard from their peers, on their own need to be more proactive in order to capitalise on what they could get out of supervision sessions. They often went away with the intention to be more organised and to take the initiative more, whether in setting the agenda, focusing more, or communicating misunderstandings and frustrations:

> I found the process of observing another supervision more valuable than I had realised! … it made me realise the importance of sending regular documents to my supervisor prior to the meetings. It also made me realise how my supervisions can sometimes veer off on tangents which are not central to the discussion, and how perhaps setting an agenda could solve this problem. I came away feeling that I also need to contribute more … I do not always have the confidence to discuss my opinion. Recognising this will hopefully allow me in future to build on this and gain more confidence.It differed from mine in that the supervisor completed the supervision record form, and very clear aims and objectives for the next meeting were mutually decided upon. Whilst my own supervision format works well for me more often than not, after this experience I will likely prepare a more detailed agenda, and send it well in advance of the supervision. I will also discuss with my supervisors in more detail what they expect me to achieve by the next supervision.
>
> [T]o be more mentally organised in order to expose my viewpoints, take advantage of the meeting, and clearly expose my frustration to my supervisor when it happens.
>
> As an international student I sometimes feel a cultural gap … what I came to know is that a student should be proactive in communication, and open to different ideas and suggestions about research, but at the same time critical enough to tease out one's misunderstandings or misconceptions – with academic vigour.

And lest all this talk of agendas and organisation sounds rather bureaucratic, and confirms the worst fears of those who feel we risk losing the 'thrills', there was also recognition of more 'organic' ways of operating (seen as effective in some but not necessarily all circumstances), as well as evidence of excitement having been experienced and communicated:

> I thought the lack of hierarchy and the 'person-centred' approach of the supervisor was extremely empowering … whilst there was no obvious structure or agenda … the organic development worked well – although in other circumstances it might not. It was fascinating to observe someone else's supervision session as I had never really thought about 'what was happening' in my own sessions before this time … I often become very anxious about supervision and feel that I need to 'perform' well enough, when perhaps I need to relax and enjoy it more.
>
> I have never engaged in a discussion of such depth in a supervision meeting. It made me think about how such a useful in-depth discussion of theory/data is achieved … total engagement in a theoretical discussion with both sides taking part. The supervisor's role seemed to be to draw out the student and to confirm her ideas while expanding on them. It felt very exciting to me, as there was an enormous amount of energy being produced as they both engaged fully with the discussion … perhaps I should be more proactive in changing my own supervisions. Having a list of questions seems one way to provoke discussions.

Students did not come away from the project with a 'blue print for good practice'. Rather they learned that there are many different ways of 'doing supervision' effectively, and they gained a recognition that what they will have in common is active 'management' of the process on the part of the student. Finally, students' comments about their participation in this two-year project validated peer observation of doctoral supervision as a methodology, with structured reflection on the experience being a vital component of the learning to be gained from it:

> Observing is a new experience for me. It was great, I love it. Their meeting was so different, so serious.
>
> It helped me to think about my own supervision. It is very useful to reflect, and I did see my own supervisor's strengths after observing somebody else's supervision.

Conclusions

Doctoral study and its supervision is a highly differentiated process and is in flux. At any one time, therefore, what 'doing supervision' means for students will differ according to a variety of factors, including: conceptions of what the PhD is 'for'; disciplinary location and the social organisation of knowledge production within it; supervisor style and how flexible this is; pedagogical issues such as the emphasis on and appropriateness of direct 'tutoring' and/or (more or less collaborative) research; mutual understandings of international and institutional cultures; the wider 'research environment' and the resources it offers; and the stage in the process the student is at, in relation to both the formal curriculum (the subject under study, methodological approaches, skills acquisition and career development) and the informal curriculum (familiarity with 'how things are done are around here' – the 'here' referring to local institutional practices and current national/political imperatives).

Until recently, what constitutes 'doing supervision' and what it looks like in practice have occupied a 'privatised' space, but there is now an emerging body of work that goes beyond interview-based studies from the supervisor perspective. Observational studies of supervisor–student interactions within supervision meetings are beginning to show how 'doing supervision' is accomplished, although there are inevitably competing interpretations of some phenomena, such as students 'failing'/refusing to 'take up turns' in talk. What is clear is that students can, and need to be, highly proactive agents within supervision, not only managing their own time, tasks, identity and career construction, and the production of the requisite 'artefacts' – but also their supervisors, and their interactions with them.

References

Acker, S., Hill, T. and Black, E. (1994) Thesis supervision in the social sciences: managed or negotiated?, *Higher Education*, 28: 483–98.

Ball, S. (1990) Management as moral technology. In Ball, S. J. (Ed.). *Foucault and Education*. London: Routledge.

Boud, D. and Lee, A. (2005) 'Peer learning' as pedagogic discourse for research education, *Studies in Higher Education*, 30(5): 501–16.

Bourner, T., Bowden, R. and Laing, S. (2001) Professional doctorates in England, *Studies in Higher Education*, 26(2): 65–83.

Broekmann, I. and Pendlebury, S. (2002) Diversity, background and the quest for home in postgraduate education, *Studies in Higher education*, 27(3): 287–95.

Burnham, P. (1994) Surviving the Viva: Unravelling the Mysteries of the PhD Oral, *Journal of Graduate Education*, 1(1): 30–34.

Butler, J. (1990) *Gender Trouble*. London: Routlege.

Cadman, K. (2000) 'Voices in the Air': evaluations of the learning experiences of international postgraduates and their supervisors, *Teaching in Higher Education*, 5(4): 475–91.

Cargill, M. (2000) Intercultural postgraduate supervision meetings: an exploratory discourse study, *Prospect*, 15(2): 28–38.

——(2004) Transferable skills within research degrees: a collaborative genre-based approach to developing publication skills and its implications for research education, *Teaching in Higher Education*, 9(1): 83–98.

Coates, N. (2004) *The 'Stranger', the 'Sojourner' and the International Student*. Paper to the Education in a Changing Environment: Scholarship, Educational Research and Development Conference, University of Salford, 13–14 September 2004.

CRAC (2002) *Profiting from postgraduate talent*. Report of a conference held at the New Connaught Rooms, London on Tuesday, 11 June 2002.

Cryer, P. (1997) *Handling Common Dilemmas in Supervision Issues in Postgraduate Supervision, Teaching and Management, Guide no 2*. London: Society for Research into Higher Education and the Times Higher Education Supplement.

Delamont, S., Atkinson, P. and Parry, O. (1997) *Supervising the PhD, A Guide to Success*. Bucks: Open University Press.

——(2000) *The Doctoral Experience, Success and Failure in Graduate School*. London and New York: Falmer Press.

Deuchar, R. (2008) Facilitator, director or critical friend?: Contradiction and congruence in doctoral supervision styles, *Teaching in Higher Education*, 13(4): 489–500.

Garfinkel, H. (1984 [1967]) *Studies in Ethnomethodology*. Cambridge: Polity Press.

Gherardi, S. (2001) From organizational learning to practice-based knowing, *Human Relations*, 54(1): 131–39.

——(in press) Telemedicine: a practice-based approach to technology, *Human Relations*.

Giddens, A. (1984) *The constitution of society: outline of the theory of structuration*. Polity Press: Cambridge.

Goode, J. (2007) Empowering or disempowering the international PhD student? Constructions of the dependent and independent learner, *British Journal of Sociology of Education*, 28(5): 589–603.

Goode, J. and Greatbatch, D. (2005) Boundary work: the production and consumption of health information and advice within service interactions between staff and callers to NHS Direct, *Journal of Consumer Culture* 5(3): 315–37.

Grant, M. (2005) Fighting for space in supervision: fantasies, fairytales, fictions and fallacies, *International Journal of Qualitative Studies in Education*, 18(3): 337–54 May–June 2005.

Haggis, T. (2002) Exploring the 'black box' of process: a comparison of theoretical notions of the 'adult learner' with accounts of postgraduate learning experience, *Studies in Higher Education*, 27(2): 207–20.

Hartley, J. and Jory, S. (2000) Lifting the veil on the viva: The experiences of PhD candidates in the UK, *Psychology Teaching Review*, 9: 76–90.

Hasrati, M. (2005) Legitimate peripheral participation and supervising PhD students, *Studies in Higher Education*, 30(5): 557–70.

Heath, L. (2006) Supervision of Professional Doctorates: Education Doctorates in English Universities, *Higher Education Review*, 38(2): 21–41.

Heath, C. and Luff, P. (2000) *Technology in action*. Cambridge University Press: Cambridge.

Heath, C. and Button, G. (2003) Special Issue on Workplace Studies: Editorial introduction, *British Journal of Sociology*, 53(2): 157–61.

Hockey, J. (1996) Strategies and tactics in the supervision of UK Social Science PhD students, *International Journal of Qualitative Studies in Education*, 9(4): 481–500.

——(2003) Practice-based research degree students in Art & Design: Identity and Adaptation, *International Journal of Art & Design Education*, 22(1): 82–91.

Holligan, C. (2005) Fact and fiction: a case history of doctoral supervision, *Educational Research*, 47(3): 267–78.

Johnson, L., Lee, A. and Green, B. (2000) The PhD and the autonomous self: Gender, rationality and postgraduate pedagogy, *Studies in Higher Education*, 25(2): 135–47.

Jones, L. and Moore, R. (1993) Education, competence and the control of expertise, *British Journal of Sociology of Education*, 14(4): 385–97.

Kamler, B. and Thomson, P. (2004) Driven to abstraction: doctoral supervision and writing pedagogies, *Teaching in Education*, 9(2):195–209.

Latour, B. (1991) *Nous n'avais jamais été modernes. Essai d'anthropologie symétrique*. Paris: La Decouverte.

Leonard, D. (2000) Transforming Doctoral Studies: Competencies and Artistry, *Higher Education in Europe*, 25(2):181–92.

Leonard, D. and Metcalfe, J. (2006) *Review of literature on the impact of working context and support on the postgraduate research student learning experience*. York: Higher Education Academy.

Li, S. and Seale, C. (2007a) Managing Criticism in PhD supervision: a qualitative case study, *Studies in Higher Education*, 32(4): 511–26.

——(2007b) Learning to do qualitative data analysis: an observational study of doctoral work, *Qualitative Health Research*, 17(10): 1442–52.

——(2008) Acquiring a Sociological Identity: an observational study of a PhD Project, *Sociology*, 42(5): 971–86.

Lunt, I. (2002) *Professional Doctorates in Education*. Online commissioned article on ESCalate website. (Available at escalate.ac.uk Accessed 2 March 2009).

Mackinnon, J. (2004) Academic Supervision: seeking metaphors and models for quality, *Journal of Further and Higher Education,* 28(4): 395–405.

Manathunga, C. (2005) The Development of Research Supervision: 'Turning the light on a private space', *International Journal for Academic Development*, 10(1): 17–30.

McMichael, P. (1992) Tales of the unexpected – supervisors' and students' perspectives on short-term projects and dissertations, *Educational Studies*, 18(3): 299–310.

Morley, L., Leonard, D. and David, M. (2002) Variations in Viva: quality and equality in British PhD assessments, *Studies in Higher Education*, 27(3): 263–73.

Mullins, G. and Kiley, M. (2002) 'It's a PhD, not a Nobel Prize': how experienced examiners assess research theses, *Studies in Higher Education*, 27(4): 369–86.

Norton, L., Harrington, K., Elander, J., Sinfield, S., Reddy, P., Pitt, E. and Aiyegbayo, O. (2005) Supporting diversity and inclusivity through writing workshops. In C. Rust (Ed.). *Improving Student Learning 12: Inclusivity and Diversity*. Oxford: The Oxford Centre for Staff and Learning Development.

Orlikowski, W. (2000) Using technologies and constituting structures: a practice-lens for studying technology in organizations, *Organization Science*, 11(4): 404–28.

Paré, A. and Le Maistre, C. (2006) Distributed mentoring in communities of practice. In P. Tynjälä, J. Välimaa and G. Boulton-Lewis (Eds), *Higher education and working life: Collaborations, confrontations and challenges*. Amsterdam: Elsevier, 129–41.

Paré, A., Starke-Meyerring, D. and McAlpine, L. (in press) The dissertation as multi-genre: Many readers, many readings. In C. Bazerman, D. Figueiredo, and A. Bonini, (Eds). *Genre in a Changing World*. West Lafayette: Parlour Press and WAC Clearinghouse.

Park, C. (2007) *Redefining the Doctorate*. York: The Higher Education Academy.

Pearson, M., and Brew, A. (2002) Research Training and Supervision Development, *Studies in Higher Education*, 27(2): 135–50.

Powell, S. (2004) *The Award of PhD by Published Work in the UK*. UK Council for Graduate Education, Lichfield, UK. (Available online from the UKCGE website www.ukcge.ac.uk/publications/reports.htm).

Premia (2004) *Access to research: institutional issues for disabled postgraduate research students*. Report produced through the HEFCE funded project 'Premia – making research education accessible' (2003–5), University of Newcastle upon Tyne.

Reckwitz, A. (2002) Toward a theory of social practices: a development in culturalist theorizing, *European Journal of Social Theory*, 5(2): 243–63.

Roberts, G. (2002) *SET for Success*. London: HM Treasury.

Stephenson, J. (2006) Managing their own programme: a case study of the first graduates of a new kind of doctorate in professional practice, *Studies in Continuing Education*, 28(1): 17–32.

Styles I. and Radloff A. (2001) The Synergistic Thesis: student and supervisor perspectives, *Journal of Further and Higher Education*, 25(1): 97–106.

Thornborrow, T., Humphreys, M. and Brown, A. D. (2006) *Researching and Supervising by Storying Around: an autoethnographic trio*. Paper at Second International Congress of Qualitative Inquiry, University of Illinois Urbana-Champaign.

Tinkler, P. and Jackson, C. (2004) *The Doctoral Examination Process*. Maidenhead: Open University Press.

Todd, E. (1997) Supervising overseas students, problem and opportunity. In D. McMamara and R. Harris (Eds), *Overseas students in higher education*. London: Routledge.

Watson, D. (2000) Lifelong learning and professional higher education. In D. Watson, T. Bourner and T. Katz (Eds), *New Directions in Professional Higher Education*. Buckingham: SRHE/Open University Press.

West, C. and Zimmerman, D. H. (1987) Doing Gender, *Gender & Society*, 1(2): 125–51.

Winter, R., Griffiths, M. and Green, K. (2000) The 'Academic' Qualities of Practice: what are the criteria for a practice-based PhD?, *Studies in Higher Education*, 25(1): 25–37.

Wisker, G., Robinson, G., Trafford, V., Warnes, M. and Creighton, E. (2003) From supervisory dialogues to successful PhDs, *Teaching in Higher Education*, 8(3): 370–83.

4

From poster to PhD

The evolution of a literature review

K. Dixon and H. Janks

A literature review evolves. At first the literature constitutes the research, then it is constituted by it. The story of the evolution of the literature review for Kerryn's research is intertwined with the story of her evolving relationship with Hilary, her research 'supervisor'. We will return to discuss and question the metaphorical implications of this curious term later.

The poster

It all began with a poster assignment that Hilary set for her students in her critical literacy masters course. Students were required to design a poster on a theorist of their choice to show how his or her work could be applied in a South African context. The purpose of the assignment was to provide masters students with the skills needed to produce and disseminate knowledge using the genre of an academic or professional conference poster.

Kerryn's theoretical starting point was Allan Luke's (1992) paper 'The Body Literate'. She was intrigued by his analysis of how bodies are trained in early literacy classrooms. She had no difficulty with the theory but was at a loss when it came to representing it visually. To help her get started Hilary suggested she find a design that could work as a template for the poster and gave her a magazine insert advertising the Apple PowerBook G3. This design opened the way for Kerryn to play with the theory she had chosen in ways that would become generative for her subsequent work.

The genre of a two-dimensional poster presented the challenge of showing bodily kinesis in three-dimensional space. In addition, the spatial limitations of a poster made it difficult to do justice to the theory.

The Apple design provided five different surfaces and enabled the use of both sides of the page. To achieve this, an A3 page is folded in half (along the dotted line in Figure 4.1) and then in half again (along the dotted line in Figure 4.2) to result in Figure 4.3.

This produces a book-cum-poster in which A is the front page, B and C are the inside of the 'book' and D is the back page. If you then open the page out E forms an A3 poster (see Figure 4.4).

Kerryn modified this design making each of A, B, C and D an A3 sheet, which when stuck together opened out to produce a large poster, four times the size of A3. Now she had a poster that was also a book, providing a wonderful visual metaphor for literacy, which she could use to demonstrate how children are taught to use their bodies to read a book and to write. Figures 4.3(a)-(e) show the actual pages of the book–poster reduced.

In Figure 4.3(a) the arrows on the front page (A) show the sense of directionality needed to read a page; labels show where you begin and end; the hand in the top right hand corner indicates where you turn the page; and the letters in the title represent children's alphabet blocks; the drawings in the word 'bodies' are the images used in the

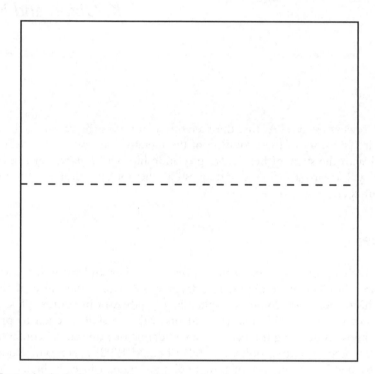

Figure 4.1 Poster Apple design instructions (Dixon and Janks).

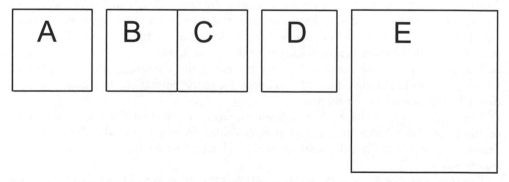

Figure 4.2 Labels for the different pages of the design when the book-poster is opened and unfolded (Dixon and Janks).

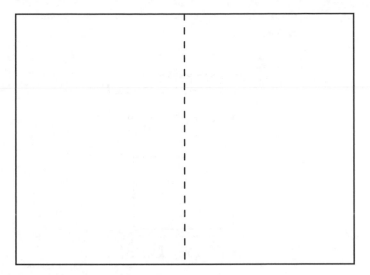

Figure 4.3 Poster Apple design instructions (Dixon and Janks).

Letterland phonics programme. Bourdieu's (1992) theories of habitus and capital are incorporated into the names of 'Allan HABITUS Luke' and Pierre CAPITAL Bourdieu' along the bottom of the page.

The second page (B) of the book (Figure 4.3(b)) shows the inscription of handwriting onto the body as well as the directionality of letters, and their spatial arrangement on the page which is conveyed by lines, arrows and fingerprints. The Escher drawing suggests both left and right hand embodiment. The third page (C) is interactive and requires readers to use their own bodies to write on the silhouette of the body shown at the top left of the page and to unscramble the puzzle-piece techno-body shown at the bottom right of the page (see Figure 4.3(c)).

Bourdieu's (1986) theory of social capital is depicted on the back page (D). In the Figure 4.3(a) the inner circle is divided into quadrants, three of the quadrants represent the subcategories of cultural capital: objectified capital, institutional capital and embodied capital. The fourth quadrant represents social capital. The images were chosen as visual symbols of these different forms of capital. These quadrants are moveable to show their relationship with economic and symbolic capital, both of which encircle them.

Figure 4.4 Poster Apple design instructions (Dixon and Janks).

Figure 4.5(a) Page A is A3 (reduced here) (Dixon and Janks).

Figure 4.5(b) Page B is A3 (reduced here) (Dixon and Janks).

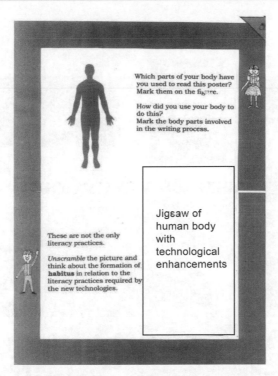

Figure 4.5(c) Page C is A3 (reduced here) (Dixon and Janks).

Figure 4.5(d) Page D is A3 (reduced here) (Dixon and Janks).

Figure 4.5(e) Large finished poster, four times the size of A3 (Actual pages of the book-poster reduced here) (Dixon and Janks).

When the book is 'opened' out, the poster (E) shows the literate bodies of real children who are depicted in the photographs. The children on the left were photographed in school and the children on the right were photographed out of school. The poster overall invites the reader to reflect on the difference between children's in-school and out-of-school embodiments. The poster within the poster – 'Rules for good listening' – was taken from the classroom in which the children on the left were photographed and it captures economically how children's in-school bodies are to be disciplined.

By the time Kerryn had finished this work she had a title for her PhD thesis: *Literacy, power and the embodied subject* (Dixon 2007), a research 'supervisor' and a theoretical framework.

The relationship between Kerryn and her 'supervisor', Hilary

In South Africa every doctoral researcher is constructed as a 'student' who needs to be 'supervised'. These naming practices are not neutral. They suggest a particular kind of relationship and set of practices. Supervision suggests the need for oversight, regulation, control, and standards setting by a superior over a subordinate or novice. It emphasises watching and monitoring and is a wonderful metaphor of what Foucault calls surveillance (Foucault 1977).

An analysis of 150 random uses of the word 'supervision' taken from the British National Corpus of 751 instances of use (sara.natcorp.ox.ac.uk/lookup.html, accessed 5 March 2009), shows that research supervision sits alongside supervision in factories, warehouses, building sites, the workplace and kitchens, where it functions to oversee workers at the bottom of the hierarchy so as to maintain discipline and quality. In these contexts supervision appears as a chain of command with supervisors supervising and being supervised. In effect, supervision is a form of governmentality that manages 'the conduct of conducts' (Dean 1999; Foucault 2002). Nine occurrences in the corpus suggest that supervisors are responsible for watching out for those for whom they are responsible: they have to protect them from health hazards and other dangerous situations. This is particularly true of the corpus references to the supervision of children and suggests a paternalistic parental relationship. What we believe is needed is a concept of a research adviser that embraces the metaphor of a fiduciary relationship (Mackinnon 2004), a relationship of trust in which the senior researcher takes responsibility for promoting the doctoral researcher's work, not his or her own interests.

How then do we understand the relationship between a senior researcher and a novice researcher? We see it as a dynamic pedagogic relationship that evolves over many years of intimate intellectual engagement. We do not use the word 'intimate' lightly. For us it captures the closeness and exposure that results from this meeting of minds.

For Hilary being a research adviser means trying to fathom how each of her doctoral researchers learns, thinks and works, as well as the kinds of emotional support they need. It also involves having to work out when to coax, when to make demands and when to back off. This is different for each of one's doctoral researchers and is always a judgement call. It changes as the relationship evolves and the research moves into different phases. This is always difficult because it requires an understanding of each researcher's personal and social circumstances, as well as their psyche. If one gets it wrong, there is a great deal at stake.

For Kerryn having an adviser was both daunting and a privilege. She had a sense that she had to prove herself worthy of the time and effort that her research adviser gave to the project. Having access to a one-on-one teacher who knew the field, who helped in the shaping and crafting of the research, who provided clarity on how research is conducted, and who had been through the ups and downs of the research process was invaluable. Because Hilary understood the project and its evolution, Kerryn knew that she could help her through the impasses, recognise her avoidance strategies and apply pressure when needed. This, of course, is easier for Kerryn to say in retrospect, and is not meant to suggest that the relationship was not uncomfortable at times and that it was not difficult to receive criticism, however constructive. For Kerryn criticism was particularly disheartening when she thought she had finished something and then had to commit more hours of rethinking and redrafting. Why the fiduciary metaphor works is because a relationship based on trust requires a leap of faith in someone else. One has to accept that at times one is so emotionally invested in the work, one cannot see it for what it is, either good or bad.

Kerryn and Hilary worked together on Kerryn's doctorate over a period of six years. During this time Kerryn moved from being a student to a university tutor to a full-time member of staff. She was young when she began with limited experience of the field, research, the world of work, professional politics, and of her own capabilities. By the time she finished she was a mature, competent, intellectually confident, self-sufficient scholar with her own novice researchers to advise. Hilary just got older, but of course learnt a great deal in the process. Bright young minds invigorate and educate older, experienced staff, and working with their fledgling ideas and their cutting-edge specialist knowledge as it deepens is one of the real joys of life in the academy.

Our relationship changed over this time. Hilary prefers a professional rather than a personal relationship with her doctoral researchers. Kerryn liked this because the intellectual relationship is so intense that clear boundaries were really important to her. Many of the metaphors of supervision in the literature represent this relationship as a partnership in which the power differential is negated. For instance, we really like Bartlett and Mercer's (2001) extended metaphors of supervision as 'cooking up an intellectual feast' (pp. 63–64), 'planting a garden' (pp. 64–66) and 'bushwalking' (pp. 66–68). While we have aspired to dealing with issues of power in our relationship in similar ways, we believe that these metaphors ignore the realities of the senior researcher's experience and institutional, intellectual, cultural and embodied capital, which the novice desires (Lacan 1989). Kerryn willingly entered into an unequal relation of power because as a Foucaultian she sees power as productive rather than oppressive (Foucault 1977; 2002). We both accept, together with Foucault, the inevitability of the knowledge/power conjunction (Foucault 1980).

Now that we are colleagues we have become really good friends socially and professionally. Our obsessive tendencies and our senses of humour make us very compatible and we now go away to write, together or alongside each other. Because of the trust already established, Kerryn has chosen Hilary as her professional mentor at work. This has been an extremely productive extension of our fiduciary relationship but it continues to recognise the power difference based on Hilary's senior status in, and experience of, the institution. This is what Kerryn wanted in a mentor whose job it is to teach her the rules of the game, including, amongst other things, how to get parking in the Senate House garage. As friends we exchange academic gossip based on our differential access in the hierarchy of the institution, our different age-related local and international academic networks and, more personally, in relation to our different stages of life experience.

Theoretical framework

If it had not been for the word 'subject' in Kerryn's title, *Literacy, Power and the Embodied Subject*, Bourdieu's theoretical work might have been the primary lens for reading the data. The word 'subject' was necessary because at that time we were working with a poststructuralist understanding of identity. Hilary knew that Kerryn needed to deepen her understanding of subjectivity, and Kerryn remembers Hilary's exact words, 'You know you are going to have to read Foucault'. The sinking feeling in Kerryn's stomach was triggered by the embodied memory of being told dismissively in a literary theory class that she had misread Foucault because she had read him as a historian when the expectation was that she would read him as a student of literature. At the time, having read only the opening of *Discipline and punish* (Foucault 1977), the required reading for that class, Kerryn did not have enough intellectual capital to defend her reading. What she took away from the class was the feeling that she could not trust herself to make sense of Foucault. In the introduction to her thesis, Kerryn described the reading of Foucault for her doctoral work as 'the return of the repressed' (Dixon 2007: 10). Students often bring their emotional history into their new intellectual relationship with their research advisers, who may have no inkling of their fears, which emanate from the past.

Because Hilary believed that Kerryn was new to Foucault, she scaffolded (Bruner 1983) her reading with a staged reading list that combined theory, commentary and applied theory. In the early stages of reading it is helpful if the adviser can provide the researcher with paths into the literature in order to make it more accessible. Kerryn worked through the following books and articles:

1 Foucault, M. (1977) *Discipline and punish.*
2 Gordon's (1980) edited collection of interviews with Foucault. *Power/knowledge selected interviews and other writings 1972–1977.*
3 Smart, B. (2002) *Michel Foucault.*
4 McHoul, A. and Grace, W. (1993) *A Foucault Primer Discourse, Power and the Subject.*
5 Dreyfus, H. and Rabinow, P. (1983) *Michel Foucault: Beyond Structuralism and Hermeneutics.*
6 Hunter, I. (1988) *Culture and Government: the emergence of literacy education* and (1994) *Rethinking the School: Subjectivity, bureaucracy, criticism.*
7 A selection of papers by Jennifer Gore (1994–98).
8 Rose, N. (1989) *Governing the Soul.*

The two primary Foucault (1977, 1980) texts were directly related to Kerryn's research and were relatively accessible. The commentaries were designed to give a broad sociological overview (Smart 2002), to focus on Foucault's work on language and discourse (McHoul and Grace 1993) and to give an overview of Foucault's *oeuvre* (Dreyfus and Rabinow 1983). Hunter and Gore were examples of applications of Foucault to education and Rose (1989) provided an example of Foucault's genealogical method and an understanding of the generativity of 'subjectivity' as a theoretical concept.

Kerryn began with the first book on the list, *Discipline and punish*, to tackle her fears head on. It was a liberating experience because she was able to read the whole book to get the big picture, rather than having to concentrate on a small section in detail as had been the demand in the literary theory course. As a doctoral researcher she constructed herself as an independent reader who could choose her own reading path through the list of recommendations, reading for her own purposes without immediately having to decide what to use or how to use it. She was free to explore a range of ideas before deciding on the fittest. The space to move in and out of texts, to stop and start, and sometimes give up provided the emotional safety net in the early stages of trying to map the theoretical landscape onto the research project. Both she and Hilary saw the reading as a recursive not a linear process.

Kerryn found reading *Discipline and punish* to be immensely pleasurable. As both a literature and history major, Kerryn found that she could mobilise the full range of her intellectual resources to appreciate Foucault. She could relish the historian's attention to detail and the literary elegance of his prose; she was no longer constrained by a pre-selected slice of text but could read the whole book and as many others as she liked. Immersing herself in Foucault, she was delighted to discover that he was indeed a historian, amongst other things.

This pleasure was the beginning of overcoming her fear of Foucault but pleasure does not bring mastery. Mastery requires concentrated, focused engagement. It is a long, hard road. Kerryn was transfixed by the primary texts but in the beginning it was the commentaries that taught her *how* to read Foucault, and provided her with an overview and leads as to what to read next. They served a purpose while Kerryn was still a novice in Foucault scholarship, enabling her to acquire both the confidence and the competence she needed. The applications of Foucault's work (Gore, Hunter and Rose) showed how his theory and his method could be used as analytical tools. Gore and Hunter modelled his application in the field of education. Rose's genealogy provided a model of Foucaultian practice, while simultaneously developing Kerryn's understanding of how subjects are produced. This combination was particularly important for Kerryn's work, which focused on the production of literate subjects in early childhood education.

Kerryn now had theorists who could help her talk about literacy (Luke), power (Luke, Foucault and Bourdieu) and the embodied (Bourdieu) subject (Foucault). In Kerryn's initial literature review, these theorists were given equal weight. The literature review required for a research proposal at Wits University is substantial enough to provide the platform for the research design and the data collection.

Description of the project

In order to examine the connections between literacy, power and the embodied subject, a preschool and a primary school in a working class suburb in Johannesburg were chosen as research sites. A multiple case study design incorporated five classrooms from four grades: Grade 00, Grade 0, Grade 1 and Grade 3. The selection of classes across early schooling enabled Kerryn to trace the continuities and shifts as children move through 'informal' preschool to more 'formal' schooling in the Foundation Phase. Data was collected over 18 months through participant observation and recorded using fieldnotes and videotape. This was supplemented with teacher interviews, artefact collection and policy documents. The thesis is underpinned by Hunter's contention that 'disciplinary practices are essential for the formation of the modern citizen' (Hunter 1994) and education is a key site in which this formation happens. In South Africa the racism of the Apartheid State worked to construct docile white subjects and attempted to eject black subjects from the State. The implications of such subject positionings resulted in the construction of resistant subjects, which has far-reaching consequences and presents challenges in the reconceptualisation of the literate citizen as constructed in postapartheid curriculum documents.

In order to understand how disciplinary power is targeted at the body in these classrooms, Foucault's four means through which discipline operates was applied to reveal constructions of the literate subject. The organisation of the spatial and temporal exposed highly routinised days in the preschool, which functioned as preparation for later schooling. Space and time are open in the preschool for experimentation with technologies of literacy. Grade 0 is a threshold year inculcating perceived school norms. In the move to formal schooling, spaces for exploration shut down as children become confined to their desks, trained to take on the habitus of skilled writers. Communal learning in open spaces in the preschool give way to the ranked and surveyed individual. Routine gives way to tasks focused on individual mastery.

This pattern is reasserted in constructions of the reading and writing subject. In contrast to the curriculum documents, literacy is perceived narrowly by teachers. A traditional skills-based model of reading predominates with a dependence on phonics. A phonics approach is particularly problematic for children whose home languages are not English. The 'reader' displays competence by reading aloud fluently with little discussion or engagement with textual features. The approach to writing mirrors this with labour-intensive corporeal training to master handwriting. This skills-based focus and minimal exposure to different texts and genres creates scribes rather than authors. The long term result of such practices result in docile or highly resistant subjects. The thesis notes that rather than increasing levels of self-regulation, the internalised practices of the early years are eroded as children reach the end of the Foundation Phase.

The literature review

There are two phases in the production of a literature review in the Wits system. It is written first for the research proposal and requires that students have an overview of the literature relevant to their project. This requires researchers to identify key points of entry into the literature(s), which in Kerryn's case was already delineated in her title. As discussed earlier her title included four key terms that we could associate with three key theorists (Luke, Foucault and Bourdieu). With this starting point she could, in addition, delve into the literature on pedagogies of literacy, conceptions of literacy, literacy and embodiment, literacy and power and literacy and subjectivity. This reading formed the basis for the literature review in the proposal.

The second phase of writing the literature review is in the thesis proper. Because the literature review has to articulate with the data analysis, Hilary prefers her students to work with the data before revising the literature review for the thesis. This does not mean that her students stop reading or thinking about the literature. In fact, trying to analyse the data helps students to find the gaps that they need to fill. At times the data analysis ground to a halt. Kerryn did not have the tools she needed to make sense of it. For example, the key terms, 'literacy', 'power', 'embodiment' and 'subjectivity' did not include a theory of bodies in time and space. What Kerryn was finding in her data was that different kinds of literacy practices routinely happened in different classroom spaces across the day. In addition, these routines and the spaces for literacy did not remain constant as students progressed from preschool to primary school, from Grade 00 to Grade 3. What was emerging was evidence that the ways in which time and space were deployed in the different classrooms were creating different conditions of possibility for the production of literate subjects. How bodies were being disciplined, always core to the project, kept taking her back to Foucault. Because of his construction of time and space as disciplinary technologies, she was able to use his work to understand the regulative force in the deployment of these modalities. Foucault was starting to loom larger than originally imagined.

Rather than rewriting her literature review prematurely, Kerryn kept notes on what she needed to add. At times, however, this was not enough. Where her analysis needed her to be on top of theoretical concepts that she had not covered in her original reading or writing, she found that it was helpful to write sections of the theory in order to understand them. These then enabled her to use these concepts in her analysis, but decisions on how to incorporate them into a coherent literature review were left until the end.

It is, of course, not enough to focus only on those theorists who provide the theoretical framework for research at this level. Kerryn read widely and deciding what to include and exclude from the final thesis was determined in the end by the direction that the project took. Mary Douglas' (1966) anthropological work on the body survived the cut because her account of the body as a set of social practices was useful for understanding the embodiment of literacy as a set of social practices. Turner's (1996) analytic framework on the geometry of bodies, together with the literature on proxemics and kinesics (Birdwhistell 1970; Antes 1996) turned out to be less useful than anticipated. The evolution of the literature review repeats Darwin's theory of the survival of the fittest. The ideas that were the fittest were the ones that were most generative in the context of the thesis itself – the ones that did not thrive did not make the cut. Fitness is not immediately discernable because it depends on how the project evolves. Only once the project takes shape does it become easier to discard material that is profoundly interesting in its own right. For example, Kerryn was so excited by Gore's work (1994; 1995; 1997; 1998), that it might have derailed her own project. Hilary helped her realise that not everything in the literature that is really good, was central to her own enquiry. Later, Kerryn came to realise that she had been seduced by the polished nature of Gore's research because her own was still in the messy stage of early conceptualisation. She was so taken with it that she forgot to assess its applicability to her own project.

As a research project achieves greater and greater definition, it becomes easier to see how the literature fits. Some of it provides secondary evidence for a claim; some of it may clarify an idea or can be referenced in passing; some of it provides direction for further research; some of it fundamentally reorganises one's interpretation of the data; much of the later reading is confirmatory. It also becomes clearer where to fit it into the thesis. Not all of it has to go into the literature review. The literature on Foucault's theory of governmentality is a case in point.

The use of literature in other chapters

Governmentality is how we think about governing. Foucault makes it clear that government cannot purely be substituted for the state. Government is not just about political structures or state management, but rather how individuals conduct/govern themselves and how groups may be directed. It is 'the conduct of conducts' (Foucault 2002: 341). The notion of conduct works on several levels that inform our understanding of government. Dean (1999: 10–11) elaborates on these meanings – 'to conduct' is to lead or direct (often with varying levels of coercion) (Foucault 2002: 341). 'To conduct oneself,' indicates a moral or ethical dimension concerning how one directs oneself in certain circumstances. Used as a noun, 'conduct' refers to behaviour or actions. The combination of these meanings implies that government is a means of shaping behaviour according to a set of norms. Government can then be defined as:

> [A]ny more or less calculated activity, undertaken by a multiplicity of authorities and agencies, employing a variety of techniques and forms of knowledge, that seeks to shape conduct by working through our desires, aspirations, interests and beliefs, for definite but shifting ends and with a diverse set of relatively unpredictable consequences, effects and outcomes.
>
> Dean 1999: 11

The idea of governmentality centres on the assumption that the ability to direct the conduct of others and ourselves implies a capacity of thought – the mentalities of government. Foucault envisages three modes of power as fundamental to modern authority: sovereign power, disciplinary power and government. Together, these forms of power target the bodies of individuals and manage and regulate populations. Living in a country where lack of respect for the law is increasing, it is easy for us to see the benefits of regulation and the unfortunate consequences of a liberation strategy that set out to make South Africa ungovernable. Once citizens refuse to be regulated it becomes extremely difficult to re-establish government.

That South Africans do not have great respect for the law, is illustrated by a newspaper article that describes traffic offenders caught in a roadblock designed to police the illegal use of cellular phones while driving.

> Sandton motorists are the worst culprits for illegally using cell phones while driving ... In a seven hour period yesterday 93 drivers were caught and fined ... During the same period in Sandton, one drunk driver was arrested, 31 drivers were stopped for driving without licenses, 82 were not using seatbelts, 40 were driving unlicensed cars, 15 had smooth tyres on their vehicles, 15 were stopped for overloading, 94 were cited for other vehicle defects, 4 were summonsed for running red robots, and 22 were cited for moving violations. Six unroadworthy vehicles were impounded.
>
> *The Star*, Thursday, 7 September 2000

At the time of writing, in 2009, the metro police are having to arrest drivers who drive on the wrong side of the road and who drive through traffic lights in order to re-establish the rules of the road. Other headlines on the same page as the article on traffic violations include:

> How Joburg security guards rip their clients off
> SAA worker fired for fraud
> Break in at Mbeki's residence: man held (Mbeki was President of the country at the time).

We believe in the possibility of a South African subject that is neither completely unregulated nor as docile as the listening subject depicted in the classroom poster in Figure 4.5e with eyes that watch, ears that listen, lips that are closed and hands and feet that are quiet. In many ways the transition from apartheid to democracy has moved from draconian over regulation of population groups to insufficient and inconsistent regulation of the entire population. In analysing literacy classrooms, the research had to confront the positive and negative consequences of regulatory practices.

Although it would have been usual to include Foucault's theory of governmentality in the literature review, we decided to use it to theorise the context. In her context chapter Kerryn provided a reading of the history of education in South Africa, against a reading of the history of apartheid and the liberation struggle in relation to Foucault's theory of governmentality. This turned out to be much more taxing and original than a section discussing the relevance of governmentality to the project in the literature review would have been. The full extent of this work survives as an as yet unpublished journal article, because in the end it had to be drastically reduced for the final context chapter. It often takes a great deal of reading and writing one's way into understanding to produce a tight, lean thesis. This process of culling and maiming is often experienced as a sense of loss because as writers we grow attached to what we have written. It is important to recognise that, like what we read, everything we write, however good, may not make the final cut.

Conclusion

This reflection on the process of producing a literature review has helped us to understand what a literature review is and is not. It is not a survey of the literature, it is not a display of one's ability to make sense of the literature, it is not a record of everything read. It is an account of the ideas that informed the project and that the project speaks back to. Phase 1 and phase 2 of the literature review can be seen as the before and after of the project: it designs the project and then is redesigned by the project. It is an articulation of how the work is positioned in the ongoing development of ideas in the field and how the researcher positions herself in the field.

Although the literature review chapter is only a fraction of the overall thesis, it is pivotal. It is key to the design of the project, the overall argument and the ways in which the data is interpreted. It provides a reference point and it is threaded through all the data analysis chapters. Kerryn's moment of transformation from novice to expert was during a seminar at which all the Foucault heavyweights at the university were presenting their readings of Foucault's work. She was astonished to discover that she understood everything they were saying and was confident that her disagreements with what they were saying were well-founded. She knew she could hold her own.

There is no one right way to select the literature or write the literature review. Kerryn could, for example, have used only Bourdieu's theory. But then she would have produced a different thesis. The role of the adviser is to send the new researcher down a number of different but relevant pathways and to follow her journey, guiding from the front at first, then travelling alongside and finally trailing behind as the researcher's knowledge outstrips her own.

References

Antes, T. (1996) Kinesics: The value of gesture in language and in the language classroom, *Foreign Language Annals*, 29: 439–48.

Bartlett, A. and Mercer, G. (2001) Mostly metaphors: theorising from a practice of supervision. In A. Bartlett and G. Mercer (Eds). *Postgraduate Research Supervision: Transforming (R)Elations*. New York: Peter Lang Publishing.

Birdwhistell, R. (1970) *Kinesics and Context: Essays on Body-Motion Communication*. Philadelphia, PA: University of Philadelphia Press.

Bourdieu, P. (1986) The forms of capital. In J. G. Richardson (Ed.). *Handbook of Theory and Research for the Sociology of Education*. New York: Greenwood Press.

——(1992) *Language and Symbolic Power*. Oxford: Polity Press.

British National Corpus. Online. (Available at sara.natcorp.ox.ac.uk/lookup.html Accessed 5 March 2009).

Bruner, J. (1983) *Child's talk. Learning to Use Language*. Oxford: Oxford University Press.

Dean, M. (1999) *Governmentality: Power and Rule in Modern Society*. London: Sage.

Dixon, K. (2007) *Literacy, Power and the Embodied Subject: literacy learning and teaching in the Foundation Phase of a Gauteng primary school*. Unpublished PhD thesis, Johannesburg: University of the Witwatersrand.

Dreyfus, H. and Rabinow, P. (1983) *Michel Foucault: Beyond Structuralism and Hermeneutics*. New York: Harvester Wheatsheaf.

Douglas, M. (1966) *Purity and Danger*. London: Routledge and Kegan Paul.

Foucault, M. (1977) *Discipline and punish the birth of the prison*. Trans. A. Sheridan, London: Penguin Books.

——(1980) *Power/Knowledge selected interviews and other writings 1972–1977*. Trans. and Ed. C. Gordan. New York: Harvester Wheatsheaf.

——(2002) The Subject and Power. In J. Faubion (Ed.). *Essential Works of Foucault 1954–1984 vol. 3*. London: Penguin Books.

Gordon, C. (Ed.). (1980) *Power/knowledge selected interviews and other writings 1972–1977*. New York: Harvester Wheatsheaf.

Gore, J. (1994) *Power and pedagogy: an empirical investigation of four sites*. Paper prepared for the Annual Meeting of the American Educational Research Association, New Orleans.

——(1995) On the continuity of power relations in pedagogy, *International Studies in Sociology of Education*, 5(2): 165–88.

——(1997) On the use of empirical research for the development of a theory of pedagogy, *Cambridge Journal of Education*, 27(2): 211–21.

——(1998) *Micro-level techniques of power in the classroom production of class, race, gender and other relations*. Paper prepared for presentation at the Annual Conference of the Australian Association for Research in Education, Adelaide, 30 November –3 December.

Hunter, I. (1988) *Culture and Government: the emergence of literacy education*. Houndsmills: Macmillan.

——(1994) *Rethinking the School: Subjectivity, bureaucracy, criticism*. Sydney: Allen and Unwin.

Lacan, J. (1989) *Ecrits: a selection*. London and New York: Routledge.

Luke, A. (1992) The Body Literate: discourse and inscription in early literacy training, *Linguistics and Education*, 4(1): 107–29.

Mackinnon, J. (2004) Academic Supervision: seeking metaphors and models for quality, *Journal of Further and Higher Education*, 28(4): 395–405.

McHoul, A. and Grace, W. (1993) *A Foucault Primer Discourse, Power and the Subject*. New York: New York University Press.

Rose, N. (1989) *Governing the Soul: The Shaping of the Private Self*. London and New York: Routledge.

Smart, B (2002) *Michel Foucault*. Revised edn, London: Routledge.

The Star. Anti-crime blitz nets 500 in Greater Joburg, Thursday, 7 September 2000.

Turner, B. (1996) *The Body and Society*. 2nd edn, London: Sage Publications.

5
Understanding doctoral research for professional practitioners

T. Evans

Introduction

In many nations, especially those with 'developed' economies, the growth in doctoral enrolments is often strongly influenced by increases in doctoral enrolments in professionally related disciplines, such as education, nursing, business and social work. (For some international comparisons of doctoral enrolments see, Evans *et al.* 2008; 2009.) Of course, not all doctoral candidates and graduates are professional practitioners in those disciplines, and likewise not all doctoral candidates who are professional practitioners in those fields undertake their doctorates in their professional disciplines. Experience suggests that it is reasonable to assume, however, that there is a considerable majority – for example, of professional educators and educational administrators – who undertake their doctorates on a topic related to their fields. These are the people – professional practitioners undertaking doctorates in their professional disciplines – who are the focus of this chapter.

Part-time study (candidature) is a common feature of professional practitioners undertaking doctorates. This is especially the case in education, which is generally the professional discipline with the highest proportion of part-time candidates; a feature that is common to many nations. In Australia, for example, in 2005, 687 students commenced doctorates in education, of whom two-thirds (455) enrolled part-time (DEST 2006). In contrast, China has a very small proportion (3.6 per cent) of part-time candidates in total, although, again, education is higher at 4.6 per cent (Ministry of Education 2007). There are difficulties, however, in interpreting what 'part-time' means internationally and in practice, these matters are discussed later.

This chapter considers the complexities involved in providing doctoral programmes for people in professional fields. It encourages students, supervisors and others to recognise and value these complexities and not to see them as difficulties from which to retreat or as risks to control.

Doctorates for the professions

As stated above, professional practitioners undertaking doctorates in their professional disciplines are the focus of this chapter. 'Professional' here is viewed broadly to include people who are engaged in a career within a field in which they are undertaking a doctorate. This focuses the discussion in this chapter on the people, rather than on the definition of what is a profession and what constitutes a professional discipline. In other contexts, such definitional debates are important and they raise some important questions and matters in understanding and interpreting national data and in shaping policy. So a caveat is required here: the chapter focuses on professional people undertaking doctorates related to their professional fields; in other contexts this operational definition would leak profusely!

In many respects, professional or practice-based doctorates are undertaken at the margins of the academy and rarely attract much attention in international reports on doctorates. For example, a recent report by the League of European Research Universities entitled 'Doctoral studies in Europe: excellence in researcher training' (LERU 2007) is strong on the importance of doctoral education for the knowledge economy, but its focus is almost entirely on PhD students undertaking their PhDs full-time in the academy and then finding work in industry. It makes only brief reference to part-time study for people in the professions, that is those who are *already working* in the knowledge economy. International, national and institutional documents and policies are slowly recognising that PhD programmes are not (just) apprenticeships for academic appointments (the destination for about 40 per cent of PhD graduates in most industrialised nations). In 2005, the European University Association (EUA 2005) produced a report entitled 'Doctoral Programmes for the European Knowledge Society' in which it noted:

> With changing demographic trends in Europe, doctoral training may be seen as part of 'life-long learning' in line with the Lisbon objectives. This, however, requires a more flexible approach with regard to both the organisation and duration of doctoral studies for part-time candidates.
>
> EUA 2005: 24

Furthermore, a UNESCO report on postgraduate education – 'Trends and Issues in Postgraduate Education: Challenges for Research' – acknowledged that doctorates 'in high demand often focus on specific work-related fields as they can lead to professional advancement' (UNESCO 2007: 7).

Although the aforementioned reports indicate that there is the emergence of recognition of the existence and potential of doctoral candidates undertaking research within their professional fields, such recognition remains swamped by the policy discourses that intrinsically assume that PhDs are undertaken by young, full-time students who, on graduation, then need to find a useful 'place' in the knowledge economy. Some colleagues and I addressed this matter in a submission to the Australian parliament through the House of Representatives Standing Committee on Industry, Science and Innovation. The Committee conducted a review and produced a report entitled 'Building Australia's Research Capacity' (House of Representatives Standing Committee on Industry, Science and Innovation 2008). The report cites part of our submission in which we said that Australia's government and institutional policies 'have a monocular policy focus on younger, full-time scholarship holders "preparing for work" which is blind to the needs and potential of the many candidates who are older, and often mid-career, part-time, salaried and in a good job' (House of Representatives Standing Committee on Industry, Science and Innovation 2008: para 5.18). Despite the widespread policy and mass media discussions of the importance of new ideas, inventions, discoveries and knowledge for

67

the future sustainable development of humanity, societies and economies; and the incentives and imperatives for universities and industry to work more closely together on research and its application – indeed, Gibbons *et al.* (1994) strongly shaped these moves through their proposition of Mode Two research 15 years ago – there is little impact on doctoral policy and pedagogy. ('Professional doctorates' are a small exception in some nations, such as Australia and the UK.) Furthermore, Florida (2003; 2005) has been very influential over policy makers, planners and others internationally in his arguments about the 'creative economy' and the environments in which creative professionals live and work. Indeed, Florida's later work (2005) noted the significance of doctoral candidates and postdoctoral fellows to the US creative economy.

One might have thought that PhD candidates working on research leading to significant and original contributions to knowledge in their professional fields would be seen as a rich vein of creative potential for future societies and economies and that governments, universities and industries would be keen to mine this lode. Pushing the analogy a bit further, it's as if they are wandering the country, metal detectors in hand but deaf to the high-pitched scream indicating 'gold'. Or maybe they can hear the scream but they don't like the digging. And 'digging' (work) there is to be done if these (potential) doctoral candidates are to yield their potential. There are two areas of work that we shall address now in this chapter that are fundamental, in my view, to providing good-quality doctoral education for professional people undertaking their doctorates in their professional fields.

Diversity

Diversity has become a 'buzz-word' of recent educational and other social policies. It is usually concerned with encouraging and ensuring appropriate representation and inclusion of the minorities in any particular society. Given education's capacity either to perpetuate differences and exclusion, or to eliminate and include them, it is no surprise that education is often a focus of such policies. Given the foundational nature of schooling for effective participation in civil society and employment, it is obvious that schooling is likely to be particularly emphasised in policies related to respecting diversity. In more recent times, the matter of diversity has affected universities and their policies and practices in the selection and support of students and staff. Although these matters have been less prevalent in policy on doctoral education, as is discussed below, there has been an increasing awareness of responsibilities concerning diversity in this respect.

Arguably, the typical primary school faces less complexity over matters of diversity with its pupils, than does the typical university with its doctoral students. Yet, I suspect that the typical primary school takes the matter more seriously, than does the typical university and this is partly reflected in the way universities exude apathy for professional people undertaking their doctorates part-time. The complex diversities embodied in such mid-career adults are usually much greater than for the five-year-olds attending primary school; the former have lived approximately half their lives, learned and thought about much, experienced likewise, and occasionally been afflicted by life's physical, health, emotional and mental misfortunes. Furthermore, a primary school usually mirrors the diversity of its local community; the doctoral students in most universities represent a wider diversity of international, national, regional and local communities. Basically, if the world's got it, a university can expect it! Intellectual impairment is generally the exception, but not entirely. The admission requirements and selection processes for doctorates act to shape the representation of people from the wider community, so, for example, the successive academic requirements of the degrees that earn admission to a PhD mean that almost invariably only highly intellectually capable people are enrolled; we also know, for example, that students' academic performance is related negatively to poverty and positively related to parents' academic achievement. In a sense this does not matter in terms of the range of diversity, rather it affects the proportions of people enrolled in doctorates from particular diverse backgrounds. That is, universities should still expect to have doctoral students from poor backgrounds with parents who did not attend university, but it is unlikely, unless there was some particular programme to redress the under representation, that the proportions would match the proportions of the poor in the national population, let alone the globe.

In a recent article (Pearson *et al.* 2008), colleagues and I analysed Australian government data on doctoral enrolments between 1996 and 2006, together with our own data from a research project (funded by the Australian Research Council) that involved, in part, producing a discipline-coded database of Australian PhD theses from 1948 to 2006. We discussed the implications for diversity in the doctoral population from these data and made the following general observation:

> From 1996 to 2004 the doctoral populations in Australia grew strongly from 22,696 to 39,531 candidates. Enrolments of women grew from 41 per cent in 1996 to 49 per cent in 2004. The age profile overall became flatter with fewer in the 30–39 age group, but with more aged over 50 years of age.
>
> Pearson *et al.* 2008: 360

In 2007, women comprised 50.2 per cent of the new doctoral enrolments in Australia, which matches trends in other industrial nations, such as Canada, the USA and the UK. There are disciplinary differences, of course, with our study showing that women are over represented in the fields of 'society and culture', 'education' and 'health', and under represented in the fields of 'natural and physical sciences' and 'management and commerce'. It is important to emphasise, however, that men and women were in all disciplines in significant numbers, as are people of all ages. Therefore, in terms of government and institutional policy related to these two broad demographic characteristics that we all share (age and sex), it is necessary to assume that doctoral candidates, in any field, will include men and women of ages from mid-20s to over 50 (most Australian universities have several doctoral candidates in their 70s and sometimes a few aged over 80).

In the aforementioned article (Pearson *et al.* 2008), the matter of enrolment modes (full-time/part-time) and types (on-campus/off-campus, sometimes called internal/ external) were discussed, both as a response to diversity within the doctoral student population, and as a form of institutional diversity (in the sense of means of offering doctorates) in itself. In some respects, the categories full-time and part-time, and on-campus and off-campus, are robust and mutually exclusive. In Australia, part-time candidature is calculated and funded by the Government and universities as half-time. Australia has a long history of distance education – across the school, college and university sectors – and so on-campus and off-campus enrolments have been part of the educational landscape and lexicon. Generally, there is little, if any, difference in funding or fees for these types of enrolment. This is especially the case for undergraduate and postgraduate coursework programmes. The research, however, shows that doctoral students float around within these categories, not just collectively, but individually, too. Research by Pearson and Ford (1997) on the 'openness and flexibility' of Australian doctoral programmes concluded that the categories masked, rather than exposed, the enrolment, study patterns and locations of doctoral students. A moment's reflection from those experienced in doctoral programmes would confirm this conclusion. For example, the anthropology, agriculture or archaeology PhD candidate enrolled full-time and on-campus who spends a substantial proportion of his/her candidature in a remote part of the world doing fieldwork does not sound very 'on-campus'; nor does the history PhD in a distant archive. In fact, the doctoral students who do their research on-campus are likely to be in the minority and to include especially those who need their university's lab or other specialist facilities. Certainly, most social and behavioural science students, including those in education, are likely to do their research (data collection) off-campus. Many full-time on-campus students may well spend part of their time working at home, especially when there is thesis writing to be done; and there are the part-time candidates who attend the campus for meetings, seminars, library work and to use specialist facilities.

Research (funded by the Australian Research Council) which I conducted with colleagues on the work of full-time and part-time PhD candidates in Australia involved, in part, a national survey of all doctoral candidates in mid-2005. We published an overview of the findings that also illustrates the complications of enrolment categories (Pearson *et al.* 2008). For example, 20 per cent of candidates changed their enrolment status between part-time and full-time, with 60 per cent or more of those who were enrolled for five years or more having changed their enrolment in this way. In the week preceding their completion of the survey, 42 per cent of respondents reported undertaking the majority of their doctoral work on-campus, 33 per cent at home, and the balance elsewhere (5 per cent gave no response). Government figures showed that 60 per cent of doctoral students were enrolled on-campus, and the balance off-campus in 2005 (see Pearson *et al.* 2008: 262), so our research showed that for a typical week of doctoral study, only 42 per cent was conducted on-campus.

Candidates' non-doctoral work responsibilities are another aspect of diversity that bears on them and, arguably, on the universities in which they enrol. The aforementioned survey (Pearson *et al.* 2008) showed that of full-time candidates 79 per cent of men and 82 per cent of women spent up to 20 hours on family and/or domestic responsibilities in the week prior to their completion of the survey; and 12 per cent of women and 9 per cent of men spent 21–40 hours. Of part-time candidates, 66 per cent of women and 78 per cent of men reported devoting up to 20 hours on domestic and/or family activities, and 18 per cent of women and 12 per cent of women devoted between 21 and 40 hours on such activities (Pearson *et al.* 2008: 21). Our research identified other trends, such as those related to age, national background, and family size, that have a bearing on the interpretation of such figures; however, these are beyond the scope of this chapter. The important considerations here are that almost all doctoral students undertake significant family and/or domestic activities each week, whether they are full-time or not. (Of full-time candidates, only 2 per cent of women and 6 per cent of men reported no such work; of part-time candidates the equivalent figures are 1 per cent and 3 per cent.) Similarly, complexities were identified in the area of paid work, both academic and non-academic, undertaken by respondents. In the week prior to completion of the survey, 35 per cent undertook paid non-academic work and 30 per cent undertook paid academic work; perhaps surprisingly, 19 per cent of respondents said they worked on academic activities but were unpaid for this work (Pearson *et al.* 2008: 17).

Two important conclusions for this chapter emanate from this research: one is that most candidates, full-time or part-time, undertake paid and unpaid work and so, it may be assumed, most of these are engaged professionally (a few, especially full-time, who are engaged in non-academic paid work may not be in what one might call 'professional' work); the other is that, not only is there diversity across the doctoral population, but also there is diversity within the categories used to describe the population. These matters have implications for both national and institutional policies, as the following quotes illustrate.

The (Australian) House of Representatives Standing Committee on Industry, Science and Innovation (2008) observed as follows:

> The Committee is apprised of the diversity of postgraduate research students and recognised that a one-size-fits-all model is not suitable for developing Australia's research capacity and strength.
>
> House of Representatives Standing Committee on Industry, Science and Innovation 2008: para 5.17

> We believe that diversity is a strength of Australian doctoral education and we call for policy that eschews homogeneity and which values diversity and flexibility.
>
> House of Representatives Standing Committee on Industry, Science and Innovation 2008: para 5.19

The Committee recognised the need for flexibility in what might be called both (government's) bureaucratic dealings and also for (institutional) doctoral pedagogies. The European University Association reached similar conclusions.

> [A] doctoral candidate was, in most cases, a person with a deep interest in research and a future career in academic research and teaching. This is not true anymore, although society still tends to maintain the stereotype of people with doctoral degrees as scholars living on the isolated worlds of academia ... there (is) a growing number of students who pursue doctoral training for professional; knowledge and skill development (for) industry, government and administration, medical and health provision, legal and financial services, NGOs, etc. There are many students who (undertake) doctoral training for personal development ... and to widen their employment opportunities ... The doctoral candidate today is a very diverse figure. Doctoral ... programmes are reflecting and tackling this reality through finding the right balance between research, which remains the core element of doctoral education, and the necessary orientation to the wider labour market.
>
> EUA 2005: 26–7

How should universities respond? And what should the new generation of doctoral candidates expect? To conclude, some suggestions are offered below.

Being professional: doctoral practices for the new professionals

Arguably, there are two fundamental problems with the way universities generally (and there are exceptions within universities: they have diversities, too!) understand and practise their doctoral administration and programmes. One is that they find it very hard to see doctoral candidates – whatever their backgrounds, expertise, seniority – as, well, students. They might be the most senior students, but they are still regulated, controlled, defined and understood as students. The other is that professional part-time doctoral candidates are mostly out-of-sight and out-of-mind. Neumann and Rodwell (2009) in their research with part-time students talk of their 'invisibility'. They are marginalised, almost invariably seen as 'different' and 'other' to the on-campus, full-time, in the lab, down the corridor, doctoral student. Part-time, students are a problem to be accom-modated or even minimised (by giving preference to enrolling full-time candidates). Their strengths (self-supporting, applied research, potential impact, industry connections) are largely ignored (somewhat ironically, as noted previously, given that universities are under increasing pressure to do useful research and work with industry) (Barnacle and Usher 2003; Evans 2002).

Some readers (supervisors, candidates, graduates) may have experienced the tensions between a high achieving professional pursuing a doctorate and the banal and bureau-cratised administrative procedures of universities. If such a candidate has an important task thrust on them at work and needs to extend a doctoral deadline, forms have to be completed, permissions granted. They don't conform to the 'normal' 'progress' of a 'typical' full-time doctoral candidate – notwithstanding that this typicality is based on myth. It is not *their* candidature it is the university's, so it will decide what time they need and may have. There are other examples, such as those that relate to the support given to doctoral students. Seminars, workshops, social events, they are all on-campus next week, never mind that many candidates work during the week, and live miles away or even overseas. There are examples where doctoral programmes within universities do much better than this; in Australia and the UK, some professional doctorate programmes do so, but one senses it is against the tide of their universities. (Professional doctorate publications and conferences in Australia and the UK have many stories from people trying to make a difference, for example, Green *et al.* 2001; Maxwell *et al.* 2005; McWilliam *et al.* 2002; www.ukcge.ac.uk/profdocs)

What is required is a professional approach by universities (administrations, managers, supervisors, etc.) and candidates. Professional, part-time candidates need to be seen as highly important and potentially very influential clients. Clients who bring their skills and expertise to bear on a research project they wish to undertake and that is likely to have a benefit in a profession or workplace. The diverse attributes and characteristics they bring are not problems to be 'worked-around', but strengths of diversity that will strengthen the quality and impact of a doctoral programme. Serving these candidates' needs should be a privilege for universities and a source of inspiration for those who work with them. Anticipating these needs and reflecting their diversity requires creative pedagogical and administrative processes. Being solely reactionary is not good profes-sional practice, although reacting promptly to unexpected matters is. It requires super-visors to recognise that the 'master–apprentice' relationship is counter productive (arguably, this is the case for all doctoral supervision). The relationship is better characterised as professional (supervisor) and client (candidate) – although some professional practices in the world beyond academe are not worth emulating. Perhaps the best way to char-acterise the relationship is as a team where the team-members have particular strengths and interests that they bring to bear to get the research done and the thesis written. In many respects, the candidate is the team-leader: it is their project. In many cases, the research will be in a professional or workplace context in which the supervisors may find it very difficult to undertake such research themselves because they are not members of that community (Evans 2007). (Elsewhere I have discussed the implications of supervising professional (part-time) candidates in their workplace-based research.)

Professional part-time candidates also need to bring their skills and expertise as professionals to bear on their candidature. I have discussed (Evans 2006) the strategies professional (part-time) candidates can use to manage their candidature. In the context of this chapter it is important that they recognise that they belong to a diverse population of doctoral candidates and that their diversities are as important as those of anyone else. That is, candidates may feel privileged to be undertaking a doctorate, they may feel particularly so if their supervisor is eminent in their field, but that does not mean they are 'just' 'peculiar' students; indeed, they are at the university mainly to *produce* knowledge not to consume it through another course of study. If candidates recognise that they are, in some respects, clients of their university, then they should expect service, and service broadly tailored to their needs; they should not apologise 'for being difficult' because they don't fit the established, ill-fitting, procedures of the university. If, however, they also adopt the view that by undertaking a doctorate they are responsible for a team being established to complete their research and thesis, then other complementary perceptions of their doctoral identity follow. They may have eminent supervisors, but these are part of the candidate's team. The candidate needs to manage them respectfully as any good team-members should be managed. Candidates need to recognise their own weaknesses and how the other team members' strengths can help them complete the whole project (e.g. with research design, research ethics, identifying literature, doctoral writing). There are also other supporters of the team, perhaps none more so than those in the library (see Macauley's (2006) discussion of the librarian as 'the candidates' forgotten friend'), but also in IT, student services, etc. A wise candidate will identify these resources to support their project and manage them professionally, too.

Conclusion

There is evidence that doctoral candidates reflect the diversities of the world and that this enables them to bring to their candidature and to universities' doctoral programmes considerable strengths as a result. Although there are some national and international reports on doctoral education that recognise these strengths, universities have been slow to respond. Yet it is universities who have much to gain by building on the diversities of doctoral candidates, especially those that are embodied in those part-time candidates who are working in their professions and undertaking related research. It has been argued that there is work to be done by universities, both administratively and pedagogically, and by candidates, in terms of managing their doctoral identity, expectations and candidature. Such work could lead to much more creative and responsive (to diversity) doctoral programmes, leading to more productive doctoral research, and, finally, to superior national research capacity residing in the skills, expertise and knowledge of the doctoral graduates.

Acknowledgements

I would like to acknowledge the contribution of my colleagues, Peter Macauley (who read and commented on an earlier draft) and Margot Pearson with whom I have worked on the research behind our publications cited here, and to Kevin Ryland (who completed his PhD with me on part-time PhD students) and to Jim Cumming (who completed his PhD on full-time PhD students) as part of one of the aforementioned projects.

References

Barnacle, R. and Usher, R. (2003) Assessing the quality of research training: the case of part-time candidates in full-time professional work, *Higher Education Research and Development*, 22: 345–58.

DEST (Department of Education Science and Training) (2006) Enrolment datasets for 1998–2005, *Higher education statistics collection*.

EUA (2005) *Doctoral Programmes for the European Knowledge Society*. Brussels: European University Association (EUA).

Evans, T. D. (2002) Part-time research students: are they producing knowledge where it counts?, *Higher Education and Research and Development,* 21: 155–65.

——(2006) Part-time candidature—balancing candidature, work and personal life. In Denholm, C. and Evans, T. D. (Eds), *Doctorates Downunder: keys to successful doctoral study in Australia and New Zealand*. Melbourne: ACER Press.

——(2007) Effective supervision of part-time candidates. In Denholm, C. and Evans, T. D. (Eds), *Supervising Doctorates Downunder: keys to effective supervision in Australia and New Zealand*. Melbourne: ACER Press.

Evans, T. D., Evans, B. and Marsh, H. (2008) Australia. In Nerad, M. and Heggelund, M. (Eds), *Toward a Global PhD: Forces and Forms in Doctoral Education Worldwide*. Seattle: CIRGE and University of Washington Press.

Evans, T. D., Gerdeman, D., Haines, I., Hall, F., Ryland, K. and Sebkova, H. (2009) Selected international comparisons of PhD enrolments and completions. In Nerad, M. and Heggelund, M. (Eds). *Changes in Doctoral Education Worldwide*. Baltimore, MD: John Hopkins University Press.

Florida, R. (2003) *The Rise of the Creative Class*. Melbourne: Pluto Press.

——(2005) *The Flight of the Creative Class: the new global competition for talent*. New York: Harper Business.

Gibbons, M., Limoges, C., Nowotny, H., Schwartzman, S., Scott, P. and Trow, M. (1994) *The New Production of Knowledge: the dynamics of science and research in contemporary societies*. London: Sage.

Green, B., Maxwell, T. W. and Shanahan, P. (Eds) (2001) *Doctoral Education And Professional Practice: The Next Generation*. Armidale: Kardoorair Press.

House of Representatives Standing Committee on Industry, Science and Innovation (2008) *Building Australia's Research Capacity*. Canberra: Parliament of the Commonwealth of Australia.

LERU (2007) *Doctoral studies in Europe: excellence in researcher training*. Leuven, Belgium: League of European Research Universities (LERU).

Macauley, P. (2006) The librarian—the candidate's forgotten friend. In Denholm, C. and Evans, T. D. (Eds). *Doctorates downunder: keys to successful doctoral candidature in Australia and New Zealand*. Melbourne: ACER Press.

Maxwell, T., Evans, T. D. and Hickey C. (Eds) 2005 *Professional Doctorates: pursuing understanding and impact*. Geelong: Deakin University www.deakin.edu.au/education/rads/conferences/publications/prodoc/index.php

McWilliam, E., Taylor, P. G., Thomson, P., Green, B., Maxwell, T., Wildy, H. and Simons, D. (2002) *Research Training in Doctoral Programs: what can be learned from professional doctorates*. Canberra: Department of Education, Science and Technology.

Ministry of Education (People's Republic of China) (2007) *Zhongguo jiaoyu tongji nianjian, 1997–2006 (Yearbook of China's Educational Statistics)*. Ministry of Education: Beijing.

Neumann, R. and Rodwell, J. (2009) The 'invisible' part-time research students: a case study of satisfaction and completion, *Studies in Higher Education*, 34: 55–68.

Pearson, M., Cumming, J., Evans, T. D., Macauley, P. and Ryland, K. (2008) *Exploring the extent and nature of the diversity of the doctoral population in Australia: a profile of the respondents to a 2005 national survey*. Paper presented at Quality in Postgraduate Research conference, Adelaide. Online. (Available at www.qpr.edu.au/papersdatabase.php?orderBy=author&byYear=2008 Accessed).

Pearson, M., Evans, T. D. and Macauley, P. (2008) Growth and diversity in doctoral education: assessing the Australian experience, *Higher Education,* 55: 357–72.

Pearson, M. and Ford, L. (1997) *Open and Flexible PhD Study and Research.* Canberra: Department of Employment, Education, Training and Youth Affairs Evaluation and Investigations Program.

UNESCO (2007*) Trends and Issues in Postgraduate Education: Challenges for Research. Final Report of the UNESCO Forum on Higher Education, Research and Knowledge.* Paris: UNESCO.

6
Critical transcultural exchanges
Educational development for supervisors

C. Manathunga

Introduction

Providing educational development for supervisors is an important part of creating vibrant and productive doctoral education cultures within universities. In particular, I think the key purpose of any form of supervisor educational development is to create a space where supervisors are able to break open this intensely private pedagogical relationship (one of the few remaining in the performative university) for discussion, debate and critique. How you go about doing this, however, is fraught with challenges and tensions. Even finding a comfortable and agreed upon language is difficult. Am I going to use the term educational, professional, staff, faculty or academic development? How might we get beyond the colonial nuances of the word 'development'? Alternative terms like 'authentic professional learning' (Webster-Wright 2009) still carry echoes of a patronising positioning of academics or supervisors as the subjected other of those who implement the development programme.

In this chapter, after trying to address some of these language issues, I suggest a theoretical framework for thinking about and enacting supervisor educational development that draws upon my work on postcolonial approaches (Manathunga 2006; 2007) and Rowland's (2003: 17; 2006) work on academic development as a 'critical interdisciplinary field'. I am hoping that this theoretical lens resonates especially with supervisors in education and the social sciences, who are well-placed to critique the neoliberal impulses inherent in notions of supervisor 'training' and educational development more generally. I then explore a range of approaches to supervisor educational development, discussing a number of curriculum design features and pedagogical strategies that might prove useful. Finally, I outline some of the ongoing issues and challenges involved in providing educational development for supervisors. I hope that all of this provokes a conversation in your school or university about supervision and how both supervisors and students can extend their understandings of this 'chaotic pedagogy' (Grant 2003: 189).

The language of educational development

I have already flagged a number of terminology issues about 'educational development' that need to be addressed before we can move on towards thinking about a theoretical framework for supervisor development. First of all, there is a huge variation in different countries about which adjective is used in front of the word development. Where educational and academic development are commonly used in the UK, Continental Europe, Australia and New Zealand (among other countries), North Americans tend to use the phrase faculty development. Then there is the broader notion of professional development, which is used not only in universities but also in other organisations. Even within countries there are internal debates about which term is the most appropriate, as a team of us investigating the history of educational development in Australia, the UK and New Zealand have discovered. In the end, I have chosen to use 'educational' development partly because it is a term that has gained enough international acceptance to be used by the International Consortium of Educational Development (ICED). I have also made this selection because I would like to emphasise the pedagogical aspects of engaging with supervisors about supervision as a form of teaching. In using the term pedagogy, I am drawing upon critical notions that understand pedagogy as the field of power relations circulating between knowledge, teachers (who may be those academics outside of faculties who facilitate educational development sessions or academics based within faculties) and learners (who may be academics based in faculties or potentially also those who facilitate educational development) (Lusted 1986; Lee and Green 1997).

This, however, does not deal with the issues created by the use of the term 'development'. As McWilliam (2002) and Manathunga (2005) have shown, development is a term overladen with colonial and neocolonial connotations. It is a word that imbues one group (usually academics located outside of faculties) with the right to 'develop' their colleagues (usually academics located within faculties). It, therefore, establishes a set of unequal power relations that are highly problematic (Manathunga 2005). When combined with the unfortunate tendency in some higher education research and in some enactments of educational development towards a deficit view of academics as teachers and towards progressivist notions of improvement and change management, it begins to sound a lot like other colonial discourses that sought to mask the violent conquering of territories and peoples with commitments to 'civilising' missions and the like. There are also a number of disturbing parallels between development work undertaken in the so-called Third (or Majority) World and that implemented in universities in the name of educational development. As McWilliam (2002: 11) argues, educational development can sometimes privilege 'generalizable, economic, technological and management knowledge' over local disciplinary knowledge and pedagogical practices.

Even more disturbing is the recent trend among government and university policy makers alike to use the term supervisor 'training' presumably to match up with notions of research 'training'. This expression clearly emphasises the extent to which narrow, instrumentalist, technicist understandings of supervision have gained ground. It carries with it the neoliberal implication that there are a set of prescribed supervision skills that supervisors can be drilled in (Manathunga *et al.* in press). At the very least, development is preferable to training because it contains within it the possibilities of growth, broadening and becoming despite its colonial overtones.

Nonetheless, the search for a replacement word for development proves to be equally impossible. One of the more recent attempts to achieve this has been undertaken by Webster-Wright (2009), who suggests that a phrase like 'authentic professional learning' might be a better alternative. Although educationalists often share broad notions of learning and even commitments to those buzz words 'life-long learning' (so beautifully deconstructed by Usher and Edwards 2007), many academics in other disciplines regard

77

'learning' as a narrow and somewhat patronising concept restricted to their own students. As a result, there are still problems associated with this substitution. So, too, anyone from a postmodernist frame of reference is likely to view with great caution the idea that any practice could be labelled 'authentic'. Therefore, I have reluctantly had to continue to use the phrase educational development here and in other writing. The best I can do is to make it part of my subtitle – behind my theoretical framework, which I will now outline.

Critical, transcultural exchange: a theoretical framework?

Very often, theoretical frameworks are missing from discussions of approaches to educational development or, if they exist, they often remain implicit or not publicly discussed. This can also occur because what counts as theory is different in different disciplines and in diverse paradigms. In some fields and approaches, a 'theory' consists of a model or can be proposed from the data itself (e.g. grounded theory). This has an impact on higher education and educational development literature because most of its proponents have 'migrated' from other disciplines (Manathunga 2007: 27) and bring with them a range of understandings about how theories are developed and what they include. Coming originally from the humanities, the theories I like to work with include a number of post-structuralist and feminist theories and postcolonial theory. In fact, there is now an active group of educational developers and higher education researchers called the Challenging Academic Development (CAD) Collective that seeks to increasingly incorporate humanities and other theories into the work of educational development (Peseta *et al.* 2005).

Because of the colonial nuances evident in educational development and its positioning in the university (discussed above), it seemed logical that postcolonial theory might offer some productive as well as deconstructive insights (Manathunga 2006). In particular, I drew on the postcolonial tropes or concepts of liminality, hybridity and unhomeliness (Bhabha 1994; Bakhtin 1981) and later transculturation (Pratt 1992) to think about how you might create a 'two-way, reciprocal, intercultural, interdisciplinary exchange' between those positioned as 'developers' and 'developees' as opposed to a one-way, deficit and transmissive approach (Manathunga 2006: 26). I argued that, because educational development occupied a threshold and uncomfortable or unhomely space between disciplines (and other 'fault lines' Rowland (2002: 52) talks about), developers and faculty-based academics actually had interdependent and hybrid subjectivities as each other's other. They were 'simultaneously powerful and powerless in their relations with each other' (Manathunga 2006: 21).

I argued that if both parties adopted an ambivalent and tentative approach to their work together in educational development, thereby sacrificing some of their expertise or authority either as pedagogical specialists or as disciplinary specialists, they might be able to 'construct transcultural, interdisciplinary, "new" but always-contested ways of seeing' supervision or any other form of teaching and learning (Manathunga 2006: 28). So, this is where my focus on transcultural exchange came from.

I also draw on Rowland's (2006) concept of educational development as a site of 'critical interdisciplinarity' to create this theoretical framework for supervisor educational development. Rowland (2006: 93) builds on Kroker's (1980) argument to define critical interdisciplinarity as 'a site of contestation between different perspectives in the attempt to come to new understandings'. He argues that this type of interdisciplinarity is 'dialectical and reflexive', it respects rather than suppresses difference, and it involves debating various disciplines' underlying 'assumptions and ideologies' (Rowland 2006: 93). Although this type of critical interdisciplinary work is fraught and difficult, it is ultimately highly productive and innovative, as my colleagues and I have argued elsewhere (Peseta *et al.* under review). Centralised educational development for supervisors offers a unique space for this critical interdisciplinary engagement. Therefore, I believe that adopting a theoretical approach that defines educational development as a critical, transcultural exchange serves as an effective philosophical underpinning to any form of supervisor educational development. I will now explore how this theoretical framework might be enacted in the curriculum design features and pedagogical strategies included in a range of supervisor development approaches.

Creating spaces for critical transcultural exchange: educational development approaches for supervisors

There are a plethora of current approaches to educational development for supervisors. The purpose of this section is to outline some of the approaches that are more likely to create spaces for the type of critical transcultural exchange between supervisors argued for above. In particular, I will focus on a number of curriculum design features and pedagogical strategies that aim to facilitate this type of exchange. First, however, it is important to consider the positioning of the person providing the educational development (who may or may not be academics outside of faculties based in educational development units).

Adopting a facilitator/participant role

Although experienced supervisors and RHD leaders (such as postgraduate co-ordinators or those responsible for the management of RHD programs) may facilitate some development programmes for supervisors, it is increasingly becoming the work of a group of people (many of whom have academic appointments and some of whom don't) who teach, research and provide service in the field of higher education. These people may be based either centrally or in faculty-specific educational development units, which may or may not work with students as well as academic staff. I, for example, have a joint academic appointment between the university's central educational development unit (Teaching and Educational Development Institute – TEDI) and the UQ Graduate School. As a result, I teach, research and provide service on supervision and doctoral education and work with both supervisors and students. I also supervise RHD students both in my original disciplines of history and politics and in my newer discipline of higher education.

Although I have growing expertise on supervision based upon my research as well as my own supervisory practice, I seek to take up a tentative and ambivalent positioning in the educational development programs I run for supervisors (Manathunga 2006; Peseta and Manathunga 2008). In other words, I believe my job in each programme is to explore in an open, questioning way the pedagogy of supervision with my colleagues. This means that I seek the positioning of facilitator/participant. A bit like a musical conductor, I orchestrate an ensemble of activities, speakers, reflective moments, discussion and debate. I provide a structure, a space and stimulus, but I do not provide the music. This is provided by the participants (and by my contributions to debates as a fellow participant). I think that adopting this facilitator/participant positioning is fundamental to achieving the kind of critical transcultural exchange that is important in supervisor educational development. However, as I say this, I am not attempting to deny the very real power dynamics that circulate within educational development so I have tried to avoid some of the terms bandied around that suggest a more naïve reading of power issues – such as co-learner, co-constructor, etc.

Curriculum design features

So let us now explore some curriculum design features that may create the space for productive (and deconstructive) supervisor educational development. First of all, I think that, although local disciplinary-based programmes are really important for both supervisors and students, highly effective critical transcultural exchanges about supervision are often best facilitated in an interdisciplinary setting. It is really important for supervisors to have the opportunity to discover more about the huge variation in disciplinary-based approaches to supervision. By either being exposed to very diverse supervision practices common in other disciplines or being required to explain your own disciplinary-based norms and assumptions about supervision, about RHD programmes and about research generally, you expand your understandings of supervision. You are also then in a better position to reaffirm some of your existing practices or to create innovative, transcultural blends of supervisory strategies. So there is a lot to be gained by engaging in interdisciplinary supervision development programs.

Then there is the question of audience. It is important to remember that students also need educational development about supervision if it is to be a positive experience for both parties. Running sessions for student groups on how to manage your supervisor is a helpful way of encouraging students to be proactive, to obtain the type of support they need from their supervisors and to understand more about what is reasonable to expect from supervisors. In schools or research centres where there is an atmosphere of trust and an inclusive research culture, joint sessions on supervision for both students and supervisors can be a highly effective way for both groups to exchange their ideas, expectations and assumptions about supervision. However, if the area is more hierarchical or competitive, such joint sessions are unlikely to be as effective. Even in a climate of trust and support, it is important to provide separate opportunities for supervisors and students as well so that they can engage in more open, critical discussions of the complex aspects of supervision pedagogy.

The other audience question relates to the levels of supervisory experience of the participants. In my experience, whether the session is at the local disciplinary level or for an interdisciplinary group, having a mixed audience of beginning and experienced supervisors is really helpful. The benefits of this are two-way. First, the beginning supervisors and the facilitator/participant gain from listening to the stories and strategies of experienced supervisors. But second, experienced supervisors also benefit from the process of making explicit their approaches in ways that they may not have had a chance to articulate before. Related to this, is also the question of what forms of educational development assist experienced supervisors to continue reflecting upon and modifying their practice in addition to the sheer benefit of increasing experience that was highlighted by Australian and Aotearoa New Zealand supervisors in a survey about influences on supervisor development (Ryland 2009). Some of the approaches that I have found helpful (which will be discussed in greater detail below) include involvement in reflective networks and mentoring programmes, specific preparation in representing excellence in supervision for promotion or supervision award application purposes and providing networks and policy fora for RHD leaders such as postgraduate co-ordinators.

In designing supervisor educational development programmes, it is important to provide a range of pedagogical experiences and settings that go beyond information sharing, awareness raising and superficial tips and tricks, which have been linked with the 'training' approach to supervisor educational development (McCormack and Pamphilon 2004). Although 'the workshop' per se has been criticised for these minimalist types of engagement about supervision, I think it is important to highlight that it really depends on the types of pedagogical strategies and activities included in the session that determine whether the experience is a superficial one or not. Related to this issue is also the need to go beyond the 'administrative framing' (Smith 2001) of supervision as only a series of roles and expectations that, once clarified, will make for an unproblematic supervisory experiences. Although these issues are important, they encompass only some of the issues that make supervision such a complex and 'chaotic pedagogy' (Grant 2003). Grant's (2003) insightful notion of the supervision relationship as a palimpsest highlights the operations of complex power dynamics and unconscious knowings and desires in supervision that need to be addressed in supervisor educational development programmes.

One programme that seeks to provide supervisors with a rich and varied engagement with many aspects of supervision pedagogy is called *Becoming an Effective Adviser*.

This programme includes five modules that are delivered over the course of a year:

- A short workshop on RHD policies and procedures (including a student panel to capture people's experiences of the 'system').
- A day-long programme called *Compassionate Rigour* that explores supervision pedagogy using a range of stimuli (e.g. activities, role plays, experienced supervisor speakers, video material, etc.).
- A mentoring programme where supervisors work with or observe experienced supervisor mentors over the course of a year and complete a reflective exercise about five key supervision experiences (first meetings; developing and refining the student's research proposal and programme; confirmation of candidature; monitoring progress and problem solving; feedback and thesis structure).
- An online module about remote or distance supervision that includes international experts' participation in a discussion forum.
- A half-day programme called *Emerging Issues*, which explores national and international RHD policies and agendas, indigenous research and supervision and an end of the programme reflective activity and action plan for the future.

Although it has been designed for beginning supervisors, many experienced supervisors elect to participate as well. The programme is supported by a substantial folder of material that includes everything from brief outlines of supervision strategies, tools and supervision activities collected from supervisors to theoretical articles on supervision pedagogy. Aspects of this programme have also been successfully delivered in other universities in Australia and in Papua New Guinea, Vietnam and Oman. The programme has also been positively externally peer-reviewed by one of the pioneers of supervisor educational development in Australia, Linda Conrad, and internally peer-reviewed by one of the participants.

Mentoring programmes have long been used as an effective form of career development and support, especially for women academics. They are also a highly effective

81

approach to supervisor educational development. This kind of supervision mentoring can occur naturally where beginning supervisors act as associate supervisors in teams with experienced supervisors. Indeed, in a recent survey of Australian and Aotearoa New Zealand supervisors, 42.7 per cent indicated that working with a more experienced colleague had influenced their development as supervisors (Ryland 2009). However, there are cases where beginning supervisors are provided with very little mentoring in these team supervision scenarios. There are also occasions where the less experienced supervisor provides most, if not all, of the actual hands-on, day-to-day supervision. This is where more formal mentoring programmes (such as the one included in the *Becoming an Effective Adviser* programme discussed above) can help. Based on an innovative mentoring programme offered at Monash University in Australia (www.mrgs.monash.edu.au/research/staff/supervision/index.html), this programme links supervisors with their more experienced colleagues through their school postgraduate co-ordinator or with supervisors in other disciplines. These supervisors can either observe their mentors in supervision meetings if the student and other team-members agree or interview or discuss supervision with their mentors. The programme also encourages schools to give newer supervisors experiences of being on Confirmation of Candidature committees. In some cases, more experienced supervisors also take part in the mentoring programme. For example, a new postgraduate co-ordinator (leader of RHD studies) asked to be placed in a mentoring relationship with an experienced postgraduate co-ordinator in another discipline.

Then there is the issue of method of delivery. Increasingly, universities are offering online supervisor educational development programmes, as well as face-to-face sessions. Having a variety, what is sometimes referred to as blended learning, as indicated in the *Becoming an Effective Adviser* programme above, is a particularly effective method because online interaction and learning is enhanced when participants have actually met in person before (Anderson and Henderson 2004; Higgins and O'Keeffe 2004). There are two key types of online programmes that are offered to supervisors. The first type are programmes offered continuously as self-directed material, where there is little or no interaction with facilitators or other participants, although online evaluations are conducted (Brew and Peseta 2004). The second type are programmes offered at particular points in time with particular cohorts in order to allow for online interaction, such as the programme described above (Manathunga and Donnelly 2009). This also facilitates the inclusion of international experts in the online discussion forum, which provides participants with a rich learning experience (Manathunga and Donnelly 2009).

Each type of approach has its own challenges. For example, in the first type of programme, in spite of the ongoing evaluation, it can be hard to trace its impact upon participants. As a result, one programme has developed an innovative final module, called the Recognition Module, that takes supervisors through a three-step process of reflection and writing a supervision case study, receiving feedback from facilitators and then producing a final piece that links these reflections with the scholarly literature on supervision and learning (Brew and Peseta 2009). The second type of approach is not flexible in terms of time because it relies on the involvement of the facilitator, a specific cohort of participants and international discussion forum guests.

Another approach is the use of supervision reflective practice groups or networks that operate more informally and continuously. An example of this includes the Learning Circle on Postgraduate Supervision (Manathunga 2005; 2006; 2008; Manathunga and Goozée 2007), which has now been renamed the RHD Supervision Network (we couldn't escape neoliberal language forever!!). This small group of supervisors, which shifts and changes as people come in and out of the group, has met four and then six times per year since 2002. Each year the participants set our agenda of supervision topics or issues and I arrange either speakers, readings or other activities (some of which are described below). Since 2006, we have conducted two of our meetings in coffee shops, which have proved to be a wonderful informal venue for discussions about supervision. Because difficult supervision problems are often discussed, the group set up its own ground rules for confidentiality and non-judgemental listening. Trust, as Emilsson and Johnsson (2007) also argue, is vital to the effective operation of the group. Acting as supervisor support group and learning collective, the group has also engaged in joint authorship of publications (e.g. Manathunga and Goozée 2007) and ongoing research projects.

Other examples of this type of approach include the Teaching Reflection and Collaboration (TRAC) groups that used to operate at Queensland University of Technology (QUT) in Australia, the new Pedagogies of Supervision seminars planned for QUT (Bruce *et al.* 2009) and the process-orientated group supervision model used in Lund University in Sweden (Emilsson and Johnsson 2007). These programmes are not without controversy (Firth and Martens 2008), but they do provide effective spaces for interdisciplinary groups of supervisors and the facilitator/participant to explore some of the more complex aspects of supervision pedagogy (Manathunga 2009 – response to Firth and Martens 2008).

Pedagogical strategies

The range of pedagogical strategies it is possible to use in supervisor educational development is huge and is only limited by your imagination and by what seems to work with different groups of supervisors. I would encourage you to go as wild as you like and try out new things. In this section, I will limit the focus to a number of less common pedagogical strategies that I believe are more likely to facilitate the type of critical, transcultural exchange that is productive (and deconstructive) for supervisor educational development.

First of all, there are a group of strategies that use writing about supervision as a form of educational development. These strategies have been outlined more fully in a forthcoming article (Manathunga *et al.* 2010) so I will just quickly sketch in why we've chosen to use writing as a form of supervisor development and briefly what each of the three approaches developed by myself (Manathunga 2005; 2006), by Brew and Peseta (2004; 2009) and by McCormack and Pamphilon (2004; and McCormack 2004; 2009) involves. Drawing upon Richardson's (2000: 923) concept of 'writing as a method of inquiry', we see writing as

> [A] way of finding out about yourself and your topic. Although we think of writing as a mode of 'telling' about the social world, writing is not just a mopping-up activity at the end of a research project. Writing is also a way of 'knowing' – a method of discovery and analysis. By writing in different ways, we discover new aspects of our topic and our relationship to it.
>
> Richardson 2000: 923

Therefore, we believe that by writing about supervision, supervisors will gain new understandings of supervision that capture not only the superficial features of this form of pedagogy, but also its complexities and irrationalities (Manathunga *et al.* 2010).

In my approach, supervisors in the Learning Circle on Postgraduate Supervision (or the RHD Supervision Network) have been given the option of writing fictional accounts of supervision, which we then discuss at the meeting. Participants have elected to write about a variety of supervision issues (e.g. interdisciplinary supervision, receiving feedback, turning points in thesis writing) from a variety of positions – as themselves, as their student, in the third person. In particular, participants highlight the evocativeness of reading and writing fictional stories about supervision and the extent to which new understandings can emerge both from the writing and the collective deconstruction of these stories (Manathunga *et al.* 2010).

In Brew and Peseta's (2004) approach, supervisors completing an online programme on supervision can elect to do a final recognition module that involves them in a three-step process. First, they write a descriptive account of their experiences of being a student and later supervisor and receive feedback from educational developers (including how they might link their account with some of the scholarly literature on supervision). Then they construct a reflective account to refine the areas they want to explore and finally they write a case study on supervision. The idea is that the case study process reflects a problem or aspect of their supervision practice that is troubling them, or that they want to develop (if they've not yet supervised). The process of reflection, feedback and writing through developing the case study is iterative. Participants begin to recognise that a student-focused approach to supervision involves the need to develop a range of strategies based on the negotiation of learning with individual students (Manathunga *et al.* 2010).

In McCormack and Pamphilon's (2004) approach, supervisors engage in a four-step process of retelling stories of their experiences as students, interactive reading of case stories of other students' learning experiences, identifying supervisory practices from these stories and then reconstructing their own supervisory practice. Because these are real stories presented in detail, they contain the messiness, difficulties, problematic endings and silences of actual supervision. Being both mirrors (we see ourselves in new ways) and windows (we look into the experiences of others), participants have found these stories very evocative, thought provoking and highly productive in building new understandings of supervision (Manathunga *et al.* 2010).

Another pedagogical strategy that may be conducive to creating a critical transcultural space to explore postgraduate supervision is the use of role plays. The range of actors and approaches is wide – from presenting videos and live dramatic performances by professional actors to involving some or all of the session participants. The approach I have found very powerful was modelled on a strategy developed by Rod Wissler (the Dean of Graduate Studies at Queensland University of Technology), whose original discipline was drama, although I am sure readers may know of other people adopting similar approaches. This involves the creation of a scenario about an aspect of supervision. In this case, I focus on the process for the confirmation of RHD candidates, which normally happens about six to nine months full-time equivalent (FTE) into a Masters of Philosophy programme and one year FTE into a PhD programme. The scenario involves the Confirmation Committee meeting for a student experiencing personal, academic and supervision difficulties. Each participant is assigned a role in the scenario, which has seven actors – a student, two supervisors, three examiners and the postgraduate co-ordinator who chairs the meeting. Together they must make a decision about whether the candidate is confirmed, is given additional time to address any concerns or removed from the programme (the official language – 'terminated' – is horrifically graphic!).

To mirror actual experiences, each participant receives a role description containing hidden agendas and details about their motivations for taking a particular stance. I have learnt from experience that you need to be careful in assigning the roles of the student (who is in a particularly vulnerable position) and the very negative examiner (who is very vocal in their cruelly critical assessment of the student). The first time I staged this role play, I inadvertently selected an inexperienced, very gentle supervisor to play the student and an educational development colleague, who embodied the hyper-critical examiner a little too well! Although it involves making highly problematic assessments about session participants, I now try to select someone who appears to be rather robust to play the student role and someone who appears to be gentle and mature to play the critical examiner role.

The power of this approach is that it vividly demonstrates how supervision and the examination of RHD students' work (even at this formative stage) is highly political and involves so many issues not just about the student's research and abilities but also about the positioning and agendas of powerful people such as supervisors, examiners and RHD leaders. Involving all participants in the scenario reminds each person of the real difficulties associated with assessing RHD students and teasing apart issues of the student's research ability and potential from their personal circumstances and the political games that are sometimes played by others. Time and time again in postscenario discussions of this activity, people highlight how the emotional and political dimensions of supervision are graphically displayed and [re]lived in the experience of enacting the role play.

Issues and challenges

As with all things pedagogical, these approaches to supervision educational development are not without problems, contestation and sometimes controversy. As I have highlighted, adopting a facilitator/participant role does not entirely address the very real issues of power and potential colonialism in educational development (Manathunga 2005; 2006). Attempts to achieve critical transcultural exchanges about supervision are never really outside of these educational development power dynamics. So, too, the issues of mandatory or voluntary supervision development programmes, the registration and potential de-registration of supervisors, and the difficulty of changing engrained, problematic supervisor or student behaviour always remain present and are not amenable to quick, easy solutions.

So, too, some of the strategies outlined above have received strident criticism. For example, Firth and Martens (2008) argued against some of these strategies and what they called 'postliberal approaches' to supervision. They have depicted some approaches as 'spiritual exercises' or 'quasi-therapeutic' endeavours aimed at 'inner transformation' (2008: 284–85). As I have indicated in response, this is not at all the case (Manathunga 2009). These strategies (some of which are outlined above) are thoroughly pedagogical and are designed to highlight some of the hidden more difficult aspects of supervision that are often expunged in supervisor educational development programmes.

An invitation

In spite of these challenges and the problematic language of educational development, I hope that this chapter has invited readers to think about ways to create critical transcultural exchanges about supervision. As indicated above, this approach to supervisor educational development is derived from my work on postcolonial approaches and Rowland's (2002; 2003; 2006) writing about academic development and seeks to address some of the problematic issues of power in educational development. In addition, I use the metaphor of being a conductor to illustrate a facilitator/participant positioning that could be helpful in implementing supervisor educational development. I have then outlined a number of curriculum design features and pedagogical strategies that may be helpful. Most of all, I hope that reading this chapter has encouraged more conversation about supervision and how supervisors and students can engage in critical transcultural exchanges to deepen their understanding of this important but complex pedagogy.

References

Anderson, N. and Henderson, M. (2004) E-PD: blended models of sustaining teacher professional development in digital literacies, *E-Learning*, 1(3): 383–94.

Bakhtin, M. (1981) Discourse in the Novel. In M. Holquist (Ed.). *The Dialogic Imagination: four essays*. Austin, TX: University of Texas Press.

Bhabha, H. (1994) *The location of culture*. London and New York: Routledge.

Brew, A., and Peseta, T. (2004) Changing postgraduate supervision practice: A programme to encourage learning through reflection and feedback, *Innovations in Education and Teaching International*, 41(1): 5–22.

Brew, A. and Peseta, T. (2009) Supervision development and recognition in a reflexive space. In D. Boud, and A. Lee (Eds). *Changing practices of doctoral education*. London: Routledge.

Bruce, C. *et al.* (2009) ALTC Fellowship: a pedagogy of supervision for the technology disciplines, http://www.altc.edu.au/altc-teaching-fellow-christine-bruce#program-summary Accessed 18 January 2010.

Emilsson, U. and Johnsson, E. (2007) Supervision of supervisors: on developing supervision in postgraduate education, *Higher Education Research and Development*, 26(2): 163–79.

Firth, A. and Martens, E. (2008) Transforming supervisors? A critique of post-liberal approaches to research supervision, *Teaching in Higher Education*, 13(3): 279–89.

Grant, B. (2003) Mapping the pleasures and risks of supervision, *Discourse: studies in the cultural politics of education*, 24(2): 175–90.

Higgins, K. and O'Keeffe, D. (2004) *An Online Digital Engineering Module Companion using Biomedical Applications*. Proceedings of the Fourth Annual Irish Educational Technology Users Conference, Waterford, May 2004.

Kroker, M. (1980) Migration from the Disciplines, *Journal of Canadian Studies*, 15(3): 3–10.

Lee, A. and Green, B. (1997) Pedagogy and disciplinarity in the "New University", *UTS Review*, 3(1): 1–25.

Lusted, D. (1986) Why pedagogy? *Screen*, 27(2): 1–14.

McCormack, C. (2004) Storying Stories: A narrative approach to in-depth interview conversations, *International Journal of Social Research Methodology*, 7(2): 219–36.

——(2009) Stories return personal narrative ways of knowing to the professional development of doctoral supervisors, *Studies in Continuing Education*, 31(2), 139–54.

McCormack, C. and Pamphilon, B. (2004) More than a confessional: Postmodern groupwork to support postgraduate supervisors' professional development. *Innovations in Education and Teaching International*, 41(1): 23–37.

McWilliam, E. (2002) Against professional development, *Journal of Educational Philosophy and Theory*, 34 (3): 289–99.

Manathunga, C. (2005) The development of research supervision: 'turning the light on a private space', *International Journal for Academic Development*, 10(1): 17–30.

——(2006) Doing educational development ambivalently: Applying post-colonial metaphors to educational development? *International Journal for Academic Development*, 11(1): 19–29.

——(2007) 'Unhomely' academic developer identities: more post-colonial explorations, *International Journal for Academic Development*, 12(1): 25–34.

Manathunga, C. (2009) Supervision as a contested space: a response, *Teaching in Higher Education*, 14(3): 341–5.

Manathunga, C. and Donnelly, R. (2009) Going global in online academic development programs. In R. Donnelly, and F. McSweeney (Eds). *Applied eLearning and eTeaching in Higher Education*. Dublin: Idea Group Inc.

Manathunga, C. and Goozée, J. (2007) Challenging the dual assumption of the 'always/already' autonomous student and effective supervisor, *Teaching in Higher Education*, 12(3): 309–22.

Manathunga, C., Peseta, T. and McCormack, C. (2010) Supervisor development through creative approaches to writing, *International Journal for Academic Development*, 15(1): 33–46.

Peseta, T., Hicks, M., Holmes, T., Manathunga, C., Sutherland, K. and Wilcox, S. (2005) The challenging academic development (CAD) collective (research note), *International Journal of Academic Development*, 10(1): 59–61.

Peseta, T. and Manathunga, C. (2008) The anxiety of making academics over: resistance and responsibility in academic development. In Morley, I. (Ed.). *The Value of Knowledge: interdisciplinary perspectives*. Oxford: Rodopi.

Peseta, T., Manathunga, C. and Jones, A. (under review) What kind of interdisciplinary space is academic development? In M. Devlin, and M. Davies (Eds). *Interdisciplinary Higher Education: Perspectives and Practicalities*. Publisher under negotiation.

Pratt, M. (1992) *Imperial eyes: Travel writing and transculturation*. London and New York: Routledge.

Richardson, L. (2000) Writing. A method of inquiry. In N. K. Denzin and Y. S. Lincoln (Eds). *Handbook of Qualitative Research*. 2nd edn. Thousand Oaks, CA: Sage.

Rowland, S. (2002) Overcoming fragmentation in professional life: the challenge for academic development, *Higher Education Quarterly*, 56(1): 52–64.

——(2003). Academic development: a practical or theoretical business? In H. Eggins, and R. Macdonald (Eds). *The scholarship of academic development*. Buckingham: SRHE and Open University Press.

——(2006) *The enquiring university*. Buckingham: OUP.

Ryland, K. (2009) *Institutional results from a survey of research training supervisors in Australia and New Zealand*. Unpublished report.

Smith, B. (2001) (Re)Framing research degree supervision as pedagogy. In A. Bartlett and G. Mercer (Eds). *Postgraduate research supervision: transforming (R)elations*. New York: Peter Lang.

Usher, R. and Edwards, R. (2007) *Lifelong learning: signs, discourses, practices*. The Netherlands: Springer.

Webster-Wright, A. (2009) Reframing professional development through understanding authentic professional learning, *Review of Educational Research*, 79(2): 702–33.

7

Negotiating the layered relations of supervision

B. M. Grant

Introducing my standpoint

> Traditionally conducted behind closed doors in spaces remote from undergraduate teaching, the intensity of the interpersonal relations of much postgraduate pedagogy is presumed but uninterrogated.
>
> McWilliam and Palmer 1995: 32

Good supervision is central to successful graduate research, yet it is a pedagogy that is poorly understood. This may be because of the assumed privacy and 'uniqueness' of each supervision (Bartlett and Mercer 2000), but also, in the literature, it is under theorised (Green and Lee 1995; McWilliam and Palmer 1995).

In my view, supervision differs from other forms of teaching and learning in higher education in its peculiarly intense and negotiated character, as well as in its requirements for a blend of pedagogical and personal relationship skills.[1] These differences arise because supervision is not only concerned with the production of a good thesis, but also with the transformation of the student into an independent researcher. This transformation is effected through an individualised working relationship between the student and an 'expert' researcher (or two), a relationship that engages student and supervisor/s in productive power relations. This view sees supervision as an ethical practice through which student and supervisor are constituted as certain kinds of human beings (Johnson *et al.* 2000).

Perhaps in part because of this ethical dimension, supervision is often problematic in practice. When working with supervisors in supervision skills workshops, I usually ask them to recall their own experiences of supervision. Frequently their memories are painful, like these:

> Both experiences ... were both quite negative experiences really. Where I was basically just thrown into the deep end ... I had to teach myself, had to give myself my own kind of emotional and intellectual support, and generally they were quite aversive experiences where I was basically left alone.
>
> Initial interview with woman supervisor A: 1

I just think that doing a PhD is probably some of the most lonely, depressing years of your life ... you can't see past the whole process and people have so much power over your life ... I often found there was conflicting and contradictory and inconsistent stuff about what I was expected to do ... [my supervision experience] was incredibly fraught and emotionally demanding, wrenching stuff.

Initial interview with woman supervisor B: 2–6

As well, through my work with students, I am aware of how poorly equipped many are to participate in the supervisory encounter. My current research, which grew out of these experiences, is kindled by the twin desires to understand my own supervision practices better and to work more creatively and effectively as an academic developer.

This chapter addresses two products of my study. I elaborate a map for supervision that is based on contemporary theories of education, as well as on my experience as supervised student, supervisor, and academic developer working with both students and supervisors. My purpose with the map is to point to the complex and unstable character of supervision. Alongside the map, to make it more 'concrete', I draw on critical discourse analysis to offer some preliminary and illustrative data from an actual supervision.

A map for supervision

A map seems a useful device for elaborating my current understanding of supervision, especially if we think of the map as palimpsest-like, a surface from which earlier layers of inscription have been partially or completely erased to make room for newer texts. The older layers occasionally intrude into the newer, interrupting their meanings. The effects of such interruptions may be misunderstandings, ambiguities, excitements, contradictions, confusions, moments of unexpected clarity, fragmentations and so on. This is what I mean when I claim that supervision is complex and unstable. It is an interesting mixture of the personal, the rational and the irrational, the social and the institutional, full of possibilities of all kinds, a source of great pleasure to some students and supervisors:

I love it. It is the best part of my job. I really enjoy it a lot.

Initial interview with woman supervisor A: 10

I do enjoy it, good fun. She enjoys it too. Oh it is just, good fun, I don't know why.

Initial interview with male student X: 7

However, it is also a source of risk, as I shall show.

When explaining each layer of the map, working from what I think of as the most recent layer to the older ones, I also offer tentative 'readings' of some 'texts' of super-vision-in-action for illustrative purposes. The texts I am analysing are the products of a supervision meeting between a supervisor and her research student. I will treat these texts as traces of the layers of the map. In analysing the texts, I have been influenced by critical discourse analysis (Fairclough 1995; Janks 1997; Kamler 1997) because it makes links between discourse-as-language and discourses as the knowledge/power formations (Foucault 1974) that enable student and supervisor to speak as 'themselves'. In this understanding, discourses (in the second sense) speak *through* supervisor and student, constituting them as certain kinds of subjects, as well as being spoken by them (as in the first sense). I have also been influenced by my training as a literature student in the reader-response tradition (Lynn 1998) of making personal meaning through the close reading of texts – although I understand 'personal' as more than individual. As the discussion progresses, my analysis will become increasingly speculative because some layers, in particular the 'older' ones, may be opaque in meaning to the person who 'produced' the text, let alone the hopeful researcher. This is because the workings of discourses occur as much outside our conscious control as within it. I think this tentativeness is a strength of my work and a necessary ingredient in any discussion of pedagogy.

Before addressing the map, I will describe some of the contextual dimensions surrounding and informing the production of the particular texts I have used to illustrate it.

Text and context

The data I analyse here are two kinds of verbal texts produced through speaking and writing. One is the transcript of a supervisor and student speaking together in an hour-long supervision meeting; the other is two sets of written notes, each made by the supervisor and student separately within 24 hours of the meeting in response to some questions I posed.

There is a rich context to the production of these texts, some of the elements of which are as follows. The immediate context is the scene of this particular supervision meeting, which is in the supervisor's office. Both supervisor and student are European-born women, the supervisor in her mid-30s, the student in her early 20s. The supervisor has read a complete first draft of the student's thesis (in a field of social science) and is giving the student feedback on it. The context is unusual in that although the thesis is due to be completed shortly the supervisor is new to the situation, having stepped in late in the day after two other (senior male) supervisors had been involved and withdrawn. Because of the late stage, there is some urgency to the supervision as there is much to be done to bring the thesis to readiness for submission and the deadline is close. (Other details that could be relevant here but for which I have no data include who asked for the meeting, how it was arranged, the room set-up, whether or not they had a drink while they met, and so on.) Another unusual feature of the meeting is that there is a tape recorder running because the supervisor has asked the student if she is willing to participate in a research project. The student has 'consented'.[2] This means that in a sense there is a third person, an observer, in the meeting. It is difficult to calculate the disruptive effects of this 'presence' and how the student and supervisor may position and reposition themselves in response to it. The supervisor writes:

> Why [did I not apologize for being so late in getting back to the student]? I wanted to keep up the appearance of Super supervisor for the tape recorder. (you, God? Etc.). Usually I do offer apologies.
>
> Notes, lines 29–30

In her comment, she suggests she is aware of my presence. However, as well as being aware of the external omniscient researcher's presence she notes her awareness of an *internalised* omniscient Other, in this case God. In other cases this internalised omniscient Other might be the Super-ego, the conscience, the head of department, the absent masters of the discipline. Although the researcher's presence may be, is even likely to be, disruptive it is not the only other possible presence in supervision. I will come back to this in my discussion of the fourth layer of the map.

Another element of the context is the department and the student's and supervisor's positions within it. The discipline is commonly a male-dominated one and, in this particular department, the supervisor is one of few women academics among many men. Yet another element is the institution. It is a large research university that is responding to fiscally difficult times by attempting to position itself as *the* elite research university in a small country with a high number of research universities per capita. One strategy the university has used in pursuit of this objective over the last decade has been to actively seek to increase the number of graduate research students. This has been successful but there has been little attention to resourcing the students and many are dissatisfied with their experiences. There had also been a recent external quality audit, which criticised the university's practices in this area in the previous year. As a result, there had been a flurry of activity on the part of the university including surveying each department to find out what resources they provided for their research students. The faculty that this department is part of had also surveyed, again by questionnaire, all its graduate students in an effort to find out what their perceptions were of their experiences. So, at this time, there was a climate of heightened sensitivity about the provisions for graduate students.

The first layer: supervisor and student

The most obvious, perhaps most visible, layer of the map represents supervision as a simple relationship between student and supervisor (Figure 7.1).

Securely founded on a belief in the fundamental rationality and autonomy of every individual, the supervisor–student relationship is institutionally mandated and thus pre-exists the individual supervisor and student. The supervisor is a knowing authority, who is also *in* authority in the sense of overseeing the student's work. The student *does not know* and therefore is in need of guidance. The relationship has a unilateral quality because its goal is that the supervisor teaches the student something – a set of research skills, an appropriate disposition with respect to the production of academic work, the skills of writing a sustained and mature piece of academic work, which is appropriate in style and substance to the values and mores of the discipline. This institutional character of supervision, although it is regulated informally as well as formally, can be made fairly transparent to the student and supervisor. Many universities, for instance, have attempted to do this by producing codes of practice that outline the responsibilities of the pair. (Elsewhere I have written a critique of the limitations of such codes (Grant 2001).)

In the transcript of the meeting, the distinctive traditional roles of supervisor and student are immediately visible – the supervisor opens the meeting and sets out the agenda. The student agrees:

> *Supervisor*: [deep breath] Okay, now let's see … try talking to this. What I've done is, um, I've written these small comments on a piece of paper and major comments, ten points yeah?
> *Student*: [overlaps] Yeah
> *Supervisor*: So shall I just go through …
> *Student*: Yeah [interrupts supervisor to agree]

Supervisor:[E]ach of them and perhaps I need to go, if you want to give examples, get examples, I will refer to the small comments [cough] and if we have time [speaking more quickly] or if you want to, we can go through the small, through the small …
Student: Mhm

Meeting transcript: 1

This opening exchange sets the scene for much of what follows. Throughout the meeting, the supervisor talks the most; she also makes the most knowing comments. The student

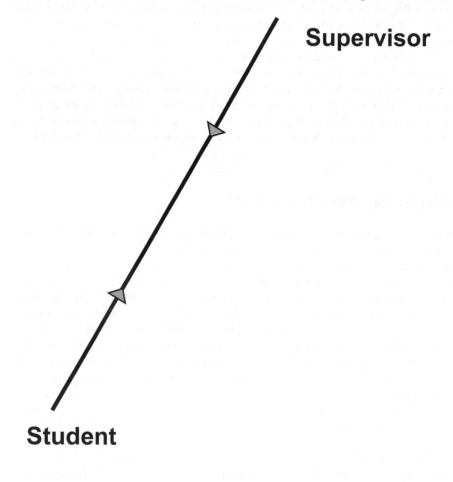

Supervisor

Student

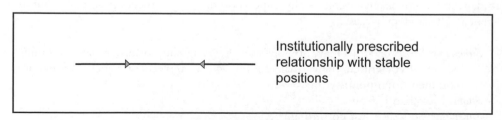

Institutionally prescribed relationship with stable positions

Figure 7.1 The first layer, supervisor and student.

readily responds with sounds of agreement that frequently overlap with the supervisor's speech; sometimes she speaks back to the supervisor to explain something further. She does not disagree with any of the comprehensive changes the supervisor suggests and she does not ask questions. Overall, their respective positions seem clear: the supervisor is an authoritative knowing teacher and the student is an agreeable and co-operative listener. However, a problematic feature of the supervision relationship so understood and enacted is that students often feel somewhat powerless and this may be exacerbated when the supervisor will also be the examiner. Yet 'power' is a dirty word and not spoken of in the codes and guidelines.

The second layer: pedagogical power relations

I want now to trace the outline of another layer that lies below the first through adding the term 'pedagogy' as it is commonly used in radical education theories. Whereas we usually think of the teaching and learning relationship as dyadic between teacher and student, in pedagogy the matrix of relationships is triadic (imagine a triangle) between teacher, student and knowledge: see Figure 7.2.

In this meaning of 'pedagogy', the relationships between teacher (supervisor), student *and* knowledge (thesis) are seen to be productive because all three are 'active, changing and changeable agencies' (Lusted 1986: 3). Equally valuable, each is *transformed* through the processes of pedagogy. In a sense, the outcome of supervision is not only to teach the student skills but also to teach the student *how* to be someone – a researcher, a scholar, an academic. Such transformation is effected through power relations that always work through the actions of an acting subject upon another acting subject (Foucault 1986). To avoid the pitfall of according all power to the supervisor, it is important to recognise that both supervisor and student have the capacity to act.

At the same time, as an institutionalised pedagogy, supervision:

[I]mposes norms for capacities and conduct, ... is organized around techniques of moral supervision, ... [and] embodies these techniques in unequal relations between the differentially constructed agents of teacher and student.

Gore 1993: 125

What does it mean to say that supervisor and student are differentially constructed? Some aspects of the institutional position of the supervisor are as follows: s/he is positioned as an experienced and successful researcher, an established authority in some area of her/his discipline, as 'finished', as an overseer of the student, as a source of various goodies including time, feedback, money, networks, recognition of the student's worth, encouragement, and sometimes as the examiner. On the other hand, the student is positioned as not knowing, insecure, inexperienced, in process, needy, consumed by the project.

In this meaning of pedagogy, the thesis as the privileged form of institutional knowledge also has a position and is implicated in power relations: it is a culturally prescribed artefact; it is meant to be big, formal, disciplined and original (yet it so often feels slippery and unknown); it will be examined according to criteria that are often not clear to the student. In relation to the thesis, a central question that supervisor and student often struggle over is whose voice should be heard there – the student's? The absent masters' of the discipline? The supervisor's? The complex matter of being a productive pedagogical

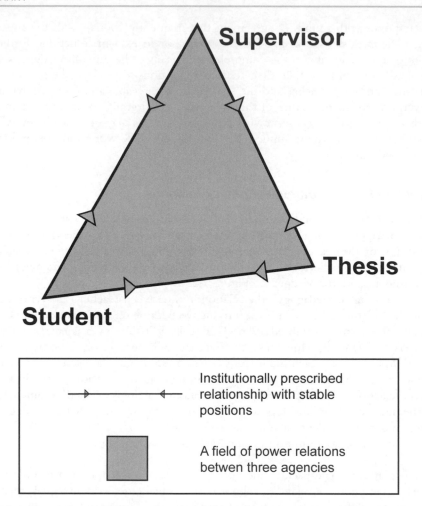

Figure 7.2 Adding the second layer, pedagogical power relations between three agencies.

power relation is often unaddressed in supervision, which is why I want to argue that this 'layer' is only occasionally visible.

When I look again at the meeting transcript, I think I can detect the power relations of pedagogy at work. For instance, much of what the supervisor has to say is about matters the student will have to do something about. Here is an exchange, quite typical, which illustrates this:

> *Supervisor*: So, we, we won't have straight away …
> *Student*: Yeah
> *Supervisor*: [T]he right question but you, I think *you need to* find an umbrella question …
> *Student*: Yeah
> *Supervisor*: [T]hat captures it all.
> *Student*: Mhmm, mhmm
> *Supervisor*: So that's one thing that *you need to do*. Aaaahm, ok, point 4 is *rewrite* your main introduction as a procedural introduction in that sense of 'I want to discuss this topic and …

Student: Right

Supervisor: [T]hen I want to discuss that topic and then I'm going to question whether I'm going to do this', rather than already as the argument so …

Student: Mhmm, mhmm

Supervisor: [Y]eah, in your introduction *write well here*, this is already an argument

Student: Ok

Supervisor: So that rather goes into the conclusion and then Chapter 5 is, ah, yeah, *rewrite your conclusion* as a substantial ahm conclusion, 'I have first argued a and then b'.

Meeting transcript: 4

The words the supervisor uses in the meeting and on the draft are intended to produce effects in the student and in her thesis. In this exchange, the supervisor is invoking disciplinary norms (indirectly, almost reluctantly) over the student's work – and over the student's body because reproducing the norms will require many hours of hard work.

However, the supervisor does not only discipline the student by directing her; she also encourages the student, hailing her as a good scholar. In so doing, she tries to engage the student's desires in the task, to 'persuade' the student to discipline herself:

Supervisor: Yeah, those are questions you probably have asked yourself at the beginning and forgotten about and now they are all come back.

Meeting transcript: 15

And later:

Supervisor: [long pause, pages turning] I had difficulties with ahm the notion of trust as it appears in chapter one …

Student: Yeah

Supervisor: [N]ot because I don't like it, cos I like it very much, but ahm there seem to be two different angles in which you build in the chapter, one is ahm following [this theorist's] model, also of the three things that build a community.

Meeting transcript: 16

The student responded to this encouragement. When asked how she felt about herself as a research student as a result of the meeting, she wrote:

Good. I feel that although there is still a lot of work to do, [the supervisor] appreciates my work and behaves in a very collegial, equal manner towards me.

Notes, lines 22–3

During the meeting, the supervisor gave the student comprehensive and detailed feedback; in fact she reshaped the structure of the student's thesis, while managing to suggest that she was just helping the student reveal what was already there. Afterwards, the student wrote that the meeting:

Motivated me greatly. I will certainly work with renewed impetus, as I now have some direction.

Notes, lines 24–5

95

In these comments we can see how the supervisor acts on the actions of her student. By previously giving her supervisor work for feedback, the student has already acted on the actions of the supervisor – the supervisor has had to discipline herself to the demanding task of reading the draft and commenting on it. Indeed, the whole interaction has this action/reaction quality, like a dance.

The third layer: diverse social positionings

But there is yet more to supervision than its 'roles' and 'duties' for supervisor and student, and its complex institutional character with tensions between discipline and freedom, dependence and independence, and its reluctance to speak of power. Supervisor and student also meet as 'individuals' who are implicated in mutual power relations that, produced through the workings of identity and their stereotypes, derive meaning from broader life experiences and social positioning (Figure 7.3).

The traces of identity are yet another layer in the map, perhaps more deeply 'buried' because much of what justifies higher education has depended on overlooking identity as an issue for its practices. These traces are found in the figures of the individuals who stand behind the labels of supervisors and student, 'real' people (variously gendered, classed, aged, ethnic, religious, sexually oriented) who *take up the positions* of student and supervisor – and a 'real' (and limited) object that takes up the (idealised) position of thesis. The relationships between the 'real' people are unpredictable and idiosyncratic. For one thing, these individuals take up their position as student or supervisor differently from how others do; they also have differing beliefs about how the other position *ought to be* taken up. More, in the intimacy of supervision, student and supervisor respond to each other as more than student and supervisor, as embodied beings who are seen as gendered, aged, ethnic, sexual, and thought to be different, same, other. Social power relations will have many effects on supervision, for instance, through posing obstacles and derailments for communication.[3] More seriously, they may provide the grounds for allegations and convictions of malpractice and abuse. In an example, Deborah Lee (1998) offers a case study from a UK university where a male supervisor is perceived by two separate women students as sexually harassing. She argues that this case study offers evidence of a supervisor's 'strategic exploitation of conditions which are actually integral and arguably necessary to this distinctive academic relationship' (Lee 1998: 299). Specifically, she suggests that this individual's institutional position as a supervisor and highly regarded researcher intersected with his social position as a heterosexual, gambling-addicted, unhappy male to produce a pattern of (unwitting?) harassing behaviour towards the women.

In the data, it is harder to trace the effects of the social positions the two people occupy and what this means for their supervision interactions. Indeed, trying to trace out the effects of social positions on the actions of individuals is always a difficult and unreliable matter:

> Often, the networks of power and social positioning in pedagogical relations can be made up of thin, stringy traces. They can be like the twisty and entwined chocolate bands running through a marbleized cake. Try to follow one of those bands. Better yet, try to extract one for a good look. It takes surgical skill.
>
> Ellsworth 1997: 7

So what follows is even more tentative than what has gone before.

One partly visible band is that of gender. I can see traces of what have been identified by linguists (Holmes 1995) as gendered language patterns – for instance, the supervisor uses many hedges in her talk, seemingly to soften the force of what she has to say:

> *Supervisor.* So *maybe if you, if you* look backwards your central question would be something like *ahm* would deliberative democracy offer a model of community?
>
> Hedges emphasised, meeting transcript: 3

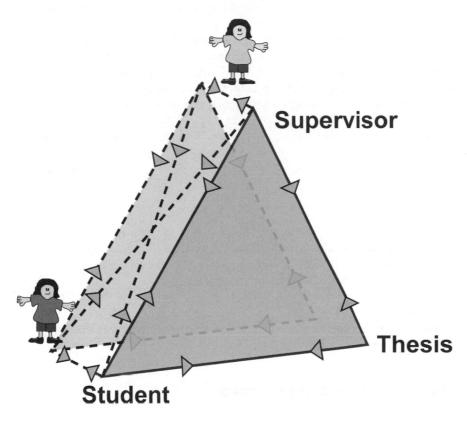

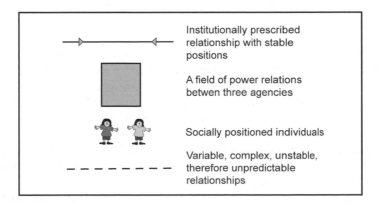

Figure 7.3 Adding in the layer of social positioning.

Likewise the student:

> *Student*: I didn't want to add much more other than *um* I *just wanted to mention* in the last two chapters the postmodern debate but just mention that there *really um* because that's where [a theorist] has her objection from but *no yeah* mainly I wanted to *just kind of* tie it all in together I think, yeah, it's quite right I've gotta actually say it, making the argument clear, writing it in every chapter.
>
> Hedges emphasised, meeting transcript: 8

This communication pattern is common for women who, in the interests of maintaining reciprocity with their listener, use many linguistic devices to signal their good intentions.

As well, right at the beginning of the meeting, the supervisor takes a deep breath, almost as if she is drawing herself up into this role. Five minutes after the meeting finished, she wrote that she thought the meeting had gone thus:

> Too fast, I spoke too fast. I was too imposing. Why am I that way always. Want to do too much for them.
>
> Notes, lines 1–2

And later, that she felt:

> First ashamed of myself as the bully. Then I started to rationalize and justify it and came out quite all right after a while. I pacify myself, otherwise it is too hard to live with myself I suppose. But it is also trying to see the other side, the advantages of a supervisor who talks and who does offer feedback.
>
> Notes, lines 67–70

What these reflections might point to are tensions some women experience in taking up positions of authority in which they easily feel overbearing and uncomfortable.

The fourth layer: eruptions of desire

Not only are student and supervisor separated from, unknowable to, each other by the 'abyssal space' (Readings 1996: 156) of difference, but they are fractured in themselves, divided between their conscious and unconscious knowing and desires, unknowable to themselves (Figure 7.4).

In the relative intensity and privacy of supervision, supervisor and student make unconscious responses to each other. They may remind each other of former significant others (and thus in some sense there are others present in the supervision meeting), of themselves even. They may have strong feelings – of gratitude, resentment, frustration, disappointment, love – because of these remindings. This is the murky realm of transference and counter transference (Frow 1988; Giblett 1992; Simon 1995; Sofoulis 1997). It is fraught by the supervisor's and student's desires – to please, to challenge, to do well, to earn glory, to demonstrate (or push towards) independence, to resist, to be respected by, to be recognised as clever, to become like, to become authoritative – desires *for* the (powerful or vulnerable) other. Often unconscious, sometimes confused and changing, these desires produce behaviours from both supervisor and student that are

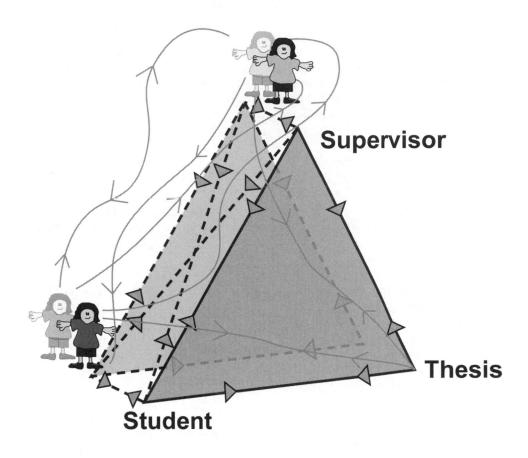

Supervisor

Thesis

Student

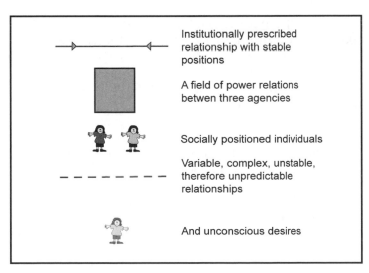

Institutionally prescribed
relationship with stable
positions

A field of power relations
between three agencies

Socially positioned individuals

Variable, complex, unstable,
therefore unpredictable
relationships

And unconscious desires

Figure 7.4 Adding in unconscious desires.

not amenable to rational explanation, that neither might wish to admit to in the public domain:

> It has not been in the interests of academics generally or their postgraduate charges to show and tell what systems of encouragements or discouragements may have been at work in the daily mentoring of 'pure' research and thesis-writing. This is not to presume transgression, but to understand that such pedagogy is dangerously untranslatable as rational inquiry made public.
>
> McWilliam and Palmer 1995: 32

Roger Simon suggests it is the very way in which we have understood and practised supervision in higher education that produces its erotic character:

> The context for learning will be erotic, where education has been historically and institutionally framed to proceed through intimate interaction and structural dependencies.
>
> Simon 1995: 100

Indeed, it may be just that character that gives supervision much of its power as a pedagogy, that makes it mean so much, particularly to the student.

If the bands of power and social positioning are difficult to trace in pedagogical relations, then how is it possible to trace the workings of desire and the unconscious? For the moment, I have decided to focus on comments or questions that suggest unexplained ambivalences and contradictions. For example, what are we to make of these comments from the supervisor:

> Too fast, I spoke too fast. I was too imposing. Why am I that way always. Want to do too much for them. ... I felt that that was awful when I was a PhD student, so why?
>
> Notes, lines 1–3

> [After the meeting, I am] exhausted. I leave the meetings always exhausted and the student doesn't have a chance to get exhausted. Bad economy.
>
> Notes, lines 8–9

Maybe she is exhausted because of the struggle to take the position of supervisor as I suggest above? Or maybe it's because she does too much of the work, that is, she performs her position 'badly' (by her own or the institution's or someone else's standards)? But, if so, why the 'always'? What drives the supervisor into a repetitively punishing pattern of interaction, one that she hated when she was a student?

The student writes that during the meeting she felt:

> Gratefulness, bit of apprehension/fear, generally very well disposed towards her, friendly, but sometimes a bit worried about her apparent coolness/distance.
>
> Notes, lines 14–16

Where does the gratitude come from? How does it affect the way she responds during the meeting? Is this why she seems so eager to agree throughout? And what about the note of dissatisfaction – what did she expect from the supervisor? What desires did she have that the supervisor left unaddressed or, more, thwarted? What were the effects of these unaddressed desires for the student? How can we find this out? Could the student answer this question even if she wanted to?

The student still felt ambivalent after the meeting was over:

> [I feel] both motivated and overwhelmed. Excited and scared.
>
> Notes, line 17

How did this ambivalence affect her work? How did it make it harder? How did it affect the way in which she understood herself as a capable scholar?

Desire and identity make supervision opaque. They are dimensions no code can regulate and no literal reading of the body can guard against. In the delicate zone between encouragement and discipline that makes up much of supervision, the workings of identity and desire provide fertile ground for misreadings, resentments, confusions. Most of us are unprepared and ill-equipped to deal with these responses when they happen. Withdrawing into stereotypes (e.g. *all* women, or Maori, or Asians are *like this*) is of little help because the politics of identity and desire cannot be literally read from the body in this way.

Layer upon layer

> Pedagogy as a social relationship is very close in. It gets right in there – in your brain, your body, your heart, in your sense of self, of the world, of others, and of possibilities and impossibilities in all those realms.
>
> Ellsworth 1997: 6

This is the map I want to offer, a map anchored to the stable institutional positions of supervisor, student and thesis but crisscrossed by unpredictable relations between selves and social positions, between reason and desire, between past experiences, present actions, and future hopes. These relations overlap and intersect, confuse and interfere with, each other. Crucially for our understanding of pedagogy, the map expands pedagogical relations beyond the supervisor–student horizon in several directions. In one direction, it expands them to include the social positions of those who take up the places of supervisor and student. These positions exert their own 'truths' of the self, shaping the ways in which individuals enact themselves as student and supervisor as well as the expectations and desires they have of each other. In the map, we find the 'interrelation and interaction of subjectivity and circumstances' that Green and Lee talk of (1995: 41).

In another direction, pedagogical relations are expanded to include the absent masters of the discipline(s) – the supervisor's peers whose voices are 'spoken' by the supervisor in her injunctions to the student. As well, the dynamic artifice of the thesis continually exerts disciplinary power along the way. The student negotiates the effects of this power relation in the struggle to write 'right'; the supervisor experiences it in the delicately balanced process of giving feedback that incites the student to independence and creativity while simultaneously patrolling the borders of disciplinary coherence. Recognising that supervision-as-pedagogy always includes the 'presence' of the absent masters and the thesis is crucial because it points to the ways in which the supervisor – subject to the norms of a discipline, responsible to the student for their (supervisor's and student's)

101

successful enactment of the properly authoritative academic self in the thesis, her/himself visible to peers in the external examination process – is unfree.

This view stands in contrast to much of the radical (feminist and critical) pedagogies literature in which the authority and power of the teacher has been read as if power is always negative in its effects, as if the teacher is the only one with power, and as if s/he is free to relinquish it. In the map I have drawn here neither supervisor nor student can escape the workings of power because it is the productive ground of supervision, it makes things happen, indeed it makes supervision what it is. In contrast to a view of polarised pedagogical power, this map suggests that both supervisor and student have power to act on the actions of the other – although with unpredictable and mixed effects. For instance, it is unlikely that the student above would have guessed at how exhausted and self-doubting her supervisor felt after their joint meeting. Similarly, the supervisor probably would not have predicted the student's ambivalence towards her, particularly given that she was stepping in at some cost to herself to assist the student complete her thesis successfully. The supervisor's power to affect the actions of the student is potentially a source of pleasure and pain to student *and* supervisor – we see the student enjoying the direction given to her by the supervisor while the supervisor is agonising over some aspects of the exercise of her power. Likewise, the student's exercise of power – through 'requiring' her supervisor to read many chapters of writing, to think hard upon it, to speak to her about her work, to take her seriously as an academic subject – is pleasurable and painful for both. However, to see power as inevitable and productive in this way does not mean that we should not scrutinise the workings of power in the form of supervisory authority – as Edward Saïd argues, all forms of authority are produced, are persuasive, suggesting themselves to be true, and all must be analysed (Saïd 1998: 874).

In the map I have drawn, we find the outlines of a sturdy triangular shape buried under the messy ephemeral lines of (too many?) relations. I do not see here the 'home-liness' (Green and Lee 1995) of teaching but rather the exoticness of strange pedagogical lands, in which every supervision inhabits a parallel world with certain regular and recognisable features but much that is new and unforeseen. People are strange to each other. Supervision comes face to face with this strangeness in an intense way and must somehow, and often does, work in spite of this. We, supervisors and students, may even be able to relish it if we can learn to tolerate its instability. The view I offer here insists on that instability, on the complexity and unpredictability of supervision-as-pedagogy, on its situated and negotiated character.

A question I have been asked is how will such a map assist supervisors and students. In attempting to map the private landscape of supervision, am I not opening a kind of Pandora's box full of fantasies and dangers for both student and supervisor? Is it not better to leave these matters of difference and desire unspoken, especially if by speaking about them I may in some sense bring them into being, through giving student and supervisor a language with which to accuse each other of maltreatment through abuse of power, or unresolved transferences?

To answer these questions, I refer to my experience over the years of listening to students' stories of supervision troubles, sometimes breakdown. I have come to think that we do need to talk about these matters because they are important for students at least. They may be useful to help them understand that many of the difficulties of supervision and ordeals of graduate research are very predictable: the 'mad' (Frow 1988) process of being a graduate research student, of committing yourself to a daunting task in the hope that you will be successful while often feeling anything but, of putting your trust, your future, in the hands of someone who on a bad day barely seems to remember your name; the possibility that intense responses to your supervisor may be about older experiences in your life than the supervision relationship itself; your increased vulnerability if you rely on your supervisor for everything, or if you over invest your supervisor with power and knowledge. These matters must also be important to the supervisor who is attempting, usually in good faith, sometimes apparently against all odds, to guide the student in this task, to assist the student to do the best s/he can, to have the most successful outcome possible.

Conclusions

In our mass higher education system, supervision can be seen as a remnant of more personalised forms of pedagogy from a time when there was greater social homogeneity between university teachers and students. Because of its personal and intimate character, there have always been many attendant pleasures and risks. Now, however, it is subject to a range of new pressures: more, and more diverse, students who have no previous experience of a close working relationship with an academic, some of whom are paying huge fees for their education, all of whom face a very competitive employment market. At the same time, many academics are dealing with the intensification of their work, and face teaching environments with dimensions of interpersonal difference for which they feel unprepared and unsupported. Meanwhile, university administrations are pushing for constant programme (and student 'market') expansion in their effort to chase funds in the battle to survive with diminishing government support. In many cases, the complex and potentially fraught pedagogy of supervision may not be withstanding these pressures particularly well.

It may be that we need to radically rethink the practices by which we credentialise, and socialise, graduate students. I think, however, we should beware simply eliminating supervision – if we do so, we may immeasurably diminish the pleasures some academics derive from their jobs and remove one of the few opportunities students have for working closely alongside an academic. A helpful repositioning of supervision may be one where its intimacy is respected without becoming a dangerous isolation. To do this, departments need to actively develop a culture where one-to-one (or two-to-one) supervision is not depended upon as the sole vehicle for the education of research students but where supervisors and students are expected to get (and provided with opportunities for) stimulus and support from the community of the department.

In a final note, I look briefly beyond supervision-as-pedagogy to the terrain of university pedagogies more widely. Although I acknowledge that supervision is a particular and peculiar pedagogical practice, many of its pleasures and risks occur in other scenes of teaching and learning – in lectures, tutorials and seminars, laboratories, online discussion groups – in any places where students and teachers interact. In particular, I suggest that this map offers a useful antidote to a view of teaching and learning that rests on the schematic simplicity of the teacher teaches (in the sense of formulating a rational plan of action) and, accordingly, the students learn (in the sense of enacting reliably and 'successfully' the objectives of the teacher's plan). This persistent view, fed by bureaucratic and managerial discourses of education, but also by the mainstream discourse of educational research itself, continues to underpin pedagogies as apparently diverse as mass lecturing and self-directed learning. Yet if an orderly sequence of teacher plans–student enacts is not how it happens in the relatively direct encounter of supervision, then it is unlikely to be happening in other university pedagogies. We need a different, perhaps more chaotic view of pedagogy, one that is capable of infusing our teaching and research practices with both an enriching optimism and a proper pessimism as to their efficacy.

Acknowledgements

Thanks to R and Z, supervisor and student, for access to their supervision relationship; to my own supervisor, Dr Alison Jones, whose support is unflagging; to Todd Brackley and Avril Bell for many useful conversations over the time of developing these ideas; to Deb Radford, Christine Herzog and Ann Smart for sharp comment and guidance; to Michelle Park for her great drawings. This article is based on a paper presented at the Improving Student Learning Strategically Conference in Manchester, September 2000.

Notes

1 My interest here is the mode of supervision in the British one-to-one tutorial tradition associated with the arts, humanities and social sciences, rather than with the physical sciences. However, from my experience of working with supervisors and students across all the disciplines for more than 10 years, I think many of the issues raised here are relevant in both domains that, at times, overlap in actual practices. Likewise, although this data came from a masters supervision, I think the challenges of negotiating layered relations between supervisor and student are relevant for doctoral supervision as well.

2 Because consent between a student and his/her supervisor is not straightforward, I met with the student to discuss her consent.

3 Contemporary theories of language and communication emphasise 'the abyssal space' (Readings 1996) between self and other in every moment of dialogue. In this sense, no communication can be guaranteed in its transparency.

References

Bartlett, A. and Mercer, G. (2000) Reconceptualizing discourses of power in postgraduate pedagogies, *Teaching in Higher Education*, 5(2): 195–204.

Ellsworth, E. (1997) *Teaching Positions: difference, pedagogy and the power of address*. New York: Teachers College Press.

Fairclough, N. (1995) *Critical Discourse Analysis: the critical study of language*. London: Longman.

Foucault, M. (1974) *The Archaeology of Knowledge*. London: Tavistock.

——(1986) The subject and power. In B. Wallis (Ed.) *Art after Modernism: rethinking representation*. New York: New Museum of Contemporary Art.

Frow, J. (1988) Discipline and discipleship, *Textual Practice*, 2: 307–23.

Giblett, R. (1992) The desire for disciples, *Paragraph*, 15(1): 136–55.

Gore, J. (1993) *The Struggle for Pedagogies: critical and feminist discourses as regimes of truth*. New York: Routledge.

Grant, B. M. (2001) Unreasonable practices: reading a code of supervision against the grain. In A. Bartlett and G. Mercer (Eds). *Postgraduate Research Supervision: transforming (r)elations*. New York: Peter Lang.

Green, B. and Lee, A. (1995) Theorizing postgraduate pedagogy, *The Australian Universities' Review*, 38(2): 40–45.

Holmes, J. (1995) *Women, Men and Politeness*. London: Longman.

Janks, H. (1997) Critical discourse analysis as a research tool, *Discourse: Studies in the Cultural Politics of Education*, 18(3): 329–42.

Johnson, L., Lee, A. and Green, B. (2000) The PhD and the autonomous self: gender, rationality and postgraduate pedagogy, *Studies in Higher Education*, 25(2): 135–47.

Kamler, B. (1997) An interview with Terry Threadgold on critical discourse analysis, *Discourse: Studies in the Cultural Politics of Education*, 18(3): 437–51.

Lee, D. (1998) Sexual harassment in PhD supervision, *Gender and Education*, 10(3): 299–312.

Lusted, D. (1986) Why pedagogy?, *Screen*, 27(5): 2–14.

Lynn, S. (1998) *Texts and Contexts: writing about literature with critical theory*. 2nd edn, New York: Longman.

McWilliam, E. and Palmer, P. (1995) Teaching tech(no)bodies: open learning and postgraduate pedagogy, *The Australian Universities' Review*, 35(2): 32–34.

Readings, B. (1996) *The University in Ruins*. Cambridge, MA: Harvard University Press.

Saïd, E. (1998) Orientalism. In J. Rivkin and M. Ryan (Eds). *Literary Theory: an anthology*. Malden MA: Blackwell Publishers Ltd.

Simon, R. (1995) Face to Face with Alterity: postmodern Jewish identity and the eros of pedagogy. In J. Gallop (Ed.). *Pedagogy as Impersonation*. New York: Routledge.

Sofoulis, Z. (1997) *What scholar would endorse me? Transference, counter-transference and postgraduate pedagogy*. Unpublished paper presented at the University of Auckland.

8
Adapting signature pedagogies in doctoral education

The case of teaching how to work with the literature

C. M. Golde

Competently working with or 'knowing' the literature of a field is important for scholarship in all disciplines, although it manifests somewhat differently in different fields. All researchers and scholars work within particular traditions and build on, modify, or overturn that which has gone before. Learning the literature requires far more than simply reading widely, regurgitating key phrases and findings, and genuflecting to seminal researchers. It is integral to any scholarly investigation. For educational research, for example,

> [T]o advance our collective understanding, a researcher or scholar needs to understand what has been done before, the strengths and weaknesses of existing studies, and what they might mean. A researcher cannot perform significant research without first understanding the literature in the field.
>
> Boote and Beile 2005: 3

Students of education and other social sciences must undertake the following (this list is not exhaustive): absorb the content of what they read, determine what is known and what needs to be known, identify important ongoing disciplinary debates, develop the judgement to discriminate between work of high quality and mediocre efforts, extract useful information on which to build, juxtapose multiple theoretical perspectives and explanations, connect research studies to one another, synthesise and reappraise others' work, connect their own thinking to that of those who have come before, and learn the stylistic conventions of written work, such as norms of what to say and what to omit (Becker 1986; Boote and Beile 2005; 2006; Delamont and Atkinson 2001; Kamler and Thomson 2006; Maxwell 2006; Richardson 2006). Learning to work with the literature, 'to canvass and interpret the field and to construct her version of its terrain', is also a form of 'identity work' in which the scholar positions herself and her own work in relation to the field (Kamler and Thomson 2006: 28–9).

Despite the fact that clear and persuasive writing is essential to, and indeed an integral part of, research and scholarship (Richardson 1998), writing well and with confidence, particularly about others' work, is a challenge for many students in every discipline (see, for example, Bolker 1998). The challenge of working with literature becomes obvious in dissertation writing, which, for many students is the first piece of sustained research. In the social sciences in which dissertations comprise one study (in contrast to the multiple paper format which is moving from the sciences into the social sciences), students are expected to write 'a substantive, thorough, sophisticated literature review' for their dissertations (Boote and Beile 2005: 3), but too many students simply report on the literature rather than building an argument based on the work that has come before theirs. 'The literature is neither used to locate their studies, nor to advance an argument about the state of the field in order to make the case for their own work', say Kamler and Thomson (2006: 32) – two experts on doctoral writing. They observe that many students seem unable to make a critique and take a stand, adding, 'This is characteristic of diffident scholars who lack authority and who are literally overwhelmed by the work of others' (p. 32). The problem may be that many students are not asked to work with literature in the ways that professional researchers do before confronting the dissertation prospectus itself. These skills are 'often neglected or taught inadequately' (Maxwell 2006: 30).

If the status quo is not working, then the question is how to teach literature work more effectively. Simply adding a class on literature reviewing or writing (see, for example, Rose and McClafferty 2001) – helpful as that is – may be insufficient. More radical rethinking of the structures of social science doctoral programmes might be in order. If working with the literature effectively is crucial for every researcher, multiple opportunities to do so before the dissertation stage should be woven through the student career. How can this be accomplished? Practices used in other programmes and fields can serve as sources of inspiration.[1] This happens routinely in research and scholarship, when theories and methods from other disciplines and enquiry traditions are borrowed and adapted. This chapter describes practices from other disciplines that might be fruitfully modified for the social sciences in which they are not well known.

Lessons from other disciplines

Disciplines differ in how research and scholarship are conducted, how the research enterprise is organised and funded, what counts as knowledge, and how knowledge claims are made and verified. Student demographics and students' post-PhD career paths also vary (see Golde and Walker 2006, for descriptions of six disciplines in the USA). So it is not surprising that the normative ways and settings in which students are taught differ from one field to the next. Some practices for teaching students are so idiosyncratic, habituated, and completely embedded in a particular discipline that they can be called 'signature pedagogies'.

The term was coined by Shulman (2005) to describe 'the characteristic forms of teaching and learning … that organize the fundamental ways in which future practitioners are educated for their new professions' (p. 52). Examples of signature pedagogies, those 'forms of instruction that leap to mind' (p. 52), include the case dialogue method of teaching in law schools and bedside teaching on daily clinical rounds in medical education.

> Signature pedagogies make a difference. They form habits of the mind, habits of the heart, and habits of the hand. … [They] prefigure the cultures of professional work and provide the early socialization into the practices and values of a field.
>
> Shulman 2005: 59

That is what they do for students. For those of us on the outside, signature pedagogies are windows into the cultures of their fields that reveal professional values. Signature pedagogies share three features: they are pervasive and routine; they entail public student performance; and they are marked by uncertainty, visibility and accountability, which raise the emotional stakes (Shulman 2005: 56–7).

Signature pedagogies are not just intriguing oddities. They are widespread across departments within a particular discipline, refined by time and practice, and they meet commonly understood pedagogical purposes. Arguably, signature pedagogies are adaptively suited – to borrow language from evolutionary biology – for the particularities of the scholarly enterprises in which they are found and therefore contribute to socialising students into disciplinary norms and identities.

In this chapter, I will describe two very different practices that share a common overarching goal of teaching students to work with the literature in the field according to the demands and standards of the discipline. They can be considered signature pedagogies in their home (and neighbouring) disciplines, one in neuroscience (the journal club) and one in English (the list examination). Of course, they are not the only activities that scholars in those fields use for this purpose. And, as will be clear, these pedagogies serve other purposes as well, making each practice particularly well suited to its discipline of origin. In the final section of the chapter, I will consider the adaptability of these practices for education and other social sciences, where they seem to be foreign but might be adapted to good effect.

Method

The practices described in this chapter came to my attention through the work of the Carnegie Initiative on the Doctorate (CID), for which I served as research director from 2001 to 2006. Sponsored by The Carnegie Foundation for the Advancement of Teaching, the CID was an action and research project working in six disciplines: chemistry, education, English, mathematics, history, and neuroscience at US universities (see Appendix A: Summary Description of the Carnegie Initiative on the Doctorate, pp. 161–75, in *The Formation of Scholars*, Walker *et al.* 2008). An outsider vantage point gave Carnegie CID staff a comparative view of the six fields. The attention to signature pedagogies developed as we saw elements of doctoral programmes that occur normally in one discipline but are unusual in others.

The research methods for this chapter are essentially observational. Over the course of the CID we heard faculty and students make passing reference to practices in their doctoral programmes that all others from the field immediately understood; but these were practices with which the CID team was unfamiliar. Naturally, we began to ask more questions to tease out the essential features of these practices. The reader might imagine that we saw many signature pedagogies, but that was not the case.[2] My discussion in this chapter is limited to practices that have the express purpose of mastery of the disciplinary literature. I interviewed faculty and graduate students who were familiar with the practices and were articulate observers. Several of them read and responded to a draft of this piece. I also reviewed the literature on the practices (journal clubs are well studied in medical education circles) as well as dozens of handbooks and webpages that describe the practices in use. Extensive literature reviews on doctoral education in English and neuroscience also provided background. It is from these sources that the cases below are drawn.

Case 1: the journal club

Journal clubs are formally organised reading groups that discuss an article found in the recent research journals. A single article is at the heart of each journal club presentation and discussion; the articles under discussion are ones deemed scientifically important. Journal clubs are conventionally multi-generational; they include faculty members, postdoctoral fellows, advanced graduate students, and novice graduate students as equal participants. Journal clubs are organised around specialised themes. For example, some of the journal clubs offered through the Neuroscience Training Program at the University of Wisconsin–Madison in the 2008–9 academic year were Axon Guidance; Neural Stem Cells and Adult Neurogenesis; and Cerebral Ischemic Damage (University of Wisconsin–Madison Neuroscience Training Program 2008).

Journal clubs are a customary part of departmental life in most biological sciences. Although they are not formal courses, journal clubs are a well-understood mechanism for teaching and learning. Participation is generally expected. One of the University of Wisconsin journal clubs advertises that it 'has met continuously since 1985' (University of Wisconsin–Madison Neuroscience Training Program 2008, 'Hearing and Donuts', para. 1). In fact, many doctoral programmes in neuroscience require participation in journal clubs (e.g. the University of Pittsburgh Centre for Neuroscience Graduate Training Program 2006, '5.6 Journal Club', para. 1). Less formally, the head of a laboratory may expect students to participate in a laboratory-based or cross-laboratory journal club.

Journal clubs typically meet weekly for approximately an hour. Each week a different person presents an article to the group, and all participants are expected to have read the article in advance. The presentation is followed by general discussion.

The process for presenting the articles is fairly standard: Summarise the article. Locate it in the larger landscape of the field. Describe the experiment in sufficient detail that the audience can understand it without becoming overly wrapped up in the details. Explain why the article is important. Critique the article: Do the data and their analysis withstand scrutiny? Are there contradictions or competing hypotheses? The discussion focuses on the big picture: the article's strengths and weaknesses, how the article extends the field, potential applications of the work, and what questions need to be answered in light of the current findings.

Neuroscience programmes often support a second kind of journal club: broad introductory ones for students in their early years. These are opportunities to read articles of historic importance and to learn the norms of journal clubs. (Such opportunities are particularly valuable in neuroscience, as students come from disparate undergraduate majors; broad introductory journal clubs are less common in more established bioscience disciplines.) Guidelines for making presentations are provided; these serve to initiate members into the norms of journal clubs. Early journal clubs also build community among graduate students, a particular challenge for neuroscience programmes whose students work in laboratories all over campus.

Feedback mechanisms can help presenters improve and often are incorporated into journal clubs for which academic credit is offered. In the University of Pittsburgh neuroscience programme, all journal club participants use a Student Journal Club Evaluation form to evaluate presenters; the form includes 13 questions covering the presenter's introduction of the topic, description of the topic, conclusion, delivery, and overall quality of the presentation, concluding with, 'As a percentage, how much of the presentation could you explain to others?'. Students also benefit from a postpresentation debriefing with the faculty co-ordinator and another faculty member who serves as an 'outside expert' for that session.

Not all journal clubs are successful. Many of the weaknesses of journal clubs are like those of any optional small-group educational activity, such as seminars or study groups. Journal clubs can face the problem of declining attendance; initial enthusiasm often wanes, particularly in the face of competing time pressures. Participant learning suffers if participants do not prepare in advance, if articles are selected and appraised without clear criteria, or if participants do not have guidance in preparing presentations (Deenadayalan *et al.* 2008; Kahn *et al.* 1999; Kahn and Gee 1999). Sometimes a few participants dominate and others, particularly non-native speakers or newcomers, remain silent. Some people are put off by the norms of heated scientific discourse, which can seem aggressive and combative.

What purposes are served by this practice?

Journal clubs have three well-understood and commonly described purposes. (Of course, the purposes may be, in each particular case, more or less important and explicit.) First and foremost, all members of journal clubs, from the most seasoned faculty member to the newest graduate student, use journal clubs to keep up with the literature. This has been the primary goal of journal clubs since they were invented in 1875 (Linzer 1987). Journal clubs provide a forum for a collective effort to promote awareness of current research findings.

Second, journal clubs teach many of the forms of sharing and evaluation of scientific findings. Students learn the written conventions for presenting science by reading articles and seeing what is well received and what obfuscates. They practise presentation skills: organising a talk, speaking to others, sharing the appropriate level of detail, and creating effective PowerPoint slides. Journal clubs also model how to discuss and critique work. Students learn to ask good questions, to respond to questions, and to disagree with others – even professors. They learn to appraise research, develop confidence in their own judgement, and, when selecting an article, determine what constitutes important work.

Third, journal clubs cross disciplinary and organisational boundaries. They are often interdepartmental or 'interlab'. Researchers in a medical school, a veterinary school, and a college of arts and sciences might share an interest in a particular brain function. Journal clubs establish connections across organisational boundaries that might otherwise be obstacles to advancing knowledge. When people come together, the resulting conversations can build bridges and establish trust.

How is this practice suited to neuroscience?

Why do all scientists, from advanced faculty to new graduate students, use journal clubs to stay current? Because journal clubs are a particularly efficient and effective way to help participants meet the three goals described above. The biological sciences have several distinguishing features to which journal clubs are particularly well suited.

First, this is an era of 'fast science'. Emerging findings make it into print very quickly; the time to publication is short (weeks or months rather than years). New information must be acquired, evaluated and incorporated into ongoing work as quickly as possible, but the vast quantity makes it nearly impossible to do so. Consequently, scientists must always be aware of new findings and have the judgement to select relevant information from the torrent of available data. Moreover, colleagues who communicate precisely and concisely are valued. All of these skills are taught in journal club.

Second, there are clear frontiers of knowledge. There is a consensus about what constitutes 'important work' so it is possible to determine which articles are of high priority.

Third, science is conducted in communal and relatively democratic ways. Scientists argue about ideas. The lively intellectual debates during journal club mimic the collaborative yet competitive culture of the laboratory.

Fourth, the norms of science must be navigated and negotiated. In principle, findings are freely shared so that others may replicate them and build on them. In reality, scientists are in competition with one another. Therefore, authors must decide when to present their science to others, garnering credit but possibly relinquishing competitive advantage. They must determine how much information is needed for publication and when to withhold some data for the next article or proposal. Scientists also frame their questions and findings to align with the political priorities of grant making and publication. These choices become visible when an article is discussed.

Finally, important problem areas evolve, and they do not always map well onto existing organisational units. Likewise, journal clubs often cross organisational boundaries. Insights from people in other fields or with different training can be critically important.

These five features of neuroscience, and indeed of most biological sciences, help to explain why journal clubs are such a widespread practice. They are an effective and efficient tool for helping senior scientists keep up with the literature, and they are equally important as a pedagogical strategy for training new scientists.

Case 2: the list

The discipline of English makes use of a very different mechanism for ensuring that students know the literature of the field. *The list* is the group of works or texts that forms the basis of the comprehensive or qualifying examination for a doctoral student in English studies.[3] Exams are usually administered in the second or third year. The list is long, typically containing 60–100 works. One work might be a collection of poems, a novel, a theoretical work, or a group of secondary sources. The examination based on the list of works demonstrates that the student has 'mastered the field'.

After this demonstration of breadth and mastery, students are expected to develop an idea (project) that they will pursue for the dissertation. The dissertation project builds on the specialty reflected in the list. (English studies scholars describe themselves as working on 'projects', not 'problems'. A project has a larger scope than a set of research experiments, and its goal is reaching understanding by developing an argument rather than arriving at a solution to a problem or an answer to a question.)

Anyone in English studies who is asked to describe the list hastens to point out that it has undergone a fundamental shift in the past two decades.[4] At one time there was a single list for all students, composed of the classics of British and American literature ('from Beowulf to Virginia Woolf'); the works were understood to represent 'genius' (Guillory 1991: 52).

Today's English doctoral students typically are expected to pass one or more 'field exams', each of which encompasses a smaller sub-set of the literature. Students and faculty members work together to define an individual list for each field, which is shaped to the students' interests and emerging expertise. Students make active choices of exclusion and inclusion in creating their lists. As stated in the Duke University English Department's graduate studies handbook, 'you should expect to play a very active role in formulating the questions you bring to texts' (Duke University Department of English 2008: 8). Although more constructed and negotiated than in the past, the lists are still relatively standardised in their own way. The theme of each list is usually dependent on a prior conceptual construction of a recognisable sub-field, such as romanticism or feminist theory, that already exists in the discipline. Thus, the works selected must not only be deemed 'major works' but also reflect the student's own position in the field.

What does it mean to display 'mastery'? The process of preparation for the comprehensive examination is a period of intensive reading and usually stretches over several months, if not an entire year. Usually the examination is oral, lasting two to three hours, and the examiners are a committee of faculty members. The examination can be on any aspect of the works on the list. It is more than an advanced quiz programme on authors, dates, plot points, and characters, although students would surely know all of those. The questions are broad and conceptual: Discuss this dynamic, compare and contrast, and the like. Emerging scholars must demonstrate that they 'know' the literature. This includes understanding the broad contexts in which works are located and understanding the evolution of the literature and of its themes and ideas.

The reading list-based examination is persistent but certainly not perfect. The shift from 'comprehensive' lists to tailored lists risks a loss of historical context and breadth, driving students too quickly to preparing for the dissertation (Delbanco 2000). As a result, students may lack a sufficiently broad foundation on which to base subsequent projects or on which to ground their teaching.

Even with focused lists, the intensive reading period can extend for many, many months. This makes it all too easy for students to disappear from the department and lose the benefit of interactions with faculty members. The structure of, and standards for, evaluating the examination itself are highly variable among programmes and individual students' committees. As a result, for some students, the examination itself can seem more like arbitrary hazing than an authentic intellectual discussion.

What purposes are served by this practice?

Three purposes are served by the creation of, and examination on, the list. First, students must self-define and defend their location in the field. To do so, they must enter into the discourse and commentaries surrounding the works of literature that have grown and evolved over time. Mastery of the list(s) is one step along the way toward definition of a professional identity, which has instrumental purposes in terms of getting a job but, more important, is about entering into a disciplinary community. The examination is 'the bridge between coursework and the dissertation', according to the English Department handbook from the University of Illinois at Urbana–Champaign. Mastering core knowledge 'makes possible productive engagement with other scholars in the field (at lectures, conferences, on e-mail discussion groups, in print, at job interviews)' (University of Illinois at Urbana–Champaign Department of English 2008, 'The Special Field Examination', para. 1).

Second, the list and the examination on the list are explicit preparation for the dissertation. It is the public foundation on which the dissertation is built. Quoting further from the University of Illinois handbook,

It enlarges knowledge of scholarship and publication opportunities in the field. By enabling students to define with increasing precision the original contributions they wish to make to the field of their choice, it lays the groundwork for and sparks momentum toward the dissertation. Constructing the list and the rationale, studying for the exam, and taking it are part of the process of defining a professional identity within the discipline.

University of Illinois at Urbana–Champaign Department of English 2008, 'The Special Field Examination', para. 1

Third, the development of the list is intimately related to the ability to teach within a broad area of the discipline. 'Your exam should also help to make you a confident and fearless teacher,' states another handbook (Duke University Department of English 2008: 8).

How is this practice suited to English?

Creating and defending a list is an important step in every English doctoral programme because it helps students to meet the three goals just described. These goals are relevant for English, the quintessential humanities field.

One feature that sets humanities scholarship apart is that it remains fundamentally solo work. Contributions to literature and analysis spring from the imagination of the individual. The list is particularly at home in a discipline that requires a scholar to understand a wide swathe of the field. Another defining characteristic of the humanities is that knowledge builds slowly over time. The contribution that a scholar makes to the discipline is not understood in terms of advancing the frontiers in the same way as in the scientific enterprise. Instead, scholarship involves conceiving new understandings and juxtapositions. One needs broad and deep foundational knowledge to enter the conversation.

Good work in the humanities is judged by its completeness, subtlety and insight. Doing work quickly, beating others to the punch, is less important than getting it right and being thorough. The humanities emphasise the written word, so scholars value nuance and elaboration. Although articles and conference papers (carefully crafted narratives that are read aloud in their entirety without PowerPoint slides) are used to work through ideas in progress, the result of a project is typically a book. This process requires time and a mature perspective developed by the careful examination and re-examination of the works at hand.

The humanities maintain a clear sense of the appropriate sequence for student work. Extensive undergraduate and graduate course work build the foundation – a foundation that is publicly defended before students begin the dissertation project. Clearly, these features are emphasised in the deliberate and time-consuming process of mastering the works on the list.

Finally, English departments are financially supported in large part by the efforts of graduate students and faculty members who teach. Scholars and faculty members are expected to have the versatility needed to teach a wide range of courses. The ability to address a broad range of texts is tested in the list defence.

Additional observations

Before turning to the question of adapting these practices into other fields, three more points should be made. First, not only do journal clubs and list-based examinations

113

advance discipline-specific versions of knowing the literature, but each serves several other purposes as well. This is not unusual in doctoral education; many programme elements serve several pedagogical purposes. Indeed, *The Formation of Scholars*, the volume on doctoral education by the Carnegie Foundation CID team, argues that all programme elements ought to be scrutinised and, when possible, reconfigured to promote student formation along several dimensions simultaneously (Walker *et al.* 2008).

Second, the reader certainly has seen how journal clubs and the examination on the list help to shape the professional identities of neuroscientists and English scholars, respectively. To return to Shulman, the implicit structure of these practices transmits professional attitudes and values (Shulman 2005: 55). One neuroscientist described journal clubs as an avenue for scientists to 'learn to play well together'. These practices are forms of legitimate peripheral participation, in which novice practitioners engage in authentic practice even while they are developing a professional identity, gradually moving to more central community membership (Lave and Wenger 1991). This is one of the most important, if generally implicit, purposes of doctoral education, instilling the 'values and intellectual leanings' of the guild in its newest members (Cronon 2006: 330).

Third, this discussion is firmly rooted in the US system of doctoral education. Several features of American doctoral programmes are assumed. Doctoral studies is a combination of coursework (in the early years) and independent research and scholarship (in the later years). The mix varies, but in the social sciences two to three years of advance coursework typically precedes the definition of a research project. The cumulative time to degree is on the order of six to eight years. The structure of the doctoral programme is largely under the control of the faculty in the programme, subject to some university-specific requirements or milestones. Because there is no higher education ministry that controls universities at the national level, this highly decentralised system is subject to considerable variation from department to department in the same field. Nevertheless, there may well be more similarities in the same field across universities, than at the same university among different disciplines and departments.

Can these practices be usefully adapted to other fields?

I have argued that journal clubs and list-based examinations are adaptively suited to the knowledge structures and conventions of their disciplines. Their stability (they must be doing something right) makes them enticing, but wholesale adoption of these practices into other fields may not be wise or feasible.

The social sciences are different from the humanities or the laboratory sciences, and their knowledge structures and practices sometimes seem like hybrids of the humanities and the sciences. Most students typically develop their own research projects and write single-study dissertations, much like students in the humanities. However, the work is more likely to be hypothesis testing and conceptualised as a research project to answer a question, akin to the sciences. Often the objects of study are people acting in the world who are not subject to controlled experiments (such as teachers and children in actual classrooms), the warrants for claims and the generalisability of findings are different from either the natural sciences or humanities.

Further complicating matters, most education graduate students are markedly different from their English or neuroscience counterparts. Coming to school in mid-career, education graduate students often are older, have complex and demanding home and work lives, and enrol on a part-time basis, making the adoption of new ways of interacting especially challenging (Eisenhart and DeHaan 2005; Golde and Walker 2006: 245–49; Labaree 2004: 83–108).

The question before us is whether either of these practices could be adapted into doctoral programmes in other disciplines to good effect. The answer may well be yes, because work at the highest level of the field requires knowing and working with the literature. The subsequent question is how to adapt these practices to take advantage of their strengths and minimise their known weaknesses. Instituting either or both of these practices into a doctoral programme, even in a revised form, demands a reallocation of faculty and student time and energy. In conducting this thought experiment, recall the key features of signature pedagogies: They are pervasive and routine, they entail public student performance, they have high emotional stakes, and they socialise students into disciplinary norms (Shulman 2005: 55–7).

Adapting journal clubs

What utility could journal clubs have in social sciences fields or education? Searching widely for relevant research findings and building on them are necessary skills for all researchers. To do so is particularly challenging in education, one of the highly inter-disciplinary learning sciences that draw from many literatures (Eisenhart and DeHaan 2005). Journal clubs are a useful tool for searching out, sharing and evaluating new findings. The current emphasis on 'scientifically based educational research' demands that new researchers develop familiarity with emerging work.

Researchers must also be able to frame meaningful yet manageable research questions. Although the ability to ask good questions is vital, formal attention is rarely paid to teaching this skill, and in some cases research problems are simply assigned. One strategy for learning what constitutes a good question is to see examples and evaluate them. Journal clubs are one of many settings in which this can happen.

But the benefits of introducing journal clubs could be far reaching, because they could advance several other goals particular to the field of education. Journal clubs would expand students' conception of what constitutes 'expected student behaviour' beyond attending classes and completing course assignments. They would connect faculty and students with shared interests and thus promote productive intellectual communities in schools of education, where all too often students interact only with the peers in their cohort group. Most important, journal clubs would help socialise students into the norms and values of the profession by immersing them in an ongoing conversation about what matters in research and practice for their fields, be it psychology, economics, sociology or education. Foregrounding and modelling scholarly argument and debate could help combat conventions of affirmation and encouragement, in which students may be reluctant to say anything that could be perceived as unsupportive or critical.

Research on journal clubs with medical residents shows that 'factors associated with high attendance and longevity [of the journal club] include mandatory attendance, availability of food, and perceived educational value by the program director' (Alguire 1998: 351). Likewise, a review of research on health-related journal clubs found that 'participant preparation appears to be a key factor to facilitate healthy and meaningful discussion' (Deenadayalan *et al.* 2008: 905). Emphasising public performance (with the high emotional stakes that it entails) requires that every student present regularly and get feedback. Developing a rubric for teaching the appraisal of article quality can increase the

115

quality of article selection and help students learn to assess research (Burstein *et al.* 1996). Incorporating such adaptations would be fairly simple and would help journal clubs succeed, becoming part of the departmental culture.

Journal club meetings would need to be strategically scheduled to make them available for students who are on campus only part-time, while still including faculty members to preserve the clubs' essential multi-generational character. The format is flexible in time and place; a journal club could meet on Saturday mornings in a coffee shop or as a Thursday evening brown-bag dinner before class. For cohort-based programmes, incorporating students from several cohorts in a topic-based journal club – say, on immigration studies, on classroom-based research, or on social psychology – could expand students' horizons and provide occasions for other kinds of peer mentorship. Given that much social science research is not a 'fast science' field, a journal club could focus on key debates in a narrowly defined area, classical works in the field, or provocative articles from other disciplines.

Adapting list-based examinations

The demand for specialised focus must be offset by attention to foundational breadth. Smaller faculties in defined social science fields may expect shared coursework of all entering doctoral students; however, the fields of education and psychology are usually divided into many areas or programmes, so that students focus very quickly on their sub-field, such as maths education or developmental psychology. Some education faculties have reorganised their curricula to include common core courses required of all students regardless of sub-field; examples are the University of Southern California, the University of North Carolina and the University of Colorado (see summaries of their work at gallery.carnegiefoundation.org/cid). Although faculty and students at many other schools of education may wish to define such a core, political obstacles might necessitate an interim strategy. (No doubt this same challenge faces large departments of psychology, economics or sociology, which may be effectively segregated by sub-field.) The middle road of negotiated lists – including classics of the field, not just texts germane to the dissertation project, and defined by the student and gatekeeping faculty experts – can establish an important shared foundation. Surely there is much that is desirable in expecting all students to read Dewey, Thorndike and Vygotsky (or whatever the correct list is!). The goal is not for students simply to read more, and more widely, but to read strategically. As Maxwell (2006) argues, 'there may be extremely relevant theories, findings, or methods in other fields or disciplines' (p. 29). Therefore, faculty guidance is essential as students craft a broad, reasonable and appropriate reading list.

Studying for list-based exams can drive students to isolate themselves, so the process must be structured to keep the intensive reading period to a reasonable duration. Retreating from the community is especially counter productive for researchers who routinely pursue team projects and publish co-authored articles. The skills of collaboration should be encouraged rather than inhibited. Requiring study groups, perhaps facilitated by advanced students who have passed the exam, would be a useful corrective.

The list is driven by a vision of the scholar in conversation with the major theorists and critics in his or her specialty. To reveal that sense of connection, the list-based oral and written examinations need to be wisely structured. For instance, imagine an examination asking students to summarise persuasively the assumptions of their sub-fields for scholars in other areas or to defend a syllabus for a course on their topic. In any case, the exams should be collectively designed, administered and monitored; faculty should debate and work together to develop appropriate questions and formats for the examination. In doing so, they can assess what students know while avoiding the problem of examinations being disconnected from the dissertation, and skirting the danger of great variation in standards and expectations among individual advisers.

Rethinking doctoral education

Neither practice is a panacea, of course, but together, journal clubs and list-based examinations could help doctoral students learn to work with the literature with the ease and sophistication of mature practitioners and professionals. And many additional elements could be introduced to meet that goal. Careful study of professional education shows the value of pedagogies that require students to perform publicly with appropriate support and feedback and to do so early and often. It is vital for education doctoral programmes to adopt, adapt and develop more sophisticated pedagogies to help students learn.

Literature work is not the only aspect of doctoral education in need of attention. The starting point could be to focus on a programmatic element (qualifying examinations) or a desired outcome (the ability to conduct credible research). In any case, what is needed is to approach the doctoral programme in a spirit of enquiry. As part of the structure of the CID we asked several questions of doctoral programme leaders: What are the goals of the doctoral programme? What knowledge, skills, and habits of mind are graduates expected to attain? Do current practices serve those goals? Would other strategies be more effective? These questions prompted rethinking in the departments participating in the CID.

But starting such conversations is not easy. One useful approach for opening the discussion about existing practices is to explore the purpose or rationale for the practice. Surprisingly enough, departments in the CID found that there was not always a shared understanding about the pedagogical purpose of elements of the doctoral programme. As I was trying to understand journal clubs and the List, I reviewed many departmental handbooks, a substantial proportion of which do not explain the thinking behind required practices and programme elements. This may be because 'everybody knows' or because practices are inherited and the department has not explicitly discussed them for some time. As a result, students often do not understand the rationale for particular practices that consequently feel arbitrary and capricious. Making the purpose of important programme requirements explicit – providing transparency – helps students keep in mind the larger picture of why they are in school and why they are going through the various 'hurdles' of the programme. These are, of course, not hazing rituals invented by malevolent faculty members, but rather well-thought-out pedagogical strategies. It is sound educational practice to make the pedagogical philosophy apparent. And if there is no consensus, this may ignite useful deliberation.

Another approach, albeit a challenging one, is to rethink 'standard' teaching and learning strategies. It may demand suspending reality and conducting a thought experiment. If, for example, qualifying exams were outlawed, what would be another way to meet the same goals as the current practice? Talking with colleagues in other disciplines is another source of inspiration. In our cross-disciplinary convenings, participants learned that, even with all of the epistemological, structural and cultural differences between disciplines, they had shared questions about the development of scholars. Questions that puzzle doctoral educators in all fields include: How do students learn to ask good questions? How to develop critical judgement? How to encourage creativity?

It is also important, perhaps more so for education than for any other discipline, that new pedagogies and programme elements be treated as educational experiments. They must be carefully assessed and the resulting knowledge shared with those in the field so that good ideas can travel and ineffective pedagogies can be avoided. In this spirit of experimentation, the college of education at the University of Texas at San Antonio instituted a journal club in the fall of 2007 with the aim of discussing current education research, and simultaneously conducted research on the implementation process and impact of the journal club. The process was not entirely smooth, but there were sufficient positive outcomes for the participants that the experiment continues (Bowers and Murakami 2008).

In the CID we learned that changing a doctoral programme is not easy. But it is important. Even a partial list of the forces buffeting universities – shifting disciplinary paradigms, shrinking public investments, rapidly changing workplaces for graduates, demands for accountability and new economic realities – reminds us that complacency is not an option. Even more important, we learned that change is possible and that scholars in other disciplines are important colleagues in the effort.

Notes

This chapter is an updated and expanded version of 'Signature Pedagogies in Doctoral Education: Are They Adaptable for the Preparation of Education Researchers?' which appeared in *Educational Researcher*, 36(6): 344–51, August/September 2007.

The original article was written while Golde was a senior scholar and research director for the Carnegie Initiative on the Doctorate at The Carnegie Foundation for the Advancement of Teaching. The other members of the Carnegie Initiative on the Doctorate team – George Walker, Andrea Conklin Bueschel, Laura Jones and Kim Rapp – were instrumental in the development of these ideas. Carnegie President Lee S. Shulman provided inspiration, guidance and early forums for my thoughts. Neuroscientists Richard Clarke and Rebecca Jakel; English studies scholars Eric Clarke, Amy Montz and David Laurence; and Carnegie scholars Rose Asera, Bridget O'Brien, Mary Taylor Huber and Andrea Conklin Bueschel gave feedback on drafts of this article. Margaret Eisenhart offered encouragement at a critical moment. An early version of the article was presented at the 2005 annual meeting of the American Educational Research Association in Montréal, on a panel that included Lee S. Shulman, Michael Feuer and Peter Bergethon. Three anonymous reviewers vastly improved this article with their thoughtful comments and ideas.

1 This is the thinking behind the extensive Promising Practices database maintained by the University of Washington. It began as part of the Re-envisioning the PhD project, funded by The Pew Charitable Trusts (www.grad.washington.edu/envision/practices/index.html).

2 Research rotations, often used in the laboratory sciences to help first year students match with a research laboratory and adviser, might also be categorised as a signature pedagogy. We describe apprenticeship as the signature pedagogy of doctoral education in *The Formation of Scholars* (Walker *et al.* 2008).

3 Terminology varies locally; exams can be called general, preliminary, comprehensive, qualifying, field or area. Examinations might be oral, written, or a combination, and there may be more than one examination.

4 Several forces converged to prompt this evolution. First, the list itself was under attack for not being inclusive on one hand and (by postmodernists) for being overly predetermined on the other (Guillory 1991). Second, the shift was a response to the continuous expansion of the field – which now includes literatures in other languages and texts from other media, such as film. Another force was the increasingly tight academic job market, which pressured students to professionalise and specialise earlier to be more competitive. Finally, the humanities are under considerable pressure to reduce the time to degree, which is longer than in the social, physical or biological sciences.

References

Alguire, P. C. (1998) A review of journal clubs in postgraduate medical education, *Journal of General Internal Medicine*, 13: 347–53.

Becker, H. S. (1986) *Writing for Social Scientists. How to start and finish your thesis, book, or article*. Chicago, IL: University of Chicago Press.

Bolker, J. (1998) *Writing a dissertation in 15 minutes a day: A guide to starting, revising, and finishing your doctoral thesis*. New York: Henry Holt.

Boote, D. N. and Beile, P. (2005) Scholars before researchers: On the centrality of the dissertation literature review in research preparation, *Educational Researcher*, 34(6): 3–15.

——(2006) On 'Literature Reviews of, and for, Educational Research': A response to the critique by Joseph Maxwell, *Educational Researcher*, 35(9): 32–35.

Bowers, A. J. and Murakami, E. (2008) *The Research Journal Club: Pedagogy of Research in the Preparation of Students in Educational Leadership*. Paper presented at the annual meeting of the University Council for Educational Administration (UCEA).

Burstein, J. L., Hollander, J. E. and Barlas, D. (1996) Enhancing the value of journal club: Use of a structured review instrument, *American Journal of Emergency Medicine*, 14(6): 561–63.

Cronon, W. (2006) Getting ready to do history. In C. M. Golde and G. E. Walker (Eds). *Envisioning the future of doctoral education: Preparing stewards of the discipline. Carnegie essays on the doctorate*. San Francisco, CA: Jossey-Bass, 327–49.

Delamont, S. and Atkinson, P. (2001) Doctoring uncertainty: Mastering craft knowledge, *Social Studies of Science*, 31(1): 87–107.

Delbanco, A. (2000) What should *PhD* mean?, *PMLA*, 115: 1205–9.

Deenadayalan, Y., Grimmer-Somers, K. and Prior, M. (2008) How to run an effective journal club: a systematic review, *Journal of Evaluation in Clinical Practice*, 14: 898–911.

Duke University Department of English (2008) *Duke English graduate studies handbook. Academic Year 2008–2009*. Online. (Available at english.duke.edu/grads/handbook/DukeEnglishGradHandbook.pdf Accessed 26 May 2009).

Eisenhart, M. and DeHaan, R. L. (2005) Doctoral preparation of scientifically based education researchers, *Educational Researcher*, 34(4): 3–13.

Golde, C. M. and Walker, G. E. (Eds) (2006) *Envisioning the future of doctoral education: Preparing stewards of the discipline. Carnegie essays on the doctorate*. San Francisco, CA: Jossey-Bass.

Guillory, J. (1991) Canon, syllabus, list: A note on the pedagogic imaginary, *Transition*, 1991(52): 36–54.

Kahn, K. S., Dwarakanath, L. S., Pakkal, M., Brace, V. and Awonuga, A. (1999) Postgraduate journal club as a means of promoting evidencebased obstetrics and gynaecology, *Journal of Obstetrics and Gynaecology*, 19: 231–34.

Kahn, K. S. and Gee, H. (1999) A new approach to teaching and learning in journal club, *Medical Teacher*, 21: 289–93.

Kamler, B. and Thomson, P. (2006) *Helping doctoral students write: Pedagogies for supervision*. New York: Routledge.

Labaree, D. F. (2004) *The trouble with ed schools*. New Haven, CT: Yale University Press.

Lave, J. and Wenger, E. (1991) *Situated learning: Legitimate peripheral participation*. Cambridge: Cambridge University Press.

Linzer, M. (1987) The journal club and medical education: Over one hundred years of unrecorded history, *Postgraduate Medical Journal*, 63: 475–78.

Maxwell, J. A. (2006) Literature reviews of, and for, educational research: A commentary on Boote and Beile's 'Scholars Before Researchers', *Educational Researcher*, 35(9): 28–31.

Richardson, L. (1998) Writing: A method of inquiry. In N. K. Denzin and Y. S. Lincoln (Eds). *Collecting and interpreting qualitative materials*. Thousand Oaks, CA: Sage, 345–71.

Richardson, V. (2006) Stewards of a field, stewards of an enterprise: The doctorate in education. In C. M. Golde and G. E. Walker (Eds). *Envisioning the future of doctoral education: Preparing stewards of the discipline. Carnegie essays on the doctorate*. San Francisco, CA: Jossey-Bass, pp. 251–67.

119

Rose, M. and McClafferty, K. A. (2001) A call for the teaching of writing in graduate education, *Educational Researcher*, 30(2): 27–33.

Shulman, L. S. (2005) Signature pedagogies in the professions, *Daedalus*, 134(3): 52–59.

University of Illinois at Urbana–Champaign Department of English (2008) *Graduate studies in English*. Online. (Available at www.english.illinois.edu/graduate/current/#purpose Accessed 26 May 2009).

University of Pittsburgh Centre for Neuroscience Graduate Training Program (2006) *PhD 06–07 guidelines*. Online. (Available st cnup.neurobio.pitt.edu/training/phd/guidelines/PHD06–07GUIDE-LINES.aspx Accessed 26 May 2009).

University of Wisconsin–Madison Neuroscience Training Program (2008) *Neuroscience journal club*. Online. (Available ntp.neuroscience.wisc.edu/program/jrnlclub.html Accessed 26 May 2009).

Walker, G. E., Golde, C. M., Jones, L., Bueschel, A. C. and Hutchings, P. (2008) *The formation of scholars: Rethinking doctoral education for the 21st century*. San Francisco, CA: Jossey-Bass.

Part 3

Challenges in supervision pedagogy/ies

Challenges arising from changing student populations

9

Supervising part-time doctoral students

Issues and challenges

J. H. Watts

Introduction

The supervision of part-time doctoral students is a long-term academic enterprise requiring stamina both on the part of the supervisor and the student. Because of the fractured identity of the part-time doctoral candidate, who is usually balancing a range of family and work commitments, strategies to support their progress have to be proactive, well planned and sensitive to the student's situation, which may well change over the course of their candidature. Much of the emphasis on good practice in research supervision, however, seems to relate to guiding full-time students through the process, most of whom are being funded for a three or four year period of intense research and scholarship. Interest in the particular challenges of supervising part-time and often 'absent' research students has not been widely debated in the literature with these students' learning and support needs not well understood. Neumann and Rodwell (2009) develop this point arguing that part-time research students are overlooked in both policy and research terms to the point that they are 'invisible'.

This chapter begins by considering some of the recent literature that debates pedagogic practice within postgraduate research education, particularly shedding light on different understandings of the supervision process, to contextualise discussion of the practical and affective elements of supervising part-time students. This will be followed by consideration of some of the characteristics of part-time students to reveal that they are by no means a homogeneous group, but rather have a plethora of circumstances and motivations that frame their identity as research students. The last sections of the chapter will present ideas about possible approaches to successful supervision of part-time doctoral students that is predicated on a student-centred perspective incorporating the concept of an interventionist pedagogic approach to supervision that operates on a fluctuating continuum of student-/supervisor-led initiative.

Current themes and debates on supervision practice

Supervision is a relationship and process – it is not a service, despite the gradual repositioning of students as customers within an increasingly market-dominated higher education sector (Waghid 2006; Deuchar 2008). Some supervisors regard relationships with their research students as essentially private ones and may resent public scrutiny of what takes place at individual supervision sessions (Taylor 2002: 143). Johnson *et al.* (2000: 135) expand on this point characterising research supervision as 'more private than any other scene of teaching and learning', noting that pedagogic practices of the PhD remain largely unscrutinised and unquestioned with the supervision role framed variously as one of facilitator, director and critical friend (Deuchar 2008).

Lee (2008) adopts a task-oriented paradigm to conceptualise the supervision role identifying five key components; the first is functional and can be understood as project management. The second is enculturation, whereby the student is encouraged to become a member of the academic community; this is closely connected to the third component of critical thinking where the student is encouraged to question and analyse their work. Emancipation is the fourth component and refers to students developing themselves and becoming independent learners; this, Lee (2008), argues will be achieved through the fifth feature, which is the establishment of a quality relationship that will serve to enthuse, inspire and nurture the student. These features of the supervision role contribute to a process aimed at producing a confident and autonomous scholarly researcher, and apply equally to both full- and part-time students. They are, however, operationalised at different stages of the candidature and, in the case of part-time students, as discussed below, may be difficult to achieve in the same measure as for their full-time peers.

Different features of the supervision relationship are an underpinning theme of recent comment on this form of teaching, focusing on issues such as learning from written feedback (Caffarella and Barnett 2000; Kumar and Stracke 2007), friendship as an authentic support tool (Waghid 2006), the management of criticism and resulting interactional difficulty within supervision (Li and Seale 2007), unequal access to research cultures (Deem and Brehony 2000) and strategies to ensure timely completions (Manathunga 2005). The issue of doctoral students becoming scholarly writers may be an ongoing concern throughout the duration of the research with Delamont *et al.* (2004) arguing that provision of writing clinics can be useful, though part-time students may have difficulty in accessing these. They also suggest that supervisors should advise students to cultivate the skills of a careful proofreader.

At the core of much of this commentary is the issue of how best to support students when problems occur and, given that problems often involve differing psychological aspects (isolation, boredom and frustration, for example), as well as the practical aspects of time management and the duration of the process, the approach that the supervisor takes has to be 'tailormade' if it is to be effective (Phillips and Pugh 2000). In recent years there has been a steady increase in the number of overseas students registering for PhDs at UK universities and the need for supervisors to engage with a wealth of personal and cultural issues for this category of (almost exclusively full-time) student is a further consideration, with potential mismatches between students' expectations and the learning and research culture they enter, a key factor (Wisker *et al.* 2003).

The term 'postgraduate' that features in the literature is not always precisely defined and neither is the term 'supervisor'. For the purposes of this discussion postgraduate refers to doctoral level, which Wisker *et al.* (2003: 384) cite as a significant leap from masters work because of the greater originality required over a greater length of time. Added to this is the feature of greater student autonomy and enhanced independent learning that is less prominent within 'taught' masters programmes, including the dissertation element.

The supervisor is understood to be the academic assigned to guide the doctoral student in all aspects of the research process; the extent to which this will also involve pastoral care of the student will differ across institutions. Rugg and Petre (2004), however, argue that it is reasonable to expect some element of empathy work to form part of the supervisor's responsibility to the student and Linden (1999) suggests that students' narratives hold considerable potential to sensitise supervisors to this aspect of their role. More often now students are being assigned a supervisory team rather than just a single supervisor, and the literature suggests that this has potential for a more enhanced experience for students, but it also has potential for problems (Rugg and Petre 2004) in terms of consistency and greater risk of fragmented communication (Taylor 2002).

Characteristics of part-time PhD students

There are different 'types' of part-time PhD student; some register as part-time out of choice electing to combine their study with other roles and responsibilities and others 'become' part-time when they do not complete within the designated full-time framework. For these students issues of transition, that can include disappointment and even a sense of failure, may be relevant. Some part-time students are drawn from the academic staff of higher education institutions and, as Denicolo (2004) points out, the supervisor/ supervisee relationship that is entered into between colleagues requires particular adaptive behaviours by both parties if the interaction is to accord with renegotiated academic boundaries (Petersen 2007), and role tensions kept to a minimum.

Part-time students tend to be older than their full-time counterparts, often balancing a range of personal and work commitments that will influence both their study behaviour and development as researchers. Phillips and Pugh (2000) argue that one of the main challenges for part-time students is the strain of having to make the psychological adjustment of constantly switching from one mindset to another, moving, for example, from their work role to their student role. Most part-time students are self-funded and, over a time span of six years (and formerly it could be as long as nine years), the annual payment of fees may become a significant issue. Even where some financial support is offered by their employers, the costs of undertaking a PhD can escalate when taking account of fieldwork, travel and book expenses. Financial pressures may extend beyond the primary concern of annual registration fees with the consequence that students are unable to attend conferences and other academic meetings unless they can access other sources of support. Part-time students may be both seen and treated as different by institutions that are more inclined to offer this kind of support to full-time students who are expected to complete quicker and so enhance the university's research profile with all that that entails in relation to, for example, the UK Research Assessment Exercise. This expectation, however, may itself be unrealistic; Latona and Browne (2001), for example, found no significant difference in completion rates for part-time students in full-time employment and full-time students, whilst Wright and Cochrane (2000) found that part-time students were more likely to complete within the equivalent of four years. This claim is further supported by Neumann and Rodwell's (2009) study, which found that part-time doctoral students had faster completion times than full-time doctoral students in equivalent-time terms.

The issues of distance and presence are other distinguishing features. Part-time students are not 'contracted' to become quasi-resident members of faculty staff contributing to reading groups, undergraduate teaching, weekly seminars or project meetings in the way that full-time students are. Some part-time students might visit the campus only twice or three times a year for supervision and/or to attend a faculty seminar or conference. Where there is such minimal face-to-face contact getting to know the student, let alone developing a productive and engaged supervisory relationship (Lee 2008), to cultivate a climate of what Waghid (2006: 427) terms 'authentic' learning, can be very challenging both for student and supervisor. Clearly one cannot generalise about the impacts of these features on the progress of part-time doctoral students precisely because each student has an individual motivation and set of circumstances that frame their study. However, because contact between supervisors and part-time students is less regular this may lead to communication problems; this issue led a colleague at a recent research supervisors' briefing at the institution where I work to comment that 'you can't expect them to drop everything to respond as you might a full-time student'. This suggests that supervisors may have differing expectations of communication frequency between full- and part-time student cohorts.

Many part-time students feel isolated and less able to access peer support in their study (Neumann and Rodwell 2009). This is hardly surprising given that the PhD process is predominantly organised around a model of three years full-time work (Phillips and Pugh 2000). As will be discussed below, I suggest that there are particular strategies that could ameliorate this but the image of the lonely part-time student who is not a full participant within the academic community remains difficult to dislodge. With isolation as an underpinning concern, discussion will now turn to ideas about different ways of approaching the supervision task in respect of these students. What emerges is that the style of supervision for part-time students is particularly influential in helping them develop their own learning.

What works and what doesn't

Suggestions for effective supervision practice in support of part-time students are now outlined and these fall broadly into three categories: communication, planning and empathy. The discussion will also include comment about strategies that are less helpful and, in some cases, potentially disruptive of the student/supervisor relationship with evidence of the delicate balance (Delamont et al. 1998) that needs to be struck between proactive interest and support and what I have chosen to term as 'harassment'.

Communication

Maintaining good communication with part-time students has been seen as difficult, essential, sporadic, 'hit and miss' and 'tricky'. Suggestions about how to operate this to actively maintain the student's connection to both the supervisor and the research culture of which they are a part involve a number of strategies. Post induction, once the student has begun to settle into their studentship, agreeing to be in email contact once a week and phone contact once a month might be a reasonable framework. The prospect, however, of weekly email contact could be experienced by some students as harassing or even threatening rather than helpful, with an associated perception that they would be expected to have made some form of 'measurable' progress on a week-by-week basis. An alternative timeframe for this contact would be an email every two to three weeks with telephone contact approximately every six weeks. This is more likely to accord with the comfort values of the busy part-time student trying to develop an appropriate pattern of integrating doctoral study with the rest of life. Also in relation to supervisors' workload this would be a more realistic expectation. I have used what I would term as a 'high frequency contact model' as well as more relaxed and infrequent contact and have found that the success of each strategy is highly dependent on both the disposition and circumstances of the individual student and also on the different stages of the student's candidature.

Given the now embedded 'E culture' of academic life, there is an increased likelihood that communication with and support of all doctoral students, both full- and part-time, will in future be transacted much more commonly across 'E' spaces (Sunderland 2002) with a concomitant decreasing dependence on the face-to-face supervision session. Where part-time students are located overseas, the use of Skype for telephone conferences is now in common use. This computer-mediated communication and its associated technologies underpin possibilities for peer learning and for individual distant students to access web-based communities of research practice other than those directed by the supervision team (Boud and Lee 2005).

Whilst the development of an appropriate model of communication should be based on the needs of the student, maintaining effective communication is the responsibility of the supervisor as part of both what the student is paying for and of the informal, if not explicit, learning contract between them. Hockey (1996), in discussing problems in supervision, has argued that establishing a formal contract as an explicit strategy is one possible way to solve supervision issues because a contract would set out the roles and responsibilities of both the student and the supervisor. That possibility aside, part-time students, with all the other aspects of their lives operating in parallel to their research, benefit from supervisor-instigated contact that aims to keep the student connected to the PhD enterprise. This contributes to both project management and the establishment of a quality relationship, two components of Lee's (2008) conceptual model discussed above. It can also be significant in encouraging enculturation that functions to incorporate the student within both their discipline and the wider academic community.

Planning

The importance of scheduling and planning, as an instrumental support for part-time students, is important in a number of ways. The first of these concerns the duration of the part-time PhD process: for students at the start of this process six years can seem endless. How the former possible nine-year span felt is difficult to imagine! With this seeming endlessness in mind the adoption of a structured 'task' approach will help keep student anxiety at bay. Breaking down tasks into achievable short-term steps to make the whole process more manageable and accessible has been described as 'scaffolding' (Collins *et al.* 1989) and is an approach that I have found to be appreciated by students. Assigning specific writing tasks is one example of this approach that develops students' critical writing skills in an incremental ongoing way (Manathunga 2005), rather than this presenting as a problem at the writing-up stage. This 'scaffolding' approach applies equally to full-time students who also may be unsure about what the next steps of the study pathway should be.

A second feature of the benefits of planning ahead is in direct response to the paucity of time available to many part-time students for attending supervision sessions, particularly the scheduling of these alongside work and family commitments. One strategy that I have found to be successful is the setting up of a schedule of supervision for the year ahead and sticking to this as a priority. Where part-time students are in their second, third and fourth years and have had the benefit of being able to rely on a pre-planned schedule, adopting this practice can build student confidence and enhance trust within the student/ supervisor relationship in an ongoing way, contributing to making the student feel valued. Supervisors as well as students can benefit from this type of advance planning, which also demonstrates their commitment to the research relationship in a very tangible way.

Empathy

The role that empathy can play in enabling the student/supervisor relationship to function effectively should not be underestimated and comprises the final topic of discussion. Because for some PhD students their research is as much a project of the self as it is one drawing on a range of practical and intellectual skills, the sense of failure that can ensue when things go wrong can feel overwhelming. The requirement of supervisors to thus engage with students about their problems will, at times, seem more a function of emotional labour (Hochschild 1983) than of pedagogical support.

This is a contested area with a range of contrasting opinion about the extent to which supervisors can or should be expected to engage with the life discourse of their part-time students. Discussion appears to centre on the perceived core responsibility of supervisors to maintain a pedagogical focus offering guidance and advice only on academic matters rather than life issues, thus 'seeing' students only in terms of their membership of the research community. Part-time students, however, often seem to want to unload at supervision other matters that appear to be unconnected to the study enterprise. Full-time students also bring personal issues such as health concerns and family and relationship problems (Manathunga 2005) to supervision, so this is not a challenge just in respect of part-time students. My view is that good practice will include supervisors responding to the life needs of part-time students, in part at least, to acknowledge that life is bound to intervene and get in the way of part-time doctoral research at some point, even if only because of its longevity. Where a particular crisis occurs, being ready to consider with the student a temporary suspension of registration can be helpful, not least because students in this position can derive some comfort from knowing that sizeable periods of unproductivity will not be counted towards the six years allowed, if registration suspension has been claimed.

A possible concern, however, is the ease with which a supervisor role can almost unwittingly mutate into a counsellor role (with supervisors ill-prepared for this additional/different role); being aware of the potential for this to occur will serve to guide individual approaches. In my experience I have found that giving students 'listening time' can make the difference, especially as students are generally not expecting supervisors to solve their personal or work problems. When students bring difficult or serious life issues to supervision one practical response might be to alter the pace of their research schedule, at least on a temporary basis, to allow them to feel that they can reclaim control and get back on track with their objectives.

Conclusion

What clearly emerges from this commentary is that part-time doctoral students have a range of support needs and these are often complex and interwoven with their 'other' roles beyond that of student. We should thus be wary of viewing this group as unitary and be prepared to adopt a responsive and 'elastic' approach to guiding their progress in the research undertaking. This suggests that for supervision to be effective it should be individualised, recognising that 'one size does not fit all'. The extent to which supervisors can enable their part-time students to achieve enculturation, critical thinking and emancipation (see Lee 2008, above) is shaped by the qualities of the individuals concerned as well as academic matters such as topic and method. Temporal aspects are also influential and recognition by supervisors that these attributes are unlikely to be gained by students in a linear way will help to maintain a sense of the different pace of the part-time doctoral undertaking.

Supervisors maintaining a pedagogic focus will help these students to address academic problems as a priority within the supervisor/supervisee dialogue, but supervisors should be realistic about the potential for this focus to be derailed by 'the personal', given the long time span of the part-time doctorate. I have referred to three particular elements of supervision practice in this chapter – communication, planning and empathy, and, although the ideas presented in respect of good practice in these areas are not new, the emphasis on the impact of these on the progress of part-time students has previously received only scant attention in the literature.

References

Boud, D. and Lee, A. (2005) 'Peer learning' as pedagogic discourse for research education, *Studies in Higher Education*, 30(5): 501–16.

Caffarella, R. S. and Barnett, B. G. (2000) Teaching doctoral students to become scholarly writers: the importance of giving and receiving critiques, *Studies in Higher Education*, 25(1): 39–52.

Collins, A., Brown, J. and Newman, S. (1989) Cognitive apprenticeship: teaching the crafts of reading, writing and mathematics. In L. Resnick (Ed.). *Knowing, Learning and Instruction: Essays in Honor of Robert Glaser*. Hillsdale, NJ: Lawrence Erlbaum Associates.

Deem, R. and Brehony, K. J. (2000) Doctoral students' access to research cultures – are some more unequal than others?, *Studies in Higher Education*, 25(2): 149–65.

Delamont, S., Atkinson, P. and Parry, O. (2004) *Supervising the Doctorate*. Maidenhead: Open University Press.

Delamont, S., Parry, O. and Atkinson, P. (1998) Creating a delicate balance: the doctoral supervisor's dilemmas, *Teaching in Higher Education*, 3(2): 157–72.

Denicolo, P. (2004) Doctoral supervision of colleagues: peeling off the veneer of satisfaction and competence, *Studies in Higher Education*, 29(6): 693–707.

Deuchar, R. (2008) Facilitator, director or critical friend? Contradiction and congruence in doctoral supervision styles, *Teaching in Higher Education*, 13(4): 489–500.

Hochschild, A. R. (1983) *The Managed Heart: the Commercialization of Human Feeling*. Berkeley, CA: University of California Press.

Hockey, J. (1996) A contractual solution to problems in the supervision of PhD degrees in the UK, *Studies in Higher Education*, 21(3): 359–71.

Johnson, L., Lee, A. and Green, B. (2000) The PhD and the autonomous self: gender, rationality and postgraduate pedagogy, *Studies in Higher Education*, 25(2): 135–47.

Kumar, V. and Stracke, E. (2007) An analysis of written feedback on a PhD thesis, *Teaching in Higher Education*, 12(4): 461–70.

Latona, K. and Browne, M. (2001) Factors associated with completion of research higher degrees, *Governmental report in 'Higher education Series'*, 37, Australian Department of Education, Training and Youth Affairs – Higher Education Division.

Lee, A. (2008) How are doctoral students supervised? Concepts of doctoral research supervision, *Studies in Higher Education*, 33(3): 267–81.

Li, S. and Seale, C. (2007) Managing criticism in PhD supervision: a qualitative case study, *Studies in Higher Education*, 32(4): 511–26.

Linden, J. (1999) The contribution of narrative to the process of supervising PhD students, *Studies in Higher Education*, 24(3): 351–69.

Manathunga, C. (2005) Early warning signs in postgraduate research education: a different approach to ensuring timely completions, *Teaching in Higher Education*, 10(2): 219–33.

Neumann, R. and Rodwell, J. (2009) The 'invisible' part-time research students: a case study of satisfaction and completion, *Studies in Higher Education*, 34(1): 55–68.

Petersen, E. B. (2007) Negotiating academicity: postgraduate research supervision as category boundary work, *Studies in Higher Education*, 32(4): 475–87.

Phillips, E. M. and Pugh, D. S. (2000) *How to get a PhD*. 3rd edn, Maidenhead: Open University Press.

Rugg, G. and Petre, M. (2004) *The Unwritten Rules of PhD Research*. Maidenhead: Open University Press.

Sunderland, J. (2002) New communication practices, identity and the psychological gap: the affective function of e-mail on a distance doctoral programme, *Studies in Higher Education*, 27(2): 233–46.

Taylor, S. (2002) Managing postgraduate research degrees. In S. Ketteridge, S. Marshall and H. Fry (Eds). *The Effective Academic – a Handbook for Enhanced Academic Practice*. London: Kogan Page.

Waghid, Y. (2006) Reclaiming freedom and friendship through postgraduate student supervision, *Teaching in Higher Education*, 11(4): 427–39.

Wisker, G., Robinson, G., Trafford, V., Warnes, M. and Creighton, E. (2003) From supervisory dialogues to successful PhDs: strategies supporting and enabling the learning conversations of staff and students at postgraduate level, *Teaching in Higher Education*, 8(3): 383–97.

Wright, T. and Cochrane, R. (2000) Factors influencing successful submission of PhD theses, *Studies in Higher Education*, 25(2): 181–95.

10

Supervising part-time doctoral students

T. Evans

Part-time doctoral students are not exceptions, unusual or aberrations in UK universities or in many universities internationally (China is a notable exception). Green (2008: 50) reports that of those commencing postgraduate research degrees (masters and doctorates) in the UK academic year 2002–3, about one-third were enrolled part-time. Similar proportions can be found in most 'developed' nations (see, for example, Evans *et al.* 2008). In education, the proportions are often reversed in such nations, with about two-thirds being enrolled part-time. Despite the significant proportion of part-time doctoral students, there is a strong tendency for people in universities, government and the media to think and write of doctoral students as people who are in their mid-20s and studying full-time in a laboratory or library somewhere on-campus. In the UK, the mean age of *commencing* doctoral students is nearly 30 years and for part-time doctoral students in education it is about 42 years. Contemporary circumstances suggest that supervising doctoral candidates in universities is likely to include a significant proportion of part-time candidates, especially in professional disciplines such as education. For the purposes of this chapter, part-time students are those who complete their doctorates principally or wholly as part-time enrolees. Typically, they are mid- to late career and working in a profession or workplace that will influence both their candidature and their topic. Of course, there are some whose family, personal, health or other circumstances necessitate or dispose them to undertake their doctorates as part-time candidates. Part-time students tend to be concentrated in the professionally related disciplines (education, health, social and behavioural sciences, IT, business).

This chapter explains the ways in which part-time students' various qualities and circumstances can be marshalled to good effect by supervisors to help them produce good doctorates that are of significant benefit beyond academe. It considers the approaches that supervisors can use to help candidates enhance the ways their employment and doctoral study work for each other. It discusses the ways in which planning and monitoring the five to six years' part-time study helps increase the benefits and reduce the effects of workplace, family and other pressures on doctoral life. This chapter presents a sequence of strategies that supervisors may adopt with part-time doctoral students to position themselves for a successful future. Such strategies include: establishing productive and effective supervisory relationships; planning the times and spaces for study; helping candidates select a topic and research design that blends with their work or other circumstances; identifying and planning for research dissemination and publication that is effective for their work and other contexts; and helping to form productive relationships with other doctoral candidates.

The benefits of supervising part-time doctoral students

Supervisors of part-time candidates may experience particular benefits over supervising full-time candidates, although there also may be some difficulties. There is, however, a considerable diversity amongst part-time students, but there are some characteristics we can generally expect. Although there are some disciplinary differences, in general, they are equally likely to be male or female. They are typically aged, at commencement, anywhere between their mid-30s and mid-50s. (So supervision is likely to involve dealing with people who are typically from mid-30s to late-50s.) They are usually employed full-time in a responsible position, sometimes in their own business. They earn a good salary, sometimes higher than their supervisors! A significant proportion of students are likely to work in a university, sometimes in the university in which they are enrolled. Some may have a job that requires travel or posting overseas. Most typically live in their own home, often with a partner or spouse. They often have obligations or responsibilities to children and/or to elderly parents. These aspects are all likely to be marked contrasts to most full-time candidates, with the exception of family responsibilities or obligations that may also affect some full-time students. Part-time students, therefore, bring to their candidature significant resources, skills, knowledge and experience that they have developed during their lives and careers. In these respects, they may be more strongly placed than, especially, the younger and least experienced supervisors. Good supervision requires recognition of, and respect for, the part-time students' strengths, and for supervisors to guide them accordingly.

One important piece of supervisory guidance is to assist part-time students with professional interests to undertake research that is related to such interests and is of direct or indirect benefit to their employer. Often part-time candidates enrol with this in mind, but there are benefits if their supervisors can ensure and endorse this approach. The consequence is that candidates are well-placed to ensure that their research has an impact in their professional or workplace context, and/or in the community. They may not appreciate this potential at the outset and they can benefit from their supervisors' encouragement to consider effective ways to inform their profession and/or workplace of their findings. A major benefit for supervisors, departments and universities is the potential for these graduates to have an impact through their research on professional and workplace contexts. By so doing, supervisors, departments and universities are able to show that these doctoral graduates have an impact in the 'real world', something which is less common for full-time students.

There are other benefits to universities having part-time students. These students tend to demand and consume fewer university resources to support their candidature than do full-time, especially international, students. Often they provide their own facilities and sometimes their employers directly or indirectly provide some resources for their study. Part of the reason for the lesser demand on university resources is that part-time students are often 'off-campus' and, therefore, provide their own office and other facilities. In addition, full-time candidates usually require scholarships for living expenses that can amount to £30,000–50,000 over the period of a PhD. Although part-time candidates have lower completion rates (that is, they are less likely to complete their doctorates than full-time students), they generally complete in slightly less equivalent time to full-time students (if we assume part-time study is half-time). On this basis, it can be said that part-time doctoral candidates are 'good value', so it is very important that we supervise them well (Evans 2002).

Considering supervision

Establishing a good working relationship with any doctoral student is essential, so it is important to do so with a new part-time student. Instead of a doctorate being akin to paid work for a full-time scholarship-holding candidate, for the part-time candidate it is usually an activity they have to squeeze-in alongside their work. In this respect, they may be part-time students to their universities, but they are far from part-time in their commitments in their lives, indeed, they are often working very long hours. In effect, they typically undertake their study in their leisure time and it is something that will occupy them (partly, but persistently) for about six years. Therefore, the university also makes a similar commitment to the candidate in terms of its physical and human resources for this period. In particular, it undertakes to provide appropriate supervision.

An implication of part-time doctoral students' six years or so of doctoral study is that they may not necessarily have the same supervisor throughout. Although it is not unusual for university staff to spend six years or more within their university, resignations or retirements (even deaths) do occur. Therefore, arrangements sometimes need to be made for a change of supervisor, which means that some new supervisors may be assuming responsibility for an existing (in this case, part-time) student.

Deciding to supervise a (new or established) part-time doctoral student is a matter that should be considered in the same terms when supervising a full-time candidate. For a potential supervisor, there are advantages and disadvantages with either mode of enrolment. Indeed, some full-time candidates change to part-time, and some part-time candidates change to full-time, so it pays not to be too fixed in one's thinking on these matters. Therefore, it is a good idea to have a phone (or face-to-face) conversation with the candidate about their proposed (or actual) doctorate before you agree to supervise. In effect, the supervisor is not only testing out the topic and personal compatibility, but also one of the main means by which supervisors will be communicating during candidature. Of course, email is probably the main way in which many ideas and drafts will be transmitted and comments provided, as happens with full-time candidates.

However, sometimes a conversation is required to discuss ideas, problems and suggestions and voice communication by phone, audio-link (or audio/video) by computer or in person is required. Supervisors need to establish early who will organise the call and the frequency of the expected communication. After the initial conversation the potential supervisor will be in a position to determine if sufficient rapport has developed and the groundwork has been laid for the next few months of candidature.

It is a good idea in this initial conversation to discuss what is involved in completing a doctorate and the sort of commitment the student will need in order to do so. In particular, a part-time doctorate is not just a matter of adding what might be seen as another part-time job to their normal working life. It is something that they can expect to intrude into their minds and, occasionally, even take over! This means that the other

133

important people in their lives will be affected whether they like it or not. It is worth suggesting that, if they have not done so, they consult their family and even the friends they may be ignoring for a few years. They may even consult colleagues and their employer, but this may be something they are reluctant to do, depending on the circumstances.

It is also important to establish whether they have the ideas that you can work with to help them produce a good doctorate. Do they understand the impact the doctorate will have on their lives? And do you both seem to be able to work together? Crucially, it is the impact on their lives that is particularly different from working with full-time candidates. Assuming these three aspects are adjudged in the affirmative and that the other requirements for enrolment are met, then the next matters to consider are after the initial enrolment has been completed.

First steps

Given that, typically, part-time candidates are mid- to late career professional people, it is important to recognise and respect their experience and expertise. It can be counter productive for a relatively junior supervisor to adopt time-management and goal-setting strategies that they may well find useful with new full-time doctoral students who have just completed their honours degrees. Many part-time candidates know how to manage time and budgets, achieve goals and schedules, and get the kids to tennis or swimming. It is oft said that to get a job done on time then give the task to a busy person. It is, therefore, important that the supervisor and the university treat part-time candidates as professionals. A more likely problem for part-time candidates is prioritisation. Work pays the bills and parenthood has personal, moral and legal imperatives, therefore, it is obvious that their doctorate is not going to be first priority. Nonetheless, it is the supervisor's job to ensure that the doctorate becomes first priority sufficiently often to be completed.

Given that it is important to respect the student's expertise and experience, a useful way to commence the first supervision engagement is with a conversation about how the candidate works and what sorts of assistance they will need from their supervisor. Some candidates are very well-organised, task-oriented and will keep themselves on schedule. They may say that what they want is advice about reading, comments on their work and ideas, and assurance that what they are doing is of a sufficient doctoral quality. In a recent study of Australian doctoral students, Pearson *et al.* (2008: 23) found that doctoral students transferred capabilities from work to study, and from study to work, during their doctorates. In particular, about 60 per cent transferred time-management and IT capabilities to their doctoral work, and over 50 per cent transferred library and writing skills to their employment. The importance and usefulness of the inter-relationships between doctoral and professional capabilities, and their development and transfer during doctoral study should not be under estimated.

Some supervisors report that written work comes in clearly, even elegantly, written and the supervisors' experiences are relatively pleasurable. Others may say that part-time students need prodding and nagging to keep their work going. This enables this type of student to say 'I have to get this done for my supervisor' (and that's why they can't go to the theatre, take the kids to football, entertain a colleague's client or paint the house). In effect, the supervisor is portrayed to others as a bit of an ogre for whom the candidates have to do work, when really it is a ruse constructed for their mutual benefits! There will be other styles of working, but these two examples indicate the subtlety that is required to manage supervision effectively and professionally.

It is expected that supervisors keep their students on schedule. Therefore, irrespective of students' approaches to their doctoral work, it is essential that supervisors monitor progress and intervene where necessary. Such intervention needs to appreciate the students' circumstances, and so flexibility is often required. However, it can be a difficult judgement to make with new students. They may say that things have been busy at work and that they will catch-up, but how does the supervisor really know that both parties similarly understand the magnitude and nature of the work involved? If the student does share their supervisor's understanding, and successful efforts are made to return to schedule, then there is a basis for the supervisor to trust the student's judgement with subsequent matters. If not, however, it is important that supervisors do not allow the problems to escalate to levels where it is difficult, or even impossible, to remedy the situation. In essence, a judgement is made about part-time candidates' competence versus their confidence. As fellow professionals, candidates should respect the supervisors' judgements and realise that supervisors have a responsibility and the expertise to exercise it.

It is useful to understand the student's family circumstances and how these may affect candidature. Some may have a spouse or partner who is most supportive and who has skills and expertise that may be brought to bear. For example, some students may come from a family with academic and/or graduate research credentials. Not only should they understand what the candidate has to do, but they may well be a useful mentor, proof-reader or stats adviser. Others may have a partner who is an English teacher or a librarian and their skills may help at particular stages. Of course, it may work the other way. There may be children who resent dad doing his doctorate instead of helping them with their homework, or husbands who think that a doctorate is an indulgence that their relationship could well do without. Depending on how things evolve, the supervisor may experience being positioned as something of a confidant or family counsellor, or at least as a sympathetic ear.

Despite the shifts in gender relations over the past decades, there remain some significant gendered differences in family and work relations that may make the balancing of work and family priorities different for men and women. It is also the case, that while we tend to think of family responsibilities as those of a parent doctoral candidate for their children, with part-time students it is common to have to deal with a student (as a son or daughter) having to cope with their elderly parents. At this point it is worth distinguishing between family and work matters that are relatively constant or regular responsibilities and priorities, and those that are unexpected or episodic to which one has to respond at the time sympathetically and flexibly. In the case of the former, the supervisor can help the student understand what needs to be negotiated so that their doctorate can be inserted and managed successfully. Essentially they need to find about 16–18 hours per week for about 45 weeks of each year in order to study. If there is no overlap or support from work, then this will mean working about two evenings per week and one day at the weekend, or working for two hours or so early mornings and a good half day at the weekend, or a few hours during the week and full-time during their holidays.

Similar to the family matters discussed above, part-time doctoral candidates' paid employment can be viewed as something that comprises regular responsibilities and priorities that need to be negotiated so that their doctorate can be inserted and managed successfully. Many candidates choose a topic that is related to their profession or workplace. In these circumstances, a supervisor may be able to help the candidate make some useful strategic decisions that ensure that some of their paid work (for example, thinking, reading, writing) may overlap with their doctorate. Every equivalent hour per week or day per month is time saved from the 'private' doctoral candidature time. Some employers will encourage (or even require) employees' further study. Although a few of these are not as helpful as they might be, often they do provide some regular study time: even as little as half a day per month is useful. Occasionally, employers may offer blocks of time, such as one or two weeks, or even one or two months. Usually this is offered later in study, after sufficient progress has been demonstrated. Particular students may arrange for unpaid leave or holidays at a time that suits their candidature and financial circumstances. It may help financially to span any unpaid leave across two tax years.

Integrating work and study

Some students have jobs that require them to work irregular hours, or travel nationally or internationally for days or weeks at a time. Supervisors can help students to see the advantages that can come from these circumstances, rather than the hindrances. For example, there is often 'time off in lieu' that can be used for study, or the time in planes and hotel rooms can be used for doctoral reading, thinking and writing. Having a laptop computer is a great advantage for any student, but especially for the highly mobile part-time student. Nowadays, universities have arrangements with publishers so that journal articles can be downloaded, data can be stored and analysed on a computer and, of course, writing is a computer art! Therefore, a laptop computer enables a part-time doctoral student to work almost anytime, anywhere they get the opportunity in their busy lives. It is *essential* that supervisors impress upon their students that regular back-ups are required and stored independently and separately from the laptop computer. For example, a back-up of an EndNote library, the data or a thesis draft should be on a separate drive or disc at university, work and/or at home, and not with the computer when it gets stolen. Ideally, all work should be stored as two independent back-up copies.

Another way in which students' employment may be of benefit is where the topic can be of benefit to the workplace, then some really good mutual benefits and efficiencies may occur. There may be matters of research and professional ethics, and of intellectual property that arise which need careful consideration. However, there are important advantages in sharing findings with colleagues, or potentially improving work-practices, quality, services and/or productivity. Several questions can be raised: If the student's research can be of direct benefit to their work, can some of their doctoral work be done at work? Is some of their paid work useful for their doctorate? Does the student read things for work that may also form part of their literature review? Can the workplace be a/the site of research? Can equipment and other material resources at work be used for the research? Often, there is an affirmative answer to these questions and the part-time student is much better-placed than their full-time on-campus peers to complete their doctorate efficiently and for it to be useful outside of academe.

Doctoral 'afterlife'

Part-time students generally rely less on their former supervisors after graduation than do their full-time peers. The latter often need help to find a job or a postdoctoral research placement and require advice on networking and finding work, as well as references from their supervisors. The former typically have jobs, networks and other referees they need to use, depending on the nature of any new position they are seeking. Also, part-time graduates are more likely to be useful to their supervisor through their professional links and new research skills. For example, in pursuing research funding opportunities with industry, commerce, the public sector or community organisations, supervisors may have very useful strategic allies in their part-time doctoral graduates who are well-placed within (even own) the businesses or organisations concerned. Likewise, when the graduates are looking for consultants, advisers or keynote speakers, their doctoral supervisor may well come to mind.

Concluding comment

From the first phone conversation or meeting, supervisors and their (potential) part-time students embark on a journey that will take about six years. The nature of part-time students, their work and their doctorates is such that supervisors are going to experience and learn things from outside of their university that most full-time candidates are unable to provide their supervisors. The value of part-time doctoral students is often unrecognised, but it something that is becoming increasingly appreciated by those 'in the know'.

References

Evans, T. D. (2002) Part-time research students: are they producing knowledge where it counts? *Higher Education Research and Development*, 21(2): 155–65.

Evans, T. D., Evans, B. and Marsh, H. (2008) Australia. In M. Nerad and M. Heggelund (Eds). *Toward a Global PhD: Forces and Forms in Doctoral Education Worldwide*. Seattle, WA: CIRGE & University of Washington Press, pp. 171–203.

Green, H. (2008) United Kingdom. In M. Nerad and M. Heggelund (Eds) *Toward a Global PhD?* Seattle, WA: University of Washington Press, 36–74.

Pearson, M., Cumming, J., Evans, T. D., Macauley, P. and Ryland, K. (2008) *Exploring the extent and nature of the diversity of the doctoral population in Australia: a profile of the respondents to a 2005 national survey*. Paper presented at the Quality in Postgraduate Research conference, Adelaide. (Available at www.qpr.edu.au/papersdatabase.php?orderBy=author&byYear=2008 Accessed 24 September 2009).

11
Fortunate travellers

Learning from the multiliterate lives of doctoral students

S. Starfield

Imagining community

The opening words of my title are borrowed from Suresh Canagarajah's (2001) essay in a collection titled 'Reflections on Multiliterate Lives' (Belcher and Connor 2001). In this edited collection, now successful multilingual academics reflect on their literate lives in English and one or more other languages. Suresh, who grew up in Sri Lanka, speaking Tamil at home and then English, is now a professor of English in the USA. Through his literacy autobiography, in which he recounts his journeys both physical, cultural and linguistic, shuttling between the different academic and private worlds of Jaffna, graduate school in the USA and his professional life as a teacher and writer, we learn much about the abilities and capacities of our students, often, perhaps thoughtlessly, or just as a convenient shorthand, labelled ESL, non-native speakers or international. The choice of the terms multiliterate and multilingual is therefore deliberate as they signal not an absence or a lack, but an accomplishment. His multiple literate lives have given Suresh a 'rich repertoire' of communicative strategies (Canagarajah 2001: 36). He views himself as a 'fortunate traveller'.

Literacy autobiographies and other reflective accounts by multilingual graduate students and academics provide supervisors with an insight into the worlds their students come from. They allow us to recontextualise discourses that position international students and others from non-English-speaking backgrounds as different, or lacking, and come to understand them as having achieved and succeeded in meeting great challenges. The situated, localised nature of becoming literate in more than one language undercuts discourses that, for example, group Asian students as an undifferentiated, homogenous grouping. Whether it be China during the cultural revolution, postwar middle class Japan or Cold War Soviet Union, we learn about the power of imagination, what Wenger (1998: 176) refers to as 'a process of expanding oneself by transcending our time and space and creating new images of the world and ourselves'. Many international students who enrol in doctoral programmes far from their home country have harnessed this power to imagine themselves becoming members of new communities 'not immediately tangible and accessible' (Kanno and Norton 2003: 241).

Guilfoyle's (2005: 2) interviews with international postgraduate research students studying in Australia clearly indicate 'an expressed desire for opportunities to develop networks'. For Guilfoyle (2005: 2), students sought 'a sense of community' through their desire for essential networks as reflected in the words of one student, 'the most important thing is to try and get yourself acquainted'. Other students' comments reflect both the desire for 'acquaintance' and the absence of contexts that facilitate it:

> One of the things I came to Australia for was the networks, developing. Get to know people, opportunities. ... I was looking to the future, get to meet people from different cultures. ... Unless you actually take the initiative yourself to get to know people, there are no structures in place to help this.
>
> Guilfoyle 2005: 2

> There needs to be somewhere to bring you together. The graduate level, the research students you are your own being, you talk with your supervisor, you don't have that much contact with colleagues. If you are someone is social you will be isolated.
>
> Cited in Guilfoyle 2005: 3

As Kanno and Norton (2003: 246) point out, imagining community has the potential to 'expand our range of possible selves' through envisioning an imagined, possible identity in the desired community. Yet for many international students, the desired community remains imagined, intangible, even once they have arrived in their destination of choice and enrolled in their doctoral programme.

George Braine (2002: 60), originally from Sri Lanka, recounts that a fellow international graduate student in his applied linguistics class at the North American university at which he completed his doctoral study, was 'traumatized with embarrassment when he was told that his English proficiency was low and was required to take full-time ESL courses for a whole year' before being allowed to take his graduate-level courses. An African student 'simply disappeared from the university' when asked to take a year of ESL classes, while a third student's academic work suffered as she missed her family. Braine (2002: 60) goes on to point out that for doctoral students, the acquisition of academic literacy is much more than simply the ability to read and write the various assigned texts. Graduate students need to build interactive relationships with their supervisors and peers and develop effective research strategies and writing skills. They must also 'adapt smoothly to the linguistic and social milieu of the host environment and to the culture of their academic departments and institutions'.

A number of studies of international students' successful and less successful transition to doctoral study suggest that the self is strongly implicated in successful transition. Furthermore, their access to their desired scholarly communities has been shown to be unequal to that of local students. The next section of this chapter considers the intricacies of identity negotiation as experienced by several international students. I then go on to summarise some of the literature on access to research culture and I conclude by examining doctoral students' accounts of mentoring-type relationships and suggest that we can learn from these accounts to support international students to more legitimate participation in the communities they seek to join.

'My own double perception of myself'

At the same time, of course, it must be acknowledged that many thesis supervisors are themselves multiliterate and that reflecting on their own successful and unsuccessful learning may assist them in guiding their own doctoral students in learning what Casanave and Li (2008) have called the 'literacy practices' of graduate school'. Such supervisors may, therefore, possess an advantage over their monolingual anglophone counterparts.

As Hirvela and Belcher (2001) point out, many of the international students who enrol in postgraduate study are already successful writers in their first language and have established a strong sense of self as a writer in this language or, in fact, in several languages. However, limited language resources can mean that writing a thesis in English and 'sounding like' the sort of person they would like to sound like becomes extremely threatening and frustrating. Established professionals or academics in their home country can experience 'extreme difficulty [...] making the transition from holding a position of professional respect in the native country to the anonymous and relatively powerless life of a graduate student in the new country' (Hirvela and Belcher 2001: 99).

The case of Fan Shen (1989), now an academic in the USA, who came to North America from Maoist China, starkly draws our attention to the very different communities and lives students may inhabit before becoming doctoral students. In a reflective piece, he writes: 'I came to English composition as a Chinese person, in the fullest sense of the term, with a Chinese identity already fully formed' (Shen 1989: 462). He enrolled in a doctoral programme in composition that has particular views about personal writing, which may differ from those of other disciplines and which fundamentally challenged his identity. The quote below encapsulates the diverse worlds of his journey:

> One day in June 1975, when I walked into the aircraft factory where I was working as an electrician, I saw many large-letter posters on the walls and many people parading around the workshops shouting slogans like 'Down with the word "I"!' and 'Trust in masses and the Party!' I then remembered that a new political campaign called 'Against Individualism' was scheduled to begin that day. Ten years later, I got back my first English composition paper at the University of Nebraska-Lincoln. The professor's first comments were: 'Why did you always use "we" instead of "I"?' and 'Your paper would be stronger if you eliminated some sentences in the passive voice'.
>
> Shen 1989: 459

Perhaps because of his interest in rhetoric and composition, Fan Shen's (1989) eloquent reflections provide a window into the identity struggles of many international students:

> To be truly 'myself', which I knew was a key to my success in learning English composition, meant *not to be my Chinese self* at all. That is to say, when I write in English I have to wrestle with and abandon (at least temporarily) the whole system of ideology which previously defined me in myself. ... In order to write good English, I knew that I had to be myself, which actually meant not to be my Chinese self. It meant that I had to create an English self and be *that* self.
>
> Shen 1989: 461

Yuriko Nagata (1999), a Japanese woman who completed graduate studies in the USA and Australia, is also acutely conscious of the pain of investing in a new self identity: 'I used to suffer from my own double perception of myself – the mature socially functioning person in my native language and the incompetent non-communicator in the target language' (Nagata 1999: 18).

140

Suresh Canagarajah (2001: 36), the self-styled 'fortunate traveller' of this chapter's title, questions whether he should 'have gone to such lengths to suppress my feelings and ethos in my early journal articles'. He sought to resolve his conflict over the extent to which he could use his 'vernacular rhetorical strengths' by 'writ[ing] myself out of my texts', but now feels that while this gained him publication in 'respectable' western academic journals, it was 'at the cost of my subjectivity'.

Joining the new community

When the new community tangibly fulfils the doctoral student's desire as in Vijay Bhatia's (2001: 43) autobiographical account of what he terms his 'apprenticeship period' as a research student at a university in the UK, the pleasure of a 'kind of initiation into the discursive practices of the academic community' is experienced. Coming from India, he likens the environment at the University of Aston, in Birmingham, to what in 'good old Indian tradition was known as *guru-kul* where students were sent as apprentices for a period of time in the company of the guru, which was anything but instruction in formalised settings'(Bhatia 2001: 42). In reading Bhatia's (2001) account, we learn how the department in which he was enrolled encouraged student participation in research, teachings and administration. Through collective sporting activity and frequent social gatherings, a sense of community was built up – 'was all part of the institutional environment'. His story highlights what Prior (1998) has noted to be the essentially contingent nature of much doctoral supervision:

> [L]earning was rarely seen as an activity confined only to supervision meetings. It was an ongoing process, which could take place anywhere: on a cricket field, in front of the TV in a video room. … or during frequent discussions sessions with the adviser and several other colleagues, some regular, others informally arranged.
>
> Bhatia 2001: 43

Bhatia (2001) went on to become a Professor of English at a Hong Kong university. Although his positive experience took place some years ago, more recent research suggests that the pressures confronting university researchers and teachers are making it more difficult to create environments of the sort in which he engaged.

Several studies (Casanave 1995; Deem and Brehony 2000; Dong 1998) have pointed to second language and international students' access to the academic research culture of their field of study, to student peer culture and to research training more generally not being equal to that of local, native English-speaking students, despite the students' strong desire to access these resources. Academic research cultures include disciplinary or interdisciplinary ideas and values, particular kinds of expert knowledge and knowledge production, cultural practices and narratives, departmental sociability and intellectual networks (Deem and Brehony 2000). Student access to these cultures and to research training appears to depend, particularly in the social sciences and humanities, on 'chance and supervisors' (Deem and Brehony 2000: 158). Knowledge of these practices is typically tacit, and therefore available to successful 'insiders' but not easily articulated by supervisors to newcomers who are 'outsiders'. Social sciences and humanities' students moreover lack the team-based environments and the opportunities for *ad hoc* interactions with the supervisor and colleagues provided by the sciences and engineering. International

141

students may be less able to access the informal learning opportunities that are important for postgraduate socialisation. Deem and Brehony (2000) found that international students mentioned informal academic networks and encouragement to attend seminars and conferences much less often than did local students and concluded that implicit exclusion may be marginalising students who are not native speakers of English and international students.

Sung (2000) identified a cluster of factors as contributing to the 'rounded socio-academic success' of a group of Taiwanese doctoral students. These included relationships with supervisors and fellow students as well as taking an active role in presentations and in departmental activities and social events. These students' successful transition to the doctoral student role is in contrast to that of Zhang, a student from Taiwan who failed to complete his doctoral studies. Zhang's 'lack of participation in campus life eliminated many opportunities for him to learn from peers outside of class ... to refine his English and to better understand his course assignments and graduate school life in general' (Schneider and Fujishima 1995: 19).

Dong's (1998) survey of over 100 first and second language students writing their masters or doctoral dissertation at two large US research universities revealed that social isolation was more of an issue for the non-native speakers of English than for their native speaker peers, despite the students typically working in a team or laboratory environment. Just over half of the second language students stated that they talked to staff and other students about their theses/dissertations either infrequently or had not yet done so, as compared to only 37 per cent of the native English speakers who had a similar response. Nearly half of the second language writers reported having no help with their writing other than from their supervisor, although many expressed a desire for native speaker help with their writing. Close to one in five of the second language students stated they had no interaction with their peers or other staff at all in regard to their writing. Dong (1998) found that the students tended to rely on students from their home countries for assistance and generally demonstrated little uptake of available resources. Dong (1998) concluded that a lack of social networks disadvantaged international students in terms of access to helpful resources and development opportunities such as publication and that the lack might be due to the poor communication skills of the students as well as to native speakers' reluctance to interact with non-native speakers, possibly because of perceived communication difficulties. Similarly, Shaw's (1991: 193) findings show that the second language thesis writers he interviewed were not making use of 'feedback from colleagues as a resource in the writing process', either for revising or for editing.

The gift of mentorship

Dong (1998) emphasises that many supervisors were not aware of the sense of isolation that many of the international students experienced. Mentorship that involves a type of apprenticeship learning, collaboration in research and writing and the establishment of trusting relationships has been identified as a key component of successful supervision in a number of studies of international research students (Belcher 1994; Braine 2002; Dong 1998; Hasrati 2005; Myles and Cheng 2003).

In Belcher's (1994) study of three international PhD students in the USA and their mentors, the most successful of the student–supervisor relationships was observed to be less hierarchical, trust-based and supportive. Although the supervisor still retained her authority, Keoungmee, the successful student, grew and developed the ability to become an independent researcher, in some ways surpassing her supervisor's expectations. Belcher (1994) suggests that it is perhaps the supervisor's conception of mentoring as 'reproducing and transforming' the student, the supervisor and the community that contributed to Keoungmee's academic development. She notes: 'The prospect of seeing Keoungmee launch future projects that her advisor had never attempted, or possibly had never even thought of, seemed to delight the advisor' (Belcher 1994: 9). Belcher (1994) concludes that:

> For some graduate students, both nonnative speakers and native speakers, it may be crucial to find a mentor who can inspire enough trust and admiration in students to encourage the risk-taking entailed in challenging and attempting to contribute to the established knowledge of a community.
>
> Belcher 1994: 9

Several of the multiliterate academics interviewed by Belcher and Connor (2001) report on the significance of mentor-type relationships with supervisors and other advisers in their own development as academics writers and as novice academics. Some, like Robert Agunga (Agunga and Belcher 2001), who shares drafts of his work with his students, have continued the supportive practices learned from their mentors with their own doctoral students. Interestingly, Lu Liu (Liu *et al.* 2008: 168), identifies 'the readiness and willingness to share his or her successful work; as the Number 1 quality of a good mentor'. Irwin Weiser, the chair of her dissertation committee, and one of the multiple mentors she acknowledges as having assisted her transition from 'confused graduate student' to 'fledgling scholar', not only shared a hard copy of his textbook proposal with his students but also disclosed his less successful academic experiences (Liu *et al.* 2008: 166). By making explicit the frequently occluded genres and tacit practices of graduate work, he facilitated the socialisation of his students into the new academic discourse community. Weiser, on the other hand, sees in Lu Liu the characteristics of a good mentee. She is proactive, seeks out support, schedules regular meetings with him and is 'enthusiastic, focused and well-organized' (Liu *et al.* 2008: 171).

Liu, who now teaches at Peking University, comments, 'I was not clear about what it meant to be a mentee' (Liu *et al.* 2008: 167). Drawing on what she learned from her multiple mentors, she now feels able to mentor her own students. Liu's mentors, who have co-authored the chapter with her, comment on how they learned to mentor new students through their own positive experiences of being a 'mentee'. They realise that 'mentoring relationships involve reciprocal sharing and risk-taking as well as regular exchanges that are satisfying to both parties' (Liu *et al.* 2008: 180). Mentoring, or what is learned through these processes, is thus a gift for both 'giver' and 'receiver'.

International doctoral students who are not native speakers of English have to cope with what Casanave and Li (2008: 3) refers to as a 'triple socialization': into the role of graduate student; the preparatory socialisation into the profession of academic (in most cases) and the 'immediate socialization into a language and culture that their mainstream peers have been immersed in for a life time'. They need to be consciously included or may remain constantly on the margins of the new community.

Even Steve Simpson, a native English speaker, feels he benefited enormously from his mentored relationship with his adviser Paul Matsuda, a Japanese native speaker (Simpson and Matsuda 2008). Simpson describes the multiple opportunities Matsuda provided for his doctoral students to engage in a range of tasks and activities authentic to the academy, yet beyond the thesis. Matsuda refers to his approach to mentoring as providing opportunities for 'attenuated authentic participation' – activities that both challenge and support the new student (Simpson and Matsuda 2008: 92). He views his role as:

- Creating opportunities for attenuated authentic performance.
- Providing resources and support to help my collaborators succeed.
- Providing examples by sharing what I have done or by inviting mentees to observe what I do.
- Introducing my mentees to the social network of professionals in my field.

Simpson and Matsuda 2008: 93

These included activities such as Simpson chairing a session or staffing an information booth at a symposium Matsuda was organising and acting as a research assistant on specific projects. Through accepting these invitations, Simpson was also able to collaborate and engage with other doctoral students in the programme. This range of activities provided Simpson with multiple 'opportunities for learning' (Simpson and Matsuda 2008: 97), as well as building his professional academic identity.

Western supervisors could perhaps reflect on some of the comments made to Brian Paltridge and a colleague in an interview study they carried out in Hong Kong. When supervisors were asked about their relationship with their students, strikingly different perceptions emerged between native English speakers' conceptualisations and those of, for example, Chinese native speakers who tended to stress the importance of a personal dimension to the advisory relationship:

> Chinese students tend to expect Chinese teachers to care for them apart from caring about their studies. … There is the Chinese cultural view that the teacher must care about the student, apart from caring about their studies.

Ohashi *et al.* 2008: 226

Interestingly, Chinese students who took part in the study held similar views, believing much more strongly than the native English-speaking students in the significance of a close personal relationship with the supervisors for successful supervision. A student commented:

> Personal doesn't mean that you get involved, or fall in love with your supervisor. However, I think that a personal relationship means you deal with each other on a more familiar basis. If you hardly know your supervisor, or your supervisor hardly knows you, it's very difficult to work together.

Ohashi *et al.* 2008: 227

Conclusion

Reading the autobiographical accounts and case studies of the multiliterate doctoral students referred to in this chapter, it has struck me how many attribute their ultimate success to chance. The challenge for supervisors and institutions is to reduce this contingency by learning from stories of transition how to better facilitate participation of new students in the doctoral community of scholars.

I would like to end this chapter with the words of two former doctoral students, both originally from Japan but now both working as academics at Australian universities. For each, the relationship with their advisor is perceived as a significant part of their achievement. Jun Ohashi (Ohashi *et al.* 2008), although acknowledging the pain of a difficult doctoral experience as an international student seeking tenure and simultaneously completing his thesis, regards himself nevertheless as a fortunate traveller:

> My PhD was not just about pursuing my academic interests. I grew as a human being, My experience, as difficult as it was, led me to a special relationship with my advisor … As hard as it was, I do not regret the journey my PhD took me on.
>
> Ohashi *et al.* 2008: 228

Similarly, Miò Bryce (2003), commented in a reflective piece;

> Doctoral supervision is a profound and lengthy joint venture involving both the supervisor and student, to nurture the development of a competent, autonomous researcher and to explore, and make a contribution to, the global academic environment. It is a demanding yet rewarding once in a lifetime experience involving two individuals' interactive, complete personal and professional commitment.
>
> Bryce 2003: 6

References

Agunga, R. and Belcher, D. (2001) How can I help make a difference? An interview with Robert Agunga. In D. Belcher and U. Connor (Eds). *Reflections on multiliterate lives*. Clevedon: Multilingual Matters.

Belcher, D. (1994). The apprenticeship approach to advanced academic literacy: graduate students and their mentors, *English for Specific Purposes*, 13(1): 23–34.

Belcher, D. and Connor, U. (2001) *Reflections on multiliterate lives*. Clevedon: Multilingual Matters.

Bhatia, V. K. (2001). Initiating into academic community: some autobiographical reflections. In D. Belcher and U. Connor (Eds). *Reflections on multiliterate lives*. Clevedon: Multilingual Matters.

Braine, G. (2002) Academic literacy and the nonnative speaker graduate student, *Journal of English for Academic Purposes*, 1: 59–68.

Bryce, M. (2003) *Defining the doctorate with Asian research students*. Proceedings of Australian Association for Research in Education (AARE), Newcastle mini-conference, October, 2003. Online. (Available at www.aare.edu.au/conf03nc/br03015z.pdf Accessed 12 March 2009).

Canagarajah, S. (2001) The fortunate traveller: shuttling between communities and literacies by economy class. In D. Belcher and U. Connor (Eds). *Reflections on Multiliterate Lives*. Clevedon: Multilingual Matters.

Casanave, C. (1995) Local interactions: constructing contexts for composing in a graduate sociology program. In D. Belcher and G. Braine (Eds). *Academic writing in a second language: essays on research and pedagogy*. Norwood, NJ: Ablex.

Casanave, C. P. and Li, X. (2008) *Learning the literacy practices of graduate school: insiders' reflections on academic enculturation*. Ann Arbor, MI: Michigan University Press.

Deem, R and Brehony, K. J. (2000) Doctoral students' access to research cultures – are some more unequal than others?, *Studies in Higher Education*, 25 (2): 149–65.

Dong, Y. R. (1998) Non-native speaker graduate students' thesis/dissertation writing in science: Self-reports by students and their advisors from two U.S. institutions, *English for Specific Purposes*, 17: 369–90.

Guilfoyle, A. M. (2005) *Developing essential networks as a source of community for international postgraduate students*. In Proceedings of the 2005 Australian Universities Quality Forum: Engaging communities. Sydney, Australia, 6–8 July 2005, Melbourne: Australian Universities Quality Agency.

Hasrati, M. (2005) Legitimate peripheral participation and supervising PhD students, *Studies in Higher Education*, 30 (5): 557–70.

Hirvela, A. and Belcher, D. (2001) Coming back to voice: The multiple voices and identities of mature multilingual writers, *Journal of Second Language Writing*, 10: 83–106.

Kanno, Y. and Norton, B. (2003) Imagined communities and educational possibilities: introduction, *Journal of Language, Identity and Education*, 2(4): 241–49.

Liu, L., Weiser, I., Silva, T., Asup, J., Selfe, C. and Hawisher, G. (2008) It takes a community of scholars to raise one: multiple mentors as key to my growth. In C. P. Casanave and X. Li (Eds). *Learning the literacy practices of graduate school: insiders' reflections on academic enculturation*. Ann Arbor, MI: Michigan University Press.

Myles, J. and Cheng, L. (2003) The social and cultural life of non-native English speaking international graduate students at a Canadian university, *Journal of English for Academic Purposes*, 2: 247–63.

Nagata, Y. (1999) Once I couldn't even spell 'PhD student', but now I *are* one! Personal experiences of an NEB student. In Y. Ryan and O. Zuber-Skerrit (Eds). *Supervising postgraduates from non-English speaking background*. Buckingham: The Society for Research into Higher Education and the Open University Press.

Ohashi, J., Ohashi, H. and Paltridge, B. (2008) Finishing the dissertation while on tenure track: enlisting support from inside and outside the academy. In C. P. Casanave and X. Li (Eds). *Learning the literacy practices of graduate school: insiders' reflections on academic enculturation*. Ann Arbor, MI: Michigan University Press.

Prior, P. (1998). *Writing/disciplinarity: a sociohistoric account of literate activity in the academy*. Mahwah, NJ: Lawrence Erlbaum.

Schneider, M. and Fujishima, N. (1995) When practice doesn't make perfect: the case of a graduate ESL student. In D. Belcher and G. Braine (Eds). *Academic writing in a second language: essays on research and pedagogy*. Norwood, NJ: Ablex.

Shaw, P. (1991) Science research students' composing processes, *English for Specific Purposes*, 10: 189–206.

Shen, F. (1989) The classroom and the wider culture: identity as a key to learning English composition, *College Composition and Communication*, 40: 459–66.

Simpson, S. and Matsuda, P. (2008) Mentoring as a long-term relationship: situated learning in a doctoral program. In C. P. Casanave and X. Li (Eds). *Learning the literacy practices of graduate school: insiders' reflections on academic enculturation*. Ann Arbor, MI: Michigan University Press.

Sung, C-I. (2000) *Investigating rounded academic success: the influence of English language proficiency, academic performance, and socio-academic interaction for Taiwanese doctoral students in the United States*. Unpublished PhD dissertation: University of Michigan.

Wenger, E. (1998) *Communities of practice: learning, meaning and identity*. Cambridge: Cambridge University Press.

12

Internationalisation of higher education

Challenges for the doctoral supervisor

A. Robinson-Pant

The number of international students being awarded British degrees is on the increase, while level of UK-based students has virtually stalled

Guardian headline, 29 January 2009

For many decades, UK universities have focused on the importance of competing for students in the global marketplace. International doctoral students make up an important source of revenue, particularly in the context of shrinking resources for research. Consequently, there has recently been exploration into the ways in which 'host' institutions and faculty can respond to the needs of international students, rather than simply assuming that adaptation should be one-way on the part of the student. This contrasts with the dominant deficit approach taken towards overseas students in the past, which focused on their problems, their lack of abilities, particularly in English language and ways to help them assimilate into UK university life (see, for instance, Dudley-Evans and Swales 1980; Kinnell 1990). Current policy on the internationalisation of higher education has the potential to take this recognition of diversity in the university classroom a step further. Moving on from an emphasis on how to improve the experiences of the individual student, many universities are now examining their own institutional practices in the light of the internationalisation agenda. What does it mean to learn, teach and conduct research in an 'international' higher educational institution? What are the implications of internationalisation for curricula, teaching and learning approaches and research practices?[1]

The doctoral supervisor is in a unique position to engage directly with these questions through their intensive one-to-one interaction with international students, many of whom will already have worked as researchers in academic institutions or government departments in their 'home' countries. As well as providing the opportunity to reflect on my pedagogical practice, I have found that supervising PhD students from countries outside the UK has led me to question many of my assumptions as a researcher.[2] By learning about another academic culture firsthand through discussions with international students in supervision meetings and seminars, I have gained new insights into research ethics, conducting and writing research within different cultural and political contexts, and strategies for working with two or more languages in research. This chapter looks at how doctoral supervisors can rise to the challenges of internationalisation: not just in terms of responding to the specific needs of international students, but also finding ways of creating a dialogic space so that supervisor and supervisee can learn more from each other.

Understanding the 'international student' and the 'international supervisor'

I have chosen to use the term 'international student' in this chapter, reflecting current policy discourse and attempts to define this group of students without the connotations of the 'other', which was implicit in earlier labels such as 'foreign' or 'overseas' student. Though the 'international' student is still often seen as a polarised opposite of the 'home' student, the term now has the potential to be redefined through the current internationalisation agenda, to include 'local students receiving an internationalized experience' (Robson and Turner 2008). As well as the tendency to assume that all international students face similar issues, many writers have unproblematically adopted cultural stereotypes when writing about teaching and learning issues. For instance, the 'Chinese student' is a common focus in the research literature, often characterised by assumptions about a passive uncritical approach to knowledge and a lack of assertiveness in classroom situations.

The individualised situation of the supervision meeting can be an ideal opportunity to begin to deconstruct such stereotypes – particularly to explore the rapid technological, political and cultural changes taking place that make it even less appropriate to generalise about the characteristics of a whole nation. Doctoral students from Malaysia, for instance, have often explained to me that we cannot generalise across their cohort, not just because of differences in ethnicity and language, but due to their different roles and institutional backgrounds. Seconded professionals stress that whether they are from a government department or a university makes a huge difference to the ways in which they will approach the PhD – how they choose their research question (and how far they had a choice about the topic), as well as factors influencing what they write, their objectives for doing a PhD and their intended audience. Many international students are not making decisions about their research question, research approach and intended outcomes, in isolation or on a solely individual basis, but have to take into account their audience and sponsors back home. Though a minority of students will have to negotiate directly with their home institutions about their research aims and methods, for others it may just be a matter of weighing up advice from their supervisor in relation to their understanding of how things work in their home context.

> Regarding the culture, my supervisors had experience with Ahmed before so they learnt about our system. There have been many Malaysian students before us so that helps.

This comment made to me by a student subtly shifted the emphasis from supervisors learning to understand 'the Malaysian student' (and any implied generalised characteristics) to the importance of supervisors learning about the context within which many Malaysian students conducted research and wrote up their PhD thesis. As this student explained, the supervisor's prior experience of other students from his country helped to facilitate their relationship with the supervisee. Although students noted how useful it had been when their supervisor had visited or even conducted research in their country, many others stressed that it was more important for the supervisor to have an open mind, listen and be ready to learn about the differences of being a researcher in their country, as compared to the UK.

With the increasing mobility of academics, it is now more likely that supervisors will also have worked in other countries or perhaps themselves were previously 'international students' in the UK or elsewhere. Such experiences can contribute unique understanding on the part of the supervisor about the process of interpreting unfamiliar academic practices, conducting research in a second language and intercultural communication. Having worked as a teacher, researcher and policy maker in Nepal for 10 years, I have often felt that I shared similar experiences to the international research students in my UK university department. However, I am also aware of the relative advantages I faced by comparison – as a Westerner, I was often privileged with more access to high-level officials and had fewer constraints on what I could do or say, as compared to Nepali colleagues. By contrast, an international student may not only face problems conducting research as an 'insider' in their home context, but may also be subject to racist attitudes or a lower status as a student in the host country. The challenge for the supervisor is to develop a situation where the student's prior knowledge and experience can become a valued resource for their research whilst in the host university context.

Developing a relationship: supervisor and supervisee

> Until now, I call him Dr. Richard as I did in [my country]. I keep calling him by title. It is a matter of courtesy and respect, not hierarchy.

Although this student knew that she could call her supervisor by his first name in the UK university, she explained to me that she preferred to use his title. However, she did not see this as signifying an unequal power relationship ('not hierarchy') but rather a form of politeness. This distinction has been reinforced for me over the years by other students who have commented on the confusing contradictions between the informality signified by forms of address and email communication between supervisor and supervisee in my department, yet the formality of having to make advance appointments to see their supervisor and produce written records of meetings. By contrast, in their home universities, they often felt they had easier access to supervisors, being able to drop in or ask for direction when they needed it. These examples illustrate how difficult it can be to interpret meaning and develop relationships in the supervision meeting – where both supervisor and supervisee are unfamiliar with each other's communicative practices.

As an 'insider' of the host culture, the supervisor is better placed to initiate a conversation about expectations regarding supervision practices in the UK university context – for instance, suggesting and asking about forms of address (for both supervisor and supervisee) and discussing openly about the best ways of managing time (again, for both parties). With the increasing tendency to formalise supervisory practices through university 'codes of practice', the student is likely to have received written guidebooks and lists of regulations. However, many students will welcome the opportunity to discuss these documents with their supervisors in the light of their previous experiences – and for their supervisors to make the ground rules more explicit. As a supervisor, I have also found it useful to talk to my students about some of the demands on my time – as they have been surprised to discover that doctoral supervision makes up only a small part of my academic life.

A major concern for many students is around how to structure their study, particularly if they have been used to more direction from their teacher. Again, this can often be regarded in terms of power relationships by the UK supervisor (that the student is used to being told what to do), but from a student's point of view might be more a question of how to interpret unfamiliar instructions. At the beginning of the PhD, the unbounded nature of the course can be a challenge for both student and supervisor – whether to read widely or begin to write about their ideas from the first week onwards. For a student studying in English as a second language, both reading and writing present particular challenges, as a student explained to me:

> This is my first time writing in English and it is slow compared to [my mother tongue]. I have to think of the precise words and sometimes I sit in front of my notebook and can only write one or two sentences.

This student was worried that, as his efforts in learning to read and write English were largely invisible to the supervisor, he would be considered as 'slow'. Like many other international students, he struggled with dilemmas over whether to try to write (and think) in his mother tongue first and then translate into English, or to carry on trying to compose directly in English. Some students felt that their supervisors did not understand the challenges of writing in a second language, particularly when they urged the student to be 'more critical' about what they read and wrote:

> All the time my supervisors insist that I should be critical, especially when reading a book. I should think what I am reading, not just read it. It is difficult when you do this in English. It is similar to [my mother tongue]. It is not a different approach, but it is difficult to be critical in another language.

The supervisor and student can start to explore practical strategies for tackling what are often dismissed as 'English language difficulties'. The student could start by reviewing literature that has been published in their own language as a first step towards writing critically about research articles in English. Even if there is little published academic literature in their mother tongue, there are likely to be policy documents and evaluation reports that can form the basis for writing initial accounts of the research context in English – which can also provide a useful starting point/orientation for the supervisor, too. I have also encouraged students to record our supervision meetings, after several students have described the difficulties of trying to write at the same time as having a discussion in English. This is easier, too, if the student makes notes in their mother tongue rather than English – I have been surprised how many people felt they should take notes in English in the supervision situation, and for their own fieldnotes when conducting ethnographic observation.

Giving and receiving feedback can be an area of concern for both supervisor and international student. For a student used to more direct forms of criticism from a teacher, words of praise followed by some negative points can be very confusing. The student usually views the supervision meeting as the occasion when they will be able to gauge their progress:

I ask every meeting with my supervisors if they are satisfied. They tell me that I am doing well but I don't know if that is the truth. Sometimes I feel that I am going very slowly.

As well as working out what the supervisor wants them to do next, the student is also trying to work out the criteria being used for assessment (which is rarely transparent for a doctoral course, even for those familiar with the academic culture). Whereas some supervisors include correction (or comments on) English language mistakes in their feedback, others do not consider this part of their role. For the student, a lack of any English corrections can be confusing as she/he wonders if this means their written English is fine as it is. Again, it is a question of starting a conversation between the supervisor and student about their (possibly) differing perspectives on the purpose and form of feedback on written drafts. Even as a supervisor, until 'co-supervision' was introduced into my department, I also had little idea about how my colleagues conducted supervision meetings or gave feedback to doctoral students. It was only when I began to interview students as part of a research project on supervising doctoral students that I realised what a diversity of practices existed in my own department – let alone across the university as a whole. Whereas some supervisors never gave written corrections or comments, only oral feedback, others would go into enormous detail, even to the extent of redrafting sections of the student's writing. My own experiences have led me to realise that academics also need to have more discussion with each other about how they 'do' supervision. This is not with the intention of 'standardising' practice, but as a first step towards developing a conversation with their supervisees about expectations and understandings of the doctoral relationship.

Teaching and learning in group settings: the 'taught' element of a PhD

Doctoral courses increasingly include seminar or lecture-based inputs on research methodology, which present different challenges for both student and lecturer as compared with the one-to-one situation of a supervision meeting. As with earlier research on the 'overseas' student, much of the literature on teaching and learning in multi-cultural higher education classrooms tended to be based on stereotypes of the 'Asian' learner who preferred rote learning and rarely contributed to group discussions. This polarising and essentialising of 'Eastern' (usually taken to be synonymous with 'Chinese') and 'Western' learning styles was influenced greatly by Hofstede's (1980) cross-cultural research in a management context. His five 'cultural dimensions' of difference (including 'individualism versus collectivism, uncertainty avoidance and power distance) can be found, for instance, in Cortazzi and Jin's (1997: 78) list contrasting 'British academic expectations' and 'Academic expectations held by Chinese and other groups': this includes 'individual orientation' as compared to 'collective consciousness', 'horizontal' versus 'hierarchical relations', 'discussion, argument, challenge' versus 'agreement, harmony, face', and 'critical evaluation' versus 'assumed acceptance'.

Whilst comparing 'Western' and 'Eastern' learning styles has helped to facilitate debate about our values, assumptions and practices around teaching and learning, recent writing by international students and lecturers offers a more complex picture, questioning such polarisation and problematising pedagogical concepts from a cultural perspective. For instance, Haggis (2003) suggested that although rote learning is often dismissed as 'surface learning', deeper understanding can be gained through memorising texts in this way. The growing literature by teachers and students from different cultural contexts offers an invaluable resource to supervisors who want to reflect critically on their practices in order to develop a more inclusive classroom (see Wu 2002; Tian and Lowe 2009; Aspland 1999; Cadman 2000).

For the potentially isolated doctoral student, regular seminars are important in providing an unusual opportunity to interact with other students from a range of cultures. As convenor of weekly seminars for research students, I found that this sometimes presented difficulties for students who were comfortable talking to their own supervisors, but had not had previous experience of taking a masters degree or other taught course in the UK. An international student explained that she found it particularly difficult to understand and interact with 'home' students in this setting:

> My main problem is to understand the others. They talk too fast with an English accent. I can understand the lecturers well. But not the other students. It's my problem, I need to improve my English. Sometimes I wanted to ask them to explain but I didn't because I thought it would stop their ideas.

Although I was aware of this problem, as the seminar facilitator, I was not sure how to improve the situation – other than by breaking down into smaller groups where students could talk to each other (and stop each other for explanations) more freely. It was only later when I presented my own research study on international students' experiences to the seminar group, that I realised the need to develop a recognised space for discussion about intercultural communication within our regular seminars. In response to my findings about the differences in teaching and learning approaches that international students had noted, we began to have a deeper and more open conversation about our experiences as members of this seminar group. Home students were in a small minority here and had also been feeling uncomfortable – for instance, they had wondered why some Chinese students had chosen to use English names in the classroom, and if it was for the home students' and lecturer's benefit. As with the supervision situation, I then understood that we needed to create the opportunity to discuss our different communicative practices more explicitly. Although differences in research approach and educational beliefs had often been the focus of our discussion, we had rarely turned our attention to our relationships as a group in these seminars.

Cadman's (2005: 353) account of the REAL (Research English as an Additional Language) programme run for first year international students at the University of Adelaide gives an insight into what it might mean in practice to prioritise 'interpersonal and classroom relationships' over 'curriculum and content material'. Within her ideal of a 'connecting' classroom, Cadman describes how a gradual move to a more collaborative teaching approach can be less 'disturbing' for some students than a sudden change: 'a "control wedge" model of curriculum design, which allows the transfer of curriculum ownership to take place gradually' (ibid.: 358). Although every higher education institution imposes particular constraints in terms of resources and time available for teaching,[3] the doctoral classroom can become a unique opportunity to develop intercultural understanding. This is not just at the level of learning to get on better together, but about gaining firsthand experience of how theoretical concepts and practices are seen from another perspective that can then influence how we carry out and write up research in our 'home' context.

Conducting field research

Having conducted ethnographic research in Nepal in my former role with development and aid agencies, I have become particularly aware of assumptions about how research should be carried out in various policy and practitioner contexts. I had come to learn, for instance, that for many NGOs in Nepal 'case study' meant a small illustrative story, rather than an in-depth exploration of a programme or institution (as is usually signalled by the term in research methodology texts). Evaluation was associated with quantitative analysis of questionnaires, even for assessing changes in people's attitudes and behaviour (such as assessing how an adult education programme had affected domestic abuse). When I began supervising international PhD students in the UK, I was surprised that they often described this resistance to or unfamiliarity with qualitative approaches such as ethnography or case study in terms of the 'cultural' differences between their country and the UK. Many saw qualitative research as a 'Western' approach requiring 'Western' values, as a student commented in his thesis: 'case study had values and approaches that differed from the values of Malaysia' (Lebar 1995: 372). As 'non-conventional' (notably, qualitative) research approaches become more widespread in their home countries, I have found that we are able to talk more about how to approach the 'cultural' differences between policy and academic research institutions – which, of course, are commonly found in the UK context, too.

I mention this similarity in terms of how academics engage with research in a policy context, because of the tendency for both supervisors and supervisees to assume that any difference between them is related to their different cultural backgrounds (in terms of geographical location/upbringing). Although a supervisor may see an important part of his/her role as explaining and ensuring that the student understands what constitutes 'good research' in the UK higher educational institution, it is important that – like teaching and learning approaches – it is not simply a question of one-way adaptation. Research ethics procedures are perhaps the most visible example of how UK ways of doing research can be uncritically imposed on other cultural contexts. As a supervisor, I have found myself sometimes acting as an advocate on behalf of an international student when the research ethics committee has advised that they obtain written consent from informants or insisted that they anonymise findings. In cultures where the relationship between researcher and the researched is based on trust – and where access is negotiated verbally rather than through written documents – our UK research governance procedures appear legalistic and may disrupt longstanding relationships between the researcher and her/his participants. Many students have commented that producing consent forms and written sheets of explanation has raised suspicions amongst people who are unused or unable to sign permission. As Tuhiwai Smith (1999) explains in relation to Maori ethical principles and research practices, such Western procedures tend to be based on assumptions of individual rather than community consent, and privilege written above oral forms of agreement.

In discussion with international students, I have also become aware of ethical issues they face that lie beyond the advice of the university research ethics committee. For instance, students working in two or more languages have been acutely aware of the ethics of translation. They emphasise how they have the responsibility to translate accurately their respondent's words and the difficulties this entails when the respondent cannot speak English and the PhD students themselves lack a 'critical friend' familiar with the languages used in their interviews. Students have also commented on the ethical responsibility they carry in deciding what to include or leave out from their thesis. In strongly hierarchical societies where there may not be freedom of speech, they are acutely aware of the dangers for themselves and their respondents in 'being critical' (on their supervisor's encouragement). Pillay wrote insightfully in her thesis about the different role that a researcher like her had to adopt in Malaysia (over a decade ago) with regard to ethics – seeing her role as not just to inform, but also to educate informants about their right to withhold information from the researcher or to refuse to participate in an interview:

> But in a country with a fledgling democracy where there is still experimentation regarding issues of open debate and the rights of individual citizens, participants would have little practice with these concepts and little training in how to exercise them. The reality may be that they do not know how to exercise their rights or feel they have the right to do so.
>
> Pillay 1995: 294

In discussions with students conducting empirical research in another country, the supervisor needs to be willing to listen and learn about the constraints and opportunities for the researcher in a different research context – particularly in relation to politics and ethics. There are practical decisions to be made, too – how can the supervisor begin to understand the analysis and interpretation if all the data has been collected in a language that she/he cannot understand? Rather than expecting the student to translate everything (interview transcripts, observation notes, etc.), the supervisor and student can develop strategies for sharing the data – such as colour coding for specific themes – and work directly with the data in the original language as far as possible. This can also become a way of transforming the relationship between supervisee and supervisor, as the student becomes the 'expert' on what to translate, when and how. Positioning myself as a 'critical friend', I have also encouraged students to share their taken-for-granted assumptions about conducting research in multilingual situations – such as code-switching and who (researcher or research participant?) has made decisions about which language to use when.

Academic literacies: reading and writing research

> That's cultural, we don't want people to think we are big and good and excellent. Presentation is all important. We don't want people to think that you think you are the best.

This student's worry about how her colleagues 'back home' will read her thesis gives an insight into the dilemmas shared by many students at the writing up stage. Although she was aware of different expectations around academic writing in the UK university, she was also concerned about the conflicting values and identity that a changed (and in this case, more personalised) writing style might convey to her home audience. In particular, I have found many students reluctant to write in the first person – seeing this as a Western practice that could be interpreted as individualistic and even 'selfish' in their home institution. A Saudi student explained to me that 'at home, it is forbidden to use the first person', and went on to describe how she had, however, tried to change her writing to first person at her supervisor's request. Although I have drawn students' attention to the fact that in other disciplinary cultures in the UK, too, it is usual to write in the third rather than first person, I am aware that this tends to be discussed in terms of 'appropriateness'. By contrast, international students who have been encouraged to write in the first person by their supervisors saw this as a challenge to their cultural beliefs and values. The above student was also worried about positioning herself as an 'expert' through critiquing published research and including her own views. Exploring the supervisor's and supervisee's approach to academic writing is thus not just a question of explaining academic conventions, such as how to reference or quote research correctly, but also about posing larger questions around the ownership and generation of knowledge.

Research on academic literacies and intercultural rhetoric has provided me with theoretical tools for analysing and understanding the literacy practices I have encountered through doctoral supervision. Challenging the idea that the Academy is 'homogeneous' with standardised ways of reading and writing research, academic literacy researchers have focused attention on how such practices vary between and within institutions (Lea and Street 1998; 2006). The implications of this approach are that within higher education, academic literacy is no longer viewed as a neutral and 'transparent' medium (Turner 2003) and teachers are urged to develop strategies for students to analyse and engage with the different literacies they encounter (Lillis 2006). International students, 'non-traditional' UK students and policy researchers moving to an academic institution have found that what counts as 'good writing' in their previous context does not necessarily 'work' in the new research culture. Rather than assuming that such students need to assimilate to the new academic culture, supervisors can help to identify differing expectations about writing in both contexts. Becoming aware of these differences is important not only for the student trying to create texts that are successful in this unfamiliar academic context, but also for the supervisor when reading students' written drafts.

The embedded assumptions about readers held by writers vary enormously across cultures (geographical, as well as institutional, cultures). Early research on 'contrastive rhetoric' revealed differences, for instance, between the ways in which an argument was constructed in different languages. Whilst English academic prose was seen as 'writer responsible' in that the various stages of an argument and structure of the piece would be clearly signposted, Connor (1996: 51) pointed out that a Finnish reader would find this demeaning and expected to make the connections unaided by the writer ('reader responsible prose'). Rather than polarising 'Eastern' and 'Western' academic prose (see Kaplan's (1966) classic analysis of the Japanese 'circular' argument as compared to the English 'linear' structure), recent researchers have instead preferred to draw on the concept of 'intercultural rhetoric' (Connor 2002; 2004; Atkinson 2004). This body of research gives an insight into how writing varies between cultural contexts without essentialising 'culture', and also provides tools for analysing how writing practices are changing in many contexts as researchers move between institutions (see Robinson-Pant 2009).

The doctoral supervisor thus needs to be aware of how assumptions about what constitutes 'good academic writing' vary greatly between academic institutions within and outside their own country. Rather than trying to characterise 'Malaysian' or 'Saudi' academic writing (in English), the supervisor can aim to take on the role of a guide, pointing out possible ways in which assumptions of the reader and writer can vary between academic contexts. This might include discussion of intended audience, voice, form, structure, style, construction of the argument, referencing conventions and accessibility of text. For the doctoral student, such critical awareness of how texts are constructed and read is essential to writing a successful thesis. For the supervisor, these insights have value beyond the supervision relationship and can influence their own academic research, writing and publishing.

Conclusion

The doctoral supervisory relationship is a key element in current attempts to internationalise higher education. As this chapter has pointed out, this is not just about how supervisors (and their institutions) can better respond to the needs of international students, but also about how supervisors and students can use this intercultural encounter to challenge their assumptions and enhance their research practice. If international students are consciously aware of the decisions they have made in adapting to the UK higher educational context, they are more likely to reflect critically on the ways in which they can adapt academic practices when they return home. Once supervisors begin to engage in dialogue with their supervisees about the differences they have encountered in the host academic culture, there can also be the potential for reflecting on and possibly transforming the dominant research practices. These may affect the host institution as a whole, for instance, a review of the institution's research ethics procedures to take account of other cultural perspectives.

With regard to academic writing practices, the implications may be even wider and be the first step towards challenging what Canagarajah (2002) has termed 'the geopolitics of academic writing'. As gatekeepers through their editor and peer-reviewer roles, 'Western' (or 'centre') academics have been influential in determining what 'good' journal writing should consist of and as a result many 'periphery'-based writers have found it difficult to publish their research. Articles may be rejected or down-graded through peer-review for citing too many references in the author's own language (rather than English – see Lillis *et al.* 2008), having very outdated references and for stylistic issues, such as an absence of authorial voice or 'non-standard' English (see Flowerdew 2001). All these features may be valued differently in academic writing elsewhere. The experience of learning firsthand through the supervision process about ways of reading and writing research in different cultural contexts can lead us to reflect more critically on the varying roles we play in maintaining academic hierarchies within our own institutions and further afield in relation to North/South inequalities.

Notes

1 For a more detailed example of integrating an 'international' perspective within university policy and practice, see Leeds Metropolitan University's 'Cross-cultural capability and global perspectives guidelines for curriculum review', available at: www.leedsmet.ac.uk/ALTre-source/cross_cultural_capability.htm

2 It should be noted that the observations in this chapter are from my perspective as a supervisor based in a School of Education in a UK university and it is not my intention that these should be taken as representative of other contexts, whether in the UK or further afield (e.g. the USA or Australia). Comments from students quoted in this chapter were collected during research projects conducted in my department (from 2003–2007) and have been anonymised. For an in-depth account of this research study, see Robinson-Pant (2005).

3 Cadman (2005: 355) also notes that in this respect 'each teaching space must be a contested site'.

References

Aspland, T. (1999) 'You learn round and I learn square': Mei's story. In Y. Ryan and O. Zuber-Skerritt (Eds). *Supervising postgraduates from non-English speaking backgrounds*. Buckingham: Society for Research into Higher Education and the Open University Press.

Atkinson, D. (2004) Contrasting rhetorics/contrasting cultures: why contrastive rhetoric needs a better conceptualization of culture, *Journal of English for Academic Purposes* 3: 277–89.

Cadman, K. (2000) 'Voices in the air': evaluations of the learning experiences of international postgraduates and their supervisors, *Teaching in Higher Education*, 5(4): 475–92.

——(2005) Towards a 'pedagogy of connection' in critical research education: a REAL story, *Journal of English for Academic Purposes*, 4: 353–67.

Canagarajah, A. S. (2002) *A Geopolitics of Academic Writing*. Pittsburgh, PA: University of Pittsburgh Press.

Connor, U. (1996) *Contrastive Rhetoric: Cross-cultural aspects of second-language writing*. Cambridge: Cambridge University Press.

——(2002) New Directions in Contrastive Rhetoric, *TESOL Quarterly*, 36(4): 493–510.

——(2004) Intercultural rhetoric: beyond texts, *Journal of English for Academic Purposes* 3: 291–304.

Cortazzi, M. and Jin, L. (1997) Communication for learning across cultures. In D. McNamara and R. Harris (Eds). *Overseas students in higher education: issues in teaching and learning*. London: Routledge.

Dudley-Evans, A. and Swales, J. (1980) Study modes and students from the Middle East. In The British Council. *109-Study modes and academic development of overseas students*. London: The British Council.

Flowerdew, J. (2001) Attitudes of journal editors to nonnative speaker contributions, *TESOL Quarterly*, 35(1): 121–50.

Haggis, T. (2003) Constructing images of ourselves? A critical investigation into 'approaches to learning' research in higher education, *British Educational Research Journal*, 29(1): 89–104.

Hofstede, G. (1980) *Culture's Consequences: International differences in work-related values*. California: Sage Publications.

Kaplan, R. (1966) Cultural thought patterns in intercultural education, *Language Learning*, 16: 1–20.

Kinnell, M. (Ed.) (1990) *The learning experiences of overseas students*. Buckingham: The Society for Research into Higher Education and the Open University Press.

Lea, M.R. and Street, B.V. (1998) Student writing in higher education: an academic literacies approach, *Studies in Higher Education*, 23(2): 157–72.

——(2006) The 'Academic Literacies' Model: theory and applications, *Theory and Practice*, 45(4): 368–77.

Lebar, O. (1995) *Evaluating initial teacher education in Malaysia: a case study*. PhD thesis, Centre for Applied Research in Education, University of East Anglia, Norwich.

Lillis, T. M. (2006) Moving towards an 'academic literacies' pedagogy: dialogues of participation. In L. Ganobcsik-Williams (Ed.). *Teaching Academic Writing in UK Higher Education: Theories, Practices and Models*. Basingstoke: Palgrave-Macmillan.

Lillis, T., Curry, M., Hewings, A. and Magyar, A. (2008) *Professional Academic Writing in a Global Context (PAW)*. Online. (Available at creet.open.ac.uk/projects/paw Accessed 16 September 2009).

Pillay, H. D. (1995) *Fragments of a vision: a case study of the implementation of an English language curriculum programme in five Malaysian secondary schools*. PhD thesis, Centre for Applied Research in Education, University of East Anglia, Norwich.

Robinson-Pant, A. (2005) *Cross-cultural Perspectives on Educational Research*. Buckingham: Open University Press.

——(2009) Changing academies: exploring international PhD students' perspectives on 'host' and 'home' universities, *Higher Education Research and Development*, 28(4) August: 417–29.

Robson, S. and Turner, Y. (2008) *Internationalization: mapping the territory*. Presentation at ESRC Seminar at Birmingham University on 16 December 2008. Online. (Available at www.education.bham.ac.uk/researchseminars/esrc/isss.shtml Accessed 16 May 2009).

Smith, L. T. (1999) *Decolonizing Methodologies. Research and Indigenous Peoples*. London and Dunedin: Zed Books/University of Otago Press.

Tian, M. and Lowe, J. (2009) Existentialist Internationalization and the Chinese Student Experience in English Universities, *Compare: a journal of comparative education*, 39(5) September.

Turner, J. (2003) Academic literacy in post-colonial times: hegemonic norms and transcultural possibilities, *Language and Intercultural Communication*, 3(3): 187–197.

Wu, S. (2002) Filling the pot or lighting the fire? Cultural variations in conceptions of pedagogy, *Teaching in Higher Education*, 7(4): 387–95.

13
International students and doctoral studies in transnational spaces

F. Rizvi

The phenomenon of international students from developing countries attending universities in developed countries for advanced research training and doctoral degrees in the social sciences is not new. During the colonial period, international students completed their PhDs from leading universities in Europe, such as Oxford, Cambridge and London in the UK and Sorbonne in France, as well as the elite research universities in the USA. Their studies were often a part of various colonial arrangements designed to develop a local elite that was sympathetic to the economic and political interests of the colonial powers. The talented students in the colonised countries benefited from various scholarship schemes, as well as a system of patronage that enabled the local ruling class to take advantage of these schemes. Many of the graduates returned home to assume significant leadership positions, often in support of colonial interests, while others stayed behind in the West.

In the postcolonial era, this pattern continued. In the 1950s, programmes such as the Colombo Plan were developed in the British Commonwealth to provide advanced technical, scientific and administrative training that was not yet available within the newly independent countries. Designed primarily as a foreign aid programme, the Colombo Plan highlighted a commitment by the richer Commonwealth countries to provide students from the developing countries opportunities to get the training that was considered necessary for the development of the social, administrative and economic infrastructure of the new nations (Oakman 2005). Scholarships were provided in a range of academic and technical fields in support of this developmental aspiration. The Colombo Plan was not, however, merely an aid programme but was also linked to the strategic interests of the West, within the broader politics of the Cold War. The Plan was grounded in an assumption that it would promote social and economic stability in the newly independent commonwealth countries, making them less likely to embrace communism.

The Colombo Plan, and similar programmes in the USA, such as the Fulbright Scheme, articulated an ideology of 'developmentalism', which implied that rapid national economic development was not possible without highly skilled labour that was technically efficient, possessing research skills needed to solve local problems. 'Development aid' in higher education was designed to 'modernise' societies through technology training and transfer. This idea of development was based on a particular perspective on modernity, involving an essentialist and linear view of historical progress, which has in recent years been widely questioned. The notion of technology transfer, for example, has largely been undermined by subsequent experience. It is now recognised that the processes of transfer are never simple, and often involve complex modes of understanding that are not generalisable across different social and economic conditions. It has also been noted that a large proportion of PhD graduates of the Colombo Plan did not return home, creating a pattern of 'brain drain' (Rizvi 2005); and even those who did found it difficult to apply their training to solve local problems and thus contribute to the national economic development in the various ways that were anticipated.

Part of the problem lay in the kind of knowledge to which the doctoral students were exposed, restricted as it was mostly to abstract concepts that were often remote from the specific requirements of the developing countries. At the same time, their research training occurred within contexts that failed to acknowledge the relations of power in which research training was embedded. Little attempt was made to provide a broader understanding of the links between colonial history and contemporary political processes and developmental requirements. As one of the earlier critics of developmentalism, Escobar (1991: 24) argued, the discourse of development has its origins in colonialism and modernisation theories, which 'choose to remain blind to the historically constituted character of development as a cultural system'. Research training similarly did not question how the broader relations of power served to define some knowledge and skills as more important than others. It thus produced scholars who often became alienated from their own cultural traditions; who acquired in their doctoral studies little understanding of the particular needs of their communities.

In recent years, the context in which doctoral studies take place has been greatly transformed not only by these postcolonial criticisms (Gupta 1998), which have largely demolished many of the epistemic and normative assumptions underlying the Western discourses of development, modernity and historical progress, but also by the processes of globalisation that have altered the social and political terrain within which universities now operate. The space within which doctoral studies now takes place has become a transnational one, characterised by multiple ties and interactions linking people and institutions across the borders of nation-states. In this chapter, I want to argue that the contemporary transnational formations have major implications for thinking about doctoral studies, not least because of the challenges they pose for doctoral students' attempts to negotiate their research aspirations, interests and experiences, and career trajectories. I want to discuss the expectations international doctoral students from the developing countries have of their research training in the social sciences; how they interpret the forms of knowledge to which they are exposed within the Western academy; how they accord a sense of legitimacy and utility to this knowledge; and the dilemmas they confront in forging their professional identities as researchers who are globally oriented but remain linked, in a variety of complicated ways, to their countries of origin.

In presenting my arguments, I draw both on my own experiences as an academic who has advised over the past 20 years a large number of international students in Australian and American universities, and also on the data I have collected from research projects that have examined issues of global mobility of students and internationalisation of higher education. These projects have sought to understand the cultural dynamics of international student experiences in both Australia and the USA, not as an aggregate account of individual experiences but as an attempt to theorise relational issues concerned with the emerging forms of transnationality. In this chapter, I use international students' own reflections on their expectations and experiences to draw a broader picture of doctoral studies within transnational spaces than is often presented in the rapidly growing literature on research training. This picture, based on five student narratives, seeks to point to the competing pressures the students face, and the ways they negotiate their experiences in order to make sense of their shifting cultural affiliations, as well as the calculations they make about the role of research training in enabling them to strategically position themselves in both national and transnational spaces.

Transnational spaces

The idea of transnational spaces is central to my analysis. It represents a conceptual optic for understanding how the world is now constituted by cross-border relationships, patterns of economic, political and cultural relations, and complex affiliations and social formations that span the world. It is used to name the multiple and messy proximities through which human societies have now become globally interconnected and interdependent. In a recent book, Steven Vertovec (2009: 3) describes transnationalism as

> [A] condition in which, despite great distances, and notwithstanding the presence of international borders (and all the laws, regulations and national narratives they represent), certain kind of relationships have been globally intensified and now take place paradoxically in a planet-spanning yet common–however virtual–arena of activity.

In this sense, the notion of transnationalism suggests systems of ties, interactions, exchanges and mobilities that spread across and span the world. It also refers to a mode of consciousness – a way of thinking about ourselves as belonging to the world as a whole (Cohen and Kennedy 2007: 58).

Vertovec (2009) discusses a number of different 'takes' on transnationalism. First, he suggests, transnationalism may be viewed as a kind of social formation spanning borders. 'Dense and highly complex networks spanning vast spaces are', he suggests, 'transforming many kinds of social, cultural, economic and political relationships' (Vertovec 2009: 5), producing a transnational public sphere that has rendered a strictly bounded sense of community obsolete. Second, Vertovec argues, transnational networks have produced a type of consciousness, marked by multiple senses of identification. Third, transnationalism involves a mode of cultural reproduction, associated with 'a fluidity of constructed styles, social institutions and everyday practices' (Vertovec 2009: 7). Fourth, transnationalism is linked to new patterns of capital formation that arguably involve globe-spanning structures or networks that have largely become disconnected from their national origins. Thus, new global systems of supply, production, marketing, investment and information management have become major drivers of transnational formations.

Fifth, transnationalism, Vertovec argues, may be viewed as a site for political engagement where cosmopolitan anti-nationalist sentiments often exist alongside reactionary ethno-nationalist notions within various diasporas, representing the dynamism of the relationships between different sites of political activity. And finally, Vertovec (2009) suggests, transnationalism has reconstructed localities as a result of the mobility of people and ideas, the practices and meanings derived from multiple geographical and historical points of origin. It has changed 'people's relations to space particularly by creating transnational 'social fields' or 'social spaces that connect and position some actors in more than one country' (Vertovec 2009: 12). Vertovec cites, with agreement, Appadurai's (1996: 213) contention that the condition of transnationalism is marked by the 'growing disjuncture between territory, subjectivity and collective social movement'.

Now, as useful as Vertovec's account of the various 'takes' on transnationalism is, its limitation lies in its failure to analyse how these 'takes' are related to each other. Although Vertovec recognises that these 'takes' are not mutually exclusive, he does not explore how, for example, global capital flows shape new modes of cultural production; how these modes define the social morphologies across systems of relationships and networks; how these systems transform the social configurations of communities, and how these configurations affect not only the cultural consciousness of people but also the calculations they make about how to position themselves within the transnational space. Also left unaddressed are questions about the ways in which transnational space is constituted by the globalisation of capitalism and the expansion of social networks that facilitate the creation of new conditions of economic and political organisation, on the one hand, and the political agency of individuals and groups of people, on the other – that is, how the transnational space is a complex product of both objective and subjective forces.

In the past two decades, an understanding of space as an objective phenomenon has been largely abandoned (Massey 2005), replaced with an idea that suggests a social grid within which objects are located, events occur and relations articulated. In this sense, space is no longer assumed to be natural, explicable solely in terms of pre-existing physical laws. Critical geographers now favour a more relational view of space, which seeks to provide an account of how it is constituted and given meaning through the various dynamics of social relations. In this way, space is no longer represented as a passive geometry, but as socio-spatial relations. It is conceived as a product of a specific set of cultural, social, political and economic interactions. It is something that is socially experienced, negotiated and named. As Massey (2005) notes, space is constituted through both social relations and material practices.

It should be stressed, however, that space is not merely a social construction. In a very helpful analysis, Soja (2000) makes a useful distinction between space and spatiality, suggesting that while not all space is socially produced all spatiality is. His analysis is thus focused both on the symbolic construction of space at the level of social imaginary and its more concrete articulation in the landscape. In this way, while a university, for example, can be minimally represented as a spatial allocation that has a physical form, it is more accurately viewed as a complex phenomenon given meaning through rules, myths, language and rituals that speak to its spatial form – it is defined by a set of social relations and cultural practices. This suggests that space is a lived, felt and experienced phenomenon that is negotiated through both larger historical relations and the contingencies of everyday life. Space is thus imbued with ideological and political content: it involves dealing with broader structures, including various contrasting representations of space and spatial practices, and working towards social imaginaries of various kinds.

This complex relational view of space provides a most useful theoretical backdrop against which to understand the contemporary drivers, forms and consequences of international student mobility, and the challenges international doctoral students confront in negotiating the transnationality of their experiences, and making calculations about how to strategically position themselves in transnational spaces they have themselves helped create. Such a spatial analysis of the global mobility of international students is useful not least because mobility is primarily a spatial notion. However, such a relational spatial analysis is helpful also because it underscores the importance of human agency, while at the same time pointing to the connections between macro-economic and geopolitical transformations and patterns of social action and calculations. It highlights the need to account for the ways in which international students interpret, engage with and negotiate various generalised processes associated with globalisation.

Significant in this discussion of transnational spaces is the manner in which the national features in the student thinking. Following such globalisation enthusiasts as Appadurai (2001), it is assumed by many that transnationalism is ushering in a new period of weakened nationalism, a postnational global cultural economy, expressed in practices both 'from above' and 'from below'. However, as Smith and Guarnizo (1998) point out, there are several reasons for doubting this claim. First, although transnational formations are certainly in evidence everywhere, these formations seldom occur outside national configurations, as, for a variety of strategic reasons, nation-states have an interest in defining their transnational connections. Nation-states are, for example, increasingly incorporating their diasporas into their nation-centred projects. Second, globally mobile people, too, seem to want to retain their national connections, both for sentimental reasons and also as a way of ensuring greater flexibility to move in between national and transnational spaces, and to enjoy opportunities emanating from such ambiguity. So far from withering away in the era of globalisation, nation-states are in fact active in promoting a particular kind of transnational subject.

If this is so then we need to ask how international doctoral students participate in these complex processes of transnationalism – how they negotiate the creation of the transnational spaces that they inhabit, becoming transnational subjects of a particular kind? How are their aspirations and expectations forged by an already formed understanding of transnationality, affected both by national discourses and those that are globally circulating? What dilemmas do they confront in negotiating these spaces, and how do they utilise various discourses to resolve tensions that are invariably an important feature of transnational processes? In what follows, I provide a number of narratives of international doctoral student experiences in order to understand the complexities of these processes, and point to the ways in which transnationalism involves a dialectic between the national and the global. I argue that such an understanding is important to universities in becoming clearer about the new practices of research training that are needed by the globally mobile students.

Student aspirations and expectations

Much has been written in recent years about the reasons students have for going abroad for their higher education (Guruz 2007). Among the reasons cited are lack of academic opportunities at home in certain disciplines and for certain ethnic groups; perceptions of better instructional quality and higher standards; following a family tradition; exposure to other cultures and intercultural understanding; possibilities of international networking; impressions of international qualifications as a marker of status and prestige; views of international education as a path to immigration; and so on. It needs to be noted, however, that these reasons relate mostly to undergraduate studies. International students interested in graduate programmes engage in a wider set of calculations that are more self-reflexive, and not driven by the preferences of parents. These calculations are informed by perceptions of transnationality, and the role higher education plays in building professional identities and forging academic careers. In this sense, doctoral student aspirations and expectations are already forged in transnational spaces.

As Aihwa Ong (2006) has pointed out, even before attending universities in the USA, many Asian graduate students have developed a strategic sense of the kind of transnational subject they wish to be. She has argued that 'flexible strategies linked to specific educational availability in different countries further normalize the production of flexible, multilingual and multicultural subjects, as well as their disembedding from a particular set of values' (Ong 2006: 153). Yet these students are often caught between the stress on individualistic skills and entrepreneurial competition, on the one hand, and on general humanistic concerns and national cultural values, on the other. Their expectations are tempered by the realisation that the ongoing internationalisation of American and Australian universities is driven as much by neoliberal market considerations as they are by specifically academic and cultural concerns. Although Ong (2006: 153) may be correct in maintaining that 'graduates of American universities the world over represent a global standard of professional excellence based on the calculative attitude and practice, articulating with egoistical individualism and self-enterprise in a spectrum of fields', she overstates the content of these calculative considerations. For the fact is that international students in the social sciences in particular develop a sense of their aspirations and expectations and negotiate their experiences abroad in a range of diverse and complicated ways. Furthermore, their calculations are affected by considerations that are both national and global.

For example, a Malaysian student, Nasir[1], I interviewed in Australia in 1999 while he was in his first year of a doctoral programme in economics at an Australian university exemplifies the multiple pressures that entered into his calculations, and the ways in which the Malaysian state sought to construct his transnational aspirations. Nasir was awarded a graduate scholarship by the Malaysian government on the strength of his outstanding performance as a lecturer at a regional Malaysian university. He had applied for a scholarship because he felt that his training abroad would strengthen his career possibilities, and provide him with the kind of education that was not available in Malaysian universities. To secure the scholarship Nasir was put through a 'long', 'difficult' and 'gruelling' process. He felt that in the end he got the scholarship because he was ethnic Malay, whose family had close links with the governing political party – United Malay National Organization (UMNO). The state was interested in promoting, he felt, mostly those students who could be more readily incorporated into the structure of Malaysian national politics.

When asked to reflect further on the selection process and how the state communicated its expectations, Nasir spoke of the state wanting him to do something that would be useful to the government in its attempts to 'modernise its economic planning processes'. The term 'modernisation' is interesting here, and points to the ways in which the Malaysia government had in the 1990s begun to pursue neoliberal economic reforms, designed to make Malaysia more competitive within the global economy. Nasir was to become an instrument of a national policy preference that sought a particular kind of transnational subject with an understanding of global processes, but who would nonetheless remain loyal to the state. Indeed, during the scholarship interview, Nasir got the impression that he was expected to come back from Australia and work for the state bureaucracy, even though he was himself more interested in teaching and research. 'I had to play the game because otherwise I would not have got the scholarship', he said. What

163

was more worrying to Nasir was his impression that the state was determined to 'keep tabs on me' throughout his time in Australia, both formally through regular reports and interviews but also informally through the appointment of a mentor, a senior Malaysian student who was himself required to report to the Malaysian government on his own as well as Nasir's progress on a regular basis.

In contrast, Neelu, a PhD student in geography at a public research university in the USA, had more autonomy to negotiate the transnational space. When interviewed in 2005, Neelu was a Fulbright scholar during the second year of her doctoral studies. She had always wanted to study in the USA and had devoted most of her studies in India in preparation for a Fulbright award, pursuing this goal with unwavering conviction and determination, learning as much about the Fulbright Scheme as she could, even going to the extreme lengths of seeking advice from former Fulbright scholars. She had realised that Fulbright officers favoured a discourse about 'cosmopolitanisation of attitudes and values'. She was thus able to recite at the interview how her transnational experiences in the USA would help her develop 'global competence', and how she would 'bring back from America an understanding of economic and cultural globalisation that was much needed in India'. She was able to speak confidently about India as an emerging power within the global knowledge economy, and about the growing relationship between India and the USA as a defining feature of the new world order.

It would be wrong to assume, however, that Neelu acted cynically, simply to secure the scholarship. On the contrary, she had internalised these beliefs, making them her own. She had fully intended to explore further new practices of thinking, judging and acting that would develop her into an enterprising global subject capable of manoeuvring herself as effectively in the field of corporate business as at a large research university. Many of her sentiments largely parodied the arguments put forward by Tom Friedman (2005) in his book, *The World is Flat*, which have been embraced enthusiastically by the new global corporate class (Robinson 2004) and with which Neelu was ready to identify. She had no problem imagining a professional career that lay outside India, and viewed her graduate education as a way of making her globally mobile, working in a transnational rather than a national space. In this way, Neelu calculations differed markedly from those of Nasir, who still privileged a commitment to national priorities, even if these were becoming reframed by the processes of globalisation.

Dilemmas of transnational experiences

Beyond the multiple considerations that lead international students to pursue their doctoral studies abroad, they also encounter a range of dilemmas during their studies. Many of these dilemmas are common to all doctoral students, but international students face additional challenges of negotiating a transnational space that is constituted not only by their aspirations and expectations but also by the forms of knowledge to which they are exposed; the ways in which they have to make sense of the significance and utility of this knowledge; and the manner in which they are positioned within the academic relations of power. In addition to the requirements of their studies, they have to learn and negotiate the structures and traditions of the Western academy. But equally important to many students are the pressures emanating from 'home', not only the formal requirements of the kind Nasir faced, but also the more informal demands of family and friends expressed as responsibilities to their countries of origin. With the availability of cheaper telephone and internet that has become the 'social glue of transnationalism' (Vertovec 2009: 54), demands of home are expressed to students on an almost daily basis. International students thus have to straddle a space somewhere between an emerging sense of cosmopolitanism, on the one hand, and national loyalty, on the other.

These dilemmas were most evident in the experiences of Kamal, a Turkish student with a PhD scholarship from the Turkish Ministry of Education. Kamal was a very serious student, with a solid background in social theory. His education in Turkey had provided Kamal with good analytical and critical skills with which to think about social changes taking place in Turkey and elsewhere. For his research he wanted to examine shifting representations of key twentieth century historical events in school textbooks widely used in Turkey. He was, therefore, correctly advised at his university in the USA to take courses in such areas as discourse analysis, critical social theory, postcolonial studies and curriculum history. His adviser saw in Kamal a potential to not only cope with complex theoretical and political issues, but also carry out an exemplary piece of critical research, for which the adviser himself was widely known. Kamal enjoyed these courses, performing brilliantly, producing papers that could have easily been published in major journals. Some of these papers showed a level of political courage that many international students hesitate to express, even if they embrace progressive and critical politics.

However, during the writing stage of his dissertation, Kamal's courage deserted him. He became increasingly concerned about the risks associated with writing a dissertation that was highly critical of the ways in which Turkish textbooks represented contentious issues. As a scholarship student, he worried about the ways in which he might be treated once he returned home. 'I am not sure how honest I can be. I don't want to risk my job chances back in Turkey', he maintained. It was not only the job prospects that worried him but also the risks he imagined in losing his friends and attracting his family's disapproval. He wondered if his critical scholarship had not in fact forced him to consider remaining in the USA. Yet this was a possibility that was also unavailable to him, as his scholarship required him to return to work in Turkey for five years. When he tried to discuss these dilemmas with other Turkish students, he did not get a sympathetic hearing from them, let alone the kind of understanding he needed. Nor did he believe his academic adviser fully appreciated his dilemma or indeed wished to become involved in what was for Kamal not only a personal matter but also a political and theoretical one. In the end, Kamal wrote a dissertation with which he was not entirely happy, and has now returned to Turkey to work at a faculty in a small regional university.

Kamal's story illustrates some of the complexities international students have to negotiate while studying for research degrees in a transnational space. It shows how the production of knowledge in the social sciences is inherently political and how these politics are exacerbated for international students subjected to conflicting pressures. These pressures, however, do not only arise in relation to the processes of knowledge production but also with respect to the ways in which international students are treated in the Western academy. The case of Marina, a doctoral student from Mexico, illustrates the ways in which international students experience marginalisation through pedagogic processes that do not always recognise their prior academic experience. Marina came to the USA to study for a doctoral degree in sociology, sponsored by her university in Mexico, where she had been a professor for over 10 years. She wished to pursue advanced research in information sciences, and had a very clear idea about her research project. While in the USA, she wanted to get opportunities to have serious scholarly conversations about her ideas with not only her fellow students but also the faculty.

165

When interviewed during the last year of her studies, as she was preparing to defend her dissertation, Marina believed she did not get these opportunities, and expressed deep disappointment about her experiences as an international student in general. To begin with, she felt slighted about the lack of recognition of her prior learning and scholarly achievements. She maintained that: 'by and large, I was treated like a young student by faculty here … more than that I felt marginalised by them, treated as if I had nothing to contribute, as if my 10 years of faculty experience was irrelevant'. Marina insisted that the faculty in the USA had not yet learnt to deal productively with mature doctoral students from abroad, and that although she was keen to benefit from her transnational experiences, the faculty did not view their engagement with doctoral students as equally important. She suspected that the faculty are unable to make a clear enough distinction between international undergraduate and graduate students, treating them both equally as objects of their patronage, not realising that international students in graduate programmes are often professionals and academics with a vast amount of experience in their country of origin.

Marina's impressions are consistent with Matus's (2006) analysis of the ways in which international graduate students are positioned within the American academy. Matus has argued that, in both policy and practice, the discourses of international students in the USA are constituted in a number of different ways. Although there is a liberal discourse of mutual benefit that surrounds internationalisation of higher education, Matus maintains, there is also a relatively hostile discourse of international students that is constructed by the Immigration and Naturalization Service (INS). This discourse positions them in a distinctive bureaucratic category, as 'non-immigrants', who are both privileged and disadvantaged at the same time – privileged because they have opportunities for higher education in the USA but disadvantaged because they lack the rights available to citizens. They occupy an in-between space. International students are also subjected to discourses of control and threat, especially since 11 September 2001, and are now subjected to surveillance and regulations that lead many to feel insecure and uncertain about the extent to which they are welcome in the USA. In this sense, the transnational space in which international doctoral students pursue their studies is constituted by a complicated set of social relations, often defined by national policy regimes.

The national enters the constitution of the transnational space for international students in another way, through their links with the diasporic communities. This is amply illustrated by the case of Meena, a student who came to a university in Melbourne from Sri Lanka to study for a doctoral degree in financial services, forgoing a lucrative corporate career in Sri Lanka. On the strength of her outstanding academic results in her masters at a British university, her studies in Australia were funded by an Australian government scholarship. Her early days in Australia were very difficult, she confided, as she had to leave her elderly parents behind in Sri Lanka. Her father died within six months of her arrival in Australia, leading her to consider abandoning her studies. She found solace and encouragement, however, in Melbourne's large Sri Lankan community. Indeed, during this time, she became closely involved in the 'diaspora' politics, which was deeply aligned to the ethnic fractions in Sri Lanka between Tamils and Sinhalese. She felt that she was forced to take sides in Australia, something she had studiously avoided in Sri Lanka itself. 'If you want to be a part of the community', she said, 'you have no option. In many ways, the [Sri Lankan] politics here is more intense and less forgiving than it is in Sri Lanka'.

Meena's participation in diasporic politics illustrates how it powerfully embodies broader trends in the changing nature of nation-states. The power of the Sri Lankan government was no less diminished for Meena in social relations in Australia, where her links with Sri Lanka became more complex, as she negotiated the transnational space constituted not only by the requirements of her studies but also a whole of host of new personal and community considerations. This complexity was further compounded by the need for her to send money to her mother, especially after the death of her father. To pay for the regular remittances, Meena had to get a part-time job in a transnational corporation, further reducing the time she could devote to her studies. For her then, the transnational space in Australia turned out to be a very difficult terrain characterised by a whole range of conflicting pressures. Towards the end of her studies these difficulties were exacerbated as she considered her options after graduation. These options ranged from working for the transnational corporation where she had a part-time job and per-haps becoming relocated to where the corporation decided she was most needed; returning home to Sri Lanka to an uncertain future; applying to immigrate in Australia where she had become an integral part of the diasporic community; or taking up an offer of a postdoctoral fellowship in the USA. This was no simple choice: it involved contrasting life trajectories that her transnational experiences in Australia had opened up for her.

Calculative logics and professional identities

What these five narratives of international doctoral students in Australia and the USA demonstrate is that their professional identities are developed around a complex set of processes that are hybrid, channelled and networked: they are formed in a diversity of self-directed ways that are socially situated in transnational spaces. The formation of their identities involves calculative logics that both require them to interpret the social spaces of their research training and also the transnational space they might occupy after their studies. Their experiences are forged in transnational social networks that suggest that their professional identities are in a state of 'becoming' rather than 'arrival' (Smith and Guarnizo 1998: 21). Professional identity formation is thus best understood as 'a dialectic of embedding and disembedding which, over time, involves an unavoidable encumber-ing, dis-encumbering, and re-enumbering of situated self'. In this way, as Smith and Guarnizo argue, and as the student narratives illustrate, identity is 'continuous but not radically discontinuous'. In a transnational space, the students retain links with home, develop new links in Australia or the USA and imagine themselves playing a role on the global stage.

It could be argued, however, that there is nothing new about these transnational practices of international students – and things were arguably similar during the Colombo Plan era, for example. However, these narratives indicate that although some international students might exhibit transnational characteristics of earlier eras, the current context is substantially different. The current transnational pressures, activities and aspirations of international research students are quite heterogeneous, and are affected by new transnational conditions shaped by global media and communication possibilities and new institutional neoliberal ideologies that have reconfigured the structure of uni-versities. The students now are also able to imagine a wider set of professional trajec-tories. These conditions are of course variably manifested among different students depending on a range of factors, including their academic background and research interests. Social sciences, in particular, have been transformed by global processes, with the recognition of the complex relations between knowledge and power across cultural traditions that are now increasingly characterised by intercultural links of various kinds (Connell 2007). International research students in the social sciences cannot avoid addressing these issues, acquiring greater self-reflexivity of not only their research questions but also the transnationality of their experiences.

The narratives of international research students presented above undermine a view popular among some recent globalisation theorists, such as Strange (1996) and Ohmae (1990) that suggests that transnational processes have weakened the nation–state, and that national cultures and political systems have lost their significance by the forces of globalisation, such as those associated with transnational capital, global media and supranational political institutions. Equally, it has been argued that transnationalism has strengthened both cross-border ethnic and religious affiliations, and also grassroots activism. These developments are often presented in celebratory terms, as increasing the possibilities of new liberatory practices (Hannerz 1996) and of cultural creativity and hydridity (Bhabha 1990). On the other hand, transnational conditions are assumed to be associated with many negative outcomes, including the consolidation of capitalist modernisation, driven by a destructive culture of consumerism, individualism and even rampant greed. Both of these perspectives on transnationalism may be found in recent writings on internationalisation of higher education, with internationalisation presented in positive terms as contributing to greater international understanding and freedom from the constraints of national prejudices in education (de Wit 1995), and also in negative terms as a site that produces a new global elite more interested in its own interests than in any commitment to the public good embodied within the national imaginary (Robinson 2004).

The student narratives show both of these positions to be misleading, because they imply a binary between the national and transnational space, and between positive and negative outcomes of transnational formations. As we have noted, national considerations enter at each of the stages of the students' transnational experiences – in the formations of their aspirations and expectations; in their experiences abroad; in the definition of the pedagogic and research; and in the development of their professional identities. Their country of origin is deeply interested in shaping the transnational subject they become, as a way of utilising their knowledge and skills in positioning the national economy within the global economy. This construction of the transnational subject is not always in line with the calculations that international students themselves make of the transnational space they want to inhabit. Australia and the USA have yet another set of expectations of the international research students, possibly as highly skilled immigrants or cultural mediators across national interests. In this way, transnational space is constituted by power relations, cultural constructions and economic interactions, but always in ways that require calculative logics.

These calculations are never easy, and have to take into account numerous conflicting demands. Some of these demands are personal, whereas others are created for international research students by the sponsoring state, such as the Malaysian government for Nasir and the US authorities for Neelu. To negotiate the complexities, both Nasir and Neelu needed an understanding of 'grounded reality' – first, the socially constructed conditions within the transnational networks they had to form and move through and, second, the policies and practices of the territorially based sending and receiving local and national states. The transnational practices thus do not take place in an abstract 'third space', located in-between national territories (Bhabha 1994), but in specific concrete spaces, by social actors whose life options are defined by local constraints and social moorings. This was clearly evident in the case of Meena, who had to negotiate a difficult terrain constituted by the competing demands of her employer, a transnational corporation, her research adviser, the Sri Lankan diaspora in Melbourne and the Sri Lankan state. For each of these students the transnational space during their studies was a space of translocal meaning making, territorial specificities, juridical control, and personal relations, articulated in transnational economic, political and cultural flows. Certainly, this is a dynamic space of personal rewards, but equally it is an uncomfortable, contested and even traumatic space that should not be romanticised in the ways in which some cultural theorists do, but recognised for what it is – full of constraints as well as opportunities.

Conclusion

This chapter describes some of the ways in which international doctoral students participate in the contemporary processes of transnationalism – how they negotiate the spaces they inhabit, and become transnational subjects of a particular kind; how their aspirations are forged by an already formed understanding of transnationality, affected both by national discourses and those that are globally circulating; and how they utilise these discourses to resolve tensions of living and working in a transnational space, and thus develop a sense of professional identity that is responsive to both the constraints and the possibilities of transnational flows and networks. I argue that international research students are highly sensitive and self-reflexive about the complexities of transnational formations as they inevitably have to negotiate competing pressures emanating from a wide variety of sources. If this is so, then I suggest that research advisers would be well advised to not only develop their own understanding of transnationality, but also help international research students to build upon their tacit familiarity with issues of transnational formations to better understand the conditions in which they are expected to produce new knowledge and forge their professional identity.

Notes

1 The names of international students in this paper are pseudo-names. Their narratives are based on research projects funded by the Australian Research Council and University of Illinois, Bureau of Educational Research, whose support is greatly appreciated.

References

Appadurai, A. (1996) *Modernity at Large: Cultural Dimensions of Globalization*. Minneapolis, MN: University of Minnesota Press.
——(2001) (Ed.) *Globalization*. Durham, NC: Duke University Press.
Bhabha, H. (1990) *Nation and Narration*. New York: Routledge.
Cohen, R. and Kennedy, P. (2007) *Global Sociology*. 2nd edn. New York: New York University Press.
Connell, R. (2007) *Southern Theory: the Global Dynamics of Knowledge in the Social Sciences*. Crows Nest: Allen and Unwin.
de Wit, H. (1995) *Internationalization of Higher Education in the United States of America and Europe: A Historical, Comparative, and Conceptual Analysis*. Westport, CT: Greenwood Press.
Escobar, A. (1991) *Encountering Development*. Princeton, NJ: Princeton University Press.
Friedman, T. (2005) *The World is Flat*. New York: Picador.

Gupta, A. (1998) *Postcolonial Development: Agriculture in the Making of Modern India*. Durham, NC: Duke University Press.

Guruz, K. (2007) *Higher Education and International Student Mobility in the Global Knowledge Economy*. Albany: New York State University Press.

Hannerz, U. (1996) *Transnational Connections: Culture, People and Places*. London: Routledge.

Massey, D. (2005) *For Space*. London; Thousand Oaks, CA: Sage.

Matus, C. (2006) Interrupting Narratives of Displacement: International Students in the United States, *Perspectives in Education*, 24(4): 81–94.

Oakman, D. (2005) *Facing Asia: A History of the Colombo Plan*. Canberra: ANU Press.

Ohmae, K. (1990) *The Borderless World*. London: Collins.

Ong, A. (2006) *Neoliberalism as Exception*. New York: Routledge.

Rizvi, F. (2005) Rethinking brain drain in the era of globalization *Asia-Pacific Journal of Education*, 25(2): 175–93.

Robinson, W. (2004) *A Theory of Global Capitalism: Production, Class, and State in a Transnational World*. Baltimore, MD: John Hopkins Press.

Smith, M. P. and Guarnizo L. (Eds) (1998) *Transnationalism from Below*. New Brunswick, NJ: Transaction Publishers.

Soja, E. (2000) *Postmetropolis: Critical Studies of Cities and Regions*. Oxford: Blackwell.

Strange, S. (1996) *The Retreat of the State: the Diffusion of Power in the World Economy*. Cambridge: Cambridge University Press.

Vertovec, S. (2009) *Transnationalism*. London: Routledge.

14

The doctorate in the life course

D. Leonard

What the doctorate has been and should become continues to be the subject of formal and informal debate in many countries and internationally. But the answers given vary according to the type of student different 'stakeholders' have in mind, and few work with a typology that includes all students.

In the UK, for instance, the various research councils and funding councils follow the government's direction in seeing education as now primarily to do with national economic development. They are, therefore, mainly concerned with the 'supply chain' of qualified researchers and their employment-related skills, and particularly with science and engineering. The national policy focus is thus largely those whose studies are funded centrally: young, 'home' (UK domiciled), mainly full-time doctoral students. The councils present the thesis as an apprenticeship piece of work.

The universities, on the other hand, are increasingly in competition with each other and each wants to raise its status and research performance by enrolling the best students who will produce original work of publishable quality. They also seek to plug some of the gaps in their funding by enrolling fee-paying postgraduates. Most are therefore happy to accept not only research council or other funded candidates but also self-funding home students (likely to be part-time) and especially international students (likely to be full-time). International students are particularly important in certain fields (economics, law, engineering and technology, business and management, social studies, mathematics and computing) where they comprise more than half of all full-time research students (Kemp *et al.* 2009: 1). They also add an interesting 'global' dimension to institutional life.

In practice, a minority of higher education institutions (HEIs) dominate both the home full-time and the international student market, with the numbers of research and masters students, subject areas of study and main countries of origin varying greatly from one university to another. Each vice-chancellor, therefore, has a somewhat different angle on which doctoral students matter most.[1]

Supervisors and professional organisations representing academic disciplines want able research students with interesting topics, especially in areas where there are shortages of home students. In the social sciences and the arts and humanities, but also in many of the sciences, these may come from a range of ages and backgrounds and many are prepared to fund their own studies out of interest. Academics stress the joys of scholarship in the doctorate, the importance of academic freedom in innovation and creativity, the necessary differences between the disciplines in the form of the transmission of knowledge, and the intellectual contribution of the thesis. They worry about external pressures to include extra elements (compulsory methodology courses, 'employment-related' skills, personal development plans, etc.) within the period of doctoral candidature while also completing in a short time, as they believe these require a narrowing of thesis topics.

What is surprising, given the stress by powerful groups on the relationship between the doctorate and employability, is how little any of these groups seem concerned with the actual prior or current work experience of those they recruit. For instance, the data collected about doctoral candidates by the Higher Education Statistics Agency (HESA); the surveys commissioned by government departments and the research and funding councils; and work by the HE Academy (including the Postgraduate Research Experience Survey) may tell us about students' age and prior higher educational qualifications and a little about their sources of funding. They may even say how many years of work experience they have had, but not what type of work it was, nor what they aspire to do in the future.[2] The same applies to the increasing quantity of marketing-related information from various institutions (including UKCISA, the International Graduate Insight Group, the UK Higher Education International Unit, The Observatory on Borderless Education, Hobsons and the British Council). The concerns of the funders or purchasers of such research are with recruitment into UK universities and what happens to students while they are within the system, not with wider contexts. Their 'analyses' are straight runs and simple binaries and basic rather than exploratory accounts – how many postgraduate researchers are full- and how many part-time, home/international, and men/women, how many in each subject area and from which main countries of domicile. Moreover, on occasion, major groups, notably part-time and/or international students, are omitted from studies as a matter of expediency. So, for instance, HEFCE omitted international students from its large-scale reanalysis of HESA data on the time to completion of the PhD (HEFCE 2005) 'because it doesn't fund them'.[3]

The delimited character of these approaches is serious because they indicate how those in power see the field, who they are concerned with and who they have in mind when making policy. They ignore the importance of other groups of doctoral students to the economic and intellectual viability of higher education as a whole, and all students' right to appropriate consideration. The items omitted may actually impact on existing government concerns, e.g. the rate of drop-out and the length of time it takes for thesis completion, and they certainly make it difficult to say much about the value added by the doctorate.[4] The restricted framing of ideas about students means not seeing what those students treated as 'other' contribute,[5] and ignoring the creative potential of the current diversity of the doctorate. Much may thereby be lost in projected moves to 'concentrate research' in a number of elite universities and to standardise processes.

This chapter will argue specifically that not considering either the prior or subsequent jobs of most UK doctoral candidates means their universities, and the country as a whole, do not benefit as they might from these students' work experiences, either in terms of knowledge transfer in and out of higher education, or the networks that could be established by the institution and the UK. Equally, that many students have a less full experience than they could and should have. They are not fully appreciated while they are studying, and the research and employment-related skills they gain are less appropriate for their future employment than they might be. If we pay attention to this, it may help future recruitment as doctoral studies become more costly (both financially and personally) and candidates come to have more and more choice of where to study (Kemp *et al.* 2009).

Existing research on UK doctoral students

Although most key reports on postgraduate students tend to treat them as blank slates on which HE writes, when we recently conducted a systematic review of the experiences of doctoral students for the HE Academy (Leonard *et al.* 2006), we found both published and 'grey' literature from the UK, which provided more holistic insights and under-standings. Even narrowing down to just publications that gave empirical information on students and their experiences, and which told us enough about their methodology to allow us to evaluate the quality of the evidence and conclusions they presented, there was still sufficient material to enable some contextualising of doctoral learning specifically in relation to employment – even though it would not be possible to present a 'student view' of the doctorate comparable to the ones given above for universities and supervisors, etc., because of their diversity.

The 120 sources that passed our rigorous screening were entered on software developed by the Evidence for Policy and Practice Information and Co-ordinating (EPPI) Centre at the Institute of Education.[6] We categorised each according to the demographic char-acteristics of the students sampled and what the texts covered in relation to their employment, study, research, domestic and financial contexts prior to, during and shortly after their doctoral studies: a total of 32 variables for each text. We could then not only construct straight counts and cross-tabulations to map the field, but also see gaps, groupings and intersecting dimensions.

Roughly a third of the literature selected was focused on pedagogy, mainly on supervision; a third on peer support; and a quarter on the viva and other forms of assessment. There was very little on drop-out. Most accounts were qualitative and most untheorised. Some only gave partial information: for example, they did not mention if students were studying full- or part-time or give any information about the location. Although a text might say if the sample included women as well as men, it very seldom discussed the significance of gender or said anything about 'race', ethnicity, social class or disability, nor how, for example, race and class effects vary by gender.

Despite its limitations, the database is rich enough to explore findings drawn from our own and others' past research and experience.[7] One such suggestion was that an impor-tant way of framing the differences among research students would be not only by aca-demic discipline and whether they study mainly full or part-time, or are home or internationally domiciled, as others have done, but also according to where the doctorate fits into the student's life trajectory. For example, in a follow-up study of alumni who gained doctorates at the Institute of Education in London in 1992, 1997 and 2002 (Leonard *et al.* 2004; 2005), we found that at least half of the 'home' part-timers were doing a doctorate, not as a prelude to a job in academe, as one stereotype of the doctoral student suggests, but rather because they had already taken a job in higher education. Similarly, experience teaching in a university in Pakistan introduced me to many women who held academic posts but were desperately trying to find the time and money to do a doctorate abroad so as to move on in their university career.

This chapter is, therefore, based on existing research included in the systematic review database, which focused on those who wrote their theses while in the early stages of an academic career. It suggests a differentiation into three sub-groups within this category:

- Home students who had moved from previous professional careers to teach in UK universities. They were then required to gain a (PhD or professional) doctorate to get tenure or promotion. On the basis of this research training they were expected to then become 'research active' in the future.
- Research officers who were writing their theses alongside employment on a funded research project, or less commonly while they were teaching assistants.
- Those who were seconded from jobs in universities abroad to study in the UK.

The texts selected are used to compare and contrast these three sub-groups and to build a brief vignette of each here.[8] It uses the category headings from the database to ask: What motivates members of this group to do a doctorate? What are their sources of support? What do they hope to get from the university and their supervisor? And what use do they make of their qualification and research findings subsequently?

Home students who move from professional careers to teach in higher education

Motivations for undertaking a doctorate

Members of this group are recruited by the university to teach (or to be registrars and senior administrators or managers) following applied work experience in education, medicine, health and social care, law, engineering or management, etc. Some are then required to undertake a doctorate, possibly as a term of probation, though many also do it for interest and self-esteem. HEIs now want their staff to hold PhDs for credibility and to provide the basis for future research activity, and those without a doctorate may feel somewhat inferior. In our alumni study, we found a 50 per cent increase between those who completed in 1992 and 2002 in the proportion mentioning this as one of their reasons for writing a thesis, especially those with jobs in lower status universities. For individuals in their 40s who have been doing part-time work in a number of different universities while trying to get a permanent post, a PhD can also contribute status or give credibility even if they stay as casual academics or work as consultants.

Staff with university posts have the advantage of generally starting with a good knowledge of the UK HE system and an overview of the current literature in their field. They may also be known to (and therefore accepted by) experienced potential supervisors. They are, therefore, likely to make well-informed decisions about where to study, based on whether they want a particular person as their supervisor or to get their degree from a particularly prestigious HEI. Their fees may be paid by their employer, or rescinded if they study in the place where they are employed. If they do study outside the university where they are employed, they have to negotiate financial support and travel for supervision and to participate in their doctoral department.

Sources of support while studying

Although they are required to undertake this form of continuing professional development, existing teaching staff are often not given much help with their doctoral studies by their university employer. Apart from fees, assistance is occasional and largely in kind ('a minor grant for part of the data collection cost and study leave for one term') – but even this is increasingly difficult to get as departmental resources are restricted. (Of course compared to the final group, foreign staff, if they do not have to pay fees, this is a major help.) But home staff do have their own offices, ICT support, reasonable salaries, academic status, administrative support, which is (or used sometimes to be) subverted to their own doctoral work, and probably also their conference fees paid when they present papers. They may also have access to some money from staff development funds (e.g. for a women researchers support group, see Hatt *et al.* 1999).

Their chief problem is lack of time. They are already teaching – and possibly also doing HE Academy or an in-house course on aspects of HE teaching. If they are in their first years of teaching, a lot of preparation is required; and in later years in academic life they will have accumulated administrative responsibilities.

They may well also have domestic responsibilities including small children or the care of elderly and disabled relatives. In our alumni study we found the doctorate being increasingly fitted alongside having children, at least by men. Of those completing in 1992, less than a quarter had small children, but in 2002 this was more than a third (more than half of men, but fewer women). Some told us they bought in paid domestic help and childcare, but unfortunately we omitted to ask about this systematically (showing we share some stereotypes of doctoral students!).

What they looked to get from the university and their supervisor

For this group, the doctorate and their supervisor occupy a different area in their lives from those who do a doctorate full-time and/or when they are young. The PhD does not become 'their whole life'. They are less dependent on their supervisor, and less critical of him or her. Some are not that interested in doing a doctorate and chose an 'easy' topic rather than one in which they are passionately interested, adopting an instrumental approach and maintaining emotional distance. But almost all become absorbed by it in the end. In general they have other sources of self-esteem: some supportive colleagues, friends, and a partner and other family members. Some use a spouse as a helper with, for example, talking through ideas, IT support, or reading and editing.

This is the group whose members are most likely to attend conferences (especially in recent cohorts) and to publish before they complete their theses. Among our alumni we found that a third published some material in professional or peer-reviewed journals or as chapters in books before they completed. If they give papers at conferences and are active in professional groups, they feel part of a network/academic community and get positive feedback.

If they do their doctorate in the institution where they work, staff doctoral candidates are quite likely to be supervised by a colleague. This may provide them with a good mentor, but it can also be difficult if the supervisory relationship breaks down or even if it is not very satisfactory (Denicolo 2004). The pair can, in addition, be in a multiplicity of other roles in relation to each other – e.g. the supervisor may be teaching on a course that the student is managing. Or other colleagues may think the supervisor is specially pleading for a lower workload for his/her 'student' in staff meetings, which may be resented and resisted. There are also issues of how close such a relationship should be, and how much each side wants to self-disclose.

Many – especially those in recent cohorts – say some of the main things they gained from doing a doctorate were skills in reading, writing, research methodology and 'doing research' (managing a project to completion), even though those were not effects they were looking for at the start of their doctorate.

Use subsequently made of the qualification and their research findings

Members of this group generally have secure jobs, but they probably have to chase up any promised promotion. Among the alumni we contacted, one in ten moved sideways into a similar job after they got their doctorate, and rather more moved up in the same field, or to a more prestigious institution, or into management, while still studying. Subsequently, the doctorate 'probably helped' their career, 'but it's hard to put a finger on just how'. There was not an immediate, direct change. Those who are motivated researchers will publish more from their thesis, but many do not, and some just move on to other projects because they are encouraged to 'bring in research money' instead.

Research officers writing their own theses alongside employment on a project

Motivations for undertaking a doctorate

Those in this group start with an interest in doing some research and/or plans to move on afterwards into an academic job or to become a career researcher. But there is some variation in the process by academic field.

In the arts and humanities and the social sciences, individuals usually start with a firm area of interest, perhaps from a masters degree, and want to carry on to investigate it further in a doctorate. Therefore, they seek a job as a research assistant on a project in a related area (or, less often in the UK, as a teaching assistant) so as to finance the degree. Others apply for jobs as research assistants on a specific project based on their having had relevant prior experience, e.g. having worked as a nurse or a volunteer abroad. Once in the job, they realise they need to do a doctorate to get ahead as a researcher, so they enrol. In either case, their status is that of a university employee on a short-term contract who is also registered to do a doctorate (usually in the same HEI).

In the sciences, however, many of those wishing to do research are initially 'given' a research studentship, either directly after a first degree or after a masters. Their status is, therefore, that of a research student member of a team – the research project having been funded with a certain number of studentships to support its work. A prospective supervisor's reputation and encouragement, and their potential bench colleagues, may be more crucial in influencing their decision to do research and to be in a certain place than the actual topic on offer (Frame and Allen 2002). Jobs at postdoctoral level in science have more in common with the status of research assistants in non-science areas – but we badly need more research on postdocs.

Sources of support while studying

Research assistants get their doctoral fees and some expenses paid and a modest salary. Those who undertook their doctorate in this way 20 years ago could work in the same job throughout the time they were working on their thesis, but later cohorts have had less job stability because the duration of projects has reduced. Their salary, therefore, often does not last as long as the time taken to complete their PhD, and they then become dependent on some other source of funding (another job, or parents or spouse) for the last year(s). Their insecure financial situation means they have worries about the future from the start of their candidacy. In our study of doctoral alumni, we found that very few of this young but relatively poor and time-pressured group had felt able to combine it with dependents or domestic responsibilities.

What they look to get from the university and their supervisor

Research assistant students are formally part of a department, but often geographically and socially isolated from it – in an office at the far end of another corridor – and do not feel they are part of the community of either teaching staff or the other research students. They are also less likely to have access to resources than staff with teaching posts. However, some respond with a proactive stance and attend seminars and volunteer to help organise events to raise their visibility and make contacts, while others simply complain.

Because many studies of 'part-time researcher' students do not, unfortunately, distinguish this group from other part-time research students (see e.g. the otherwise useful study by VITAE 2009a), we cannot say if they feel as isolated as non-staff part-time students, or if they are more, or less, satisfied with the research environment provided for them than other part-timers, nor how good they (or their supervisor/project director) are generally at establishing peer support and networks in the academic community.

Research assistants (and doctoral student team members in the sciences) are very dependent on the personality and status of their project director, who may also be (one of) their supervisor(s). They face all the issues discussed in the previous vignette in relation to supervision by a colleague, but in spades. Acker (1999) found they are especially likely to complain of infrequent meetings to talk about their doctorate with their supervisor in the social sciences, and in our study of education students we also got some of the sharpest critiques of supervision/ management from this group. In addition, its members may be using some of the data they gathered as part of the project on which they are employed for their thesis. This helps with fieldwork costs and time, but requires careful negotiation to clarify which work is the student's own. It may also mean that the researcher does not choose his or her topic freely. However, if research assistants do decide to do something different from the project on which they are working for their thesis, they have to reconcile dual demands and may not get the same support if they want to present on 'their own topic' at conferences, or with publishing.

In the sciences where people are working in a laboratory situation (and remembering that not all science doctoral candidates are in this situation), research associates and technical staff are generally around and supportive. They are an important source of technical advice for junior staff members and for postdocs, too (Wright and Lodwick 1989; Delamont et al. 1997; Pole et al. 1997). Supervision here may be partly a collective responsibility, there is also not the same expectation of, or importance attached to, choosing one's topic and approach, publications are multi-authored, and there is generally a shorter time to completion – all of which result in greater student satisfaction.

The use subsequently made of their qualification and research findings

Acker suggests this group of research students is the one most disaffected with academe in the social sciences and the most likely to leave after they get their doctorates (Acker

1999). Very few seek to become generic career researchers. In our alumni study, their numbers were small but we also found that although they might go on to do a post-doctoral job, they then left academia, or else they undertook further training in related but practical fields. Some later returned to HE or education-related public or private sector organisations (we contacted them between two and 12 years after they completed), but others become self-employed consultants. They did not work in research.

Students seconded from jobs in universities abroad

Motivations for undertaking a doctorate

Many international research students in the UK have gained masters degrees in their home country or in the UK, and some, especially those working in academia or research centres abroad, have wanted to undertake a research degree for a long time. The experience of a PhD is essential for them to move beyond the rank of lecturer, and prestigious doctorates are not obtainable locally. I have supervised several African women research students, for instance, who had experienced particularly heavy discrimination in their home universities and wanted doctorates to get promotion. They also sought to explore how women had improved their lot in the West, with a view to transporting (and transforming) relevant concepts and practices. Both men and women from overseas are also often committed to using their doctorate to contribute to national advancement generally.

Sources of support while studying

All foreign students have to be proactive and determined to organise the special experience of getting a doctorate in the UK. The majority, the two-thirds of post-graduate research students who come from outside the EU, pay substantial fees as well as the high costs of living here. They have to seek either financial support from their employer or their home government, or competitive scholarships from British sources. The latter are much thinner on the ground than in the USA, Australia, France and Germany, because, despite their declared commitment to getting the best students and to internationalisation, UK universities support few international students, and there are very limited UK government funding schemes (see Kemp et al. 2009, sections 5.16, 5.17).

Overseas students, therefore, often depend heavily on gifts and loans from their extended family and/or draw on savings. Most use multiple sources; and more of them than is generally recognised get part-time jobs while they are in the UK. Up to 80 per cent of international research students in some UK universities undertake part-time work; and 38 per cent are registered as part-time (survey of HEIs in Kemp et al. 2009: 53). Getting such work has been helped by changes in visa requirements, but what is available may well not be constructively related to the subject they are studying, and it may also be more acceptable for men than for women (Leonard and Rab in press).

US research suggests foreign research students are less likely to get temporary jobs within the university than home students: they are less likely to get the informal tasks that professors can hand out, and are much less likely to be given any formal teaching (Nerad and Stewart 1991).

Those who get funding from employers abroad may continue on their previous salaries, but these are cut into by the exchange rates and cost of living in the UK. British Council and other scholarships are relatively generous. But almost all international students experience a markedly lower standard of private and public living during the years they are studying.

Such students generally do not have children with them when they start their doctorate and (if they have any) leave them with relatives. They may bring them later with a relative or servant to take care of them – if they can get a visa for the carer. But doctoral studies often mean periods missing families and cultural familiarities, even if improved travel and communications technology helps with homesickness. When they return home they find social life has moved on and reintegration can be difficult, again especially for women.

What they look to get from the university and their supervisor

These research students are themselves experienced teachers, but in another culture, and may be critical of what they find in the UK. They expect – indeed they have eagerly come to learn – a different teaching style and a critical approach, even if they sometimes find it hard to adjust to the actuality. But, in addition to good teaching from experts, they would like to have at least a shared office, good computing or lab equipment, internet access, help with their English language skills, an international office that will sort out problems, and some organised social activities. At home, if it is a low to medium income country, they may have had one or more personal assistants and several teaching assistants. They are thrown if they not only have to do their own photocopying, but can also only do restricted amounts of it without paying dearly; or if there is little subsidised accommodation near campus for those with families. They do not appreciate living in accommodation alongside and sharing social facilities with undergraduates. They expect to be treated differently from other students as a mark of their superior, doctoral student status. They may think UK universities should not be taking on more students than they can properly cope with. (These are the ones, presumably, which UK HE management describe as 'having unrealistic expectations'.) International students welcome some directed teaching and feel the courses now provided give value for money. On the other hand, they often cannot afford to go to conferences and so miss out on networking and publishing opportunities. Editors of journals, for instance, do not hear them talk about their work and so do not offer the morale boosting suggestion that the student submits a piece.

International students probably have a highly and mutually respectful attitude to their supervisor; but resent how little attention they get from other staff in UK departments (e.g. there is seldom recognition of, knowledge about, or interest in their home country, nor does anyone, except their supervisor, know what, sometimes prestigious, jobs they hold at home). At departmental events, the UK staff tend to talk to each other rather than to their colleagues' research students. The students also say that their peer group consists largely of other international, rather than British students.

Like many home students, international students may well not attend departmental seminars, partly because they have a narrow definition of what is 'relevant' to them, and also because they are less likely than home students to be encouraged to do so. Some events that might seem friendly and hospitable to UK staff, for example, evening meetings in people's houses, are found intimidating, especially by those with English as a second language (Deem and Brehony 2000). There may be the added embarrassment for those who have officially been teaching in English but are then confronted by their inadequacies/non-standard usage/non-academic writing style when in the UK.

They generally feel under great pressure for time as well as money, including a sense of what they owe (employers and family) back home. This may lead to counter-productive activities, for example, sitting alone at their computers for hours on end trying to work 'hard enough' and missing out on serendipitous discovery of materials or approaches and meeting visiting scholars relevant to their thesis argument. They do not often see themselves as having a possible role in contributing to the (department, institution or national) academic community while they are in the UK.

The use subsequently made of their qualification and research findings

Most international students who study in the UK return 'home', even if they might like to stay on for a while after they get their doctorate (Tremblay 2005). They have jobs held open for them to which they return, and often get promotion. But they disappear from the UK radar. HESA, in its graduate destinations statistics, groups together all foreign students who 'return overseas' and gives no occupational information on them. Consequently, any accounts based on secondary analysis of HESA data, such as the UK GRAD study of *What do PhDs do?* (UK GRAD Programme 2006) and the follow up, *What do Researchers do? First destinations of doctoral graduates by subject* (VITAE 2009b), also omit them.[9]

Many international students find it hard to maintain a research profile and to get articles from their thesis accepted for international peer-review journals once they are home. Some join alumni organisations (e.g. run by their UK university or by the British Council) and maintain a strong sense of attachment to their supervisors and the UK, but without these providing much intellectual outlet.

Concluding comments

This account has sought to counter the presumption that individuals do a doctorate and then get a job in higher education, by stressing that significant numbers of students already have jobs in higher education before they start their doctorate. It has also focused on how the doctorate fits into the lives of these 'early career' academics (who may well not be young[10]), rather than the usual perspective of how their lives fit around the doctorate. In so doing it has shown how, despite policy makers expressed concern with the doctorate in terms of the continuing supply of skilled researchers for national economic development and enhancing employability, the data their agents gather and the research they fund has to date been relatively unconcerned with students' actual employment before and after their doctorates, and cannot tell us what changes a doctorate makes to a career trajectory. Focusing on the elite of home, full-time, mainly science students, who come direct from their first degree and masters, has made politicians and research and funding councils overlook UK universities' strength in drawing in many with outside work and international experience. These 'non-traditional' research students are, moreover, prepared to pay (or someone other than the UK government or university is prepared to pay) for their intellectual development and for their 'original contribution to knowledge'.

It may, of course, be argued that 'non-stereotypical' research students are both the numerical minority and of less importance than the 'full-time, young, home students in key disciplines' who are the focus of government concern. But the argument about relative numbers in key areas no longer holds – witness the importance and contribution of international students in engineering and technology, business and management, and mathematics and computing noted above. The incidence of different types of student enrolment and the importance of part-time, older, home students certainly varies by subject area and from one university to another; but for some subject areas and many locally and vocationally focused universities, they are essential.

This chapter also outlined three different contexts for the doctorate in the lives of those already employed in higher education. These will be familiar to many supervisors, but the details provided here from existing qualitative research help to develop a typology, even if the data available is not as full as we might want, and even if there may also be other groups of 'non-stereotypical' research students whose characteristics equally merit better definition and inclusion – notably those who do a doctorate alongside other jobs. (This last group has come into focus partly through work on the professional doctorate and from some other countries, notably Australia.) For the moment, it is hard to estimate the frequency with which the doctorate is undertaken during, rather than at the start of a career, and specifically the incidence of the three groups traced here, because of the shortcomings in the official UK data. Nor can we evaluate the importance of – the value added by – getting a doctorate because we do not know individuals' jobs and earnings and satisfaction before and after their doctoral candidature.

It is worth noting, however, that in our follow-up of the doctoral graduates at one UK postgraduate research institution, we found more than half the international students were employed in universities when they started their doctorate; as were nearly half of home students. Only 5 per cent of our respondents were research officers, writing their theses alongside employment on a funded research project – which surprised us. (However, as this group tends to be disaffected, it is possible that fewer responded to our questionnaire.) These incidences may be a characteristic of education as a field, but until HESA and others ask the right questions, and we all start to think in terms of research student market segmentation generally, we will not know.

We do know, however, that almost half of all research students in the UK, and half of all new full-timers, are currently from abroad (35 per cent of from outside the EU, 15 per cent from other EU countries and 50 per cent from the UK, HEFCE 2009). While we do not know how many of them have jobs in universities in their home countries, and it is unlikely to be the case for the majority of those from China, India, Germany and Greece as they have less than two years prior work experience when they arrive, it may well be the case for many of those from Malaysia, Pakistan, Taiwan, Thailand and the USA, who have been in employment for three or more years (Kemp *et al.* 2009, Annex 1 Figure 43). In any event, if we are serious about building international ties with other universities, we should cherish and learn much more from those who will be senior members of universities worldwide in the near future.

Focusing on UK research candidates who already have jobs when they do their doctorates, and especially jobs in universities, throws new light on moves to harmonise European higher education: namely the 'Bologna Process'. In the UK it has been customary to cast doctoral candidates firmly as 'students', rather than as employed by their university, even those who are working as assistants on projects with funding awarded to the university. But in this we are out of step with most of the EU. (Or as Margaret Thatcher would have said, most of the EU is out of step with us.) A European Universities Association (EUA) survey in 2006 found that among the 37 member countries participating in the Bologna Process, the status of a doctoral candidate is 'mixed' in 22: that is to say, they are officially recognised as both students and employees. In nine they are seen only as students and in three only as employees (cited in Bitusikova 2009). The EUA itself argues that the status of doctoral candidates should be that of an 'early stage researcher', and both it and Eurodoc (the European council of doctoral candidates and young researchers), and the UK-based VITAE (formerly UK GRAD), eschew the title of doctoral 'student' and prefer either 'doctoral candidates' or just 'researchers'. They argue that doctoral 'candidates' should have not only a wage but also healthcare, pension and social security provision.

But work presented here suggests that perhaps we should be a bit wary of a 'mixed' location, given the experiences particularly of UK research assistant doctoral candidates, but also home and international university teachers doing doctorates. Not all staff members doing doctorates are located in the same way and some seem better placed and more content than others. We should build in some safeguards and try to accentuate the positive.

Finally, the material presented here leads to the question of how policies recently introduced, or being proposed, by powerful groups outside the universities, with young, science students in mind, suit those who are not so young and across the disciplines. Are the generic research methodology and compulsory 'employment-related skills' courses now being provided equally appropriate for all groups? Or do they need something more individually tailored? Just suggesting students with past work experience can choose not to attend course elements that provide basic work-related skills, rather than providing special, more advanced courses, appropriate for various different countries, is short-changing many students.

Equally, there may be some (unintended but) positive consequences of recent developments that could be highlighted more and built on – though we need systematic research to indicate these, as well as just 'examples of good practice'. For instance, our alumni research found that international students appreciated the methodology courses much more than the home students (for whom the research councils originally intended them), both because they helped make overt many previously implicit understandings, and because they provided a supportive cohort of students in the first year. We suspect they are also useful because they can use them for teaching at home.

Perhaps we could use those who are currently registered to do their PhDs to help us more in course development? So, for example, in discussions of time management, we could include different conceptions of time, and acknowledge the different demands on and resources available elsewhere in universities and research centres from what exists in the UK. This would enrich both the varied overseas doctoral 'community' and the 'home' members' experiences, and encourage more transfer of knowledge in and out of UK universities in an organic way. The (relatively few) follow-up studies by funders of those they have supported in studying in the UK in the past, show how strong and important such two-way links can be initially, and how long they may continue over time.

Notes

1 UUK issued a report on inter-university variation in respect of taught postgraduates that stressed this (UUK 2009a), but the companion report on the doctorate (UUK 2009b) unfortunately says little on differences between HEIs.
2 See, for instance, DIUS 2008; HEFCE 2005; 2009; Kulej and Park 2008.

3 Response to a question at the seminar to launch this report.

4 This is aside from, but related to, another important question: the issue of 'widening participation' at graduate level and particularly the social class background of home and international graduate students.

5 On the contribution of international doctoral students to the US economy, see Chellaraj *et al.* 2004.

6 This database is publicly accessible and searchable by keywords in the Research Evidence in Education Library (REEL) on the EPPI-Centre website. For fuller details of the methodology, see Leonard *et al.* (2006) section 2.5 pp. 16–18 and appendix 4 pp. 66–67.

7 Thanks to the colleagues who worked with me on this: my co-Principal Investigator Janet Metcalfe, researchers Rosa Becker and Jennifer Evans, and staff in the EPPI-Centre. This chapter is based on my own subsequent analysis of our data.

8 Extensive referencing has been avoided for ease of reading, but the descriptions are tightly based on accounts in the database texts, together with material from other work of mine where indicated.

9 Note that quite a number of UK domiciled doctoral graduates also move to work abroad, and they are equally not tracked.

10 Among research students starting in 2004–5, the mean age of full-timers was 27.3 years and part-timers 37.6 (HEFCE 2009, section 53). Numbers of young starters are declining.

References

Acker, S. (1999) Students and supervisors: the ambiguous relationship, *Review of Australian Research in Education*, 5: 75–94.

Bitusikova, A. (2009) New challenges in doctoral education in Europe. In D. Boud and A. Lee (Eds). *Changing Practices of Doctoral Education*. London and New York: Routledge.

Chellaraj, G., Maskus, K. E. and Matloo, A. (2004). The Contribution of Skilled Immigration and International Graduate Students to U.S. Innovation, *World Bank Policy Research Working Paper*, World Bank.

Deem, R. and Brehony, K. (2000) 'Doctoral students' access to research cultures – are some more unequal than others?, *Studies in Higher education*, 25(2): 149–65.

Delamont, S., Atkinson, P. and Parry, O. (1997) *Supervising the PhD: a guide to success*. Buckingham: SRHE and Open university Press.

Denicolo, P. (2004) Doctoral supervision of colleagues: peeling away the veneer of satisfaction and competence, *Studies in Higher Education*, 29(6): 693–707.

DIUS (2008) Higher Degrees: Postgraduate study in the UK 2000/01 to 2005/6, DIUS Research Report 08 16.

Frame, I. A. and Allen, L. (2002) A flexible approach to PhD research training, *Quality Assurance in Education*, 10(2): 98–103.

Hatt, S., Kent, J. and Britton, C. (Eds) (1999) *Women, Research and Careers*. Basingstoke: Macmillan Press.

HEFCE (2005) *PhD Research Degrees: entry and completion*. London: Higher Education Funding Council for England.

——(2009) *PhD study: starters to doctoral degree courses in UK higher education institutions between 1996–97 and 2005–05*. Issues paper, Higher Education Funding Council for England.

Kemp, N., Archer, W., Gilligan, C. and Humfrey, C. (2009) *The UK's Competitive Advantage: the market for international research students*, London: UK Higher Education International Unit.

Kulej, M. and Park, C. (2008) *Postgraduate Research Experience Survey 2008*. The Higher Education Academy.

Leonard, D., Becker, R. and Coate, K. (2004) Continuing professional and career development: the doctoral experience of education alumni at a UK university, *Studies in Continuing Education*, 26(3): 369–85.

——(2005) 'To prove myself at the highest level': the benefits of doctoral study, *Higher Education Research and Development*, 24(2): 135–50.

Leonard, D., Metcalfe, J., Becker, R. and Evans, J. (2006) *Review of the Literature on the Doctoral Experience*. York: HE Academy.

Leonard, D. and Rab, M. (in press) The inter-relationship of employment, marriage and higher education among Pakistani students in the UK. In E. Unterhalter and V. Carpentier (Eds). *Whose interests are we serving? Global inequalities and higher education*. Basingstoke: Palgrave.

Nerad, M. and Stewart, C. I. (1991) *Assessing Doctoral Student Experience: gender and departmental culture*. Paper presented to annual conference of the Association for Institutional Research, San Francisco.

Nishio, A. (2001) *Issues facing Japanese postgraduate students studying at the University of London with special reference to gender*. Institute of Education University of London.

Pole, C., Sprokkereef, A., Burgess, R., and Lakin, E. (1997) Supervision of doctoral students in the natural sciences: expectations and experiences, *Assessment and Evaluation in Higher Education*, 22(1): 49–63.

Tremblay, K. (2005) Academic mobility and immigration, *Journal of International Education*, 9(3): 196–228.

UK GRAD Programme (2006) *What do PhDs Do? Analysis of the first destinations for PhD graduates 2004*. Cambridge: UK GRAD Programme.

UUK (2009a) *Taught Postgraduate Students: market trends and opportunities*. London: Universities UK.

——(2009b) *Promoting the UK doctorate: opportunities and challenges*. London: Universities UK in association with VITAE.

VITAE (2009a) *Understanding the part-time researcher experience*. Online. (Available at vitae.ac.uk/CMS/files/upload/part-time%20researcher%20experience.pdf Accessed 1 June 2009).

——(2009b) *What do Researchers do? First destinations of doctoral graduates by subject*. Cambridge: CRAC, the Career Development Organization.

Wright, I. and Lodwick, R. (1989) The process of the PhD: a study of the first year of doctoral study, *Research Papers in Education*, 4: 22–56.

15

Rhythms of place

Time and space in the doctoral experience

S. Middleton

Spatial questions are central in academic work. As a supervisor of doctoral students, a manager of doctoral programmes, and a researcher on higher education, I have heard countless stories from doctoral graduates about 'finding time', 'clearing space', or 'making room.' As Harvey (1996: 267) argues, 'space may be forgotten as an analytical category open to questioning, but it is omnipresent as an unquestioned category in everything we do'.

Academic life is replete with spatial language. Thesis-writers are required to *locate* their research in epistemological or abstract space: to *position* research topics, questions, methodologies and theories in recognised *fields* or disciplines. The conceptual, interpersonal, financial and professional components of disciplines are globally constructed, coalescing around and forging connections between international, national, regional and local hubs, including conferences and journals. Disciplines rank and reward; according differential status to individuals, research units, paradigms and publications where 'The language of exclusion is by and large spatial; who's in, who's out, at the heart, on the margins' (Gulson and Symes 2007: 99). Doctoral students' engagements with disciplines are face-to-face, in print, and online. As learning spaces, the disciplines of the twenty-first century have been reconfigured by 'the interactive effects of globalisation and the ICT revolution' (Ferguson and Seddon 2007: 117).

Students' and supervisors' intellectual identifications and professional affinities with these 'fields' are overlaid by the organisational categories of the institutions in which they are enrolled or employed. Institutions classify students and staff according to administrative categories (such as programmes and subjects) and locate them geographically in buildings assigned to faculties and departments. As Bernstein (2000) indicates, organisational divisions within institutions do not always coincide with researchers' wider professional disciplinary affiliations. Students whose topics do not neatly fit the organisation's departmental structure may find themselves torn, straddling multiple institutional locations.

The locational complexities of doctoral work are evident in the following extract from an interview with Dee, a PhD graduate in education.[1] Dee was enrolled in an education faculty in which she was also a member of staff:

> The first six months were terribly angst driven. I wandered around reading way out, this great breadth of Pacific Ocean reading, in order to try and write something that

was fine and focussed and blazing – only to find that I couldn't bridge the gap between the Pacific Ocean of reading to this fine line of academic writing. And that was painful – trying to tame the ocean, trying to pull it into something that was going to be really focussed. That took six months and I felt like I was wasting time. I could hear the clock, 'tick, tick, tick.' And I could feel my anxiety levels rising 'cause I was on study leave to begin it and I just felt it was going nowhere. I got very fit. I went for lots of runs. After each run I would think, 'I've got it now and I know where I am going,' only to go and do a classroom observation and find that I was more confused than ever.

As both an employee and a student, Dee was administratively, epistemologically, and physically located in the discipline/faculty/profession of education. Struggling to confine her project within a recognised field in this discipline, Dee confronted the possibility that her freely ranging reading and thinking were too 'way out' for academic purposes. Dee had to draw, and follow a 'fine line.' She also wanted to retain her creative flare – her 'blaze' of originality. Dee's location in New Zealand informed her metaphor: she fears her flame will be extinguished in the vast Pacific Ocean. Dee felt out of control, buffeted by untameable external forces. Scientific linearity eluded her. Dee's experience was of drowning: bodily pain, anxiety, and confusion.

Bureaucratic mappings of time threatened to enclose Dee's untamed mental, emotional and psychological landscapes. Reading, fieldwork and writing had to keep time with the rhythms of academic calendars and regulatory timeframes. Fieldwork in primary schools must accommodate school, as well as university timeframes. Conceptual mappings in the discipline's literature did not match the categories suggested by classroom observations. As a member of academic staff, Dee was required to complete fieldwork during study leave, at the end of which satisfactory progress must be proven to her employers, who were also her supervisors.

Dee could no longer indulge in free 'wandering' intellectually or physically. She adopted an ascetic approach to mind and body in the hope that running might discipline dreaming, pull diffuse thoughts into linear form. Dee's running body carved metaphorical pathways: between the abstractions of academic knowledge, a university's bureaucratic configurations, the schools in which she carried out fieldwork, and the poetic imagery of her emotional/spiritual underworld.

To explore Dee's and similar stories, it is useful to bring together geographical and educational theories. In particular, I shall draw on Lefebvre (1974), who is increasingly identified as 'an overarching presence in the educational appropriation of spatial theories with many researchers referring to his work on perceived, conceived, and lived space' (Gulson and Symes 2007: 101). The following section introduces this typology. The second section discusses 'dwelling in the disciplines' as configured in university departments. Thesis work is seldom contained within academia's designated spaces: it infuses students' domestic and wider community contexts. Usually conceptualised as private spaces beyond the gaze of educational theory, these 'other' sites of doctoral work are addressed in section three. I conclude by reviewing students' strategies for managing time and space.

Thinking spaces

Perceived spaces are those of everyday social practice, of bodily movements and habit. From infancy bodily orientations in space become 'the practical basis of the perception of the outside world' (Lefebvre 1974: 38). Spatial experimentations of infancy underpin adult skills such as sitting on chairs, negotiating corridors, reaching for books. Dee's running body would 'instinctively' swerve to avoid trees, recognise her home and her street, 'know' how to cross kerbs and climb hills.

Lefebvre (1974: 205) urged social scientists to 'envision a sort of "rhythm analysis" which could address itself to the concrete analysis of rhythms, and perhaps even to their use (or appropriation)'. He wrote

> Perceived spaces, those of bodily and everyday social practice, have their own rhythms. Some of these are easy to identify: breathing, the heartbeat, thirst, hunger and the need for sleep are cases in point. Others, however, such as those of sexuality, fertility, social life, or thought, are relatively obscure.
>
> Lefebvre 1974: 205

'Natural' (seasonal, diurnal or bodily) rhythms are overlaid with cultural rituals and conventions: festivals, rites of passage, routines and so on. During doctoral research and writing, students continue to celebrate holy days and holidays, attend tangi [funerals], fall ill or give birth. The primal bodily beats and social rhythms of everyday life continue to reverberate throughout the doctoral experience.

Conceived spaces (also referred to as abstract or mental spaces) are appropriations. Legally mandated enclosures by the state or of capital (public or private property) conceived spaces include those 'of cartographers, urban planners or property speculators' (Shields 2004: 210). Their codified representations are *representations of space*: 'In order to dominate space, technology introduces a new form into a pre-existing space – generally a rectilinear form such as a mesh-work or chequerwork' (Lefebvre 1974: 139). Maps, floor plans, blueprints, models, flow-charts, timetables, taxonomies, grading or ranking systems – hallmarks of education at all levels – are representations of [abstract] space. University campuses (physical, landscaped and built) are the architectural manifestations of such representations. As in other industrial-bureaucratic organisations, university life is patterned by the rhythms and tempos of academic years, working days, degree timeframes and examination deadlines.

Academic disciplines can usefully be seen as conceived spaces. Positioned in relation to a discipline or interdisciplinary field, a thesis is oriented substantively, conceptually and methodologically towards an audience of specialists. The doctoral process involves learning to identify and address such an audience. As global discursive practices, the scientific, humanities and professional disciplines are in many ways 'not bound to geographical landscapes and physical points of reference' (Popkewitz and Brennan 1998: 12). However, thesis topics, methods and conceptual tools are inevitably enabled, constrained and 'flavoured' by their writers' geographical settings (in nations, regions, institutions and so on) and their socio/cultural positioning within those locations (socio-economic and cultural background, gender, etc.).

Student's national-historical locations influence their theses in multiple ways. For example, New Zealand was colonised in the Victorian 'Age of Empire'. Although scientific and educational theories and methods were even then global phenomena, metropolitan England was their originating and legitimating authority. Indigenous peoples, such as New Zealand Māori, were made objects of scientific as well as political domination (Smith 1999). Harvey (1996: 49) writes:

Beyond the spatial limits of civilisation there were untamed people and untamed nature to be incorporated into the imperial system. Attitudes to people on these peripheries were ambivalent, however. While this was regarded with disgust or fear if they violated the space of the colonisers, they were also idealised or romanticised

Today's disciplines bear traces of these colonial origins (McKinley 2005). From New Zealand, Smith (1997: 203) writes that the educational 'battleground for Māori is spatial. It is about theoretical spaces, pedagogical spaces, structural spaces'. Barbara, a doctoral graduate and university staff member, described her cultural orientation as Māori and her discipline's positioning of her as Māori as conflicting:

> When you say, 'My orientation is Māori and this is how [my discipline] applies and fits', you're actually on the other side of the fence saying, 'Hang on, this is how you apply it to me' and so there's that resistance from academia and from the profession of [discipline] to say, 'No, you should be fitting around what we have'. So there's that kind of tension.[2]

Barbara's story exemplifies Bernstein's (2000) distinction between external identities (projected by authorities) and internal identities (introjected by the student). The official identities of academics (staff and students) are projected across conceived space: via statutes, regulations, handbooks, templates, contracts, examinations and grading systems. Academic/professional identity formation is 'a continuous and reflexive process, a synthesis of (internal) self definition and the (external) definition of oneself offered by others' (Henkel 2005: 157). Doctoral students' disciplinary identities 'are forged through embodied relations which are extended geographically as well as historically' (Massey 2004). These are unstable, as academic 'identifications are never fully made; they are incessantly reconstituted and, as such are subject to the volatile logic of iterability' (Butler 1993: 105). Doctoral success requires repeated endorsements in the form of feedback from supervisors, success in the examination process, having papers accepted by prestigious conferences and journals.

Doctoral theses involve performances (citations) of disciplinary conventions (Butler 1993). Disciplines are scripted, cited and mapped in international, national and regional forums such as learned societies, journals and conferences. The economic and political powerbrokers of the English-speaking world remain hubs of epistemological dominance: the status hierarchies within international research organisations, the global rankings of institutions and journals, the ebbs and flows of theoretical and methodological fashion. In countries on academe's 'periphery', writing for 'overseas' high-status conferences, journals or thesis examiners can involve feelings of dislocation. In very small countries, theses are still sent overseas for examination. Indigenous students within such countries may experience an intensified academic marginality, having to translate everyday cultural knowledge for their local as well as the international gate-keeping authorities.

I have argued that students' disciplinary affinities, cultural and personal identities may intersect in complex and contradictory ways with the financial and administrative categories whereby institutions allocate students to programmes, distribute resources to their departments, and locate them in buildings (Bernstein 2000). An education specialist, Dee struggled to accommodate her creative impulse and her personal life to the rhythms of bureaucracy: study leave, the academic year, primary school timetables, and degree regulations. Barbara identified a gap between cultural and disciplinary meanings, trying to bend resistant academic frameworks around her cultural standpoint. The poetic language used by both students evokes Lefebvre's (1974) idea of *lived* space (also referred to as *third space*). Lived spaces are infused with the symbolic meanings of biographical and cultural legacy. Lived spaces encompass the pre-linguistic imagery, symbols and dreams of earliest infancy. At a cultural, collective, level, lived space is the mainspring of mythology, spirituality and the imaginary. From lived spaces emanate the *representational spaces* of poetry and the arts.

In academic contexts, these representational spaces are conceptualised as objects of disciplinary enquiry: 'Ethnologists, anthropologists and psychoanalysts are students of such representational spaces' (Lefebvre 1974: 43). Until the 1990s, only a tiny academic elite entered doctoral study. In today's mass higher education systems, a wide range of professionals is undertaking PhDs or professional doctorates (Green *et al.* 2001). Increasing proportions of doctoral students are of cultural, national or socioeconomic backgrounds whose previous visibility in a discipline may have been as objects, rather than subjects (or authors) of their research enquiries (Smith 1999). Such students may feel 'out of place' in academic settings, and experience a splitting between mind and body, the abstract (conceived) from the lived.

Dwelling in the disciplines

The lived – this 'third space' of the imaginary, the speculative, and the artistic – cannot be fully codified or repressed by the abstract representations of the conceived. Atakohu, a Māori doctoral graduate, described how her 'doctoral journey was prompted by *he moe tapu*, which is a sacred vision. At the core was the advancement of Māori.' Another Māori graduate, Mere, described her powerful spiritual sense of the historical tribal and colonial-era violence that had taken place on what was now her university campus. She changed departments because her original department building:

> [S]tands on old war grounds. I don't know if that's the reason why the [department] can't gel. I suspect it is. I mean I had to karakia … [chant traditional prayers]. That's one of the war grounds. That's one of the battle sites and you feel it. You walk on there, but you karakia first. I was quite relieved to get away from there because I felt safe in the Māori Studies Department.

As Merleau-Ponty (1962: viii) argued, 'all my knowledge of the world, even my scientific knowledge, is gained from my own particular point of view, or from some experience of the world without which the symbols of science would be meaningless'. Social class can 'locate' a doctoral student in deeply felt ways (Middleton 2003). Wendy, a mature student, was also employed as a tutor in her University Education Department. As a child from a working class family, Wendy had felt alienated from the academic 'high culture' of secondary school and now, as a doctoral student, felt attracted to neo-Marxist theories that gave voice to this experience. For Wendy, social class was not simply a disembodied statistical abstraction; it was agonisingly lived. Wendy's supervisors (for whom she was also a junior teaching assistant) invited her to join their reading group:

> I didn't understand what was going on. I couldn't really read the language most of the time. I struggled with the jargon of that academic education because it didn't

mean anything to me. While I was a good reader, I had never had to deal with this very academic language before. I found that incredibly difficult.

Another working class student, Peggy had grown up in a religiously repressive household. Denied access to books as a child, her rebellion had taken the form of secret reading. Having recently escaped a violent marriage, Peggy saw her doctorate as a promise of individual freedom. Instead, her field, the sociology of education, was focused on:

[W]hy working class people fail. I thought, 'You bastards! You're sitting there saying how people fail and you're not empowering anybody'. I looked at some post-modern stuff and I thought, 'Fuck this! It doesn't actually tell me how to change any policies!' Theories that say that this rationality's as good as that rationality did fuck all for me. It just made me so angry after what I've been through. I thought, 'All you intellectuals sitting there – you don't know shit!'

Seeking freedom in an emotional as well as an epistemological sense, Peggy negotiated a physical move and a bureaucratic reclassification within the conceived, transferring her enrolment to a philosophy department. The libertarian individualism Peggy encountered there counteracted the psychic and interpersonal feelings of alienation she had experienced in neo-Marxist sociology of education.

Max moved in the opposite direction – out of philosophy and into education. With a working class background, Max could not feel at home in the philosophy department, describing it as a: 'privileged little enclave, a kind of pale imitation of the progression of the public school system in Britain where people talked in funny voices about questions which bore no relationship to their own context'. Max *lived* at a deep emotional level questions studied in the education department as 'the politics of knowledge.' From the point of view of the university hierarchy, his move out of philosophy ('at the top of the university hierarchy') and into education was a move 'down' to 'the bottom of the hierarchy of subjects'.

Doctoral study involves identification with a discipline or interdisciplinary field. This involves becoming familiar with its *abstract* spaces: its theoretical/epistemological composition and its professional/bureaucratic modes of organisation. It also involves familiarity with the *perceived* spaces of a university campus and its departmental buildings. But doctoral students also experience their disciplines as lived spaces. Their fields of knowledge are not only experienced as disembodied abstractions: as *lived* spaces they can 'express human thought, fantasy and desire. They are also institutionally based, materially constrained, experientially grounded manifestations of social and power relations' (Harvey 1996: 80).

A thesis in the house.

In his discussion of 'spatial imaginings' (representational spaces), Lefebvre (1974: 121) referred to Bachelard's study of literary images of house and home as primal repositories for 'thoughts, memories and dreams … The binding principle in this integration is the daydream. Past, present and future give the house different dynamisms, which often interfere, at times opposing, at time stimulating one another' (Bachelard 1994: 26). Often depicted as such 'private' space, the home can also be viewed sociologically as structured by wider social relations of reproduction and of production: 'the division of labour has repercussions upon the family and is of a piece with it; conversely, the organisation of the family interferes with the division of labour' (Lefebvre 1974: 32).

Virginia Woolf's (2002) portrayal of the Hyde Park house in which she lived as a child in London in an upper middle-class family around the turn of the twentieth century illustrates how gendered class relations configured the domestic geography of an intellectual household. The tea table was:

> [T]he centre, the heart of the family. It was the centre to which the sons returned from their work in the evening; the hearth whose fire was tended by the mother, pouring out tea. In the same way, the bedroom – the double bedded bedroom on the first floor was the sexual centre, the birth centre, the death centre of the house.
>
> Woolf 2002: 125

With the help of servants, the mother's (downstairs) work involved care of the body, presiding over the fire, pouring tea for returning sons, performing social rituals demanded by Victorian convention. Upstairs, cut off from such menial concerns, was her 'father's great study ... entirely booklined ... the brain of the house' (Woolf 2002: 125). The floor-plan was vertical, segmented by the body (female) – mind (male) split. Woolf (2002: 125) wrote: 'The division in our life was curious. Downstairs there was pure convention, upstairs pure intellect'.

Woolf's (2002) story, written when women were denied university education, depicts the scholar as monadic and male, thinking and writing in seclusion. It exemplifies the enlightenment persona of 'man of letters' and its architectural accommodation through 'the insertion of truly private and individualised male space – the study-into the house' (Harvey 1996: 228). In Woolf's (2002) home there was a close association 'between daily reality (daily routine) and urban reality (the routes and networks which link up the places set aside for work, "private life" and leisure)' (Lefebvre 1974: 38). Architectural space (the layout, functions and occupancy of rooms) and the rhythms of nature (day–night, the seasons) were overlaid with the 'mesh-works' of the conceived (working days, gender roles).

Today in some countries, women dominate doctoral enrolments in at least some academic disciplines. The complex gender relations of the twenty-first century are played out in a wide range variety of domestic arrangements. Students residing in flats or hostels may regard themselves as living 'away from home'. Doctoral candidates may be single or partnered, with or without children or other dependants. Couples may share domestic tasks equally, or have designated roles and responsibilities, and these arrangements shape how time and space are configured within households.

Some resist bringing thesis work home. Gordon wrote 'mostly in my office at the university, because I tried to keep a division between work and home'. James wrote his thesis at home, but in a designated 'little detached den outside the house'. Isolating himself during family time proved painful. James's adult children 'can still remember their mother saying, "Don't disrupt Daddy, he's working on his PhD" [...] Daddy was working on his PhD, he was buried away out in his study'. During weekdays James worked as a university lecturer, work he did not bring home, confining teaching and administration tasks to weekday working hours on campus. James did not take PhD work into his university office: 'I found that I had to keep the two things separate'. Felix created 'space' at home through organising time:

> I worked incredible crazy hours. I set up an office in a bedroom so that I never went away from the house to work apart from my standard work hours because I wanted to keep the family connection and not always be seen to be away somewhere.

Mary brought her thesis into the centre of home activities:

> I've got a study, but I don't use it because I'm attuned to working at the table. I don't mind a bit of noise and music and people coming in and out. I grew up in a big family where you had to work like that.

Christine:

> became quite adept ... at managing to write in my study with five rather large kids thumping around the rest of the house. I can write for half an hour and get up and bake a batch of scones and go back and write for another hour.

Kate, a full-time doctoral student, and her self-employed husband shared responsibility for their children and the housework. Kate:

> walked the kids to school and then would come back and start work. That was a demarcation to the beginning of the day. That worked really well. And I'd find it really hard, if I didn't walk them to school, to actually get started.

The 'conceived space' of a school day legally mandated the relocation of Kate's children from domestic to public space and her academic work kept time with these school-day rhythms. For Kate this walk was a ritual, a daily 'rite of passage': she left home as (embodied) 'mother' and returned home in the persona of 'intellectual'.

Woolf's (2002) intellectual household was a bastion of Edwardian upper middle class privilege and gender inequality: upstairs was the domain of the intellectual and masculine and downstairs of the manual/embodied and feminine. The sons went 'out' to work. Mediated by public school hours, the rhythms of Kate's day enabled differential appropriations of the 'same' architectural 'place' (various rooms in her family home) as, at different times, domestic and intellectual space. In both stories, households mediate the wider gender relations of their time and place: 'the personal space defined by the self and the intimate spaces of the home are integral elements of social space. These private spaces of the home have a relationship with the public spaces of geography' (Sibley 1995: 71).

While this 'public–private' binary is characteristic of Western society, the 'home and family' affiliations of students from 'other' cultural groups may encompass larger temporal/spatial territories. For example,

> For Māori there are several ways of identifying one's indigenous 'community.' One commonly used way is to introduce yourself by naming the mountain, the river, the tribal ancestor, the tribe and the family. Through this form of introduction you locate yourself in a set of identities which have been framed geographically, politically and genealogically.
>
> Smith 1999: 126

Sometimes 'given' topics (and/or funding) by their tribal authorities, indigenous students may be held accountable to these as well as to academia. The lived spaces of tribe and extended family may superimpose uneasily across the borders between disciplines:

> '[T]he community' is regarded is being a much more intimate, human and self-defined space, in a research sense, to 'the field.' 'Community' conveys a much more intimate, human and self-defined space, whereas 'field' assumes a space 'out there' where people may or may not be present. What community research relies upon and validates is that the community itself makes its own definitions.
>
> Smith 1999: 126

A society is 'a space and an architecture of concepts, forms and laws whose abstract truth is imposed on the reality of the senses, of bodies, of wishes and desires' (Lefebvre 1974: 103). Within universities, everyday life 'is lived directly before it is conceptualised; but the speculative primacy of the conceived over the lived causes "practice" to disappear along with life, and so does very little justice to the "unconscious" level of lived experience per se' (Lefebvre 1974: 34).

Managing time and space

Lefebvre (1974: 40) writes: 'That the lived, the conceived and the perceived realms should be interconnected, so that the "subject", the individual member of a social group may move from one to another without confusion – so much is a logical necessity'. Doctoral students' everyday involvements with the emotive-imaginary, the bureaucratic-abstract and the embodied-habitual dimensions of doctoral study are not seamless. Some of their strategies to address tensions between them will conclude this chapter.

Limiting the thesis to the realm of the 'conceived' (conceptualising it as 'just a quali-fication and not my life's work') can limit its impact at home. Research design might even be influenced by family considerations. Peter chose a quantitative methodology because: 'I was determined for my family's sake to do the thing in three or four years or not at all. It wasn't worth ten years' sacrifice – it had to be done quickly'. Others delayed or spaced having children around thesis timeframes.

The complex structures of twenty-first century postmodern families are reflected in students' parenting arrangements. Shared custody arrangements between households were accommodated through allocating thesis time on a weekly or fortnightly basis according to the presence or absence of children. Maureen's stepdaughter 'came every other weekend. This sometimes was tricky in terms of the space because she was [sleeping] in my study'. Describing her stepdaughter as a 'high achieving' secondary school student, Maureen 'put the computer in the kitchen and we would study together.' Jeanette, a divorcée, shared custody with her ex-husband on a week-about basis:

> [I]n my non child week I worked hard – I had no children, no relationship, no social life and that's how I got it done pretty quickly. So I wasn't trying to juggle everything all the time. Though the week that I had the children I didn't do any PhD work.

Jeanette performed 'mother' and 'student' in alternate weeks.

When writing her final drafts, Jeanette adopted a 'clinical' approach, writing one page per day:

> I knew how long it had to be and I divided it by the number of days I had left. I knew it had to grow by that much a day so I wouldn't go to bed at night until it had! The children understood this and would ask, 'Have you done your page yet Mum?'

If she had been unable to complete her page during daytime hours, Jeanette wrote 'after the children had gone to bed. I was also getting up at 5.00am.' Ring-fencing her thesis in this way made it manageable: 'It was a part of what I was doing. I was passionate about it, but I was equally able to put it aside and treat it like any other task that needed to be done'.

Other theses overflowed the rational borders of the conceived. Lola's 'marriage just about disappeared' because of 'the depth that I was getting into my topic. My partner wasn't interested enough'. Although physically present, such students felt mentally 'absent' from family: 'I was physically there, but my brain wasn't' and 'kids were sick of it'. Margaret, a working class student, 'used to touch the stones of the university and say, "Wow, this is fantastic! I can't believe I'm here!" I felt so lucky and loved the learning so much'. Reversing the erotic/rational split, Margaret chose thesis over marriage: 'My husband said, "You have to make a choice!" And I made it like that! No second thoughts … I didn't want to spend any more time with him'. Conceptualising her thesis as an *oeuvre*, or major creative work, Margaret saw it as a chance to realise wider fantasies and dreams.

Lefebvre (1974: 205) intended 'rhythm analysis' to bring researchers 'closer to a pedagogy of appropriation (the appropriation of the body, as of spatial practice)'. Articulated to the realm of the conceived, doctoral pedagogy involves 'a sustained process whereby somebody(s) acquires new forms or develops existing forms of conduct, knowledge, practice and criteria from somebody(s) or something deemed to be an appropriate provider and evaluator' (Bernstein 2000: 78). Pedagogical practices 'provide for acquirers the principles for the production of what counts as the legitimate text. The legitimate text is any realisation on the part of the acquirer which attracts evaluation' (Bernstein 2000: xiv). The conferral of a doctorate is acknowledgement of the thesis as 'legitimate text' in academe's conceived spaces.

Ruth, a multi-media performance artist, wanted to create a new kind of space – academia's prioritising of the conceived over the lived left her little room for artistic expression as a mode of thesis presentation. Of 'mixed' descent, Ruth had been brought up in a strict church environment and denied knowledge of her Māori cultural heritage. University exposed her first to feminist, and later to kaupapa Māori theory. Ruth's interest in female spirituality conflicted with the version of Christianity espoused by male tribal elders. Her thesis would burst through boundaries within and between academic and tribal traditions:

> There's a lot of young Māori working with new digital media because it's a liberating place to work. When they make tāonga [treasures] or make art work, it's not judged in the way that raranga [traditional weaving] or whakairo [woodcarving] is. It doesn't have those set rules. The elders can't talk to the medium, so you're not going to be hit by what I call the 'Māori art mafia' for what you're doing. So it's

safe in that respect. In respect to the gallery system (which is predominantly Pākeha), they won't talk to the Māori content. So it's kind of a safe place to play ... Māori are using new media to communicate the essence of what is Te Ao Māori, the essence of Māori ... You can have sound, image, moving image, object, space, all these — you can be quite immersive. You can get someone to walk into a room and completely change their environment, take them to another place physically, even.

When 'conceived' spaces of the university (epistemological classifications, departmental divisions, architectural configurations and interpersonal groupings) do not fit the epistemological, spiritual, familial and conceptual resources students need to address, research and write about cutting-edge topics, supervision is stretched over the 'edges' of disciplinary comfort zones. With multiple, cross-departmental supervision arrangements, students' work and disciplinary identities become splintered, fragmented across disparate departments and disciplines with no integration or coherence. Some are marginalised out of the institution, but others draw power from the critical edge, shouting loudly back to the academy from its interstices, critiquing and challenging, creating dynamic and revolutionary works.

Notes

1 In 1998–9 I interviewed 57 of the 183 who had completed a PhD in education in New Zealand. My analysis was published as a monograph (Middleton 2001). Although this is currently out of print, shorter articles discussing aspects of this study include a book chapter (Middleton 2003) and a journal article (Middleton 2007). Dee's story and most of the interview extracts in this paper are taken from this study.

2 The Māori students' stories are extracts from my own interviews carried out as part of a team researching 'The supervision of Māori doctoral students'. The team, based at the University of Auckland's Nga Pae o te Maramtanga consists of Associate Professor Elizabeth McKinley, Dr Barbara Grant and Emeritus Professor Les Williams (Auckland University), Dr Kathie Irwin (Te Puni Kokere, formerly of Te Wananga o Awanui a Rangi) and myself. The project was funded by the New Zealand Ministry of Education's Teaching and Learning Research Initiative (TLRI) Fund.

References

Bachelard, G. (1994) *The poetics of space*. Boston, MA: Beacon Press.

Bernstein, B. (2000) *Pedagogy, symbolic control and identity: Theory, research, critique*. Lanham, MD: Rowman and Littlefield.

Butler, J. (1993) *Bodies that matter*. London: Routledge.

Ferguson, K. and Seddon, T. (2007) Decentred education: Suggestions for framing a socio-spatial agenda, *Critical studies in education*, 48(1): 111–29.

Green, B, Maxwell, T. and Shanahan, P. (Eds) (2001) *Doctoral education and professional practice: The next generation*. Armidale: Kardoorair Press.

Gulson, K. L. and Symes, C. (2007) Knowing one's place: space, theory, education, *Critical studies in education*, 48(1): 97–110.

Harvey, D. (1996) *Justice, nature and the politics of difference*. Oxford: Basil Blackwell.

Henkel, M. (2005) Academic identity and autonomy in a changing policy environment, *Higher education*, 49: 155–76.

Lefebvre, H. (1974) *The production of space*. Oxford: Blackwell.

195

Massey, D. (2004) Geographies of responsibility, *Geografiska Annaler* 86 B (1):5–18.

McKinley, L. (2005) Brown bodies, white coats: Postcolonialism, Maori women and science, *Discourse: Studies in the cultural politics of education*, 26(4): 481–96.

Merleau-Ponty, M. (1962) *Phenomenology of perception*. London: Routledge and Kegan Paul.

Middleton, S. (2001) *Educating researchers: New Zealand Education PhDs 1948–1998*, 'State of the Art' Monograph, No 7. Palmerston North: New Zealand Association for Research in Education.

——(2003) Top of their class? On the subject of 'Education' doctorates. In M. Tambouku and S. Ball (Eds). *Dangerous encounters: Genealogy and ethnography*. London: Peter Lang.

——(2007) The place of theory: Locating the New Zealand 'Education' PhD experience, *British journal of sociology of education*, 28(1): 69–87.

Popkewitz, T and Brennan, M. (1998) Restructuring of social and political theory in education: Foucault and the social epistemology of school practices. In T. Popkewitz and M. Brennan (Eds). *Foucault's challenge: Discourse, knowledge and power in education*. New York: Teachers' College Press, Columbia.

Shields, R. (2004) Henri Lefebvre. In P. Hubbard, R. Kitchin and G. Valentine (Eds). *Key thinkers on space and place*. London: Sage.

Sibley, D. (1995) *Geographies of exclusion*. London: Routledge.

Smith, L. T. (1997) Decolonising intellectual identity: Maori/Woman/Academic. In M. Peters (Ed.). *Cultural politics and the university*. Palmerston North: The Dunmore Press.

——(1999) *Decolonising methodologies: Research and indigenous peoples*. Dunedin, London: Zed Books.

Woolf, V. (2002) *Moments of being: Autobiographical writings*, London: Random House.

16

Global social justice, critical policy and doctoral pedagogical spaces

E. Unterhalter

In 2000, virtually every country in the world adopted the Millennium Development Goals (MDGs) and the Dakar Programme of Action on Education for All (EFA). These outlined a global commitment to ambitious targets for addressing aspects of poverty and injustice, with a particular focus on education. Implementing or expanding the MDGs and EFA programme entails a vision of global social justice that makes particular assumptions about curriculum and approaches to learning and teaching in higher education. If the MDGs and the EFA goals are to be realised, higher education institutions in every country in the world need to produce professionals who can teach in, research and manage national systems for quality education. Furthermore, as the declarations put forward ideas about international collaborations to achieve their goals, they suggest the need for more than just technical skills or understanding of how to implement them, pointing to the importance of investigating and practising new forms of global relationship. How can doctoral pedagogic spaces be utilised to respond to this?

Although the MDGs are more limited in scope than the aspirations expressed in the Universal Declaration of Human Rights of 1948, and lack concern with some key areas of inequality (particularly participation in decision making, gender justice and a wider measure of poverty than income), they were, nonetheless, an attempt to register problems of hunger, lack of health and education as concerns of the whole world, not just of the countries or peoples who suffered these deprivations. This implies that higher education institutions must engage with ideas about global social justice, not just in specialist courses about international relations or development studies, but as part of 'core business' in the formation of graduates and professionals. Although consideration of how to approach this has become an emerging area of scholarship (e.g. Nussbaum 1997; Walker 2006; Banks 2007; Takagi 2009; Unterhalter and Carpentier 2010 forthcoming), less specialist attention has been given to the development of research communities and doctoral pedagogies as a distinctive space for engagement with global justice and public policy.

As global justice itself remains a highly contested terrain (Brock and Brighouse 2005; McGrew and Held 2007), it is clear that there will be no simple formula that can guide the development of doctoral pedagogies to support investigation or practice. Nonetheless, Kenway and Fahey (2008) provide very generative insights regarding the development of an ethical imagination to deal with the challenges of conducting research, given both the complexities of the globalised world and as part of a vision of social justice and change. In discussions with six critical scholars of globalisation, Kenway and Fahey draw out how each has developed a critical policy stance, and 'a defiant research imagination'. Each scholar – Arjun Appadurai, Raewyn Connell, Doreen Massey, Aihwa Ong, Fazal Rivzi, and Saskia Sassen – has a particular position on global justice and public policy engagement. These range from Appadurai's critique of global flows of misery and the maldistribution of hope, to Sassen's stress on the significance of understanding the particulars of locale in order to root different meanings of cosmopolitan. Each also has a personal story about how particular experiences and approaches nurtured the development of a research imagination. Each also reflects on the ways they work with their own doctoral students. Kenway and Fahey note that much current doctoral training, which emphasises the logic of positivist representation, does not produce the conditions to develop the form of research imagination these scholars describe. They stress both the ontological and epistemological ruptures research students might need to be encouraged to risk in order to engage with questions of global justice. These entail generating uncomfortable thoughts, understanding the importance of examining unexamined habits and the significance of striving for complexity (Kenway and Fahey 2008; 2009)

This chapter reflects on the use of a particular doctoral pedagogical space to prompt an examination of professional engagement, public policy dialogue and global justice in education. It considers responses to this initiative highlighting some difficult questions about practice. However, in concluding, I consider what resources my current work in progress on higher education pedagogies, equity, cosmopolitanism, transversal dialogue and global social justice (Unterhalter 2008a; 2008b; 2009a; 2009b; 2010 forthcoming) might add to the insights generated in Kenway and Fahey's (2008) work in order to elaborate some possible shifts in practice to enhance an engagement with doctoral students on the diverse issues entailed by public policy and global justice.

Critical reflection and research imaginations in an international doctoral classroom

In 2003, the course team developing a component of the International Education Doctorate (EdD) at the Institute of Education, University of London, worked on a particular pedagogical approach to enhance critical reflection on the notion of 'the international' that would orient students to some understanding of questions of global justice and critical engagement with public policy on the MDGs and EFA. The education components of the MDGs had set a number of targets to be met by 2015, which include primary education completed by all children and equal numbers of girls and boys in all levels of schooling and higher education (United Nations 2000). These complemented the Dakar Programme of Action on Education for All (EFA), adopted by a very large number of governments in 2000, focusing on free, compulsory, quality schooling, and improvements in adult literacy and early childhood provision (UNESCO 2000). In developing the international education course we wished to alert students to the ways in which existing global and national education policy draws on particular 'rules of the game' and try to elicit deeper understandings of global justice. We thus aimed to develop an approach to teaching research that was not narrowly technical and that encouraged a critical and questioning stance. Our intentions were somewhat similar to the imaginative defiance Kenway and Fahey (2008; 2009) have sketched, although we did not at that date have the vocabulary now provided on this theme.

A computer game *Classroom Challenge* was developed between 2003 and 2005 as the key pedagogic device for this.[1] As all students on the International EdD were encouraged to draw, to some extent, on their professional experience in developing their research approach. We encouraged both consideration of the public policy issues entailed in thinking about global justice and some critical engagement with practice. Part of the assessment task for the course was thus to:

> Develop a strategic reflection on the 'world view' implicit in Classroom Challenge (the Education for All game). Make some concrete suggestions drawing on relevant literature or your professional experience about an alternative way to frame this game.
>
> International EdD 2004: see Crawford and Unterhalter 2004

Students taking the course were thus required to think about an aspect of global justice as portrayed in *Classroom Challenge* and to reflect critically on the rules that shaped the game, the process of playing the game in a doctoral classroom with other research students, and the ways in which the game did or did not connect with their real life experiences.

This pedagogic practice was intended to orient the curriculum towards international concerns and provide a platform for key professionals to articulate ideas relating to global justice and critical policy analysis. Students were invited to problematise both their professional experience and some of the assumptions about truth, error, economic, social and cultural capital expressed in the game. We intended that some of the theoretical resources provided through studying debates relating to comparative education and global justice would allow students to go below the surface in exploring these questions. The boundary between rules and game play was precisely what we wished students to examine in order to deepen understanding of the international and forms of global connection.

Five types of country at different stages or levels of development are identified in the game using measures of human development and education provision drawing on UNDP, UNICEF and UNESCO statistics. All are trying to reach EFA by 2015, but they start from different places and have differential resources in curriculum, teaching, school conditions and learning materials. Some difficulties relate to the situation the government of each country faces in 2005, when the game begins, some result from the success or failure of improvements the players try to effect, some are randomly generated by the changing global economic situation, and others by unforeseen events, represented each turn by a chance card, which brings benefits or drawbacks. (Crawford and Unterhalter 2005: 3). In playing the game, students can make improvements to the education system, but have to consider whether they can pay for these and sustain the reforms. They can also try to reform the process of discussion, decision making, community involvement and commitment to equality, but existing historical conditions constrain or facilitate this. There are various mechanisms for drawing on financial or technical resources from other countries. At the end of the game a log allows them to see how far they have come towards EFA and how they have fared in relation to the other countries playing the game.

Student engagements with *Classroom Challenge*

Students enrolled on the International EdD come from every continent, range in age from early 30s to late 50s and comprise approximately half women and half men. Some have positions of considerable seniority in schools, international organisations, or as freelance consultants, whereas others have had more experience of day-to-day teaching. Earlier work (Unterhalter 2009a) analyses some major themes that emerged in student assignments about the global justice issues raised by *Classroom Challenge*. In summary, three broad approaches are evident. The first concerns the extent to which the game and the process of playing the game as a learning activity does or does not reflect what is written about putting EFA policy into practice or bringing about education change. This theme talks to issues about higher education as a differentiated site of learning from professional practice. It positions a particular boundary for classrooms, learning resources and computer gaming with regard to learning about the real world of global justice and policy applications or their failures. The second theme concerns critical engagements with the epistemology and values of 'playing' a game with such weighty matters and highlights problematic assumptions the game makes, against which the students can establish quite 'comfortable' critiques. The third theme raises problems concerned with a pedagogy of learning about other people's problems and questions whether a simulation game, concerned primarily with resource accumulation, gives sufficient insight into the complexity and discomfort of the narratives required to develop dispositions concerned with global justice among cohorts of doctoral students.

The question of realism

A recurrent theme through much student writing was that the game was realistic It reflected how richer countries, with access to money and skill, could more easily achieve EFA than those 'with the greatest need'. The game thus mirrored the injustices of current global inequalities and the grave consequences of not achieving EFA in the poorest countries. In much student writing the game was deemed realistic in the difficulties it presented in achieving education reforms or in ensuring that changes in education provision translated into improving the prospect for EFA. Many students commented on the frustration of not being able to effect reforms that made good sense. Others highlighted how the technology of the computer game mirrored the process of putting plans into action in organisations. The ways in which the game portrayed global processes for distributing finance, assessing reform or attending to injustice, all of which generally fail to take adequate account of the needs of those in particular countries, struck a chord with many students reflecting their experience of management regimes and professional lives in a range of different contexts.

But for all the students who felt the game was realistic with regard to what they had read about EFA or their own experiences of education reform, there were as many who felt the game was unrealistic. Amongst reasons given were that it failed to model all the complexity of the relations between governments, civil society and international donors. It did not take account of salient factors such as natural disasters, war, dramatic changes in government, the interconnections between health and education, regionalism, differential planning for urban and rural education provision, or the consequences of improved gender equality in school and improving women's lives and gender equality in a society. Some students felt that the rules of the game with regard to the outcome of a particular action did not enhance learning. (In the game the outcome of actions depends on a complex interplay between prevailing context, the levels of participation in decision making and chance). For some students this was too random, and they felt the game should relate more directly to what is known through research about different experiences of putting policy for EFA into practice.

The extent to which the game is or is not like real life or could ever be so, raises issues about the boundaries between education institutions as sites of teaching and learning and professional practice as a site of learning and action. It can be seen that for students who felt the game was realistic and unrealistic what was salient was the ways in which it confirmed or failed to confirm what they had read or experienced. Thus the very process of reflection in an environment that is constructed and not natural seems an important part of doctoral teaching to think about global justice. The boundary between professional practice, policy and study – established through lectures, seminars, reading and the artificiality of the computer game with its attendant commentary – seems to assist consideration of global justice understood in somewhat conventional terms as a set of historical problems for which there are reasonable solutions. The distance offered through the mixture of realism and critical reflection on the rules of the game seems to offer an opportunity to address the differentiation between sites of learning, but it does not seem to go beyond familiar ways students use other learning resources to confirm or expand ideas and experience.

Global justice as a game with rules?

For all the students who appreciated the ways in which the game modelled reality, there were many who were frustrated by the notion of a 'game', and a number of cogent comments were made of the limited ways in which the game represented the process of discussion and dialogue. Written into the rules of *Classroom Challenge* is an assumption that more participation by communities, public discussion and enlarging freedoms will improve the chances of attaining EFA by 2015. This is represented in the game by the political culture modifier. If political culture increases, reforms have a better chance of taking effect. Thus, the game attempts to express, in limited ways, an approach to global justice drawing on the capability approach with its stress on democratic deliberation (Sen 1999; Nussbaum 2000). But a common criticism is that the game fails to give any space for listening to the voices of those engaged with EFA. While the political culture modifier is available as a reward for increasing discussion and participation, there is no space in the gameplay to consult teachers, children, parents, administrators or voters and respond to their concerns outside the narrow parameters set by the rules of the game.

It appears that the catchall action of 'improve political culture' available every turn the game was played does not open up reflection on how this might happen. The very linear ways in which the process of democratic deliberation is portrayed in the game probably obscures the critical dialogical questions. The problems about the complexity of discussions and action across different forms of community with different processes of expressing belonging, explored in analytical and empirical depth in the work of Nira Yuval-Davis (1997; 2006a; 2006b) for example, and a range of writers on democracy, participation and equity in education (McCowan 2009; Zajda *et al.* 2008) provide rich resources for thinking about these issues with doctoral students, which the technology of a computer game as a pedagogic resource somehow pre-empts.

201

A further perennial criticism has been that the game fails to make questions of culture a concern of global justice. In student writing this critique takes a number of forms. One is that the game models only the improvements in relation to culture that are written about through Western scholarship, thus there is an assumption in the 'rules of the game' that local cultures need to collaborate with a national or global culture of education reform and that attaining EFA is a universal goal. A second form of cultural critique is that there is an assumption in the game that the cultures associated with education are superior to the cultures associated with lack of education. Inherent in these critiques is the perception that the game suggests a particular form of global justice that ignores local contexts.

These criticisms are, in a way, at an opposite pole to those commentaries that appreciated the game for its realism, or the space it provides to consider practice. These comments do not point to ways in which the game could be enhanced by adding particular features, but question the very rationale of a game, the assumptions about truth it presents and the ways in which particular experiences are valued above others. In making these comments these students suggest that the online resources provide a position against which students can define themselves, work out their own view of global justice and thus situate themselves more reflectively and critically.

Learning through other people's problems

But whether students take a position of appreciating or questioning the game, the issue remains as to whether this form of resource takes them beyond conventional patterns of learning and discussion. The depth of the global inequalities the course deals with and the complexity of the problems of developing global justice constantly confront the staff with difficulties in how both to depict and organise insight. Making connections to the lives of the poorest people in the world is particularly difficult in a doctoral classroom where virtually all students and staff associate largely with elites, and have very little knowledge of poverty and lack of education. We all, despite our professional positions, have only fragmentary insight into the range of political and economic practices associated with enacting global justice.

Commenting on playing the game many students echoed my observations as a teacher of the significance of the 'dynamic' discussions between classmates. But a number highlighted that the procedures of the game were 'mechanical' in that you take an action and it has a consequence, for which there is a rationale (even though some of this is random). Some suggested the need to introduce a more flexible approach to rule making, as is now possible given new virtual worlds in gaming. Others wondered about different modes of interaction, not just with the countries playing the game and fellow classmates. However, over and above developing potential for new internet interactivity, there is a problem about the 'flatness' of the human relationships presented. Some students suggested the need to help players build 'emotional involvement' through knowledge of 'the human factor in the country they are assigned to' in order to develop 'more hope and optimism than is currently possible'. A number commented that improvements should provide ongoing access to relevant information as each turn of the game progressed, or the chance to research different approaches to reform between turns.

It can be seen that the position of professional with access to information, reflection from experience, clearly delimited terms of reference for actions, and awareness of enlarging professional insight are seen by students as very important prerequisites for acting effectively in support of EFA and global justice. The imaginative repertoire they use does not use tropes inflected by sensibility of the shame of lack of education, the pains of hunger or illness, or outrage at the inequalities of global maldistribution. In this they confirm Kenway and Fahey's assertion that a defiant research imagination, which invites radical ruptures with present ways of understanding globalisation is not being produced by much current doctoral training (Kenway and Fahey 2008). Indeed, it could be that *Classroom Challenge* fails to prompt enough questioning of comfortable professional identities and their consequence for a revisioned global justice.

On the one hand one can argue that this is a drawback of the learning associated with *Classroom Challenge*. It does not give students access to the real life consequences of failing to provide EFA by 2015. It provides understanding only within already well-established rules of professional practice, and to the extent that students become emotionally involved with game play, it is with their own experiences as players not with the experiences of teachers, managers, parents or students in the countries struggling to achieve EFA.

On the other hand one must pose the question whether the sensibilities cultivated by narratives of hardship or the depth and complexity of social situation will improve professional engagement. The critics of globalisation interviewed by Kenway and Fahey (2008), spoke of their pedagogic practice with doctoral students as encouraging uncomfortable thought, examining unexamined habits and striving for complexity. Members of the course team on *International Education* would probably concur that they share these aspirations. But the very rule-bound environment of the computer game appears too restrictive a format to cultivate some of the human engagements required by the challenges of global social justice. Identifying games of truth and error through the course assignment thus elicits complex and considered writing, but may not be a profound enough learning experience to build deep commitments with regard to global justice.

Conclusion

This chapter has outlined how doctoral students engaged with the pedagogical space provided by the International Education course in the International EdD to position themselves in relation to questions of global justice and changing public policy. Their responses range from diligent use of the boundary between educational space and 'real world' practice, to critical commentaries on assumptions of reflection and distance. However, the step of 'avoiding unreflexive worldliness' (Kenway and Fahey 2008) was one it was difficult for students to take.

It thus appears that a very significant challenge in developing doctoral pedagogic spaces for engagements with questions of global justice and public policy reform requires what I have called elsewhere pedagogies of construction and connection (Unterhalter 2010). These draw on ideas about what I have termed equity from below, and listening to often excluded voices, and equity from the middle, that is making assessments and evaluations about particular actions or forms of information in the light of the social relationships of knowledge production and use. These pedagogies are likely to be more tolerant of aspects of positivism than Kenway and Fahey (2008) believe is justified. They acknowledge the importance of quantitative work as well as critical examination in addressing poverty or gender inequality as matters of global justice and policy reform. Nonetheless, consciously deploying pedagogic repertoires that draw on these approaches with doctoral students might allow them to move beyond established professional identities and take the difficult questions of global justice and public policy not as their teachers' but as their own.

Notes

1 For a more detailed description of the computer game and student response see Unterhalter 2009a.

References

Banks, J. (Ed.) (2007) *Diversity and Citizenship Education: Global Perspectives*. San Francisco: Jossey-Bass.

Brock, G. and Brighouse, H. (2005) *The Political Philosophy of Cosmopolitanism*. Cambridge: Cambridge University Press.

Crawford, J. and Unterhalter, E. (2005) *Classroom Challenge: The Education for All Game*. London: Institute of Education, University of London.

——(2004) *International Education. Course Handbook*. London: Institute of Education, University of London.

Kenway, J. and Fahey, J. (Eds) (2008) *Globalizing the research imagination*. London: Routledge.

——(2009) A Transgressive Global Research Imagination, *Thesis Eleven*, 96(1): 109–27.

McCowan, T. (2009) *Rethinking Citizenship Education: a Curriculum for Participatory Democracy*. London: Continuum.

McGrew, A. and Held, D. (2007) *Globalization theory: Approaches & controversies*. Cambridge: Polity.

Nussbaum, M. (1997) *Cultivating Humanity: A Classical Defense of Reform in Liberal Education*. Cambridge, MA: Harvard University Press.

——(2000) *Women and Human Development: The Capabilities Approach*. Cambridge: Cambridge University Press.

Sen, A. (1999) *Development as freedom*. Oxford: Oxford University Press.

Takagi, H. (2009) Internationalization of undergraduate curricula: The gap between ideas and practice in Japan, *London Review of Education*, 7(1): 31–9.

UNESCO (2000) *The Dakar framework for action*. Paris: UNESCO.

United Nations (2000) *Millennium Declaration*. New York: United Nations.

Unterhalter, E. (2008a) Cosmopolitanism, global social justice and gender equality in education, *Compare*, 38(5): 539–54.

——(2008b) *Considering equality and equity in higher education pedagogies*. Paper prepared for Colloquium on Higher Education Pedagogies, University of Nottingham, May.

——(2009a) Global justice or other people's problems? Computer gaming and critical reflection in an international classroom, *London Review of Education*, 7(1): 41–53.

——(2009b) Translations and transversal dialogues: an examination of mobilities associated with gender, education and global poverty reduction, *Comparative Education*, 45(3): 329–45.

——(2010) Equality and equity in higher education pedagogies in the context of globalization. In E. Unterhalter and V. Carpentier (Eds). *Whose interests are you serving? Global inequalities and higher education*. London: Palgrave Macmillan.

Unterhalter, E and Carpentier, V. (Eds) (2010) *Whose interests are you serving? Global inequalities and higher education*. London: Palgrave Macmillan.

Walker, M. (2006) *Higher education pedagogies*. Maidenhead: Open University Press.

Yuval-Davis, N. (1997) *Gender and Nation*. London: Sage.

——(2006a) Human/Women's rights and feminist transversal politics. In M. M. Ferree and A. M. Tripp (Eds). *Global Feminisms: transnational Women's Activism, organizing and Human Rights*. New York: New York University Press.

——(2006b) Intersectionality and feminist politics, *European Journal of Women's Studies*, 13(3):193–209.

Zajda, J, Davies, L. and Majhanovich, S. (Eds) (2008) Comparative and Global Pedagogies: Equity, Access and Democracy in Education (Vol. 2) of the Series *Globalization, Comparative Education and Policy Research*. Dordrecht: Springer.

17

Coming to terms with research practice

Riding the emotional rollercoaster of doctoral research studies

A. Morrison-Saunders, S. A. Moore, M. Hughes and D. Newsome

Emotions are an integral part of the doctoral process. A range of emotions are common and to be expected. How do emotions affect the doctoral process for doctoral both students and their supervisors? And how can they be made to work positively for all concerned? This chapter explores the role that emotions play in the doctoral process and how students can benefit from reflecting on this issue. The role of emotions at the beginning, middle and end of a doctoral programme is explored along with some of the emotions that arise from the supervisor/doctoral student relationship.

Introduction

The academic demands and rigours in carrying out doctorate research are clear, or they will become so as doctoral students grapple with the challenge of 'making an original contribution to knowledge'. But what about the emotional ups and downs and challenges that a doctorate programme of study also poses? It is exciting to embark on research programmes that will result in one of the highest academic qualifications obtainable with the eventual prospect of being able to add the 'Dr' prefix to one's name (or the suffix 'PhD' as some customs have it). This is a typical emotional starting point for many, if not all, doctoral candidates. But candidates can also expect to experience many other emotions directly related to undertaking doctoral research.

This chapter discusses the emotional rollercoaster ride that students are likely to experience during their doctoral research. The aim is to focus on the nature and role that emotions play in the doctoral process, and to develop strategies and approaches that can be used to help manage these emotions with the aim of helping students work more successfully towards their goals. Extensive guidance exists on strategies for conducting doctoral study that are usually outcome–oriented; in this study by focusing on 'emotions' we are most concerned with the personal response to doctoral undertakings rather than the research undertakings themselves.

This chapter has its origins in a workshop that the authors (and several others) initiated in 2002. The workshop was designed by three academic staff who had completed their PhDs within the previous six years, along with three doctoral candidates whom they were supervising. The students were at various stages in their research, with one in the first year of study, one in the third year and the other within weeks of submitting a thesis for examination. The six participants had varied backgrounds with ages at PhD commencement ranging from 25 to 42, and three males and three females. The PhD topics covered a broad range of disciplines within the environmental science field (including soil science, environmental management of industry, policy analysis, tourism and surveys of visitors to national parks and analysis of their behaviour). All six, however, recognised similarities in their emotional experiences associated with their doctoral studies.

Preparation for this first workshop involved the six 'facilitators' collectively developing and then responding to three self-reflective questions. These were:

1. How would you graph your emotions over the duration of your PhD?
2. What emotions did you experience during your data collection and fieldwork activities? How did you manage/not manage them? How could you have made your emotions work better for you in your data gathering/fieldwork?
3. How did you manage your emotions? Could you have managed them better in hindsight? Who helped you in this management? Who/what could have helped you?

The responses were collated and used to consolidate similarities and discuss solutions and strategies for management of emotions. The workshop included activities, in which participants reflect on the role of emotions in their own doctoral studies, interspersed with presentations in which the facilitators shared their experiences.

This first workshop was well received, and a series of participative workshops with doctoral students and academics followed. At these workshops at least three of the facilitators shared accounts of their personal emotional journey through their doctorate studies and then invited participants to reflect on and share their experiences. It became very apparent from the workshops that doctorate students from all manner of disciplines shared or had similar emotional experiences. A common emotional trajectory with respect to various stages in research programmes began to emerge. These workshops have been run at the Australian Association for Social Research annual conference (Moore *et al.* 2002), the Murdoch University Doctoral Forum (in 2002, 2004 and 2005), the Murdoch University Environmental Science Doctoral Forum (in 2004), Teaching and Learning Forum[1] (in 2003 and 2005; Morrison-Saunders *et al.* 2005) and Council for Australian University Tourism and Hospitality Education conference (Hughes 2009).

This chapter presents the collective findings of the personal reflections of the authors, their learning from the workshops and a literature review. The literature review revealed that although little exists explicitly on the topic of emotions in doctoral research, related material suggests this is an important aspect for achieving success and developing a confident researcher identity. Following a review of literature, presented as 'lessons learned', this chapter explores the emotions associated with the beginning, middle and end of the doctoral studies. The chapter concludes with a suite of approaches for managing emotions that doctoral candidates might personally apply and benefit from during their studies.

Lessons from the literature

The importance of the role of the supervisor, and the student–supervisor relationship has been frequently identified as a key issue in the success of the doctoral process (Cullen *et al.*

1994; Cryer 1997; Graves 1997), and clearly this relationship may have an important emotional dimension to it. Acknowledging some of the psychological and emotional aspects that may be encountered in the doctoral process, such as enthusiasm, isolation, boredom, frustration, anxiety and euphoria, Phillips and Pugh (1994) proposed that part of the supervisor–student relationship should incorporate a helpful psychological 'contract'. Graves (1997) suggested that students should share any worries about their research or other factors that might affect it with their supervisor(s), and Cryer (1997) made a case for supervisors to have some involvement in their students' personal problems. However, he suggested setting limits on time and emotional energy spent, with an awareness of when students should be directed to further professional help.

Denicolo and Pope (1994) noted the solitary but challenging and rewarding nature of doctoral research work, its pressures and conflicts with simultaneous roles the student maintains with associated feelings such as guilt and anger that may arise. They suggested the need for supervisor involvement in addressing such personal issues and concerns throughout their students' candidature. Emotions experienced in the doctoral process may relate to student success with respect to completion rates. For example, West *et al.* (1988) noted maintenance of motivation and enthusiasm rated as one of the greatest problems encountered with the doctoral process in a survey of 26 PhD graduates from Monash University, Australia. In contrast to this Rudd (1985) reported issues such as boredom, disenchantment, laziness and 'work ethic' were considered factors in failure or delays in completion of the PhD in only a small minority of cases.

Some important consideration of the role of emotion in the doctoral process can be found in work on a number of sub-types of anxiety. This includes library and statistics anxiety; the feelings of intimidation, discomfort and/or fear students describe when starting an information search that requires using an academic library or use of statistical methods to analyse datasets. Library anxiety has been recognised in undergraduate and postgraduate students (e.g. Onwuegbuzie and Jiao 1998; Jerabek *et al.* 2001). In some cases it may be debilitating to the extent it becomes difficult to write research proposals, a potential stumbling block for continuation of research study (Onwuegbuzie 1997). Some of the research suggests library anxiety may be related to the learning mode preferences of individual students (Onwuegbuzie and Jiao 1998; Jiao and Onwuegbuzie 1999). It also seems to occur at higher levels for students who perceive that they have to keep up with particular standards or expectations of others (Jiao and Onwuegbuzie 1998). Students who perceive that they have lower levels of scholastic competence, intellectual ability and creativity also tend to have high levels of statistics anxiety (Onwuegbuzie 2000). Much of this work, however, is focused on the characteristics of the learner, rather than on ways of managing emotions.

For a better understanding of the potential role of emotions in the doctoral process, some idea of how the emotions will affect or impact on the student's ability to progress with their research would be useful. The small number of studies into the role of emotions and doctoral students is reflected in understandings of emotions in education more generally. Few studies of the role of emotions on learning, other than of test anxiety and attribution theory, were undertaken prior to the 1990s (Pekrun *et al.* 2002). Although test anxiety has long been recognised as being inversely related to performance in certain conditions (Hembree 1988), it is of little relevance to the doctoral situation. Pekrun *et al.* (2002) demonstrated the important but complex roles of both positive (e.g. enjoyment, hope, pride, relief) and negative emotions (e.g. anger, anxiety, hopelessness, shame and boredom) on motivation and learning in school and undergraduate university students.

The emotions related in significant ways to motivation, effort, learning strategy use, self-regulation and academic achievement. The positive emotions, with the exception of relief, were correlated with higher achievement and the negative with lower achievement. Negative emotions were elevated in students who dropped out of their studies compared with those who completed, although the direction of causality could not be implied in the results (Pekrun *et al.* 2002).

Reactions to emotions are often complex and individual. Shame reactions to perceived failure in undergraduate students who did not achieve the result they wanted were found to result in increased motivation and effort in some students, but equal or reduced performance in others (Turner *et al.* 2002). Individual factors relating to esteem, self-efficacy, and goal-related processes seem to account for differences in individual responses. Individual responses to emotions were also noted by Pekrun *et al.* (2002). For example, some individuals were positively motivated by anxiety whereas others were negatively motivated. Goals seem to have an important role in emotional responses and emotional regulation as they provide direction, comparison points (e.g. 'Where am I in relation to my goal?') and the need to make judgements about goals within the context of other, perhaps conflicting goals, with the result that emotional responses develop (Schutz and Davis 2000).

Doctoral students, as a cohort, are likely to have different characteristics when compared to school or undergraduate students. They have a proven record of academic achievement and could be expected to have more positive views of self-efficacy, be better motivated, and are perhaps also more likely to have self-regulatory strategies, learning strategies and strong study skills, compared with cohorts of school or undergraduate students. The links between emotions, goals and motivation described in these recent studies, are likely to be of relevance to the doctoral cohort where motivation and its maintenance are recognised as an issue (West *et al.* 1988).

Emotions experienced during the doctoral process

A PhD is a very individual process; a finding that was repeatedly reiterated in the workshops and which evokes a variety of emotional responses. As a doctoral candidate is required to make an original contribution to knowledge, this necessitates the candidate conducting a new or unique study of some kind. This virtually ensures that they work largely independently in an individual manner. However, the responses at these workshops suggested that the emotional states experienced by any individual doctoral candidate are likely to have common themes with those of other doctoral students. During the various occasions that these workshops were presented to doctoral students, many of the participants empathised with the facilitators' experiences and shared similar accounts. The overwhelming feeling in the room was always one of great relief that other doctoral students have experienced similar emotional reactions to the doctoral process: that despite the individuality of a doctoral study, there are common shared experiences and feelings.

Emotions recorded during the doctoral process included: anxiety, boredom, excitement, fear, frustration, elation, satisfaction, loneliness and even what some described as 'slight insanity'. Over the period of candidature each student typically experiences a plethora of emotions with swings from negative to positive and back at varied time scales, described by one participant as an 'emotional rollercoaster'. More than one emotion could be experienced simultaneously. It was clear that these highs and lows are a normal part of the doctoral process. The rollercoaster can be usefully considered as having early, middle and end phases.

Early phase

Both positive and negative emotional states are evoked at the beginning of the PhD; however, positive emotions (including elation and enthusiasm) seem to dominate initially. Initial elation was related to factors such as being accepted as a doctoral candidate, or being awarded a scholarship to undertake PhD studies. Enthusiasm was linked to the challenge and anticipation of undertaking the research in an area that the candidate was interested in and considered relevant and important. Older doctoral candidates, returning to studies following many years (sometimes decades) in the workforce, reported feelings of excitement but at the same time were daunted by fears of returning to study. These fears appeared to be exacerbated when surrounded by younger (and more confident) colleagues and by information and technology-related issues (e.g. the sheer volume of literature and information technology skills necessary to access it). One particular 'mature' age student returning to study after a number of years in the workforce made the realisation during one workshop that it would be helpful to find a mentor (not necessarily from their discipline area) to help them adapt to and progress through the doctoral process.

Most of the negative emotions recorded in the early phase related to the initial major challenges of the project. Bewilderment and confusion were associated with:

- Deciding where to start, especially in tackling the body of literature that needed to be understood and reflected upon
- Focusing on a research area that would be manageable
- Focusing on a project that would make a valuable contribution to the field
- Ensuring that the research will be sufficiently original to fulfil the requirements of a doctorate; and
- Determining an approach for the project.

Anxiety could also be recorded in relation to these issues, and the additional concern of establishing a positive working relationship with the supervisor(s).

Although negative emotions were evident in this early phase of the PhD, they are not necessarily problematic at this stage. Emotions can interact in quite complex ways with motivation, goals and performance. According to a cognitive-motivational model (Pekrun *et al.* 2002), positive and negative emotions may additionally be viewed as activating or deactivating based on their effects on motivation and performance. Based on the authors' self-reflections and the views presented at the workshops, these negative emotions described in this early phase are more likely to be activating than deactivating, being viewed as part of the challenge. At this stage most doctoral students describe a high level of motivation for the task ahead, and are looking forward to 'getting their teeth into the project'.

Middle phase

Negative emotions were more prominent in the middle phase of doctoral programmes than in the early phase. Emotions include frustration, boredom, guilt and loneliness/

isolation. A large part of the work in this middle stage revolved around data collection including fieldwork activities. These are discussed in more detail later in this section. The negative emotions in this stage were often associated with the realisation of the size of the project and the amount of time and effort required (e.g. by comparison, earlier undergraduate experiences are of much shorter timescale). By this stage a doctoral student may have experienced a number of issues such as:

- Encountering a research dead end, or the need to change direction with some aspect of the project
- Things not always working out as planned
- Things taking longer than planned; or
- Administrative requirements, such as budgets, progress reports or ethics approvals, causing slowing or stalling.

These issues were associated with feelings of frustration.

The repetitive nature of ongoing literature searches, or writing and rewriting drafts (for some participants) also gave rise to frustration, and even boredom. By this time a doctoral student has been working for some time, as an individual, on a large and challenging project. Feelings of isolation and loneliness were more likely to be recorded now than in the initial stages. The most common result described for this stage then seemed to occur, this was a slump in enthusiasm and associated motivation. Feelings of boredom, often about half way through the doctoral programme, along with isolation, associated with dampened enthusiasm and output have been noted elsewhere (Phillips and Pugh 1994).

Another cause of negative emotions related to employment – many doctoral students undertake some casual teaching, or engage in some other employment for all or part of their candidature. These activities can be very distracting and time-consuming, especially as work engagements have strict deadlines whereas doctoral activities could be viewed as having no real deadline. A result is that doctoral activities frequently get relegated to second place (albeit temporarily), leading to feelings of guilt and frustration.

Because of the intensity and diversity of emotions associated with data collection, more detailed comments are provided here. Gathering data is a core activity in many doctoral programmes, whether it is via laboratory, field or archival research. This is a major activity in terms of time and effort, and is associated with both positive and negative emotions. The main positive emotion is excitement, and this seems to relate to a number of underlying factors:

- The initial thrill of being able to apply the theoretical ideas in a practical situation
- A sense of progress in actually getting real data after the time spent planning and designing the project
- As the data collection progressed there was satisfaction that a body of data was accumulating, or if patterns began to show in the data that supported the initial ideas; and
- The excitement and joy of simply being 'in the field', as enjoyment of a particular environment or activity may have been one of the initial reasons for choosing the topic for doctoral study.

The excitement noted in relation to data collection is typically tempered by a number of negative emotions: notably fear, frustration, and to some extent loneliness. Fear appears to have been related to two underlying factors – fear of the unknown, and beliefs regarding one's own self-efficacy. All of the facilitators of the initial workshop (and this includes the authors of this chapter) experienced some degree of fear prior to and during initial trips. This fear of the unknown could relate to the remoteness of the field area, being in a strange new place, concerns about a lack of success, or an inability to gain access to experts or information. Belief in one's self-efficacy became critical if data collection relied on interviewing experts or members of the public. Interviewing experts was associated with fears that they might not approve of the research, whereas for members of the public there were concerns related to cultural differences (e.g. how to communicate effectively with Japanese tourists visiting a national park). Participants in the workshops engaged in other types of research reported similar fears, although the research settings and particulars were different.

Frustrations with data collection fall into two areas. The first concerns the need to collect large amounts of data within a tight time schedule. Students in workshops reported feeling rushed, things not going as planned, and forgetting important equipment. One of the workshop participants experienced significant frustration and self-directed anger after setting off on a major field expedition only to discover when they got there (a whole day's driving later) that they had left vital equipment back at the university and had to return and start all over again. Frustration was also associated with the fatigue of the demanding (emotionally or physically) and repetitive business of data collection. The second area of frustration concerns participants who were involved in large-scale surveys and had enlisted the help of volunteers for data collection. If some volunteers were not collecting data according to the instructions then the data would potentially be flawed, giving rise to frustrations.

A number of the participants noted loneliness during the data collection stage of their PhD. This was a particular issue for those working in remote settings, or at least away from home. In these circumstances the issue was most serious 'after hours' when there was no one to socialise with. A science student on fieldwork in remote locations working very long hours alone (having had the frustration of not being able to attract volunteers to accompany him) reported that he found himself feeling slightly 'crazy' and deprived of human company.

Negative emotions seem to be common and prominent during the middle phase of the doctoral process. Whereas the negative motions in the early phase are not necessarily problematic, they may pose more significant dangers in this middle phase. The feelings of frustration and boredom, and the underlying issues such as the repetitive nature of the work and realisation of the size of the project, have the potential to become deactivating in their effects on motivation and performance. During this phase, a slump in productivity and procrastination over doctoral tasks is a real possibility. Managing negative emotions during this phase, including data collection, appears essential for maintaining motivation, avoiding a slump in productivity, and ensuring progress towards long-term goals. It may even be important for more fundamental reasons concerning health and well being. For example, a psychology student workshop participant, who was preparing to collect data that would involve observations of and interviews with victims of domestic violence, realised that she would need to take care to 'look after herself' emotionally during this demanding process. Up until that point, she had only given consideration to the practical design and academic content aspects of her research.

It is also vitally important to acknowledge the positive emotions associated with this data collection phase. These can potentially counter the deactivating effects of some of the negative emotions. A key example here is the excitement of building a body of data as a progress marker towards the ultimate goal of achieving the doctorate, and is one factor that is likely to have an activating effect on performance and motivation.

End phase

The end stage of doctoral studies is also characterised by a mix of strongly felt negative and positive emotions. Negative emotions include fear, frustration, anxiety, boredom, and panic; whereas positive emotions include elation and satisfaction. This stage for most doctoral candidates comprises mainly data analysis and writing up (although due to the nature of individual projects, some candidates have advanced drafts of parts of their thesis by this stage).

During the writing up phase most candidates seem to experience satisfaction and elation when final drafts of thesis chapters and eventually, the entire thesis, are completed. But on the way to achieving this some also experience strong negative emotions (frustration and boredom) associated with the need to think and write about the project constantly. Fear of failure is common. Often this is based on concerns that the research will not contribute anything new to the candidate's particular field or specialty. This emphasises the need for supervisors to ensure their students clearly understand the different ways in which it is possible to make an original contribution (Phillips 1994).

Anxiety arose in relation to a number of issues, for example, whether the work really justifies the conclusions made. Anxiety can also emerge if students feel their work contradicts expert opinion in their field. Making such assertions requires considerable confidence. This was particularly an issue if candidates were questioning the established views of experts likely to examine their thesis. Although not common practice in Australian universities, the requirement to mount a thesis defence is an obvious source of anxiety for doctoral students in the final stages of their programmes.

Frustrations were often reported with respect to the relationship and tensions between the student and the supervisor. Usually these related to the usefulness of guidance provided by the supervisor, and aspects of feedback on thesis drafts. Problems were noted where the supervisor was not able to discuss issues in the thesis at the depth required by the candidate because they were not sufficiently close to the research area themselves, or where they requested the inclusion of additional material (e.g. data analysis or literature reviews) or changed their mind about how to approach a particular problem. Frustrations also arose when students had to wait, for what they considered unreasonable periods, for supervisors to provide feedback and guidance on thesis drafts.

For those candidates who have been the recipient of a scholarship, the end of funding could be associated with feelings of panic. Although this might be expected to have a negative and debilitating effect on motivation, the opposite, a strong motivation to finish, was apparent. Although some of the negative emotions (e.g. boredom) characterising this phase are potentially deactivating in their effects on motivation to complete the doctorate, they may to a large part be countered by the mix of other positive, and negative but motivationally activating, emotions. At this stage the long-term goal of the PhD is closer, which in itself can be highly motivating. Some students do, however, falter at this stage, and it is not unknown for students to withdraw their candidature even in this final phase of their research programme. The support of an understanding and helpful supervisor can be critical.

In most Australian universities, the doctoral thesis is submitted for examination by independent and external reviewers; a process that typically takes months (it is akin to the peer-review process utilised by academic journals). Submission of the thesis was generally described by workshop participants as anti-climactic rather than celebratory, as it is surrounded by the completion of many mundane and administrative tasks. The situation is surely much different when a thesis defence takes place. Feelings of relief, pride and elation at completing the task were also reported.

In some respects it is completion of the thesis that stands as the single most significant outcome accomplishment. Thereafter comes a period of restlessness, and for some a deep anxiety while awaiting the outcome of the examination process. It is as though the candidate is trapped in limbo. All doctoral research activity has ceased abruptly after three or more years of continuous focus and life is meant to somehow return to 'normal', but meanwhile the outcome is unknown. There is little candidates can do to manage this situation other than to be aware of it in advance.

An ongoing issue throughout the doctoral process emphasised by both the workshop facilitators and participants concerns the difficulty of trying to explain to friends, family and colleagues what the chosen doctoral studies were about. Also in some cultures, such as Australia, the value of academic pursuits may be under appreciated so the societal benefits of doctoral research may not be acknowledged or supported by friends and families. The important challenge for all doctoral students (and indeed all researchers) is to learn how to talk about their research in ways that engage all that they come into contact with.

Strategies for managing emotions

The doctoral process is clearly associated with varied and changing emotional states. The positive emotions described previously are not likely to cause problems on the way to achieving a PhD as the main goal. Negative emotions are potentially a danger, but are not always a problem. In some circumstances they can result in an increase in motivation. However, students need to be aware of those negative emotions that deactivate from the task and long-term goal of the PhD.

Many of the following strategies are suggested for doctoral students. Some, however, require inputs from peers, the supervisor or other individuals. The supervisor has an undeniably important role in the management of the student's emotional responses (particularly as some of the emotional responses will be related to aspects of the working relationship that is developed). And it is essential that supervisors as well as students are able to recognise and deal with the emotional aspects of the doctoral process.

The following strategies are suggested for doctoral students:

- Participate in forums and discussion groups with peers. These may also involve the supervisor(s). Sharing experiences and ideas is beneficial both emotionally and intellectually. It helps to break down feelings of isolation as shared experiences allow a student to realise that their experiences are a normal part of the doctoral process. The value of self-reflection and discussion groups/forums has been noted elsewhere. Burnett (1999) described the advantages of a meeting as a collaborative cohort for students who were at the 'all but dissertation' status in the coursework/research doctoral studies. These included reduced isolation for some students, a greater likelihood of completion, and skill and knowledge acquisition especially for writing and editing. The benefits to doctoral students of self-help and peer-support groups (Phillips and Pugh 1994) and supervisory groups (Elphinstone and Schweitzer 1998) have also been recognised.

- Talk to experts from the research area and, if it is appropriate within the structure of the project, publish journal papers during candidature (this may not always be possible or desirable). Both will help to reaffirm that what a student is doing is important and interesting, which should help with motivation. They are also a good source of feedback on the direction and progress of the research.

- Avoid working (exclusively) at home. Feelings of isolation may be reinforced if a student works at home most of the time. On the other hand, having to share offices with other doctoral students at a university seems to be the norm, and these environments can be noisy and distracting, reducing students' capacities to be productive. Working at home then becomes more attractive. If this is the case, be aware of isolation issues; if they emerge take measures to counter them.

- Construct a timetable for major activities and milestones, including both academic tasks and administrative requirements such as progress reports. A timetable helps to provide motivation and a sense of direction. It also allows progress towards the long-term goal of the doctoral programme to be measured. The timetable should be realistic, and a student should be encouraged to keep to it, perhaps rewarding themselves if they do.

- Carefully plan and organise data collection and fieldwork trips well in advance. This way at least some of the potential frustrations can be avoided. (For example, plan budgets, arrange vehicles, food and clothing, make equipment lists and check each item off as it is packed, and ensure that all equipment is working properly).

- Be prepared for possible frustrations when methods are trialled. Initial methods or techniques may need to be modified to make them more effective or efficient.

- Take breaks and holidays. It is important to make time for breaks from the PhD, so include them in the timetable. Holidays allow for relaxation and rejuvenation. A break from 'the grind' and standing back a little from the project may have the additional benefit of producing new ideas or inspirations. If the routine has led to feelings of boredom, or there is a tendency to procrastinate over the PhD (as one of our participants noted 'cleaning the fridge, garden, office, etc. is much more appealing than writing') then set aside a specific time to do something different or rejuvenating, before returning to the more 'mundane'. Rudd (1985) commented that some students work too hard and 'might have been more successful if they had eased up a little'.

- Socialise while in the field or on data collection trips. This may be achieved by living in shared accommodation, through contacts with local staff or organisations associated with your research, or even visiting a local pub occasionally. Having a friend or relative along can really help, especially if they are able to assist with the research as well. Avoid taking along anyone who is likely to be a distraction from your work, for example if they are likely to become bored waiting around whilst you engage in data collection activities and put pressure on you to hurry up or stop work altogether.

- If the field trips are lengthy, timetable some time off to do something not related to the research. As with taking holidays during a PhD, it is important to relax and rejuvenate.

- Choose examiners[2] that the student judges may be supportive or accepting of their thesis findings and approaches.

215

- Be ready to adjust the explanation of what the doctoral project is about according to the audience. It is useful to have a simple explanation as well as a more detailed answer. The simplification of concepts and emphasising practical benefits of the project can be helpful; for example, describing it as a regular job avoids embarrassing or uncomfortable situations and can overcome the tendency to be labelled as being in an 'ivory tower' or a 'boffin' or other similar derisory comment.

A critical precursor to the implementation of any coping strategy is an awareness that emotional highs and lows are a normal aspect of the doctoral process. Thus, it is critical that both doctoral students and supervisors are aware of the issues surrounding these emotions. Overall, there is a need for open communication about emotions. A student needs to be honest with their supervisor about their feelings and their progress. The supervisor needs to be able to provide guidance, encouragement and strategies. Emotions also need to be seen as a way of acknowledging the many different challenges of the doctoral process (O'Leary 2001).

Supervisors also need to be aware of how their own actions and interactions can in fact be a part of the 'problem' or solution – students may wish to explicitly address such matters in discussions with their supervisors. Issues surrounding communication, academic pressures and supervisor availability may translate into emotional responses in students. Grant and Graham (1999) stressed the important role of supervision and its quality, and considered it vital that students have an active role in the supervision process, despite the marked power differences. Furthermore, the supervisor needs to fulfil their academic responsibilities appropriately, for example by providing feedback and guidance on thesis drafts within an acceptable time. Maintaining clear communication is also vital, a point stressed by Phillips (1994) with the caution that misunderstandings are very common.

Negative emotions may remain, despite the use of many management strategies. Self-reflection on the causes of these emotions may help the individual to deal with them. As Parsons (2001) comments, finding one's own strategies to deal with feelings is positive, and a good training for the professional life that would follow a doctorate.

Conclusions

This chapter has drawn on a novel approach to understanding the emotions associated with the PhD process by using self-reflection by a group of six academics combined with learning from a subsequent series of workshops run over almost half a decade. Collectively, these activities have documented the emotional rollercoaster of doctoral research studies. Emotional swings are experienced by all candidates. Even those for whom the doctoral process is overall a very positive experience, some negative emotions are encountered. This chapter addresses the three phases of research and associated emotions and what form these emotions are likely to take. Negative emotions are most likely in the middle phase and are often associated with data collection. Recommendations for managing these emotions include encouraging students in their self-management as well as 'managing' those around them. There appear to be great benefits to doctoral students in becoming aware of their own emotions and the particular role of these in their own doctoral research programmes. Self-reflection is critical.

Acknowledgements

An earlier version of this chapter (aligned towards doctoral supervisors) was published as Morrison-Saunders *et al.* (2005). Thanks to Jane Newsome, Amanda Smith and Kate Rodger for their input.

Notes

1 The Teaching and Learning Forum is a series of conferences initiated in 1992, held annually in Perth, Australia, by the five Western Australian universities making up the TL Forum partners (see otl.curtin.edu.au/tlf/tlf-pubs.html).
2 In Australia, the doctoral candidate is often asked to nominate a list of potential examiners from which the supervisor or a university committee makes the final selection.

References

Burnett, P. C. (1999) The supervision of doctoral dissertations using a collaborative cohort model, *Counsellor Education and Supervision*, 39(1): 46–52.
Cullen, D. J., Pearson, M., Saha, L. J. and Spear, R. H. (1994) *Establishing Effective PhD Supervision*. Canberra: Australian Government Publishing Service.
Cryer, P. (1997) Handling common dilemmas in supervision. Issues in Doctoral Supervision, *Teaching and Management*, No. 2, London, UK: The Society for Research into Higher Education & The Times Educational Supplement.
Denicolo, P. and Pope, M. (1994) The doctoral's journey. In O. Zuber-Skerritt and Y. Ryan (Eds). *Quality in Doctoral Education*. London: Kogan Page, pp. 120–33.
Elphinstone, L. and Schweitzer, R. (1998) *How to Get a Research Degree: A Survival Guide*. St Leonards, NSW: Allen & Unwin.
Grant, B. and Graham, A. (1999) Naming the game: Reconstructing graduate supervision, *Teaching in Higher Education*, 4(1): 77–89.
Graves, N (1997) Problems of supervision. In N. Graves and V. Varma (Eds). *Working for a Doctorate – A Guide for the Humanities and Social Sciences*. London: Routledge, pp. 76–95.
Hembree, R. (1988) Correlates, causes, effects, and treatment of test anxiety, *Review of Educational Research*, 58(1): 47–77.
Hughes, M. (2009) *The emotional lifecycle of a PhD*. Council for Australian University Tourism and Hospitality Education Conference: Bill Faulkner PhD Workshop, 10 February 2009, Esplanade Hotel Fremantle, Western Australia.
Jerabek, J. A., Meyer, L. S. and Kordinak, S. T. (2001) 'Library anxiety' and 'computer anxiety': Measures, validity, and research implications, *Library and Information Science Research*, 23(3): 277–89.
Jiao, Q. G. and Onwuegbuzie, A. J. (1998) Perfectionism and library anxiety among graduate students, *Journal of Academic Librarianship*, 24(5): 365–71.
——(1999) Identifying library anxiety through students' learning-modality preferences, *Library Quarterly*, 69(2): 202–16.
Moore, S., Rodger, K., Hughes, M., Morrison-Saunders, A., Smith, A. and Newsome, D. (2002) *Making our emotions work for us in doctoral studies*. Workshop paper presented at Worlds of Research Coinciding and Colliding, Annual Conference of the Australian Association of Social Research, 1–4 October, Hydro-Majestic – Blue Mountains, NSW.
Morrison-Saunders, A., Moore, S., Newsome, D. and Newsome, J. (2005) Reflecting on the role of emotions in the PhD process. In *The Reflective Practitioner*, Proceedings of the 14th Annual Teaching Learning Forum, 3–4 February 2005. Perth: Murdoch University. Online. (Available at lsn.curtin.edu.au/tlf/tlf2005/refereed/morrison-saunders.html).

O'Leary, Z. (2001) Conversations from the kitchen. In A. Bartlett and G. Mercer (Eds). *Eruptions. Vol 11. Doctoral Research Supervision – Transforming (R)Elations*. New York: Peter Land Publishing Inc, 195–98.

Onwuegbuzie, A. J. (1997) Writing a research proposal: The role of library anxiety, statistics anxiety, and composition anxiety, *Library and Information Science Research*, 19: 5–33.

——(2000) Statistics anxiety and the role of self-perceptions, *Journal of Educational Research*, 93(5): 323–30.

Onwuegbuzie, A. J. and Jiao, Q. G. (1998) Understanding library-anxious graduate students, *Library Review*, 47(4): 217–24.

Parsons, M. (2001) The dark side of a PhD: Learning the lesson that supervisors don't teach. In A. Bartlett and G. Mercer (Eds). *Eruptions. Vol 11. Doctoral Research Supervision – Transforming (R)Elations*. New York: Peter Land Publishing Inc, pp. 189–93.

Pekrun, R., Goetz, T., Titz, W. and Perry, R. P. (2002) Academic emotions in students' self-regulated learning and achievement: A programme of qualitative and quantitative research, *Educational Psychologist*, 37(2): 91–105.

Phillips, E. (1994) Avoiding communication breakdown. In O. Zuber-Skerritt and Y. Ryan (Eds). *Quality in Doctoral Education*. London: Kogan Page, pp. 134–42.

Phillips, M. and Pugh, D. S. (1994) *How to Get a PhD – A Handbook for Students and Their Supervisors*. 2nd edn. Buckingham: Open University Press.

Rudd, E. (1985) *A New Look at Doctoral Failure*. Guildford: The Society for Research into Higher Education & NFER–NELSON.

Schutz, P. A. and Davis, H. A. (2000) Emotions and self-regulation during test taking, *Educational Psychologist*, 35(4), 243–56.

Turner, J. E., Husman, J. and Schallert, D. L. (2002) The importance of students' goals in their emotional experience of academic failure: Investigating the precursors and consequences of shame, *Educational Psychologist*, 37(2): 79–89.

West, L., Hore, T. and Beard, S. (1988) What makes a successful graduate student? In *Assistance for Doctoral Students: Achieving Better Outcomes*. Paper delivered at a seminar held in Canberra, 1–2 December 1987. Canberra: Department of Education, Training and Youth Affairs, pp. 45–64.

18

Doctoral education in global times

'Scholarly quality' as practical ethics in research

T. Seddon

Doctoral qualifications were first awarded in Australia after the Second World War. What it meant to be a doctoral student was largely framed by English doctoral traditions. The award of a PhD hinged on the preparation of a substantial thesis that made a significant and original contribution to knowledge. This performance was judged against the standards of closed disciplinary communities. In the 1990s, partly prompted by policy pressures on universities, the pattern of doctoral education began to change. Experiments in doctoral education proliferated. Knowledge communities beyond the academy were acknowledged and disciplinarity became more open. The establishment of professional doctorates and subsequent integration of coursework into some PhD programmes prompted questions about the performances required by doctoral students to qualify as a 'Doctor'.

In 2000 I examined these shifts in doctoral education, asking what is 'doctoral' in doctoral education? In this chapter I revisit this question but now with the benefit of hindsight and awareness of new challenges confronting doctoral education. My thesis is that the 'contribution to knowledge' is still the key criteria in the award of a doctoral degree, but the notion of 'scholarly quality' is increasingly anchored in the practices of research and identity of the researcher. In this respect, 'scholarly quality' defines and foregrounds a practical ethic in research work. The effect is to generalise doctoral education. It is no longer just a preparation for research in academic workplaces but serves as a more ubiquitous professional education for working with knowledge across dispersed workplaces.

The chapter is organised in three parts. I begin by reviewing the earlier study that drew attention to the changing terms and conditions of doctoral education and its effect in focusing research assessment on research practice. Next, I extend that review by documenting third and fourth generation doctoral programmes. The former is a 'life-long learning' doctorate described in the literature. The latter is an empirically based case in which I participated. Finally, I look across these doctoral education experiments to further elaborate the idea of 'scholarly quality' that defines the doctoral in doctoral education.

'Scholarly quality' in doctoral education

In 1991 Monash University established one of the early education professional doctorate programmes in Australia. This initiative prompted significant reflection on research education

219

and its pedagogy in PhDs as well as masters-level research education. The initial EdD experiment opened the way to other experiments in research education, including activities to support research induction, the collectivisation of research education through cohorts and cluster supervision, and collaborative cross-national doctoral education initiatives.

These experiments at Monash were part of a wider intellectual movement reflecting on the nature of doctoral education (Green *et al.* 2001). It developed particularly in applied scholarly fields where students enrolling in doctoral programmes do not fit the stereotypical image of a doctoral student or where doctoral education does not take the structured form of laboratory-based research degrees (Evans and Pearson 1999). They cut across established practices in doctoral education and made the meaning of criteria that governed the award of 'Doctor' somewhat slippery.

In 2000 I tried to problematise these developments by asking what was 'doctoral' about doctoral education (Seddon 2001). In that paper I reviewed professional doctorate programmes emerging in Australia in the field of education. I suggested that the shift from first to second generation professional doctorates presented academics with significant dilemmas. First generation professional doctorates retained many features of a conventional PhD (e.g. substantial written work that codified a 'contribution to knowledge'). By contrast, second generation professional doctorates were more oriented to workforce development. I captured these dilemmas as follows:

> [H]ow to resolve the priority between teaching and learning; how to organize provision between old and new learning sites; how to position professional doctorates in the press for modernization and tradition [in universities]; and how to be an academic in an institution of knowledge that is gradually being eroded by funding cuts and public sector reform.
>
> Seddon 2001: 329

Working through these dilemmas, I suggested that professional doctorates were shifting the character of doctoral education. Their purposes were being reoriented in line with changes in work and policy commitments to life-long learning. Doctoral education was being relocated into learning spaces at the interface between academic, professional and workplace knowledges. These were exposed places where traditional public sector research practices and ethics rubbed up against privately oriented ways of knowing and producing knowledge. This location required students to cross knowledge boundaries and negotiate their positions relative to these different knowledge communities.

These terms and conditions of doctoral education, I argued, could be accommodated if researchers recognised and sustained 'academic knowledge production ethics'. I drew on the comments of an EdD examiner, who had asked one of my students for revisions, to articulate my sense that doctoral education should be judged 'as a way of doing academic knowledge production'. The examiner had written:

> I believe that work at [a doctoral level] is differentiated from other kinds of thinking and writing by its scholarly quality. In other words, there needs to be a level of intellectual rigour and discipline that is sustained throughout the work. ... There are several ways this can be done:
>
> • By making clear and transparent the methods through which data were created, interpreted and analyzed;

- By making clear and transparent the train of reasoning and analysis through which conclusions, models or theories are developed;
- Through rigorous critique and use of the literature; [and]
- By entering the discipline of 'critical subjectivity' through which the assumptions, values and processes of the researcher themselves [sic] become the subject of research.

With the benefits of hindsight, almost 10 years on, it is clear that the development of professional doctorates acknowledged growing tensions in research. These tensions have become more significant as governments have implemented policies that build knowledge economies and reorient societies towards life-long learning. These policy trajectories privileged 'learning' as a fundamental competence for citizens, communities and societies (Kuhn 2007), but understood in ways that prioritised incremental increases in knowledge that are in tension with established processes of academic work and the signage of education (Seddon 2009).

Given these tensions, experimentation around doctoral education provided a useful way of navigating through the reform agenda. Doctoral education experiments supported an interrogation of research as a particular kind of praxis that works with and builds knowledge in many different contexts. This way of understanding research recognised that knowledge is contextualised through knowledge politics. It helped to unlock the specification of 'contribution to knowledge' from forms that were particularly suited to academic contexts and recontextualise research performance in forms that were more appropriate in other contexts. In this way, the function of doctoral education programmes in developing high-level research capacities was maintained while their form varied.

The effect of these reorientations around doctoral education has:

1. Recognised research as work: research is an intellectual labour process whose outcomes are constituted and constrained by the terms and conditions of intellectual work (Connell 1983). The structure and culture of research work is shaped and steered through policy frameworks and regulatory arrangements that are embedded in distinctive discourse communities. These knowledge frames delineate and distinguish normative research performances as well as priorities in the way they are materialised as products. Orienting doctoral education towards more diverse and open practices of producing knowledge provides a way through these external constraints on research.

2. Prioritised practical ethics in doctoral-level work: it makes sense to emphasise the quality of research practice as the performance criterion demonstrating research capacity. This is the value of the EdD examiner's comment. She names 'scholarly quality' as the basis for judging researcher practices and defines a preferred way of being a researcher. Her definition foregrounds practical ethics in research work, with research products seen, secondarily, as a consequence of and proxy for good practice. This way of capturing the research performances that distinguish doctoral-level work reinvokes social practices that are 'only possible within a set of relationships that support and permit honest inquiry, knowledge production and critique' (Doecke and Seddon 2002).

3. Focused doctoral education on student's self work: judging doctoral-level work in terms of scholarly quality refocuses doctoral education on a student's way of being a researcher. It encourages pedagogical attention to student's capacity for self-work;

the critically self-reflexive formation of identity that is alert to positioning within relations of power and its practical effects in the world (Chappell *et al.* 2003). Doctoral education programmes help students to: become more conscious of knowledge processes; enable them to question the way they mobilise discourses; consider whether their rendering of knowledge is desirable; and act in ways that construct or modulate relationships through this process of rendering experience as knowledge (Chappell *et al.* 2003: 17). Such reflections reveal the way knowledge is a cultural infrastructure that organises the social and orders self-other relationships through everyday life.

4. Encouraged occupational identity as researchers: doctoral education is not just a technical preparation in doing research but a professional education in being a researcher in a globally distributed occupation of research. Like other occupations, researchers make their work and are made by it. Their occupational jurisdiction, now and in the future, depends on inter- and intra-professional negotiation of professional license (permission to carry on certain activities) and mandate (the elbow room while doing the work of research) (Abbott 1988).

So how has the form of doctoral education changed and what kinds of research practice are endorsed as indicators of 'scholarly quality'? In the next section I review four generations of doctoral education to further clarify the practical ethics that define 'doctoral' in doctoral education.

Four generations of doctoral education

The character of different doctoral education programmes offers insights into the research practices negotiated and approved as 'doctoral-level' within academic communities. The institutionalisation of these practices define what counts as doctoral research performance and, therefore, establishes a more detailed conceptualisation of 'scholarly quality'.

The key features of these programmes and their specification of 'contribution to knowledge' are summarised in Table 18.1. My assumption is that the purpose of these programmes, their design and the way they define contribution to knowledge, is an indication of what is being privileged in the development of researcher's practical ethics. The profiles on which Table 18.1 is based are outlined after the table. The first three brief profiles are based on secondary literature. The fourth profile is longer because it documents a cross-national doctoral education experiment (in which I participated) that has not been reported in the literature.

Doctoral education profiles

First generation professional doctorate programmes retained a relatively conventional academic focus. A thesis or substantial written portfolio was the main vehicle for demonstrating capacity for scholarly research. The Monash and Deakin EdDs illustrated these approaches. They opened up doctoral education by adding coursework to the preparation of written work. These developments recognised that students required some formalised instruction in research and, as busy professionals, would benefit from a more socialised learning environment than conventionally occurred in individualised student–supervisor relationships. These changes were anchored by the specification of doctoral

Table 18.1 Four generations of doctoral education

Criteria	1st	2nd	3rd	4th
Purpose	Informed professional practice	Workforce development	Lifelong learning	Global professional education
Space for learning	Academic	Workplace-professional	Self-designed	Trans-local
Knowledge resources	Engagement with academic knowledge	Mobilization of transdisciplinary knowledge	Mobilizing and justifying relevant academic-professional knowledge resources	Fixed and mobile academic, professional, community knowledges
Pedagogical technology	Supervisor	Peer collaboration	Engaging with relevant communities	*Paedia* of place and dialogue through difference
Contribution to knowledge	Written product codifying knowledge	Communication of knowledge in relevant peer formats	Legitimation of knowledge within knowledge politics	Self-reflexivity about location and effects in knowledge geopolitics

purpose. Candidates were still examined on their 'contribution to knowledge' but this was understood to be knowledge relevant to professional practice, rather than to academic scholarship – the great conversation that progressed through discipline communities. The written products drew out and codified the knowledge that had been generated in the course of the research enquiry and writing process.

Second generation doctoral programmes shifted their primary focus towards workforce development. Doctoral study was relocated to the boundary zone between the university and workplaces and professional communities. Doctoral education was framed through engagement with academic and professional-workplace knowledge and experience. For instance, the University of Western Sydney model required students to produce a portfolio made up of written products but also participate in a programme of seminars, meetings and conferences that were focused on professional learning and peer review (Baumgart and Linfoot 1998). The locus of learning was a boundary zone in which knowledge building was more open and accountable to social interests beyond the academy. This relocation meant that learners worked within a learning space characterised by Mode 2 transdisciplinary knowledge production (Lee *et al.* 2000). They engaged with a 'hybrid curriculum' to develop their skills and capacities for research in applied settings. The traditional individualised student–supervisor pedagogical technology was replaced by more collaborative learning relations, which acknowledged all participants as learners as well as experts in their own domains of practice. The university provided a context of support and input to facilitate learning and codification of knowledge. Performance necessary for the award of doctorate privileged the development of working knowledge and skills. It acknowledged the diversity of practices through which knowing was demonstrated, oral as well as written performance. It judged those performances as communications within and contributions to professional and workplace communities.

Third generation doctoral programmes moved towards a learner-centred approach. Rather than privileging academic or workplace-professional communities, these programmes vested responsibility for learning and for legitimation of knowledge performances with the student. Middlesex University illustrates this approach. It has framed doctoral education within a life-long learning perspective that was 'learner-centred and

223

experience-led' (Stephenson *et al.* 2004). Like second generation doctorates, it mobilised transdisciplinary knowledges that had developed and been researched in relevant communities of practice but shifted the locus of control from the university and workplace-profession to the learners themselves. The programme emphasised self-regulated learning tailored to learners' own agendas, supported by the university. The students engaged in critical reviews of their own professional experience and achievements as a basis for generating a range of products, specified by the student, for final assessment. This work was conducted in dialogue with a member of their relevant professional community. The products of this work could take many forms, including reports, books, guidelines and regulations for programmes of action. These products, plus a critical commentary on the learner's overall achievements provided the basis for judging the quality of research against standards that were common for all doctoral degrees, PhD as well as professional doctorate. The contribution to knowledge was not simply a body of work but was demonstrated through the embodiment of that work in a comprehensive professional career. That career involved prior learning, professional experience and final products, and also the capacity to navigate effectively within the politics of knowledge that enabled these professionals to justify and legitimise their work with knowledge. The outcome was a contribution to knowledge that also recognised the learner's enhanced credibility, the impact on their capabilities in different contexts and their capacity for ongoing self-directed learning (Stephenson *et al.* 2004).

Fourth generation doctoral programmes, I want to suggest, take up the challenges of preparing globally mobile researchers. They are proliferating particularly in response to Europe's mobility agenda but are also evident in other places around the world. These initiatives acknowledge the diversity of disciplinary, workplace and professional knowledge communities and also the way these communities are framed by national cultures and jurisdictions (Nóvoa 2000). There is, therefore a geopolitical ordering of research between nation-states, so ways of producing and projecting knowledge have different effects and impacts in different places in the world.

These geopolitics of knowledge are tensioned in two ways. First, there are power relations between 'metropoles' and 'Souths' (Connell 2007). The former are recognised and endorsed loci of knowledge building; the latter are 'others' that tend to receive and apply knowledge. This tension in knowledge building does not just exist within the academy but is a feature and a locus for active politics across and within economies and societies. Second, there are also power relations in the application of knowledge that hinges on the politics of representation. Research as a form of work is oriented towards the production of truths but it can be used in many different ways by different agencies: as contextualised 'really useful knowledge' or as a mode of governing (Nóvoa and Yariv-Marshal 2003). These applications show the way the work of research constitutes a knowledge infra-structure that enables and orders identities, their relations and capacities to act in the world.

Globally mobile researchers must navigate these complex multi-scalar tensions in their research. Doctoral education programmes are developing to support this kind of learning. CROSSLIFE, a cross-cultural collaboration in life-long learning and work (CROSSLIFE 2008), is one example

Doctoral education for globally connected researchers

CROSSLIFE was a European ERASMUS curriculum development project that aimed to 'revitalise academic apprenticeship'. The six-country university partnership[1] developed a research education programme for masters and doctoral students in the field of education and work. It was distinguished by an active commitment to simulate global conditions at every level of the project: planning by the university partners, tutoring by university staff, and learning by students and tutors in three cross-national workshops.

This collaborative project was nested in the VET and Culture network. These networked activities brought senior and junior researchers interested in life-long learning and work together. They were drawn from different countries, disciplinary traditions and occupational fields. Many of the junior researchers in VET and Culture and CROSS-LIFE were experienced professionals who worked in adult and vocational education and had enrolled in research degree programmes. Some were doing doctorates or research masters, others were enrolled in coursework masters programmes but had interests in research.

The planning group comprised academics from each of the six partner universities. There was a co-ordinator but collaborative planning was the preferred *modus operandi*. This approach to planning was slow because in the global space constructed through this project, there were no prior conventions or protocols to guide our work. Rather each member of the planning group had equal status and right to speak but each spoke out of a different national research culture and often out of different occupational and disciplinary cultures, too (Kraus and Sultana 2008).

CROSSLIFE was developed as a five-step study plan offering research students in life-long learning and work the opportunity to do global research. The five steps nested in home university doctoral programmes. They included pre-workshop activities in home groups within each university, the three cross-national workshops, which each required preparation and postworkshop journalling, and the integration of outcomes in thesis writing. In practice, full institutional embedding was not possible so localised solutions were found in each university. For example, Monash established a parallel cohort research masters programme and invited students to also participate in the CROSSLIFE activities. Two of these students took up the invitation, along with five enrolled in other doctoral and masters research programmes.

The three workshops were organised around content and process themes. The idea of 'travelling knowledge' provided the broad content focus. Its effects were explored in terms of institutionalisation of national systems (London workshop, November 2007), organisation of work and workforces (Tampere, Finland, March 2008) and teaching and learning (Malta, September 2008). Through these substantive issues, students and tutors (mostly also members of the planning group) engaged in process learning necessary in cross-cultural collaborative work.

Ultimately cultures, their spatialisation and geopolitical ordering, became the context of this doctoral education programme. The Malta workshop brief illustrates these features (Sultana 2008). The nature of the programme is outlined under five headings:

- *Purpose:* The aim of the Malta workshop was to explore pedagogical ideas that do or do not travel across boundaries and also develop research capacities and insights into cross-cultural collaborations. This agenda was organised through studies of contradictions in teaching and learning when established education practice confronts 'travelling pedagogies'. The meanings of these terms were constructed in terms of learning as communication. The workshop brief presented education as a process of developing capacities for communication that build relationships between self and other. This work of attaining 'communion' with others far and wide is now dramatically enhanced and supported by the new information technology. The

225

'endeavour to reach out beyond ourselves, to start conversations that lead to improved understanding of the "other"' is the heart of 'pedagogy'. Yet, the brief notes, 'travelling pedagogies' cut across these culturally embedded and spatialised processes in the wake of the developing knowledge economy. They promote and develop knowledge and skills in different contexts (e.g. work-based learning, education through 'edutainment'), recognise learning whenever and wherever it happens (e. g. through the Accreditation of Prior Experiential Learning). They involve teachers in formal, informal and non-formal learning situations (e.g. coach, mentor) and use methods to make learning available everywhere (e.g. mobile, open and distance learning). Learners also confront new roles, being expected to engage with life-long learning – in strategic and self-directed ways. So what does this juxtaposition mean for processes of teaching and learning? What competence and capacities do educators and researchers need in globalised life-long learning and work?

- *Knowledge communities:* The workshop sat at the interface of global–local academic, professional and embedded community knowledges. Students were invited to consider these knowledges and the way they were troubled by contradictions between established and travelling pedagogies. Learning how to communicate with other, differently located groups, means carefully engaging through languages provided by small-l (linguistic) and large-L (scientific and disciplinary knowledge) communities. ICTs are another 'language'. They permit boundary-crossing in geographical and other ways but also frame language practices in line with the cultural conventions of their designers (e.g. Microsoft). Travelling ideas, and the technologies through which they move, disrupt established education and research because these institutions of knowledge have developed within distinct national cultures and jurisdictions.

- *Learning space:* The workshop was organised as an intense week-long interrogation of these fixed and travelling ideas, the way they were embodied and their contradictory effects in education and research. Malta, as a place, provided the *paideia or* learning context. The brief notes that Malta's:

> '[E]xotic/strange' quality as an island in/of the geographic/economic 'south' may shift participants out of cognitive and habitual comfort zones: it will certainly speak to us differently, obliging us to ask questions, confront the self, think of our own cultural assumptions and ways of creating meaning as we face life's challenges. We will work with this 'otherness' by immersing ourselves in a village, and see how this 'interpellates' us. We will be guided by anthropologists and social scientists, who have honed their skills in listening to the heartbeat of communities. *The invitation and challenge is to develop a deeper understanding of culture—thus building bridges between 'us' and 'them' as well as to generate deeper insights about the 'paideic' practices embedded in communities, as well as about indigenous knowledge.*
>
> Sultana 2008

- *Pedagogical technology:* Engaging with this *paideia* of place, students were encouraged to consider embedded and travelling pedagogies and the way they intersected in cross-boundary teaching and learning. Through interactive and tutor-led sessions, the workshop interrogated these contradictory fixed and mobile pedagogical forms. Participants considered the way pedagogies anchored in national traditions interfaced with the travelling ideas carried through globally mobile pedagogic technologies – workplace learning initiatives, computer games and also the non-Maltese tutors and students who participated in CROSSLIFE. Those of us who travelled to Malta were mobile pedagogies that rubbed up against Maltese and other participants, all of whom were formed within their own national education and knowledge traditions.

The design and process of the workshop created a trans-local space for learning. Fixed identities–entities anchored in Malta and mobile identities–entities that travelled into Malta were mobilised as a technology for experiential and scholarly learning and research. In this learning space, participants experienced communication complexities across cultures of nation, class, gender, occupation and discipline. They learned to respect the difficulties of this intellectual and relational work, and the importance of creating safe spaces to work through these learning relationships. They began to codify the terms and conditions for complex cross-boundary engagements and the capacities and capabilities necessary for this work.

- *Contribution to knowledge:* The outcomes of this doctoral education programme showed that participants developed an increased sensitivity to self and other, and the way knowledge and research shape meanings. For example, one student commented:

> The Birghu walkabout-ethnographic activity stopped me dead in my tracks and it seems to me that it was the sequencing of activities related to the expedition that was crucial to the delivery of the full impact of what it means to do cross cultural, border work. The 'expedition' was followed by a forum with an historian, a priest and a sociologist, then a reflective group exercise and evaluation and presentation of our findings and artifacts. This was an incredibly valuable exercise for me as it forced me to question the analyses, the assumptions and evaluations we make, and are in fact trained to make, as academic researchers and what this means in cross cultural settings. I am much more mindful of interpreting and evaluating observations as 'evidence'.
>
> A3

Participants grasped the way knowledge acts as an infrastructure for everyday life. This cultural infrastructure is spatialised geopolitically, constructs relations between self and other, and therefore contributes to the social ordering of the world. Students reflected on these insights through cross-national dialogue in relation to their own research topics and professional working lives. They revealed different ways of understanding places and the politics that constitutes them. Through these differences they opened up productively critical perspectives on international and Australian developments. For instance one Australian student commented on the way CROSSLIFE broadened perspectives:

> The shared yet distinct understandings and questions about VET, pedagogically and culturally, has provided me with a more considered approach to my education work in both research and practice. As a researcher I have become more cognisant of the planetary aspects of vocational education. Vocational education is a sea of learning traditions and practices about making and producing. Hearing from and talking with people from Finland, Germany, Switzerland, Malta, the UK and other countries provided me with insights into how vocational education as it is organized nationally and through international policy discourses, is constantly being made anew through changes to production and consumption.
>
> A2

227

Another reflected on her own professional experience and the way CROSSLIFE provided some distance on daily experiences:

> I am in a setting where institutional mergers and significant organizational change are currently underway, putting pressure on professional learning, relationships and self-efficacy of colleagues. The experiences of Crosslife have enabled me to be metacognitive about the processes in which we are engaged, to understand and analyze 'glitches' in terms of the challenges presented by cultural boundary-crossing, in its broader sense.
>
> A1

The general assessment was that CROSSLIFE helped participants to grasp the significance of research in the world and their own agency as researchers:

> I did not learn what I expected (theoretical knowledge) but I learned more than expected in terms of insight in academic work, project making, cross-cultural interaction, group processes, as well as capability of working in this setting myself.
>
> E1

> CROSSLIFE raised some critical questions and issues not only about collaboration, about doing academic work in cross cultural settings and about the ways that ideas travel in a global context but also about the bounded spaces of institutional and workplace learning, theory and practice and about doing academic work in interdisciplinary settings. My experience of CROSSLIFE impacts on the framing of my own PhD research particularly in terms of my approach to methodology, and the crafting of my research design and method. By questioning the bounded spaces of academic research and writing I hope to raise questions about how collaboration and cross boundary work problematizes academic research traditions of method and methodology in education
>
> A3

CROSSLIFE created a doctoral education programme in a simulated global space. It mobilised trans-local resources that enabled junior and senior researchers to grasp the geopolitics of knowledge and the significance of research as work, which produces cultural infrastructures that constitute the socio-spatial ordering of the world. The programme enabled researchers to understand research as cultural work, grasp their involvement as research identities, and recognise their agency in these knowledge geopolitics and their effects in the world.

Doctoral education as an occupational agenda

This chapter has reviewed a series of experiments in doctoral education to clarify what counts as 'doctoral' in doctoral education. I suggest that these experiments have unlocked the forms of research performance that are endorsed as indicators of doctoral level work but also clarified the idea of 'scholarly quality' that justifies a 'contribution to knowledge' for the award of 'Doctor'.

This idea of 'scholarly quality' captures practical ethics that define doctoral-level research. The analysis suggests that doctoral research can be distinguished by research performances that:

- Demonstrate honest transparency, reason and care, critical reflexivity and attention to the social effects of knowledge building in all research activities and products
- Recognise the cultural embeddedness of knowledge in knowledge communities and its social effects as a cultural infrastructure in everyday lives
- Work in ways necessary to justify and legitimise research and its outcomes relative to those knowledge communities
- Grasp the geopolitical ordering of knowledge, its applications and effects in the world; and
- Use knowledge, which is also power, responsibly to understand and inform the world, its ways of knowing and ways of acting in relation to self and others.

Doctoral education is the place where students develop their research identity and are inducted into these practical research ethics. Drawing out the idea of 'scholarly quality', therefore, provides a guide to researcher preparation, the specification of professional expertise in working with knowledge, and a basis for negotiating the professional license and mandate of research as an occupation. The challenge for those engaged in doctoral education is to support and teach students so they develop their research capacities in socially responsible ways, which recognise the way knowledge and power can be used to support everyday living in complex, mobile and poly-vocal communities, which together make a secure and sustainable world.

Notes

1 Danish Pedagogical University, Copenhagen; Tampere, Finland; Institute of Education, London; Malta; Zurich; and Monash, Melbourne.

References

Abbott, A. (1988) *The system of professions: an essay on the division of expert labour.* Chicago, IL: University of Chicago Press.

Baumgart, N. and Linfoot, K. (1998) The professional doctorate in education: a new model. In T. Maxwell and P. J. Shanahan (Eds). *Professional Doctorates: Innovations in teaching and research.* Armidale: University of New England, pp. 115–22.

Chappell, C., Rhodes, K., Solomon, N., Tennant, M. and Yates, L. (2003) *Reconstructing the lifelong learner: pedagogy and identity in individual, organizational, and social change.* London: Routledge Falmer.

Connell, R. W. (1983) Intellectuals and intellectual work, in *Which Way is Up?*, Sydney: Allen and Unwin.

Connell, R. (2007) *Southern Theory: The global dynamics of knowledge in social science.* Sydney: Allen and Unwin.

CROSSLIFE (2008) *Cross-cultural collaboration in lifelong learning and work, project summary report.* Online. (Available at www.education.monash.edu.au/research/projects/crosslife Accessed 5 August 2009).

Doecke, B and Seddon, T. (2002) Research Education: Whose Space for Learning? *Australian Education Researcher*, 29(3): 85–100.

Evans, T. and Pearson, M. (1999) Off-campus doctoral research and study in Australia: Emerging issues and practices. In A. Holbrook and S. Johnston (Eds). *Supervision of postgraduate research in Education, Review of Australian Research in Education No 5.* Melbourne: Australian Association for Research in Education.

Green, B., Maxwell, T. W. and Shanahan, P. (2001) *Doctoral Education and Professional Practice: The Next Generation?* Armidale: Kardoorair Press.

Kraus, K. and Sultana, R. (2008) Problematizing 'cross-cultural' collaboration: Critical incidents in higher education settings, *Mediterranean Journal of Educational Studies* 13(1). Online. (Available at www.um. edu.mt/ – data/assets/pdf_file/0008/47663/Kraus_Sultana_13_1_2008.pdf. Accessed 13 March 2009).

Kuhn, M. (2007) *New Society Models for a New Millenium: The learning society in Europe and beyond.* New York: Peter Lang.

Lee, A., Green, B. and Brennan, M. (2000) Organizational knowledge, professional practice and the professional doctorate at work. In J. Garrick and C. Rhodes (Eds). *Research and Knowledge at Work,* London: Routledge, 117–36.

Nóvoa, A. (2000) *Ways of Thinking about Education in Europe.* Keynote paper presented at the European Conference on Educational Research, Edinburgh, 20–23 September 2000.

Nóvoa, A. and Yariv-Marshal, T. (2003) Comparative research in education: a mode of governance or a historical journey?, *Comparative Education,* 39(4): 423–38.

Seddon, T. (2001) What's doctoral about doctoral education?. In *Third International Professional Doctorates Conference,* University of New England, Armidale, NSW.

——(2009) Knowledge economy: Policy discourse and cultural resources. In M. Simons, M. Olssen and M. Peters (Eds). *Re-reading education policies: Studying the policy agenda of the 21st century.* Rotterdam: Sense.

Stephenson, J., Malloch, M., Cairns, L. and Costley, C. (2004) *Towards a third generation of professional doctorates managed by the learners themselves?* Paper presented at the Deakin conference on Professional Doctorates, Melbourne: Deakin University, 25–26 November.

Sultana, R. (2008) *Cross-cultural/cross-boundary pedagogies … How travelling ideas are changing our ways of teaching and learning.* Malta Workshop briefing paper, CROSSLIFE project.

19

The truth is *not* out there

Becoming 'undetective' in social and educational enquiry

N. Gough

Crime fiction and social enquiry: intertextual continuities

In this chapter I explore the proposition that positioned readings of crime fiction can usefully inform understandings of research methodology in social and educational enquiry.[1] Like Cleo Cherryholmes (1993: 1), I want to break the 'silence of the research literature on the textuality of research findings' by attending to *some* of the 'many ways to read and interpret and criticize' research texts. Consider, for example, the intertextual continuities between research methods texts and crime fiction implied by variations on the word 'investigate' in the following passages:

> Most qualitative researchers maintain a stance best described as 'investigative'.
>
> Lancy 1993: 30

> In undertaking educational research, the first problem is to find a problem to investigate.
>
> Burns 1994: 17

> [T]here is that word again – 'investigate' – invoking the crime narrative, that investigatory hermeneutic which seeks to reveal, disclose, to *know*, and thence, so the myth goes, to empower.
>
> Munt 1994: 173

If the word 'investigate' invokes a crime narrative, then those of us who 'investigate' questions, problems and issues that are not (at least in any obvious sense) 'criminal', should be able to identify the similarities, differences and continuities between our practices and criminal investigation. I attempt to do this by reading crime stories in terms of the 'investigatory hermeneutics' they share with forms of educational enquiry, and by reading research stories in terms of the literary tropes (analogies, metaphors, synecdoches, etc.) and textual structures they share with crime fiction. I emphasise that my primary purpose is to explore the hermeneutic and semiotic codes *shared* by educational enquiry and crime fiction rather than to demonstrate the generativity (or otherwise) of constructing the fictional investigation of crime as a metaphor for educational research. In this respect, my project complements, but also extends beyond, the work of other writers who have explored this particular metaphor in regard to social enquiry (e.g. Moring 2001) or who argue the merits of understanding qualitative research metaphorically as, for example, jazz (Oldfather and West 1994) and dance (Janesick 1994; 1998; 2001). I am not merely asserting that educational enquiry *resembles* the fictional investigation of crime, but also that readers and writers of research texts and crime stories are materially connected by the cultural articulations of the discourses and sign systems in which they are interpellated. I also emphasise that both detective stories and research texts are, as Cherryholmes (1993: 2) writes of the latter, 'subject to multiple readings', and thus recognise that the readings I offer here are partial and incomplete. Nevertheless, I argue that generating intertextual relationships between research literature and other literary forms is pertinent to such activities as supervising research students, teaching graduate programmes in research methodology, interpreting research reports, and choosing textual strategies for narrating research.

I discern three types of intertextual continuity that connect stories of educational enquiry with detective fiction, and I explore each of them here. First, and perhaps most obviously, research reports resemble detective stories insofar as they narrate quests to determine 'the truth' about something that is problematic or puzzling – stories in which 'investigators' seek (to reiterate Munt's terms) 'to reveal, disclose, to *know*, and … to empower'. In considering this analogy, my concern is with the extent to which the characteristic investigatory methods of fictional detectives resemble forms of educational enquiry. Second, following Umberto Eco's (1984: 2) characterisation of the novel as 'a machine for generating interpretations', I consider the extent to which the characteristic ways in which detective stories generate interpretations resemble the textual 'machineries' used in the discursive production of educational research. Third, I consider some of the ways in which recent transformations of both detective fiction and educational enquiry can be understood as comparable – and intertextually linked – manifestations of cultural and discursive shifts signified by various notions of postmodernism and postmodernity.

Watching the detectives

For more than a century, detective fiction has both modelled and offered critiques of culturally privileged forms of social enquiry, although the extent to which detective stories indeed provide critical positions on dominant social institutions and discourses is a matter for debate. For example, in *Delightful Murder: A Social History of the Crime Story*, Ernest Mandel (1984: 84) argues that the 'original detective story' (exemplified by Sherlock Holmes stories) is 'the purest, most elementary expression of bourgeois society'. Conversely, in *Uncommon Cultures: Popular Cultures and Post-Modernism*, Jim Collins (1989: 35) argues that the proliferation of crime fiction in the nineteenth century represented a widespread disillusionment with the state. Nevertheless, when teaching research methodology coursework, I invite students to consider undertaking educational research by 'watching the detectives'[2] – that is, by imagining educational enquiries conducted in the manner of fictional detectives with whom they are familiar and by comparing the methods deployed in investigating fictional crimes with various paradigms or traditions of social enquiry.

Even a fairly superficial analysis reveals that educational research has not necessarily kept pace with developments in the methods of fictional detection that have accompanied the cultural changes of the late modern era. Much educational research still privileges scientific rationalism even though its stereotypical personifications in fiction – notably Sherlock Holmes and other heroes of the classic 'logic and deduction' detective story[3] – are no longer taken for granted as appropriate models of how we can or should obtain worthwhile knowledge of the world. During the 1920s and 1930s the detachment and 'objectivity' of Holmes's method of enquiry began to give way to a variety of more involved and subjective approaches. For example, Agatha Christie's Miss Marple, who first appeared in *The Murder at the Vicarage* (1930), investigates crimes in the manner of an ethnographer: her detailed observations (thick descriptions) of life in the village of St Mary Mead provide her with a grounded theory of human behaviour, which she deploys to solve mysteries both within that community and elsewhere. 'Hard-boiled' detectives such as Dashiell Hammett's (1930) Sam Spade and Raymond Chandler's (1939) Philip Marlowe display a different kind of involvement and subjectivity; often they are deeply implicated (as actors rather than spectators) in the mysteries they are called upon to explicate. Also, Marlowe and his successors usually tell their stories in the first person, a change in narrative perspective that further problematised the role of the participant-observer in the dialectic of truth versus deception decades before interpretivist styles of enquiry seriously challenged positivistic social science. From the 1960s, an increasing number of fictional detectives have adopted socially critical standpoints such as feminism, exemplified in different ways by Amanda Cross's (1964) Kate Fansler and Sara Paretsky's (1982) V. I. Warshawski. Via their journals and other writings, a number of my students have reported that they have been pleasantly surprised by the generativity of making such comparisons. For example, students who have read many 'cosy' mysteries for recreation, have found it intriguing to speculate on how the investigative methods of Agatha Christie's Miss Marple might translate into educational research and compare these with, say, the approaches taken by Amanda Cross's Kate Fansler. Such comparisons bring into sharp focus the differences between (and different consequences of) essentialist and interactionist interpretations of human behaviour.

However, methods of fictional detection are not strictly analogous to the forms of social enquiry that they superficially resemble. For example, although Sherlock Holmes often emulates procedures stereotypically associated with research in the natural sciences, the relationships between 'facts' and the meanings that can be ascribed to them are very different for fictional detectives and natural scientists. The 'facts' that natural scientists 'discover' are usually *produced* in circumstances designed and more or less controlled by scientists themselves and thus are already the result of many acts of interpretation. Conversely, the 'facts' to which fictional detectives ascribe meaning usually result from deliberate acts of deception by guilty parties. But the problem of deception – deliberate or otherwise – is by no means irrelevant to educational research, especially when it comes to interpreting what students and/or teachers say and/or do when they are being observed or interviewed or are responding to questionnaires. As a methodological issue, the possibility of deception often is subsumed by questions about 'authenticity' – questions frequently raised in circumstances involving research subjects who are clearly less powerful or privileged than the researchers, as in much research on minority groups (see, for example, Foster 1994; 1999). Critics of such research argue that we cannot assume that people who see themselves as oppressed, exploited or marginalised by culturally dominant groups will necessarily tell the truth when interrogated by members of those groups. However, the question of whether or not researchers are being 'told the truth' in the course of their investigations might be pertinent in many more situations than these criticisms suggest.

One of Sherlock Holmes's well-known dialogues exemplifies another way in which the classic fictional detective departs from conventional understandings of scientific rationalism:

> 'Is there any other point to which you would wish to draw my attention?'
> 'To the curious incident of the dog in the night-time'.
> 'The dog did nothing in the night time'.
> 'That was the curious incident', remarked Sherlock Holmes.[4]

Holmes's willingness to apprehend and ascribe meaning to a silence – to perceive the absence of a trace as itself a trace – is a disposition that, in retrospect, seems more in keeping with recent critical and postcritical discourses of social enquiry than with nineteenth century conceptions of 'scientific method'. However, in terms of the broad analogies that can be constructed between fictional crime investigation and social enquiry, it might be more significant to note that this dialogue is just one among many instances of a fictional detective's methods – often represented as eccentric or idiosyncratic – being compared with the more conventional methods used by the police, usually to the latter's disadvantage. Variations on this kind of comparison are also found in the 'police procedural' type of crime novel, where the more 'successful' detectives are often those whose methods are in some kind of conflict (ranging from subtle subversion to outright rebellion) with bureaucratised versions of 'official' knowledge.[5] For example, Sheri Kinney (1998) bases her argument for using experiential knowledge and unobtrusive observations in educational enquiry on a comparison of the methods used by the (unsuccessful) police detective and the (successful) amateur investigators in Alfred Hitchcock's (1954) *Rear Window*.[6] We can use such characteristics of crime fiction to frame and generate questions about educational enquiry, including questions about the relative strengths and limitations of individualistic and collectivist forms of enquiry and the merits and demerits of institutionalising research efforts. Is there, for example, any place for 'private investigations' in educational research? Under what circumstances, if any, might it be defensible to assert, as a popular song puts it, that 'this is *my* investigation – it's not a public inquiry' (Knopfler 1982)?

Although it is important to raise such questions in the study and critique of educational research methodologies, I emphasise that, as a pedagogical strategy, I see 'watching the [fictional] detectives' chiefly as an accessible and pleasurable preliminary to exploring more significant questions that arise from watching (as it were) the ways in which stories of fictional detection generate interpretations.

Crime fictions as model narratives of enquiry

The meanings that any given text generates are, at least in part, a function of the storytelling genre in which authors and readers perceive it to be situated. When we read an article in the *International Journal of Applied Semiotics* or a chapter in *The Routledge Doctoral Student's Companion*, we mobilise a very different set of expectations and intertextual referents from those we bring to reading a crime novel or watching a mystery on television. Each storytelling practice incorporates a particular selection of narrative strategies and conventions, the implicit or explicit knowledge of which influences the author's craft, the audience's expectations and the meanings that they mutually construct. However, given that both research reports and crime stories are narratives of enquiry, it seems reasonable to ask if we can learn anything by comparing them.

According to Roland Barthes (1978), the crime story sets up a central enigma to be explicated by the detective and/or the reader. Indeed, as Slavoj Zizek (1992: 58) writes, detective fiction can be understood as a quest to tell a story that concludes not when the solution to the mystery is revealed but when the detective is able to tell 'the true story' of the mystery in the form of a coherent linear narrative:

> What we have at the beginning is a void, a blank of the unexplained, more properly, of the *unnarrated* (How did it happen? What happened on the night of the murder?). The story encircles this blank, it is set in motion by the detective's attempt to reconstruct the missing narrative by interpreting the clues. In this way, we reach the proper beginning only at the very end, when the detective is finally able to narrate the whole story in its 'normal,' linear form, to reconstruct 'what really happened,' by filling in all the blanks.

The classic form of detective fiction usually reconstructs this 'missing narrative' in the form of a historical recount. The author – through the voice of an 'omniscient' narrator or the detective's Watsonian companion – opens what Dennis Porter (1981: 24) calls a 'logico-temporal gap' between the time of the crime's commission and the time of its telling. The function of the detective *and the narrative* is to close that gap and restore the logical temporal order. In hard-boiled crime fiction the 'missing narrative' is more likely to reconstruct a map of social order or disorder. The detective him/herself usually narrates these stories in the first person and the 'gaps' the narrative opens tend, at least metaphorically, to be spatial. For example, Fredric Jameson (1983: 131) notes that the form of Raymond Chandler's books reflects an initial 'separation of people from each other, their need to be linked by some external force (in this case the detective) if they are ever to be fitted together as parts of the same picture puzzle'.

Such differences in narrative perspective and strategy between classic and hard-boiled crime fiction have clear parallels in social and educational enquiry. These include the shift away from impersonal styles of reporting – the supposedly 'objective' accounts in which the researcher's presence in the text is disguised or hidden – towards textual strategies that foreground the subjectivity of the narrator and the ways in which she or he is implicated in, and indeed responsible for, the story. As crime fiction and educational research have developed during the past half-century, authors in both fields seem to have become more self-conscious of the inherent reflexivity of their respective narrative forms – increasingly aware that they are telling stories of quests to tell stories. If we accept Katherine Hayles's (1990: 285) view of cultural dynamics, in which 'issues become energized in theories because they are replicated from and reproduced in the social', then these parallels are not coincidental but, rather, reflect the multiple discursive currents and feedback loops through which the production of educational theories and popular fictions are culturally connected.

Similar currents and feedback loops also operate in the *consumption* of educational theory and popular fiction and thus it seems reasonable to ask how our approaches to reading and writing educational research might be influenced by what we learn about structuring narratives of enquiry from reading crime fiction. As Eco (1984: 54–57) suggests, our curiosity about 'the structure of conjecture as such' is one plausible explanation for the popularity of crime fiction:

> I believe people like thrillers not because there are corpses or because there is a final celebratory triumph of order (intellectual, social, legal, and moral) over the disorder of evil. The fact is that the crime novel represents a kind of conjecture, pure and simple. But medical diagnosis, scientific research, metaphysical inquiry are also examples of conjecture. After all, the fundamental question of philosophy (like that of psychoanalysis) is the same as the question of the detective novel: who is guilty? To know this (to think you know this), you have to conjecture that all the events have a logic, the logic that the guilty party has imposed on them. Every story of investigation and of conjecture tells us something that we have always been close to knowing (pseudo-Heideggerian reference).

It is not difficult to make a case for asserting that 'the fundamental question' animating much educational enquiry is also 'the same as the question of the detective novel: who is guilty?' For example, much socially critical educational research – feminist, neo-Marxist, anti-racist, postcolonialist – seeks to identify 'who is guilty' of reproducing a given society's structural inequalities through its education system. To determine this, critical educational researchers 'have to conjecture that all the events [the power relations and material conditions that constitute structural inequalities] have a logic, the logic that the guilty party has imposed on them' – the 'guilty party' being (as many such researchers 'have always been close to knowing') the patriarchal hegemony constructed by white, middle-class, Eurocentric, heterosexual, able-bodied men and their fellow travellers. William Reid (1981: 165) succinctly captures the notion that critical research in education 'tells us something that we have always been close to knowing' in his characterisation of what he calls 'radical' curriculum enquiry:

> The assumptions underlying such work ... are: that no worthwhile curriculum improvement is possible without a radical transformation of social and political institutions; that abstract concepts like 'class', 'capitalism' or 'hegemony' are, in some way, 'real' and provide the key to what is wrong with society; that the needed remedies are already known, at least in principle, and that the function of research and theorizing is to increase the power of already known facts.

The analogy between critical educational research and crime fiction can be taken further. As Zizek (1992: 53–54) writes, 'the scene of the crime with which the detective is confronted is ... as a rule, a false image put together by the murderer in order to efface the traces of his [sic] act'; the scene's 'organic, natural quality is a lure, and the detective's task is to denature it' by decoding the 'doubly inscribed' signifying materials that become known as 'clues'. These doubly inscribed signifiers are sometimes verbal, as in the Sherlock Holmes story in which a murderer uses a dying woman's words – 'It was ... the speckled band!' – to throw suspicion on gipsies camped nearby. The 'true story' is told when Holmes is able to read 'band' as a synonym for 'ribbon' rather than 'gang'.[7] However, in most crime stories, the doubly inscribed signifying materials are non-linguistic although, as Zizek (1992: 54) asserts, they are nevertheless 'already structured like a language' because they are elements of a story written by the guilty party. Critical educational researchers are similarly concerned with decoding doubly inscribed data. They do not 'read' events such as the participation rates or achievement levels of girls in mathematics as part of the educational scene's 'organic, natural quality' but set out 'to denature it', to reveal the 'true' structure of the story inscribed by the guilty party. For example, in 'Ned Ludd was framed', Pat Thomson (1998) offers an alternative inter-pretation of the historical events and circumstances that produced the term 'Luddite' as a pejorative description of someone reluctant to take up new technologies. Thomson suggests that the story of the Luddites as misguided vandals is 'framed' by a dominant discourse that silences and forecloses debate on social and technological change by reinforcing a simple binary opposition between those who are for and against 'progress'.[8]

Another reason for the 'clues' at the scene of a fictional crime already being 'structured like a language' is that the scene is indeed written by an author whose intent is not so much to delude the fictional detective and the fictional representatives of 'official' knowledge but, rather, to mystify the 'real' reader. The 'false' solution that entices readers is so ubiquitous as a narrative strategy in detective fiction that Zizek (1992: 54, 57) concludes that it a 'structural necessity' of the genre:

> The status of the false solution is epistemologically internal to the detective's final, true solution. The key to the detective's procedure is that the relation to the first, false solutions is not simply an external one: the detective does not apprehend them as simple obstacles to be cast away in order to obtain the truth, rather it is only *through* them that he can arrive at the truth, for there is no path leading immedi-ately to the truth … The detective does not simply disregard the meaning of the false scene: he [sic] pushes it to the point of self-reference, i.e., to the point at which it becomes obvious that its sole meaning consists in the fact that (others think) it possesses some meaning.

I have no systematic empirical evidence to support the view that the 'false' solution is also a 'structural necessity' of the stories produced in the traditions of critical (or, for that matter, any other forms of) educational research. But the rhetorical strategy of demol-ishing a so-called straw argument in order to advance a counter argument is hardly unknown in the literature of educational enquiry. Moreover, given that postpositivist educational researchers tend to assume that the objects of their enquiries are social con-structions rather than 'naturally occurring' phenomena, it seems likely that the narrative structures of conjecture that they deploy are indeed analogous to those of crime fiction,[9] and might be recognised as such by some researchers.

For example, in their editorial introduction to *Rethinking Curriculum Studies: A Radical Approach*, Martin Lawn and Len Barton (1981: 17) raise the possibility of approaching curriculum enquiry in a manner that 'owes something to the attitude and procedure of Dashiell Hammett's detective, the "Continental Op"'.[10] They elaborate this position by quoting from Steven Marcus's (1977: 15–16) introduction to a collection of Hammett's Continental Op stories:

> The Op is called in or sent out on a case. Something has been stolen, some dire circumstance is impending, someone has been murdered − it doesn't matter. The Op interviews the person or persons most immediately accessible. They may be innocent or guilty − it doesn't matter; it is an indifferent circumstance. Guilty or innocent, they provide the Op with an account of what they really know, of what

they assert really happened. The Op begins to investigate; he compares these accounts with others that he gathers; he snoops about; he does research; he shadows people, arranges confrontations between those who want to avoid one another, and so on. What he soon discovers is that the 'reality' that anyone involved will swear to is in fact itself a construction, a fabrication, a fiction, a faked and alternate reality – and that it has been gotten together before he ever arrived on the scene. And the Op's work therefore is to deconstruct, decompose, deplot and defictionalize that 'reality' and to construct or reconstruct out of it a true fiction, i.e., an account of what 'really' happened.[11]

When I first read Lawn and Barton's text in the early 1980s I was not aware that a literary scholar like Marcus might have intended the word 'deconstruct' to signify something more than common English usage suggested at the time – a compound verb in which the prefix 'de-' signalled either the removal or reversal of 'construct'.[12] Certainly, neither Lawn and Barton nor any of the other contributors to their collection made any reference to Derrida's work or to literary and philosophical understandings of deconstruction or poststructuralism and their implications for curriculum enquiry. But when I returned to Lawn and Barton's (1981) text in the early 1990s I knew that Marcus's (1977) assertion that 'the Op's work … is to deconstruct' *could* have referred to Derrida's (1972: 271) sense of deconstruction as 'being alert to the implications, to the historical sedimentation of the language we use'. This speculation seems reasonable, given that Marcus was a professor of English and Comparative Literature at Columbia University, and that by the time he wrote his introduction to *The Continental Op* Derrida was well-known among US literary theorists (see, for example, de Man 1971).[13] Nevertheless, I doubted the suggestion (intended or not) that the Continental Op worked as a Derridean deconstructionist (or that Hammett's stories might represent Derridean deconstruction at work), because my readings of crime fiction (and related literary criticism) up to that time led me to suspect that crime fiction was an irredeemably modernist genre. However, my curiosity as to whether or not a poststructuralist mode of detective fiction might be possible (and, if so, what it might look like) initially motivated and guided the enquiries documented in this chapter.

If narratives of educational enquiry are structurally analogous to crime stories, then it seems reasonable to suppose that those of us who write educational research might find some clues to the improvement of our textual practices by examining some of the more innovative and adventurous examples of crime fiction. During the past 30 years or so, one relatively superficial innovation has been to characterise the detective as a much less stereotyped identity – many more fictional detectives than previously are something other than white, middle class, Eurocentric, heterosexual, able-bodied men. However, it seems to me that relatively few of the stories categorised as, say, feminist detective fiction depart markedly from the dominant narrative forms of the genre. Possible exceptions include the Kate Fansler stories written by 'Amanda Cross', a pseudonym of Carolyn Heilbrun, a distinguished feminist academic whose publications include studies of the representation of women in literary fiction, biography and autobiography (see, for example, Heilbrun 1989; 1997; 1999). Like Heilbrun, Kate Fansler is a professor of English literature and the mystery novels in which she features can be read as critiques of taken-for-granted representations of the storylines that give substance and pattern to the dominant cultural discourses into which women's subjectivities are interpellated.[14] In a similar way, Julianne Moss (1999; 2003) interprets the practice of inclusive schooling in

Tasmania, Australia, between 1996 and 1998 as an 'educational detective story' – a quest to expose the relations of dominance perpetuated by the special education knowledge tradition.[15]

Another phase in the development of detective fiction that seems to have preceded an analogous transformation of educational research is the emergence of what William Spanos (1987: 154) calls the 'anti-detective story': stories that 'evoke the impulse to "detect" … in order to violently frustrate it by refusing to solve the crime'.[16] Anti-detective stories can be interpreted as one manifestation of the wider cultural transformations subsumed by the concept of postmodernism. As Jeanne Ewert (1990: 167) writes, 'the detective novel is eminently suited to postmodern manipulation because its tacit dependence on the hermeneutic code offers the possibility of disabling that code' (p. 167). Although postmodernist scepticism towards modernist versions of rationality and agency supports Stefano Tani's (1984) suggestion that the classic detective story is 'doomed', literary postmodernism continues to provide explicit and implicit narrative models of 'detection' – of methodological and textual enquiry strategies. Thus, explicating continuities between educational enquiry and postmodernist anti-detective fiction might be one way of framing educational research as a postmodernist textual practice.

Postmodernisms and fictional 'detection'

To some extent, the detective story is not so much *a* modernist form of storytelling but *the* quintessential modernist genre. Brian McHale (1992: 146) argues that an 'epistemological dominant' characterises modernist fiction, with the typical plot being organised as 'a quest for a missing or hidden item of knowledge'. Thus, in its structure and thematics, 'a modernist novel looks like a detective story', centrally concerned with 'problems of the accessibility and circulation of knowledge, the individual mind's grappling with an elusive or occluded reality' (McHale 1992: 147). The detective is the archetype of the modernist subject – a quest(ion)ing 'cognitive hero', an 'agent of *recognitions* … reduced synecdochically to the organ of visual perception, the (private) eye', seeking to understand the *universe*, a unified and objective world. Modernist fiction can offer multiple perspectives on the world, but does so without disturbing the essential unity of the self: 'each perspective is lodged in a subjectivity which is itself relatively coherent, relatively centred and stable' (McHale 1992: 254).

By contrast, McHale (1992: 247) asserts that an 'ontological dominant' characterises postmodernist fiction – stories in which neither the world nor our selves are assumed to be unitary. Rather, postmodernist fiction explores the possibility that we function in an ontologically plural *multi*-verse of experience – that selves and worlds operate in many modalities. According to McHale, the characteristic genre of postmodernism is SF – an acronym for something much more complex than many popular stereotypes of 'science fiction'[17] – with its stock-in-trade of a potentially infinite variety of bodily forms, beings and cultures:

> [W]hile epistemologically-oriented fiction (modernism, detective fiction) is preoccupied with questions such as: what is there to know about the world? and who knows, and how reliably? How is knowledge transmitted, to whom, and how reliably?, etc., ontologically-oriented fiction (postmodernism, SF) is preoccupied

with questions such as: what is a world? How is a world constituted? Are there alternative worlds, and if so, how are they constituted? How do different worlds, and different kinds of world, differ, and what happens when one passes from one world to another, etc.?

McHale 1992: 247

I explore elsewhere questions about what narratives of educational research might look like if they were modelled on SF rather than detective fiction (see, for example, Gough 2001; 2004; 2007; 2008). Here, it will suffice to note that SF narrates ontological enquiries by such strategies as exposing a plurality of worlds by staging confrontations among them (or focusing attention on boundaries between them) rather than by personifying enquiry in the figure of a detective. Indeed, as Scott Bukatman (1993) notes, SF detective stories have rarely enjoyed success. The combination is difficult because the boundary between possible and 'impossible' in SF is so flexible and, because SF stories often presume some imagined future event or technological innovation, the 'solution' to the mystery may involve an unforeseeable twist (aliens, a time machine).[18] Douglas Adams's (1987; 1988) novels, *Dirk Gently's Holistic Detective Agency* and *The Long Dark Tea-Time of the Soul*, are rare instances of SF and detective genres being blended, albeit in the guise of humorous parodies of both.[19] However, Adams's Dirk Gently novels are also examples of the anti-detective story, which, in the light of McHale's reasoning, can be read as a postmodernist literary deconstruction of modern fiction's paradigmatic genre.

One of the most celebrated anti-detective stories is Umberto Eco's (1983b) novel, *The Name of the Rose*, which takes some well-known examples of generic detective fiction as its intertextual models,[20] but − as Eco (1984: 54) puts it − 'is a mystery in which very little is discovered and the detective is defeated'.[21] In *The Name of the Rose*, Eco uses the narrative form of detective fiction to deconstruct, disrupt and undermine the rationality of the models of conjecture that the genre conventionally provides − which is why, as Eco (1984: 57) writes, his 'basic story (whodunit?) ramifies into so many other stories, all stories of other conjectures, all linked with the structure of conjecture as such'. Eco provides a physical model of conjecturality in the abbey's labyrinthine library but also demonstrates that his detective − William of Baskerville − cannot decipher the complex social milieu of the abbey by assuming that it has a comparably logical (albeit complicated) structure. Following Gilles Deleuze and Félix Guattari (1983), Eco (1984: 57–58) likens 'the structure of conjecture' to the infinite networks of a rhizome rather than to the finite (and hierarchical) roots and branches of a tree:

> The rhizome is so constructed that every path can be connected with every other one. It has no center, no periphery, no exit, because it is potentially infinite. The space of conjecture is a rhizome space ... the world in which William realizes he is living already has a rhizome structure: that is, it can be structured but is never structured definitively ... it is impossible for there to be *a* story.

Other anti-detective stories that exemplify this indefinite 'structure of conjecture' include Paul Auster's (1987) *New York Trilogy* and Sophie Calle's (1999) remarkable *Double Game*.[22] Peter Høeg (1993: 410) emphatically makes a similar point in the final paragraph of *Miss Smilla's Feeling for Snow*.[23] 'Tell us, they'll come and say to me. So we may understand and close the case. They're wrong. It's only what you do not understand that you can come to a conclusion about. There will be no conclusion'.

Thus, the anti-detective story not only subverts the rationality of the investigatory methods modelled by conventional detective fiction but also denies the defensibility of dominant cultural expectations (such as a desire for *the* 'true' story) that animate such investigations. The literature of educational enquiry is replete with examples of researchers not understanding what they come to conclusions about, lured by the possibility of telling 'one true story' and encouraged by the cultural pervasiveness of detective stories as intertextual models of how research should be narrated. The significance of anti-detective stories for social and educational enquiry is that they model ways of narrating research differently and, furthermore, they might help us to reshape our expectations about what it is possible and desirable to narrate. For example, Valerie Harwood (2001: 151) names 'being undetective' as a deliberate strategy for 'working in ways that do not nourish searches for truth' but at the same time sustaining an 'obligation to truth'. She quotes the narrator of *The Name of the Rose* who observes that 'William was not at all interested in the truth, which is nothing but the adjustment between the thing and the intellect. On the contrary, he amused himself by imagining how many possibilities were possible' (Eco 1983b: 306). Harwood suggests that asking 'how many possibilities are possible?' is an 'undetective' way to create 'vigilance to truth' without searching for *the* truth.[24] I prefer to formulate Harwood's strategy as *becoming* undetective because I am disposed to accept Deleuze and Guattari's (1987; 1994) insistence that we should not see our lives and work in the fixed and immobile terms of 'being' but, rather, that 'all life is a plane of becoming, and … the perception of fixed beings … is an effect of becoming' (Colebrook 2002: xx)

The pedagogical usefulness of *The Name of the Rose* in studying research methodology is enhanced by comparing the postmodernism of the novel and the modernism of Jean-Jacques Annaud's film version. As McHale (1992: 149) observes:

> [T]he William of Baskerville whom we encounter in the film is a *successful* detective. He suffers a defeat, of course, in the burning of the library and particularly of the lost volume of Aristotle; but he has not been defeated *as a detective*, but rather (like Sherlock Holmes himself in story after story) vindicated in the end. By contrast, Eco's original William of Baskerville conspicuously *fails* as a detective. He discovers the truth, yes, but by stumbling upon it, not by a successful chain of deductions.

William's failures as an exemplary modernist detective allow the novel to foreground productive narrative strategies from postmodernist repertoires. Consider the following interchange between William and his 'Watson', Adso:[25]

> 'What I did not understand was the relation among signs … I behaved stubbornly, pursuing a semblance of order, when I should have known well that there is no order in the universe.'
>   'But in imagining an erroneous order you still found something … '
>   'What you say is very fine Adso, and I thank you. The order that our mind imagines is like a net, or like a ladder, built to attain something. But afterward you must throw the ladder away, because you discover that, even if it was useful, it was meaningless … The only truths that are useful are instruments to be thrown away'.

> Eco 1983b: 492

William could equally well be describing the changes wrought by poststructuralism in the relationships between investigatory methods – 'detection' – and objects of social enquiry. Once we have 'found something' with the ladders and nets – the 'erroneous order' – we have imagined, they can be thrown away because, in deconstruction, the method precedes the problem and is 'meaningless' once it has served its purpose of foregrounding the effects of our uses of language in constituting that problem. But whereas structuralist ladders and nets lead us towards closure and a semblance of 'order in the universe', poststructuralist ladders and nets are temporary markers of ongoing processes of reconfiguration, leading not to closure but to new openings. *The Name of the Rose* is itself such an 'erroneous order', which Eco emphasises by using metafictional narrative strategies – strategies that expose his story's status as text and as fiction – to destabilise the projected world of the novel, thus drawing attention to the very processes by which it is constructed both as a world to be explored and the means of its own exploration.

Thus, after poststructuralism, I consider that undertaking educational research in ways that are analogous to the methods of Sherlock Holmes, Miss Marple, Philip Marlowe, V. I. Warshawski, Dirk Gently, Kate Fansler, or even William of Baskerville, are no longer defensible. We should be able to find more generative inspirations for our practice by 'watching the *un*detectives', including the authors of SF and other postmodernist fictions whose work probes the mysteries of the word-worlds they (and we) inscribe.

Acknowledgments

I thank Annette Gough, Bill Green, Antoinette Oberg and Pat Thomson for introducing me to authors and detectives who might otherwise have eluded my enquiries.

Notes

1 To avoid the longwindedness of constantly referring to both social enquiry *and* educational enquiry I will generally use only one of these terms, with the understanding that I intend social enquiry always to include educational enquiry. I draw most of the examples of research texts and methods to which I refer from the areas of educational enquiry in which I practise, but emphasise that they are also examples of social enquiry writ large.

2 This phrase is the title of a popular song by Elvis Costello (1977) – one among many instances of the tropes and images of detective fiction spreading beyond the common forms of popular narrative media that constitute the genre (novels, comics, movies, etc.).

3 Note, however, that a strong case can be made for reading Holmes's method as *abduction* rather than deduction (see, for example, Umberto Eco 1983a).

4 From 'The adventure of Silver Blaze', first published in *The Strand Magazine* Vol. IV December 1892 and reprinted in Doyle (1986: 271–96).

5 The US television drama series *House* provides a more recent example (from 2004) of the unorthodox investigator – in this case medical diagnostician Dr Gregory House – who clashes with authority (the hospital's administrators). As a character, House has clear similarities to Sherlock Holmes: both are drug users, aloof and largely friendless.

6 Kinney initially wrote this essay for a research methodology course I taught at the University of Victoria, Canada, in August 1995.

7 'The adventure of the speckled band', first published in *The Strand Magazine* Vol. III February 1892 and reprinted in Doyle (1986: 194–209).

8 Thomson's essay was written for a research methodology course that I taught at Deakin University, Australia, in 1996.

9 One point at which this analogy might break down is in ascribing such qualities as 'guilt' and 'deception' to the agents of the 'false' solution.

10 'Op' is a colloquial abbreviation of 'operative'; thus, the 'Continental Op' is a private investigator employed as an operative of the Continental Detective Agency. The Continental Op's creator, Dashiell Hammett, served as an operative for the Pinkerton National Detective Agency from 1915 to 1921.

11 Lawn and Barton (1981) incorrectly attribute this quotation to Hammett rather than to Marcus.

12 The seventh edition of *The Concise Oxford Dictionary* (1982) has no separate entry for 'deconstruct' as it does, for example, for 'decompose'.

13 John Caputo (1997: 205) notes that 'Derrida was first welcomed to the USA by literary theorists, first at Johns Hopkins University in the 1960s and then in the 1970s at Yale and Cornell. Caputo indicates that US philosophers 'caught on to Derrida' sometime later, and their disputes with literary theorists' readings of Derrida were not represented in print until the early 1980s. Poststructuralism and deconstruction had little impact in US educational theory and curriculum studies until scholars such as Cherryholmes (1987; 1988) began to publish their 'poststructural investigations' in the mid- to late 1980s. According to Pinar and Reynolds (1992: 245), two Quebecois scholars – Jacques Daignault and Clermont Gauthier – were, for most of the 1980s, 'the only curricularists working post-structurally'.

14 In this judgement I depart from Munt (1994), who sees the Kate Fansler stories chiefly as expressions of liberal feminism. Although I agree that the gender politics of these stories might appear to be relatively conservative, I also believe that they make sufficient gestures towards poststructuralist conceptions of narrative framing – including subtle dispersals of the subject, and hints of multi-vocality – to interpret their textual politics as being rather more adventurous.

15 Moss undertook the doctoral research reported in her 1999 dissertation under my supervision.

16 Few of the examples of anti-detective stories that Spanos cites – including Franz Kafka's *The Trial* and Graham Greene's *Brighton Rock* – evoke the detective fiction genre per se, but all were written prior to 1960 and it is noteworthy that Spanos sees them as relatively early gestures towards the postmodernist literary imagination.

17 As Donna Haraway (1989: 5) explains, SF designates 'a complex emerging narrative field in which the boundaries between science fiction (conventionally, sf) and fantasy became highly permeable in confusing ways, commercially and linguistically'; SF also signifies 'an increasingly heterodox array of writing, reading, and marketing practices indicated by a proliferation of "sf" phrases: speculative fiction, science fiction, science fantasy, speculative futures, speculative fabulation'.

18 Larry Niven (1976) summarises some of the difficulties that authors face in writing hybrid SF/ detective stories. The distinctions that McHale draws between the detective and SF genres are demonstrated particularly clearly by George Alec Effinger (1988) whose SF detective, Marîd Audran, literally and materially embodies the shift from epistemological to ontological investigation when he deliberately shifts his mode of 'being' by augmenting and modifying his brain functions through the use of neural implants.

19 Parody is symptomatic of other attempts to postmodernise detective fiction. As Munt (1994: 173) explains: 'The few feminist crime novels appropriating a post-modern aesthetic express their sense of play and experimentation through parody'.

20 These include, for example, Conan Doyle's *The Hound of the Baskervilles*, Dorothy Sayers's *Gaudy Night* and Edgar Allan Poe's 'The purloined letter'.

21 By way of reflecting on my own textual strategies, I must point out here that I am not privileging Eco's interpretation of *The Name of the Rose* merely because he wrote it. I agree with the spirit of (Eco's 1984) dictum that 'The author should die once he [sic] has finished writing. So as not to trouble the path of the text' (p. 7). I quote Eco for the same reasons that I use or paraphrase other authors' words: because their formulations and interpretations are agreeable to me and because I am self-consciously writing in a genre of academic journalism characterised by the rhetorical deployment of frequent quotations and citations. For a thorough analysis of *The Name of the Rose*, both as detective fiction and as an example of 'the literature of semiotic possibility', see Peter Trifonas (1999).

22 Sophie Calle is a photographer and installation artist whose work explicitly resembles that of spies and detectives, including unobtrusive surveillance of herself and others. For example, Calle (1999: 122–23) writes that she produced one exhibition by having her mother hire a detective agency 'to follow me, to report my daily activities, and to provide photographic evidence of my existence'. Parts of *Double Game* are playful collaborations with novelist Paul Auster. In *Leviathan*, Auster (1992) used

episodes from Calle's life to create a character named Maria. In *Double Game*, Calle responds by enacting some of Maria's character sketches while Auster switches roles with Calle by putting her under observation. Calle pushes the play of art imitating art imitating life further by asking Auster to invent an entirely fictitious character whose 'scripted life' she follows. *Double Game* has three parts. Part I is 'the life of Maria and how it influenced the life of Sophie' (Calle 1999: 10–11), Part II is 'the life of Sophie and how it influenced the life of Maria' (34–5), and Part III is 'one of the many ways of mingling fact with fiction, or how to try to become a character out of a novel' (233–4). In *Double Game*, Calle deconstructs not only the detective 'story' but also the *performance* of both detective and author.

23 Published in North America as *Smilla's Sense of Snow*.
24 Harwood acknowledges that her 'undetective' strategy borrows from, and extends, my earlier formulations (Noel Gough 1994b; 1996; 1998) of the inter-relationships between fictional genres and educational enquiry.
25 Elsewhere (Noel Gough, 1994a), I have used excerpts from this passage to frame a comparison of the ways in which the concept of order is manifested in phenomenological and poststructuralist curriculum inquiry.

References

Adams, D. (1987) *Dirk Gently's Holistic Detective Agency*. New York: Pocket Books.
——(1988) *The Long Dark Tea-Time of the Soul*. New York: Pocket Books.
Auster, P. (1987) *The New York Trilogy: City of Glass, Ghosts, The Locked Room*. London: Faber and Faber.
——(1992) *Leviathan*. New York: Penguin.
Barthes, R. (1978) *A Lover's Discourse: Fragments*. Trans. R. Hurley. New York: Hill & Wang.
Bukatman, S. (1993) *Terminal Identity: The Virtual Subject in Postmodern Science Fiction*. Durham, NC and London: Duke University Press.
Burns, R. B. (1994) *Introduction to Research Methods*. Melbourne: Longman Cheshire.
Calle, S. (1999) *Double Game*. London: Violette Editions.
Caputo, J. D. (Ed.) (1997) *Deconstruction in a Nutshell: A Conversation with Jacques Derrida* (with a Commentary). New York: Fordham University Press.
Chandler, R. (1939) *The Big Sleep*. New York: Knopf.
Cherryholmes, C. (1987) A social project for curriculum: post-structural perspectives, *Journal of Curriculum Studies*, 19(4): 295–316.
——(1988) *Power and Criticism: Poststructural Investigations in Education*. New York: Teachers College Press.
——(1993) Reading research, *Journal of Curriculum Studies*, 25(1): 1–32.
Christie, A. (1930) *The Murder at the Vicarage*. New York: Dodd, Mead & Company.
Colebrook, C. (2002) *Understanding Deleuze*. Crows Nest NSW: Allen & Unwin.
Collins, J. (1989) *Uncommon Cultures: Popular Cultures and Post-Modernism*. London: Routledge.
Costello, E. (1977) *Watching the detectives* [Song]. London: Columbia Records.
Cross, A. (1964) *In the Last Analysis*. New York: Ballantine.
de Man, P. (1971) *Blindness and Insight: Essays in the Rhetoric of Contemporary Criticism*. New York: Oxford University Press.
Deleuze, G. and Guattari, F. (1983) *On the Line*. Trans J. Johnston, New York: Semiotext(e).
——(1987) *A Thousand Plateaus: Capitalism and Schizophrenia*. Trans B. Massumi. Minneapolis, MN: University of Minnesota Press.
——(1994) *What is Philosophy?* Trans G. Burchell and H. Tomlinson. London: Verso.
Derrida, J. (1972) Discussion: structure, sign and play in the discourse of the human sciences. In R. Macksey and E. Donato (Eds). *The Structuralist Controversy: The Languages Of Criticism and the Sciences of Man*. Baltimore, MD: The Johns Hopkins University Press, pp. 230–41.
Doyle, A. C. (1986) *The Complete Illustrated Sherlock Holmes*. Ware: Omega Books.
Eco, U. (1983a) Horns, hooves, insteps: some hypotheses on three types of abduction. In U. Eco and T. A. Sebeok (Eds). *The Sign of Three: Dupin, Holmes, Peirce*. Bloomington and Indianapolis: Indiana University Press, pp. 198–220.

——(1983b) *The Name of the Rose*. Trans W. Weaver, London: Secker & Warburg. (Originally published in Italy under the title *Il nome della rosa* by Gruppo Editoriale Fabbri Bompiani, Sonzogno Etas S.p.A., Milano, 1980).

——(1984) *Postscript to The Name of the Rose*. Trans W. Weaver. New York: Harcourt, Brace and Jovanovich.

Effinger, G. A. (1988) *When Gravity Fails*. New York: Bantam Books (first published by Arbor House 1986).

Ewert, J. C. (1990) Lost in the hermeneutic funhouse: Patrick Modiano's postmodern detective. In R. G. Walker and J. M. Frazer (Eds). *The Cunning Craft*. Macomb, IL: Western Illinois University Press, pp. 166–73.

Foster, M. (1994) The power to know one thing is never the power to know all things: methodological notes on two studies of Black American teachers. In A. Gitlin (Ed.). *Power and Method: Political Activism and Educational Research*. New York and London: Routledge, 129–46.

——(1999) Race, class, and gender in education research: surveying the political terrain, *Educational Policy*, 13(1): 77–85.

Gough, N. (1994a) Imagining an erroneous order: understanding curriculum as phenomenological and deconstructed text, *Journal of Curriculum Studies*, 26(5): 553–68.

——(1994b) Narration, reflection, diffraction: aspects of fiction in educational inquiry, *Australian Educational Researcher*, 21(3): 47–76.

——(1996) *Plotting research: educational inquiry's continuities with detective fiction*. Unpublished manuscript, Geelong, Victoria.

——(1998) Reflections and diffractions: functions of fiction in curriculum inquiry. In W. F. Pinar (Ed.). *Curriculum: Toward New Identities*. New York: Garland, pp. 94–127.

——(2001) Teaching in the *(Crash)* zone: manifesting cultural studies in science education. In J. A. Weaver, M. Morris and P. Appelbaum (Eds). *(Post) Modern Science (Education): Propositions and Alternative Paths*. New York: Peter Lang, 249–73.

——(2004) Narrative experiments: manifesting cyborgs in curriculum inquiry. In J. A. Weaver, K. Anijar and T. Daspit (Eds). *Science Fiction Curriculum, Cyborg Teachers, and Youth Culture(s)*. New York: Peter Lang, 89–108.

——(2007) Rhizosemiotic play and the generativity of fiction, *Complicity: An International Journal of Complexity and Education*, 4(1): 119–24.

——(2008) Narrative experiments and imaginative inquiry, *South African Journal of Education*, 28(3): 335–49.

Hammett, D. (1930) *The Maltese Falcon*. New York: Knopf.

Haraway, D. J. (1989) *Primate Visions: Gender, Race, and Nature in the World of Modern Science*. New York: Routledge.

Harwood, V. (2001) Foucault, narrative and the subjugated subject: doing research with a grid of sensibility, *Australian Educational Researcher*, 28(3): 141–66.

Hayles, N. K. (1990) *Chaos Bound: Orderly Disorder in Contemporary Literature and Science*. Ithaca, NY: Cornell University Press.

Heilbrun, C. G. (1989) *Writing a Woman's Life*. London: The Women's Press.

——(1997) *The Last Gift of Time: Life Beyond Sixty*. New York: Ballantine Books.

——(1999) *Women's Lives: The View from the Threshold*. Toronto: University of Toronto Press.

Høeg, P. (1993) *Miss Smilla's Feeling for Snow*. Trans F. David, London: Flamingo.

Jameson, F. (1983) On Chandler. In G. W. Most and W. W. Stowe (Eds). *The Poetics of Murder: Detective Fiction and Literary Theory*. New York: Harcourt Brace Jovanovich, 122–48.

Janesick, V. J. (1994) The dance of qualitative research design: metaphor, methodolatry, and meaning. In N. K. Denzin and Y. S. Lincoln (Eds). *Handbook of Qualitative Research*. Thousand Oaks, CA: Sage Publications, pp. 209–19.

——(1998) *'Stretching' Exercises for Qualitative Researchers*. Thousand Oaks, CA: Sage Publications.

——(2001) Intuition and creativity: a pas de deux for qualitative researchers, *Qualitative Inquiry*, 7(5): 531–40.

245

Kinney, S. (1998) Looking into *Rear Window*: experiential knowledge in educational inquiry. In J. Mousley, N. Gough, M. Robson and D. Colquhoun (Eds). *Horizons, Images and Experiences: The Research Stories Collection*. Geelong: Deakin University, 135–45.

Knopfler, M. (1982) *Private investigations* [Song]. London: Rondor Music International Inc.

Lancy, D. F. (1993) *Qualitative Research in Education: An Introduction to the Major Traditions*. New York and London: Longman.

Lawn, M. and Barton, L. (Eds) (1981) *Rethinking Curriculum Studies: A Radical Approach*. London: Croom Helm.

Mandel, E. (1984) *Delightful Murder: A Social History of the Crime Story*. Minneapolis, MN: University of Minnesota Press.

Marcus, S. (1977) Introduction. In D. Hammett *The Continental Op*. London: Pan Books, pp. 723.

McHale, B. (1992) *Constructing Postmodernism*. London and New York: Routledge.

Moring, I. (2001) Detecting the fictional problem solvers in time and space: metaphors guiding qualitative analysis and interpretation, *Qualitative Inquiry*, 7(3): 346–69.

Moss, J. (1999) *Inclusive schooling: contexts, texts and politics*. Unpublished Doctor of Philosophy, Deakin University, Geelong.

——(2003) Inclusive schooling policy: an educational detective story?, *Australian Educational Researcher*, 30(1): 63–81.

Munt, S. R. (1994) *Murder by the Book? Feminism and the Crime Novel*. London and New York: Routledge.

Niven, L. (1976) Afterword: The last word about SF/detectives. In *The Long ARM of Gil Hamilton*. New York: Ballantine Books, pp. 177–82.

Oldfather, P. and West, J. (1994) Qualitative research as jazz, *Educational Researcher*, 23(8): 22–6.

Paretsky, S. (1982) *Indemnity Only*. New York: Dial Press.

Pinar, W. F. and Reynolds, W. M. (1992) Appendix: Genealogical notes – the history of phenomenology and post-structuralism in curriculum studies. In W. F. Pinar and W. M. Reynolds (Eds). *Understanding Curriculum as Phenomenological and Deconstructed Text* (pp. 237–61). New York: Teachers College Press.

Porter, D. (1981) *The Pursuit of Crime: Art and Ideology in Detective Fiction*. New Haven, CT: Yale University Press.

Reid, W. A. (1981) The deliberative approach to the study of the curriculum and its relation to critical pluralism. In M. Lawn and L. Barton (Eds). *Rethinking Curriculum Studies*. London: Croom Helm, pp. 160–87.

Spanos, W. (1987) *Repetitions: The Postmodern Occasion in Literature and Culture*. Baton Rouge, LA: Louisiana State University Press.

Tani, S. (1984) *The Doomed Detective: The Contribution of the Detective Novel to Postmodern American and Italian Fiction*. Carbondale, IL: Southern Illinois University Press.

Thomson, P. (1998) Ned Ludd was framed. In J. Mousley, N. Gough, M. Robson and D. Colquhoun (Eds). *Horizons, Images and Experiences: The Research Stories Collection*. Geelong: Deakin University, pp. 146–50.

Trifonas, P. (1999) Crafting the literature of semiotic possibility: from the metaphysical to the detective story, *The Name of the Rose*. *International Journal of Applied Semiotics*, 1(1): 27–58.

Zizek, S. (1992) *Looking Awry: An Introduction to Jacques Lacan through Popular Culture*. Cambridge, MA: The MIT Press.

20

A personal reflection on doctoral supervision from a feminist perspective

M. E. David

I reflect on my professional life as a social scientist and educational researcher, including being a supervisor of about 50 doctoral students, in this chapter. I use my own intellectual autobiography as a basis for this reflection. This kind of personal reflection and narrative style of writing, based on the concept of stories and qualitative research is now a relatively commonplace approach in the social sciences (Deem 1996; Frame and Burnett 2007; Sikes 2006; 2008; Weiler and Middleton 1999; Weiler 2008; Weiner 1994). Whilst there are many versions of reflections and personal reflexivity, they are all attempts to locate 'the personal' in the wider social and political context of social relationships as understood in the social sciences (Wright Mills 1959). It has slowly emerged from the so-called biographic or personal turn (Chamberlayne *et al.* 2000) dating from the early 1990s. Most recently, the Economic and Social Research Council have recommended a narrative style for writing the end of award research project reports (2009; Society Today website www.esrc.ac.uk/ESRCInfoCentre/index.aspx).

I have used personal reflection in several previous studies, such as my extended account in *Personal and Political: feminisms, sociology and family lives* (David 2003a). In an essay entitled *Personal Learning on Professional Doctorates: Feminist and Women's Contributions to Higher Education* (David 2007), I considered the development of doctoral education, and my reflections on developing a professional doctorate in education. These have been conscious attempts to use feminist theorising to locate my own personal journey in relation to those of others of similar generation and gender.

Developments in narrative writing and personal reflections, often drawing on feminist perspectives, and emerging social scientific approaches, have grown apace during my academic life, which spans over 40 years. As I noted in *Personal and Political*, this approach to academic writing was not de rigeur when I started out life as a social scientist. Indeed it was completely other, and expectations were that one wrote in the third person, as if that made one more objective. Indeed, subjectivity was frowned upon, and social scientific methods tended to focus on either quantitative approaches, or qualitative methods within a positivist framework. Value commitments, and the pursuit of social and/or gender justice were certainly not recognised as appropriate to the academic or scholarly endeavour (David 2005).

Thus, my professional life as an academic social scientist has witnessed dramatic changes, which have indeed been linked to wider socio-political developments, too. I have also tried to illustrate how these wider changes are linked together with a feminist project in higher education in a couple of essays written together with Sue Clegg (Clegg and David 2006; David and Clegg 2008). I have also attempted to develop a specific and feminist analysis of doctoral education and studies together with Diana Leonard and Louise Morley (Morley *et al.* 2002; 2003), although our aim to develop a research project on doctoral assessment through an investigation of the viva voce was not successful.

My own doctoral work in socio-political context

When I embarked on an academic career, back in the second half of the 1960s, becoming a professional social scientist did not necessarily entail undertaking a doctorate of philosophy or PhD. Indeed, I obtained three posts as a research officer at various colleges of the University of London without the necessity to have undertaken a doctorate and only with an undergraduate degree in sociology. I was a researcher at the postgraduate Institute of Psychiatry (part of the then University of London) on a US–UK comparative study of mental illness, followed by being a researcher in the Department of Social Administration at the London School of Economics, on a study of gambling, work and leisure and finally a research officer in the Department of Economics at Queen Mary, University of London, on a study of local educational planning (David 1977).

It was only after a year as a visiting research associate on a comparative study of educational decision making (David 1975) at Harvard University's Graduate School of Education, that the necessity of obtaining a doctorate became abundantly clear. I returned to the UK, to a lecturing post in educational policy and social administration at the University of Bristol, obtained without having a doctorate. I decided that I wanted to convert some of my previous educational research, conducted as a research officer on a then Social Sciences Research Council (SSRC) project into local education authority (LEA) planning into a doctorate. This was very much to the surprise of my mentor and 'supervisor', Professor, now Lord, Maurice Peston. He did not have a doctorate and yet was a very successful academic economist and founder of the Economics Department within one of the growing colleges of the University of London. His riposte to my request was: 'Why do you want one of those?', to which my reply was that I wanted to be able to become an international scholar. Without a PhD, research or indeed teaching and becoming an academic in the USA, for example, would be impossible. Thus, I obtained my PhD in the spring of 1975. This was later published as *Reform, Reaction and Resources: the 3 Rs of Educational Planning* (David 1977).

The emergence of doctoral studies as part of the expansion of social sciences

My obtaining a PhD was thus happenstance and relatively unusual for a social scientist of my generation in the UK. Although it was already the usual path for natural scientists to pursue a doctorate followed by postdoctoral fellowships as a prelude to becoming a fully fledged academic in UK universities this was not the case for either the social sciences or humanities. Several of my colleagues and associates of my generation have indeed become very successful and senior academics, and part of the senior administration of universities, including becoming deans, and vice chancellors, without having studied for or obtained a doctorate. It is also notable how many social scientists, especially women, of my generation have obtained PhDs by what might now be considered unconventional routes, for example obtaining a doctorate by publication (e.g. Arnot 2002), or by an extended period of research (e.g. Anna Pollert, who published her study *Girls, Wives, Factory Lives* (1981) before obtaining a PhD). Moreover, as I will mention below, the development of new and distinctive forms of doctorate, such as professional doctorates in education, have been developed to accommodate a range of different career paths into and through higher education. These often mirror the careers of women as professionals and educators.

However, it is also important to mention here how obtaining a PhD helped to assure me of what was entailed in undertaking such a research project and how therefore to become an appropriate supervisor and mentor for doctoral supervision. Of course, this has also become a professional learning experience and development for me, as much as it has for the students that I have had the privilege to supervise. I turn now to my learning to become a doctoral supervisor. I will then move on to how the process of doctoral supervision has become formalised over the last couple of decades, along with the growth of diverse forms of doctorate, both nationally and internationally.

On becoming a doctoral supervisor, and graduate studies officer, Bristol-fashion

I returned to the UK from an exciting and exhilarating year in the USA, albeit that it was also a very taxing time intellectually, to my first full-time academic post at the University of Bristol. My previous positions had been as a contract researcher, on externally funded research projects. Given the high reputation of the university in the UK if not in the USA, I was very excited by my new opportunities to develop a professional career as a social scientist. Given the controversial political times, too, of emerging social movements for equality and liberation against a backdrop of social repression and regulation of the Conservative administrations I became passionately involved in both my academic work and developing women's studies within and outside the university (see David 2003a, chapter 3 entitled 'Feminist move into the Academy' pp. 61–83; and chapter 4 'New Right Turn and Feminism in the Academy "Bristol Fashion"' pp 83–105).

My job as a lecturer in the School of Applied Social Studies entailed developing undergraduate courses in education and social administration, and also teaching on a postgraduate diploma for students wishing to become professional social administrators or social workers, including in child care. Together with women colleagues in both my own department and in other departments within the social sciences faculty of the university, we began to develop an array of undergraduate and postgraduate courses on understanding social and sexual divisions in society. This included the emerging forms of women's studies and the fundamental question of the history of education as underpinning these developing issues. We were part of an international social movement that later became known as 'second wave feminism' (Weiler and David 2008). We also became a group of academics who taught on courses outside the university, extra-murally or for the workers' educational movement.

My first doctoral students: early feminist studies in motherhood or sisterhood?

Most significantly, however, was that we were joined as an emerging collective of academic colleagues by other women who were undertaking doctoral or research studies on specific funded research projects. Whilst it was relatively unusual to undertake a doctorate as a prelude to an academic career, it was not completely unknown, and during this period of the late 1970s, I acquired about half a dozen students to supervise either jointly or singly. There were three, in particular, who were my personal supervisees, and who worked together in their interests in emerging feminist studies or work on reclaiming women's history. Having completed successfully their PhDs, they have gone on to have highly successful academic careers: Linda Ward, now Professor of Disability and Social Policy at the University, Myna Trustram who has become a curator of women's museums, and Gill Blunden, now Professor Gillian Blunden-Grant, Dean of the Faculty of Health and Life Sciences at de Montfort University. Their substantive topics were somewhat different with Linda interested in the history of birth control and family planning in the 1920s; Myna interested in nineteenth century history of women's relation to the army, especially in terms of women's health (Trustram 1985); and Gill the one most concerned with the history of women's education at the turn of the twentieth century and in relation to local economies and women's work (Blunden 1983).

Clearly, Gill's substantive work was closest to my own. We worked collaboratively and she helped me to develop my own studies of the history of education, which also related to my undergraduate teaching on education and social policy (David 1980). However, given the lack of knowledge about the terrain of women's social and intellectual histories and involvement, as academic social scientists and relatively early career researchers, we relished the challenge of forging new ways of understanding and developing new women's histories and understandings. Indeed, we learnt and researched together, although at times my role as a supervisor felt more maternal than sisterly, and one of equals. This was neither paternalism nor patriarchy, although the power relations were complex and sometimes contested. Gill, Linda and Myna were all only a few years younger than me, and perhaps that is why the early women's movement took on the slogan about sisterhood being 'powerful' (Morgan 1970). A decade later, the idea of sisterhood as being a part of feminist practices either within or outside the academy was heavily critiqued by Juliet Mitchell and Ann Oakley and subsequently (1976; 1986; 1997).

The idea of motherhood and the maternal role was, however, one that was being critiqued and developed with respect to women's roles within the family (Oakley 1974; 1976; 1979) and in relation to research practices (Oakley 1981). Indeed, Ann Oakley's 'Interviewing women: a contradiction in terms' became a classic text for qualitative research methods in the 1980s. The question of the caring role of women in relation not only to children and men in the family, but also as it began to influence women's roles outside the family and in work, especially educational work, became a commonplace of feminist social research (David 2003a, op. cit.).

For example, the French term for nursery and early childhood education – *ecole maternelle* – gave the lie to women's roles both inside and outside the home. Thus, it was a relatively familiar role for myself and other women supervisors to play in relation to our doctoral students, although little has been written about this except Sara Delamont's work with colleagues on supervising the doctorate (Delamont *et al.* 1998; 1998/2005). Subsequently, feminists began to draw more on psychoanalytic ideas for understanding social relationships. For instance Chodorow's (1978) *The Reproduction of Mothering: psychoanalysis and the sociology of gender* also became a classic study of its kind during this period. Ideas about sibling rivalry also abounded (Dunn and Kendrick 1982; Dunn 1984). Whilst these were normally being developed in relation to studies of children in families, with the benefit of hindsight, it is not hard to discern the sibling rivalry between my first three excellent doctoral students, especially in relation also to my learning to adopt a maternal role as a supervisor.

The viva voce: formalising doctoral assessment in UK social sciences

Perhaps the most significant display of the maternal role was in relation to the doctoral examination and assessment process. When I was examined for my PhD in the University of London the regulations were that the viva voce should consist of an external examiner and the supervisor in the role as internal examiner. Indeed, my own viva voce was incredibly, for nowadays, unusual. My external examiner at the time was on secondment as an economic adviser to the Treasury and thus my viva was held in his office in the UK Government's Treasury at 9 a.m. It was an informal and relatively brief occasion, although the questions asked were rather difficult and incisive. I certainly felt that I was grilled by two rather patriarchal and somewhat paternal figures; and grateful for their approval of my work.

A similar set of regulations were in place at the University of Bristol in the 1970s and early 1980s. However, there was a question raised about whether the supervisor should be present, or whether the process should consist only of the external examiner. Once the external examiners had been chosen, selected in negotiation with the students themselves, all three of my early students wanted to be examined alone. It was an interesting reflection on their desire to prove themselves as having grown up, and not needing the mother's care and attention. Their examinations were then very closed and private affairs, and equally informal as mine had been.

Another analogy with the maternal role is that the process of producing a doctoral thesis is somewhat akin to being pregnant and giving birth. Thus, actually going into labour can be a prolonged and difficult process of confinement. Letting go, and producing a perfect baby, are conflicting processes. These analogies were present at the time. They have continued to pervade the changing processes of doctoral supervision and examination (Tinckler and Jackson 2004).

Patriarchal concepts also abounded when I became the inaugural Graduate Studies Officer (GSO) in the Faculty of Social Sciences at Bristol. The role was created to deal with the growing number of postgraduate research students in a growing faculty, with new subjects or disciplines and interdisciplinary social science studies developing. The role was subordinate to that of the Dean of the Faculty, given the smaller scale of postgraduate students compared to that of undergraduate studies within the faculty.

Patriarchal responsibilities for original doctoral research?

The role of GSO grew out of the process by which the then Faculty Board was responsible for approving the titles of the thesis, brought to the board's attention by the supervisor rather than the student; another parental responsibility perhaps? For the most part, the responsibilities related to ensuring the adequacy of titles, and related supervision, and supervisors, including dealing with the occasional conflicts that emerge between students and supervisors, and in the process of selection of external examiners for the viva voce. Here, the questions hinged on whether or not the examiners could and should be known to the students and selected by or for them. Again, the orthodoxy had been one of paternalism, namely that the supervisors should decide on examiners as objectively as possible. This would ensure that there was no collusion, and that the student's work would be evaluated dispassionately, in the secret garden of the viva voce.

What was not then attended to, perhaps because of the paucity of female research students, and an even smaller number of female academics, was the potential for harassment and abuse, including sexual, in these processes. However, one of the changes that was raised during this period, was the need for examiners to be chosen with respect to, and sympathy for, not only the disciplinary boundaries, but also the intellectual approach to the subject matter. The question of whether the external examiner was in sympathy with the particular approach and perspective became of particular significance in this process. Doing feminist or gender work was a significant challenge to the orthodoxies of the time. This was first expressed most clearly in relation to thesis titles, but became a more challenging dilemma in relation to the selection of sympathetic or so-called objective examiners.

Formalising doctoral supervision and examination in the 1990s

As the expansion of higher education gathered pace during the last two decades of the twentieth century (see, for example, Rosado and David 2006; Weiner 2009; David et al. 2009 in press), so too did the growth of postgraduate and research or doctoral students. By the end of the twentieth century there were as many postgraduate students as there had been undergraduates 40 years earlier. The numbers of undergraduates had quadrupled to two million in the UK, with many international and overseas students. This process of so-called massification, or the move from elite, to mass, to universal higher education (Trow 2005), has been discussed in a diversity of ways, but in particular with the process of marketisation and regulation. Morley's (2003) critique of the processes of equality, quality and power in higher education remains one of the most trenchant critiques of these changes largely with respect to undergraduate studies.

The formalisation of doctoral supervision and examination, in relation to expansion, took many forms (Morley et al. 2002). In the first place, there was the question of new universities, created in 1992 under the Further and Higher Education Act, receiving research degree awarding powers, as part of their becoming independent universities. Until 1992, powers of awarding degrees, including doctorates, had usually been vested in the Council for National Academic Awards (CNAA) rather than the universities themselves. Some of these former polytechnics had achieved research and undergraduate degree awarding powers, in the mid- to late 1980s, as part of the changing processes.

South Bank, for example, where I was appointed Head of the Department of Social Sciences in 1985, already had both sets of degree-awarding powers. Nevertheless, its security as an independent higher education institution, was much less assured than Bristol's had been. Thus, the regulations for research or doctoral degrees were far more formalised than those that I had previously experienced.

However, given that I was by then a relatively experienced supervisor, with almost 10 successful supervisions to my name, I was treated with a great deal of respect and dignity. I was almost immediately appointed to the rather prestigious Research Degrees Committee for all subjects across the college, responsible for regulating all the arrangements for supervision, progress and upgrading, and examination, including appointing external examiners. The college was largely a science, technology and engineering institution, and had very extensive and bureaucratic procedures for research degrees. Some years later, when the structures of the college were reorganised, I became chair of the sub-committee for research degrees in humanities and social sciences (in other words, for all the non-science, technology and engineering subjects).

This was a tremendous change, and allowed for the flowering of a variety of new approaches to doctoral research within and across the social sciences. Whilst the regulations for supervision and examination were far more formal than they had been in the traditional universities, this to some extent allowed for a more open and transparent process of supervision, including the requirement for joint supervision and for both independent internal and external examiners. The processes of joint supervision also meant that it was possible for the more experienced and senior supervisor to mentor and help the less experienced to become independent and also to be eligible to become an external examiner.

Mothering work: supervising feminist educational studies and methodologies?

During my time at South Bank, I also had the privilege of supervising a number of excellent feminist social and educational research students. I began to feel that this kind of research supervision and collaborative working relations was my métier. Indeed, having successfully supervised three feminist doctoral students, we produced a book together about our research entitled *Mothers and Education: Inside Out? Exploring Family-Education Policy and Experience* (David *et al.* 1993). These three research students were all so-called mature women students when they embarked upon their doctorates. Indeed, this was the focus of Ros Edwards' study, which was also published separately (Edwards 1993). Mary Hughes was active as an adult educator, and had several previous publications, and wrote about feminist adult education. Jane Ribbens was interested in mothering in relation to young children and her thesis developed these concerns, and was also published separately (Ribbens 1995).

An even more significant issue to emerge, however, during this period of work, was the development of the concept of feminist methodology as applied to social and educational research. Thus, Ros and Jane went onto to develop their analysis through a group they organised called the women's workshop, made up of feminist doctoral researchers (Ribbens and Edwards 1998).

Collaborative feminist research amongst groups of doctoral students thus became the norm rather than the exception. Diane Reay, now Professor of Education at Cambridge University, also came as a mature student to study mothers and their relations with schooling. Her thesis was published as *Class work: mothers' involvement in their children's primary schooling* (Reay 1998). Together with Ros Edwards and another of our research students – Kay Standing – and a researcher on one of our funded projects – we began to develop further methodological and substantive analyses of mothering in relation to education and schooling. Thus, two collaborative essays were produced from this work (David *et al.* 1996; 1997).

Thus, doctoral supervision and collaborative feminist educational research had become an exciting and exhilarating aspect of the funded and informal research undertaken at what became South Bank University, and its Social Sciences research centre of excellence. This indeed was what Ann Oakley called her similar, and even more productive, research centre at the London University Institute of Education, namely the Eppi-centre. Supervision of feminist doctoral research had thus come in from out of the margins, to coin a phrase used by Sylvia Walby and Jane Aaron (1991) in discussing the whole question of women's studies.

The regularisation of our passionate feminist research:

During the 1990s there was a flowering of women's studies, including the development of critiques of doctoral studies from a feminist perspective. For example, Diana Leonard provided intellectual leadership for feminist studies in education, for teachers and doctoral studies. Her *A Woman's Guide to Doctoral Studies* (Leonard 2001) provides an extended critique of developments in postgraduate studies from a feminist perspective. Similarly Tinckler and Jackson (2004) have developed a careful analysis of the doctoral process from a feminist and gender perspective.

However, at the same time the regularisation of our passionate feminist research was developing apace within the UK academy. On the one hand, there was an exciting initiative, by Bob Burgess, to set up the UK Council on Graduate Education, and aim to co-ordinate policy developments and practices across all universities in the UK. The organisation succeeded in becoming a membership organisation of all universities with graduate supervision. It even began to publish reports on developments and initiatives across the country, drawing comparisons and contrasts with other international developments, particularly in Europe.

On the other hand, the government also came to formulate new codes of practice and regulations through the funding of research through the research councils, and also the higher education funding councils, which also formalised the supervision and examination of doctorates. Whilst these made the processes more open and transparent, the dangers of the secret garden of the viva voce remained hazardous. Moreover, regularisation led to inequitable funding mechanisms for different types of student, in terms of subject, age and type of university. Thus, the possibilities of funding for part-time and mature, most usually women, students became more rather than less difficult. Yet these kinds of diverse students continued to grow and emerge.

Developing professional doctorates: the example of the Keele education doctorate

At the turn of the century, I was appointed to an exciting new position as Professor of Policy Studies in Education, at the University of Keele, with the specific remit to develop what were becoming very commonplace in the older universities – professional doctorates. These were mushrooming as universities continued to expand around the social sciences and humanities, especially. There were a range of different types of professional doctorate as Andrew Brown, Ingrid Lunt and colleagues (Brown *et al.* 2004) have shown, from those in creative arts, design and the humanities, to new professional areas such as business and management, as well as the practice of education.

Such professional doctorates developed more quickly, through different funding mechanisms, in former commonwealth and Anglophone countries such as Australia, Canada and New Zealand. Indeed, a biennial conference on professional doctorates was inaugurated in Australia towards the end of the millennium (McWilliam 2002; McWilliam *et al.* 2002). In the USA, doctorates in specific subjects had also begun to emerge on rather different lines. In some universities, where the practice of research advice was rather different from the UK, doctorates in education, as academic rather than professional, degrees begun to emerge (David 2003b) This is part of a wider movement of change around new forms of teaching and learning across education, including higher education (see David 2009 in press).

A key distinction between professional and traditional academic doctorates in the UK was to be the range of taught elements. Whilst taught components had always been a feature of doctorates in the USA, this had not conventionally been the case in the UK. Thus, the possibilities were tremendous as to how to develop a professional doctorate, although gauging the market for such developments was quite a problematic question. As I have noted in my essay in Sagaria's edited volume (David 2007) at Keele, we decided upon two distinctive approaches. One was to develop a professional doctorate for education policy practitioners, such as people working in local or central government agencies concerned with policy developments. This was because as a faculty and department we had considerable expertise and experience with a range of masters courses for educational policy practitioners.

The other development was to build on the expertise in working with mature women students within a range of educational settings, such as teachers in schools, further and higher education, including other and newer universities. In this course we targeted those students interested in exploring issues of gender in relation to education and management, theoretically and methodologically. We, thus, named the doctoral programme Gender and Educational Management or GEM. Indeed we found recruitment to this latter programme somewhat easier, and also the students that we recruited stayed the course and completed their thesis work, despite it appearing rather demanding given their busy lives and jobs.

Examples of some of our successful students include a lecturer in health policy and management at Keele itself who completed a thesis on health and sex education in the Caribbean, with the specific example of Guyana. Another was a former head teacher turned lecturer in education at the Aga Khan University first in Kenya, then in Karachi in Pakistan and now in Tanzania. Her work was on educational professionals and their attitudes to different types of gender policies in schools. Yet another example was of the head of a university faculty undertaking a study, from a psychoanalytic perspective, of the roles of academics, women especially at her university.

A key feature of the professional doctorate in education is the extent to which one's professional setting can and is the basis for one's thesis study. Thus, being able to theorise and develop an understanding of professional practice from one's own standpoint has become germane to these programmes (Brown *et al.* 2004). The origins of the developments of this standpoint perspective are complex and contradictory. With Sue Clegg I have developed an analysis of the genealogies of 'the project of the personal' (Clegg and David 2006; David and Clegg 2008). At least two strands include the political project from second wave feminism, and the strand of the creation of the neoliberal, employable subject. Feminist ideas about 'the personal as political' have, for instance, become part of standpoint theory and developed within feminist methodology (Smith 1987).

Conclusions: changing higher education in global socio-economic contexts

The geography and shape of higher education, including the place of postgraduate doctoral education and feminist studies within doctorates has been transformed over the course of the last four decades. That transformation is in part because of the wider, global economic and political developments, including international economic competition. This has meant that the place of higher education within international economies has also been transformed. As the feminist Sheila Slaughter and Gary Rhoades (Slaughter and Rhoades 2004) have argued, for the USA the fundamental changes amount to what they now call 'academic capitalism'. They demonstrate how fundamental international movements of students are, especially in becoming part of the academic labour markets in the USA (ibid.). They argue that this creates increasing inequalities between the developed and developing nations. Whilst the global economic recession may put a break on these developments to some extent, they are powerful forces that seem difficult to stem.

A second issue of importance is how influential the development of the social sciences, and especially feminist work within the social sciences, has become to the transformations of higher education and its practices. This had started with the development of doctorates, and doctoral studies, as Diana Leonard (2001) has argued so cogently. Early feminist theses added to the stock of feminist knowledge and understanding, as well as methodological developments.

Similarly, more recently, the international growth and development of professional doctorates, especially but not only within education, has also been an important sign of changing forms of higher education. Thus, feminist pedagogies and practices are no longer only in the margins of higher education, although they may remain in the interstices of many of the more elite and traditional universities and subjects within the UK (Weiner 2009). However, the internationalisation of higher education, and global developments in ICT, has influenced the extent of methodological, theoretical and substantive developments. Thus, the internationalisation of diverse systems of external examinations and the viva voce, in particular, have led to both the diversification and yet stratification of feminist work and doctoral studies. This then ranges across the so-called global north, including the USA, UK, Australia and New Zealand, by comparison with the south, and the developments of doctoral studies in Africa and Asia as key instances (Morley and Lugg 2009).

Feminist studies and methodologies are now a key element in the pedagogies and practices of higher education (David 2005; Weiner 2006), including influencing doctoral work. However, this is not an unalloyed good, as systems of patriarchal domination and power relations, including through sexual harassment and abuse continue to have their place (Leathwood and Read 2008). Yet, in conclusion, it must be noted that the trends in gender transformations in working lives are a key feature of the social and economic global changes into the twenty-first century.

References

Arnot, M. (2002) *Reproducing Gender? Critical Essays on educational theory and feminist politics*. London: RoutledgeFalmer.

Bazeley, P. (1999) Continuing research by PhD graduates, *Higher Education Quaterly*, 53(4): 333–52.

Blunden, G. (1983) Typing in the Tech. In D. Gleeson (Ed.). *Further Education*. London: Routledge.

Brown, A., Lunt, I., Scott, D. and Thorne, L. (2004) *Professional doctorates: Integrating Professional and Academic Knowledge*. Buckingham: Open University Press.

Chamberlayne, P., Bornat, J. and Wengraf, T. (Eds) (2000) *The biographic turn in the social sciences*. London: Routledge.

Chiang, I. (2003) Learning experience of doctoral students in UK universities, *International Journal of Sociology and Social Policy*, 23(1/2): 4–32.

Chodorow, N. (1978) *The Reproduction of Mothering: psychoanalysis and the sociology of gender*. Berkeley CA: University of California Press.

Clegg, S. and David, M.E. (2006) Passion, Pedagogies and the Project of the Personal in Higher Education, *21st Century Society: Journal of the Academy of Social Sciences*, 1(2) (October): 149–67.

David, M.E. (1975) *School Rule in the USA: A Case Study of Participation in Budgeting* (with a foreword by Professor Nathan Glazer, Harvard). Cambridge, MA: Ballinger, 152.

——(1977) *Reform, Reaction and Resources: the 3 Rs of Educational Planning*. London: NFER.

——(1980) *The State, the Family and Education*. Series on Radical Social Policy. London: Routledge and Kegan Paul.

——(2003a) *Personal and Political: feminisms, sociology and family lives*. Stoke-on-Trent: Trentham Books.

——(2003b) *Feminist Contributions to Doctoral Education in Britain: Feminist Knowledge in the New Knowledge Economy*. Included in the conference proceedings of the 4th International Biennial Conference on Professional Doctorates 'Research Training for the Knowledge Economy', held at University of Queensland, Brisbane, Australia, 29–30 November 2002, E. McWilliam (Ed.), pp. 39–53.

——(2005) Feminist Values and Feminist Sociology as Contributions to Higher Education. In S. Robinson and C. Katalushi (Eds). *Values in Higher Education*, Leeds: Aureus publishing company on behalf of the University of Leeds for the centenary, pp. 107–17.

——(2007) Personal Learning on Professional Doctorates: Feminist and Women's Contributions to Higher Education. In M. A. D. Sagaria (Ed.). *Women, Universities and Change*. London: Palgrave Macmillan.

——(Ed.) (2009 in press) *Improving Learning by Widening Participation in Higher Education*. In the Improving Learning series. London: Routledge.

David, M. E., Edwards, R., Hughes, M. and Ribbens, J. (1993) *Mothers and Education: Inside Out? Exploring Family-Education Policy and Experience*. London: Macmillan.

David, M. E., Davies, J., Edwards, R., Reay, D. and Standing, K. (1996) Mothering, Reflexivity and Feminist Methodology. In L. Morley and V. Walsh (Eds). *Breaking Boundaries: Women in Higher Education*. London: Taylor and Francis, 208–23.

——(1997) Choice within Constraints: Mothers and Schooling, *Gender and Education*, 9(4): 397–410.

David, M. E and Clegg, S. (2008) Power, Pedagogy & Personalization in global higher education: the occlusion of second wave feminism? In special issue of *Discourse, The Cultural Politics of Education* December 29(4): 483–98.

Deem, R. (1996) Border Territories: a journey through sociology, education and women's studies, *British Journal of Sociology of Education*, 17(2): 5–19.

Delamont, S., Atkinson, P. and Parry, O. (1998) Creating a delicate balance: The doctoral supervisor's dilemmas, *Teaching in Higher Education*, 3(2): 157–72.

——(1998/2005) *Supervising the PhD: a guide to success*. Buckingham: SRHE and Open University Press.

Dunn, J. and Kendrick, C. (1982) *Siblings: Love, envy and understanding*. Cambridge, MA: Harvard University Press.

Dunn, J. (1984) *Sisters and brothers*. Cambridge, MA: Harvard University Press. London: Fontana.

257

Edwards, R. (1993) *Mature Women Students: separating or connecting family and education*. London: Taylor and Francis.

Frame, P. and Burnett, J. (Eds) (2007) *Using Auto/Biography in Learning and Teaching*. SEDA Paper 120, p.5, foreword by M. E. David, London: SEDA (Staff Development Association).

Holdaway, E., Debois, C. and Winchester, I. (1995) Supervision of Graduate Students, *The Canadian Journals of Higher Education*, 25(3): 1–29.

Leathwood, C. and Read, B. (2008) *Gender and the changing face of higher education*. Buckingham: SRHE and Open University Press.

Leonard, D. (2001) *A Woman's Guide to Doctoral Studies*. Buckingham: Open University Press.

McWilliam, E. (Ed.) (2002) *Fourth international biennial conference on professional doctorates: research training for the knowledge economy conference proceedings*. Brisbane: Australia Queensland University of Technology.

McWilliam, E., Thomson, P., Green, B., Maxwell, T., Wildy, H. and Simons, D. (2002) *Research Training in Doctoral programmes: What can be learnt from professional doctorates?* Canberra: ACT Commonwealth of Australia Department of Education, Science and Training.

Marsh, H., Rowe, K. and Martin, A. (2002) PhD Students' evaluations of research supervisors, *Journal of Higher Education*, 73(33): 13–34.

Mitchell, J. and Oakley, A. (Eds) (1976) *The Rights and Wrongs of Women*. Harmondsworth: Penguin.

——(Eds) (1986) *What is Feminism?* Harmondsworth: Penguin.

——(1997) *Who's afraid of Feminism? Seeing through the Backlash*. Harmondsworth: Penguin.

Morgan, R. (Ed.) (1970) *Sisterhood is powerful*. New York: Random House (ISBN 0-394-70539-4).

Morley, L. (2003) *Quality and power in higher education*. Buckingham: Open University Press.

Morley, L., Leonard, D. and David, M. E. (2002) Variations in Vivas: Quality and Equality in British PhD Assessments, *Studies in Higher Education*, 27(3): 263–73.

——(2003) Quality and Equality in British PhD assessment. In special issue edited by H. Green and S. Powell. *Quality Assurance in Education* 11(2): 64–72 (won a prize for the best article in 2003 issues).

Morley, L. and Lugg, R. (2009) Mapping Meritocracy: intersecting gender, poverty and higher educational opportunity structures, *Higher Education Policy*, 22(1) (March): 37–60.

Oakley, A. (1974) *A sociology of housework*. London: Martin Robertson.

——(1976) *Housewife*. London: Penguin.

——(1979) *Becoming a mother*. Oxford: Martin Robertson.

——(1981) Interviewing women: a contradiction in terms. In H. Roberts (Ed.). *Doing Feminist Research*. London: Routledge.

Pollert, A. (1981) *Girls, Wives, Factory Lives*. London: Palgrave Macmillan.

Prosser, M. and Trigwell, K. (1999) *Understanding Learning and Teaching: The Experience in Higher Education*. Buckingham: SRHE and Open University Press.

Ramsden, P. (1991) A performance indicator of teaching quality in higher indication: The course experience questionnairre, *Studies in Higher Education*, 16: 129–50.

Ramsden, P., Conrad, L., Ginns, P. and Prosser, M. (2003) *Students' and Supervisors' Experiences of the Context for Postgraduate Study*. Paper presented at the *10th Conference of European Association for Research into Learning and Instruction*, Padua, August.

Reay, D. (1998) *Class work: mothers' involvement in their children's primary schooling*. London: UCL Press.

Ribbens, J. (1995) *Mothers and their Children: A Feminist sociology of child-rearing*. London: Sage.

Ribbens, J. and Edwards, R. (Eds) (1998) *Feminist Dilemmas and Qualitative Research Public Knowledge and Private Lives*. London: Sage.

Rosado, L. D. and David, M. E. (2006) A massive university or a university for the masses? Continuity and Change in Higher Education in Spain and England, *Journal of Education Policy*, 3(3): 343–64.

Sikes, P. (2006) Scandalous Stories and Dangerous Liaisons: When Male Teachers and Female Pupils Fall in Love, *Sex Education*, 6(3): 265–80.

——(2008) At the Eye of the Storm: An Academic(s) Experience of Moral Panic, *Qualitative Inquiry*, 14 (2): 235–53.

Slaughter, S. and Rhoades, G. (2004) *Academic capitalism and the new economy: Markets, State and Higher Education*. Baltimore, MD: John Hopkins University Press.

Smith, D. E. (1987) *The Everyday world as Problematic: A feminist sociology*. London: Martin Robertson.

Tinckler, P. and Jackson, C. (2004) *The Doctoral Examination Process*. Buckingham: SRHE and Open University Press.

Trigwell, K. and Ashwin, P. (2005) *Postgraduate Researches Students' Experience of Learning at the University of Oxford*. Oxford: University of Oxford.

Trow, M. (2005) Reflections on the Transition from elite to mass to universal access: forma and phases of higher education in modern societies since WW II. In P. Altbach (Ed.). *International Handbook of Higher Education*. Rotterdam Holland: Kluwer (now Springer).

Trustram, M. (1985) *Women of the Regiment: marriage in the Victorian army*. Cambridge: Cambridge University Press.

Walby, S. and Aaron, J. (Eds) (1991) *Out of the Margins: Women's Studies in the nineties*. London: Falmer Press.

Weiler, K. (2008) The feminist imagination and educational research, *Discourse: Studies in the Cultural Politics of Education*, 29(4): 499–509.

Weiler, K. and David, M. (2008) The personal and political: second wave feminism and educational research: introduction, *Discourse, Studies in the Cultural Politics of Education* (special issue on Second Wave Feminism), 29(4) (December): 433–5.

Weiler, K. and Middleton, S. (1999) *Telling Women's Lives: Narrative Inquiries in History of Women's Education*. Buckingham: Open University Press.

Weiner, G. (1994) Feminisms and Education. Buckingham: Open University Press.

——(2006) Out of the Ruins: feminist pedagogy in recovery. In B. Francis, L. Smulyan and C. Skelton (Eds). *International Handbook of Gender and Education*. London: Sage, pp. 79–92.

——(2009) More Difficult Times Ahead? The Impact of Patriarchy and Globalization on Gender In/Equality in Higher Education. In D. Stephens (Ed.). *Higher Education and International Capacity Building. Twenty Five Years of Higher Education Links,* Oxford: Symposium (ISBN 978-1-873927-22-9).

Wright Mills, C. (1959) *The Sociological Imagination*. Harmondsworth: Penguin.

21

Writing in, writing out

Doctoral writing as peer work

C. Aitchison and A. Lee

The context of our teaching and thinking about doctoral writing is the rapidly altering landscape of research and research education. This is a space of 'growth and expansion, changes in modes of knowledge production, modes of institutional and state governance, in forms of doctoral programmes and in pedagogies' (Boud and Lee 2009: 1). Universities are responding to a wide range of changed circumstances and students are experiencing altered forms of doctoral education and a heightened awareness of the impacts on them of greater international competition for graduate researchers.

In this landscape, writing and publishing have assumed a greater visibility and significance since we first wrote together about doctoral writing (Aitchison and Lee 2006). For example, there has been a growing number of reports of innovation in the support of doctoral writing, a recent and particular feature of which has been an attention to pedagogies that assist researchers to increase productivity and publication output (Kamler 2008; Kamler and Thomson 2006; Lee and Aitchison 2009; Aitchison *et al.* 2010). It would seem that much of this concern is driven by institutional desires to increase productivity-based income. What is less well documented are details of how these newer writing-focused pedagogies actually work for research students as they move from novice to experienced researchers, and how, in doing so, they are drawn into diverse sets of relations with networks of different kinds of peers.

In this chapter we build on our earlier work on writing groups as a pedagogy that promotes a writing-focused experience of research study and doctoral learning. As practitioner-researchers we draw on our combined experiences as supervisors, writing teachers and researchers working with doctoral students across a variety of disciplines and doctoral programmes. In particular here, we are concerned to show the ways in which writing groups facilitate an experience of doctoral research as participation in a network of peer relations: in the first instance within the writing group community itself, and then gradually more broadly, and ultimately with networks of other scholars.

To facilitate this intention, our discussion is focused on transcription data of interactions within an actual writing group meeting. We present, for the purposes of exploring the dynamics of peer work, two distinct modes of exchange, which we call 'writing in' and 'writing out'. These refer to the twin tasks of writing for self and the group, and, writing for the broader network of peer review to which doctoral writing is ultimately directed, that is external examination and scholarly publication. In any instance of writing and writing group exchange, both these foci are present and closely intertwined, of course, but for our purposes we artificially separate them to distinguish aspects we believe are helpful in building effective pedagogic interventions with students.

We then outline key characteristics and practices of writing groups in order to elaborate a conceptual framework for the idea of doctoral writing as 'peer work', building on the discussion of peer learning in the context of doctoral study developed by Boud and Lee (2005). There is little empirical research on students engaging in work on doctoral writing, so the material here offers a unique window into a conception of writing as intensely social, emotional and personal, as well as formal and public, involving dynamics of fear and desire (Simon 1992; Lee and Boud 2003), as well as intellectual understanding and skill development. We will see how writing is not something that is separable from reading, learning, sense making, understanding, theory building and positioning of self within the field of study. Rather, it is a site where these matters are played out in the textual work of dissertation writing. The segments of talk engaged by group members presented in this chapter show how these complexities are rendered visible and explicit.

Introducing the group

The writing group we analyse in this chapter consists of doctoral students from various disciplines, who had been meeting together, facilitated by Claire, for about six months at the time this recording was made. According to normal practice for such groups, two pieces of writing, previously circulated by email from Matthew and Amy, were to be discussed.

When forwarding his writing to the group, Matthew wrote: 'I would appreciate your comments on clarity of argument and the logical development of ideas'. At the meeting Matthew tells us that he is uncertain about some of the finer theoretical distinctions in his methodological framework, and, about his writing style. Typical of writing group meetings, in the discussion of Matthew's work, comments on details such as spelling mistakes and punctuation sit alongside more complex theoretical issues, how Matthew's position fits within his own scholarly community, his use of referencing, how various bits relate to other sections in the thesis, how his writing compares to others in the field, and so on.

Amy's writing is only four pages. It is new writing that will be an introductory piece to her dissertation. She has been struggling to realign her thinking following some major disruptions in the data collection. She is worried that she hasn't explained her stance very well, and she tells us: 'It's the first, it's a very, very, very first draft, an argument. So, yeah, I'm not really looking for micro edits at this stage'.

In both discussions there are broadly two kinds of conversations occurring. First, people are interested in the writing and the meanings as presented to the group itself, but there is also a parallel conversation about the other readers that Amy and Matthew are writing for.

Writing in: writing for the self and for the group

Writing groups are social constructions – they are communities of people who come together to discuss writing. This sociality stands in contrast to enduring notions of an individual writer/researcher working independently on their dissertation or their publications. Research students typically seek out writing groups as an antidote to isolation, and, because they expect the group environment will motivate them to write more, and through feedback, to write better (Aitchison 2009b). For doctoral students, especially those in humanities and social sciences where team-based research is less common, opportunities to participate in a community of writing scholars may be limited.

Our experience of writing groups mostly involves ongoing, facilitated and voluntary groups of six to eight committed people that meet fortnightly. Supervisors generally support the attendance of these students but are not actively involved. When writing groups are voluntary arrangements of doctoral students working together on their own writing, normal institutional hierarchies of power, assessment, and teaching and learning arrangements are disrupted and contested. A writing group can work as a 'safety' zone, a supported space, where members can experiment together, take risks and engage in forms of self-disclosure that can contribute to meaningful learning.

The following transcripts allow us to analyse how writing groups provide an opportunity for peers to engage in exploratory talk that facilitates this kind of learning. In the following two excerpts, the group talks about Matthew's text at hand, and reflects more generally on what kinds of writers, and kinds of writing they value. We begin this segment when Matthew responds to a compliment about his writing:

> *Louise*: I like your writing style, it's very easy to read. It's very easy to follow and it's clear. I can understand what you're saying.
> *Matthew*: I just look at it and keep on thinking … ah, I'd prefer if it was so complex only Einstein could understand it, because I think it's a failure when it's easy to read.
> *All*: No!!
> *Louise*: No – that means that you've turned something that's really difficult into something that …
> *Jane:* I think it's harder to write in everyday language.

In the writing group community in our example, there is only one scientific writer, and, despite a range of disciplinary backgrounds (including performing arts, welfare, botany, policy studies, natural sciences), they share a common project to progress their doctoral studies through writing their dissertation. As a group they write to a considerable extent for each other – bringing their work, sharing their vulnerabilities, hopes and desires. We see this vividly when the group responds immediately and universally 'No!!' to Matthew's desire to write so that 'only Einstein could understand it'. They speak as members of a community whose preference is for writing that is 'easy to read'. In fact Louise equates liking a style of writing with its readability. As a group they disagree that complexity necessarily equates with good writing. Matthew ranks his writing against an external standard; he implies that his dream is to make a significant intellectual contribution, that is, one that would be appreciated by the world's best. For this group on this day, there is quite a lot of talk and dreaming about what kind of writers they have been, they are, and they wish to become.

In the second half of the meeting, when the group looks at Amy's writing, they are more critical:

> *Louise*: Is it possibly a little rich?
> *Amy*: Yeah.

Louise: It's almost too much in one bite.

Jane: Yeah.

Catherine: It just needs some revision I suppose. I mean there is a lot you're saying – and it is enticing, but then I think; 'What?'.

[Amy shares her own anxiety about her writing:]

Amy: It is really, it is, … what I find really scary is I come from a humanities background and I know my writing looks very flowery to a lot of social scientists

Matthew: No.

Amy: So … but I can't …

Catherine: It's not flowery.

Catherine: It's just a bit packed.

Louise: And that's where I think structure really needs to be your friend.

Amy: Yeah, it's not my friend at the moment. Because I just don't know what I'm doing quite frankly, half the time.

Karen: In a way I look at this, and I kind of say this is almost something that you can analyse for so many things. Because you've got new ideas, it has a flow of writing and I really enjoyed the flow of this, but you know, you could, I would, be tempted to analyse it for what are the main things that I want to talk about here, and then rearrange it in a way, around that.

Catherine: It's like an abstract in a way for the whole thesis.

In contrast to their views on Matthew's writing, the group finds Amy's writing dense; 'possibly a little rich'. The group conveys responses thoughtfully by using hedging: 'possibly' and 'a little', and by reintroducing a cake metaphor they have used in earlier discussions: 'too much in one bite' and 'it's enticing'. The group is being honest in its critique and it is doing so with solidarity and concern.

For both these authors, Amy and Matthew, there is a sense of uncertainty about their writing. They are between the comfort of what is known, that is, their former ways of writing; and a concern that these older ways may no longer be suitable. Amy's explanation for her current mode of writing is historical: 'I come from a humanities background'. Amy and Matthew seem to be searching for a new writerly identity to match their new status as doctoral students. We can feel Amy's relief when it is confirmed that her writing is not 'too flowery'. We can also feel the pain and the torment she expresses about not writing as well as she'd like to: 'I just don't know what I'm doing quite frankly, half the time'. Bringing their writing to the group has been an important mechanism by which both authors have been able to get a sense of how their changing writing is being received. The group acts as a zone for testing out newer writerly identities.

These conversations are exploratory, and personal, exposing vulnerabilities and building on early investigations of the role of writing in constructing a scholarly identity. They are not sophisticated analyses of grammar or rhetoric but much more part of a process of coming to understand self and text, and the relations between thinking, writing and communicating. In these interactions we can see the group members working as a community of peers in which power is dispersed. Everyone participates in the discussion and there is a marked attention to the interpersonal dimensions of critical review; for example, members use hedging, metaphor, humour and self-revelation simultaneously building a sense of group cohesion and intimacy.

For doctoral students, writing groups provide a space to learn about the scholarly conventions away from the (real or imagined) burden of assessment and expectation so often associated with supervisor–student interactions. This conception of writing groups as some kind of 'safety zone' is especially poignant for novice writers unfamiliar with the requirements and conventions of doctoral-level academic writing and academic publishing. Sharing writing for critique amongst peers is quite different to the experience of sending writing off into an unfamiliar zone of unknown readers, practices and conventions. In writing groups the stakes are lower, as the readers are neither gate-keepers nor assessors and students recognise this as a freedom to try out different kinds of writing.

In evaluations, students explain the psycho-social benefits of working in groups: 'I find it a gentler way. If I come here first, you can say where the gaps are, and I can fix them before I send it off' and 'I get the chance to practise in the writing group (Aitchison 2009a: 261). Such evaluative comments eloquently point out the value of joining with others who are similarly placed, of the emotional support and confidence building that comes from sharing experiences and 'journeying' together.

Writing out: imagining the expanded group of peers

Writing group members do not simply write for each other, of course. Even as the group members talk about their own writing, there is a constant comparison with other writers. Their notions of themselves as writers are infused with knowledge of other writers. In the following transcript, reference is made to the characteristics of numerous academic and non-academic authors including Lewis Carroll, Shakespeare, Kissinger, Churchill, James Joyce, Foucault, Fairclough, Durkheim, Wodak and Beck.

Our research shows how, as these doctoral students seek to develop their writerly identity, they look to other writers as models for comparison or for emulation. As research students become more familiar with their scholarly or disciplinary communities, and especially if they plan to write for publication, they actively refer to published scholars in their field. When writing groups encourage experimentation and discussion, they can further assist students to extend their repertoire of writing.

Matthew's chapter commences with a quote from Lewis Carroll and another from Shakespeare. He has done this explicitly to test out the reaction of the group, as can be seen from the excerpt below. The first response from his peers is personal – 'I loved that; it's great!'. But it's not long before someone refers to practices within Matthew's disciplinary community, thus giving a different kind of authority and legitimacy to Matthew's experiment:

> *Matthew*: It's an introductory sort of … It's just a thing I've always liked.
> *Claire*: I think it's fabulous that we have Alice in Wonderland from the very outset.
> *Catherine*: I loved that. It's great.
> *Louise*: I liked that too.
> *Matthew*: I'm not sure … I just liked it; so I thought 'Bugger it, just put it in!'. Stick them both in.
> *Catherine*: I think particularly Lewis Carroll is more apt than the Shakespeare.
> *Louise*: I've seen other social constructionist writers use Carroll. It's very – it's a really nice way of setting it up.

We can see from the nature of the interactions over the texts students bring to the group that peer learning is both unpredictable and reciprocal. In the exchange above, Louise shares her knowledge about how other social constructionist writers draw on Carroll. In the exchange that follows, another student expresses her interest in learning from others, even proposing a 'Foucault lunch'. In their discussion it is clear there are different levels of expertise and interest in Foucault's work: some like him, some do not, some will use Foucault and others will not. What is common is an interest in, and a shared respect for each other's knowledge and preparedness to share that knowledge.

> *Louise:* You don't support Foucault?
> *Karen:* I don't like Foucault, but I like the way you're using him.
> *Matthew:* Marxists don't like him, and there are others that don't like him.
> *Amy:* Well, I feel guilty for not using Foucault by now!
> *Matthew:* He's boring, it's hard to read.
> *Louise:* But I think that's the thing, isn't it, it's like agency and structure is like a Marxist framework. It's interesting. Well, let's have a Foucault lunch.
> *Karen:* I don't know if some of us would have much to do with Foucault or not.
> *Matthew:* You see, I can read Durkheim all day, but most French philosophers at that time I think, Foucault, Derrida. Derrida; it's that dense, … you should read Foucault for 'Crime and Punishment'.
> *Amy:* I try, … the intricate language that he uses just illustrates it so well, it's excellent.
> *Amy:* [turning to Matthew's writing] There is no 'we', you're using that here
> *Matthew:* Yeah, ok. It's just the language people use in social constructionism as a way of slapping each other around the head.
> *Karen:* Yes, no, they do.

There is a contrast between the discussion above and the initial one about writing and writers. Earlier, Shakespeare and Carroll were invoked in a light-hearted way, explicitly as an experiment: 'I liked it; so I thought "Bugger it, just put it in!"'. As middle-stage doctoral candidates, these students recognise that experimenting with Carroll and Shakespeare quotations as chapter starters is a relatively low stakes decision, and largely a matter of personal choice. On the other hand, the discussion above shows that the group regards decisions about major scholarly writers as carrying critical implications for the whole project. As academic scholars, group members felt impelled to declare their position vis-à-vis Foucault: 'I don't like Foucault'; 'I feel guilty for not using Foucault'; 'It's interesting', and so on. Individual responses interface with, and are prescribed by their imagined external scholarly community with its own pre-existing conversations and concerns. The group talk reflects their developing need to connect with this wider network of scholars in a knowledgeable way. Again we can see how the group operates as a kind of private place – so safe that members feel entirely free to express strong, even irreverent personal views.

As we recall, Amy and Matthew initially asked the group for feedback on their developing ideas *and* early stage writing. The segment above illustrates, for these becoming scholars, the close interconnectivity between ideas, and writing, and writers. Matthew and Amy make comments that reflect their personal struggles to understand the ideas of theorists alongside observations about writing. In one breath Matthew says of Foucault: 'He's boring, it's hard to read', while Amy says 'I try, … the intricate language that he uses just illustrates it so well, it's excellent'.

As a community, this group of peers create, critique and satirise other, imagined, communities of scholars. The writing group members share observations about how other scholars use language, and how they write and communicate in a way that informs their own world with expanded possibilities about ways of writing.

There is a great deal being negotiated and exchanged here and the boundaries between writing and thinking, writing and learning, writing and reading, the intellectual and the social, the theoretical and the personal, self and other, are constantly crossed and renegotiated. These conversations function in part as a kind of 'exernalisation' of thoughts, fears, forms of identification and aspiration – as well as theory testing and more formal intellectual work. Matthew, for example, is attempting to clarify the difference between constructivism and constructionism, while Amy is continuing to explore her attraction to 'dense' theoretical writing. Conversations about other writers, within and outside the academy, are intimately connected to the project of becoming a scholar – learning to write for the self, beyond the self for the immediate group, and into one's own broader scholarly community.

Writing groups as peer learning

Whether writing groups are made up of students or academics, whether they exist for the support of thesis or publication writing, whether they are defined course-length or more informal ongoing groups, their success depends on their ability to meet the needs of the group members. In our experience, writing groups are most effective when they are actively supported institutionally, either at the department level or university-wide via a Learning Centre or the like; and when they are facilitated by a person with expertise in writing.

A skilled facilitator will be able to help build the necessary sense of community and mutuality that facilitates learning (Lee and Boud 2003; Aitchison and Lee 2006) by directly focusing on specific learning objectives, and by attending to organisational and management matters (Aitchison 2010). Typical organisational tasks include such things as recruiting and allocating members to groups with a view to maintaining diversity, over-seeing the submission of student texts over time, monitoring attendance, participation and group dynamics. Multi-disciplinary groups that include students at different stages in their doctoral study offer the richest environment for peer learning – but they can also be relatively difficult to sustain. Groups that are well organised with transparent and routine practices are more likely to be able to be respond to the diverse and often changing needs of doctoral students over the period of their study. When the facilitator is responsible for recruiting and introducing new members, they will be better able to maintain group cohesion and the long-term viability of groups.

In particular, it is important that the routines and practices for giving and receiving of feedback on peers' writing are well established. For example, a common practice will be for group members to circulate their writing four to seven days prior to meetings, enabling peers enough time to read and critique the volunteered text before they meet. Meetings of two and a half hours' duration generally give enough time for two texts to be discussed, as well as allowing for spontaneous facilitator-directed 'mini lessons' on language-focused aspects such as researcher voice, discipline-specific citation practices, points of grammar, or for example, for sharing peers' publication experiences. More often, the facilitator will 'lead from behind', monitoring group discussions to balance and/or direct critique and to maintain the focus on language – especially by scaffolding and modelling commentary on the complex ways that language works to raise questions of identity, to play with ideas and ultimately to take these ideas to the public.

In our experience, writing groups for doctoral students are powerful, rewarding and productive learning environments. In these writing groups, the community is made up of peers each undertaking their own unique research projects, often from different disciplines and with different scholarly traditions, and with different levels of familiarity with academic writing and scholarship. This diversity characterises doctoral writing groups and distinguishes the associated pedagogical practices from other kinds of collaborative learning formulations. When groups are facilitated by a language specialists, the individual students are positioned as the 'experts', being the authority on their own project and horizontalising relationships. Thus, students themselves take responsibility for their learning by nominating what and when they choose to bring writing to the group. Also, if students are expected to indicate what kind of feedback they require, they learn to identify their own writing strengths and weaknesses. In writing groups peers report that learning flows from receiving feedback on their writing, from instruction and pedagogical resources engineered by the facilitator, and also from giving feedback on others' writing. Hence, a key task for the facilitator is to ensure that there are ample opportunities to share text as well as to engage in the critique of peers' work.

When peer learning is foregrounded as the critical pedagogical mechanism for learning, peers learn about writing by participating in the processes and practices of writing for, and with each other, and by participating in the review and critique of that writing. The focus on writing enables the production of knowledge to be an organic part of the research process, and for writing to be integrated into the research over the entire endeavour. Ultimately, however, the work of doctoral students is defined by their common objective to write for other communities outside the group. The writing group is the first but not the ultimate target reading audience; rather it acts as an intermediate space for testing out interactions with other networks of scholarly peers. This idea of an expanding network of interdependent social relations that radiates outward from a particular text is taken by Barbara Kamler and Pat Thomson in their use of Fairclough's three dimensions of discourse (Kamler and Thomson 2006). It is certainly evidenced in the transcripts above.

In writing groups individuals learn from peers in the fullest sense of doing and practising the range of activities endemic to scholarly practice; that is, through peer review, 'The institution of peer review ... is both indexical of, and productive of, what comes to be accepted as good research among licensed members of scholarly communities.' (Boud and Lee 2005: 510). At the same time, peers also share their personal experiences and know-how about their institution, their disciplinary and research expertise, and their writing practices and processes including publication experiences.

Conclusion

Doctoral study is making new demands on institutions, students and their supervisors whereby research writing has to be placed at the centre of research candidature. Writing groups are an effective pedagogical approach for addressing this need. The literature frequently asserts that writing groups result in improvements to the writing productivity and quality for participants (Aitchison and Lee 2006; Caffarella and Barnett 2000; Grant and Knowles 2000; Lee and Boud 2003; Maher *et al.* 2008; Murray and Mackay 1998; Murray and Moore 2006). Although most of these reports are based on small–scale studies and participant self–reporting, the frequency and consistency of these claims is persuasive. Certainly the widely held belief that participation in writing groups will bring about increased output and improved writing quality is the most common reason given for joining such groups (Aitchison 2003; 2009a; Larcombe *et al.* 2007; Maher *et al.* 2008), and there is no doubt that institutional support for writing groups is based on this premise.

In this chapter we have highlighted how doctoral writing groups that provide researchers opportunities to work with peers at different stages of candidature and with different disciplinary or methodological orientations, provide intermediary spaces where students can learn and experiment together. This pedagogical space enables doctoral writers to develop knowledge and knowhow for advanced scholarly writing *while* advancing their research project. In writing groups, writing is construed as a social practice, normalising writing, enabling it to be 'the practice as well as the site of production and exchange of knowledge' (Aitchison and Lee 2006: 266) rather than stigmatising it as an 'end–on', post–research activity or as problematic and difficult.

The particular aspect of sociality examined in this chapter is an expanded understanding of 'peer learning' in the semi–formal setting of the writing group. This extended use of the term 'peer' refers to both the relations of group members with each other – all are students learning together – and the institution of 'peer review' in academic writing, where international communities of scholars participate in building and maintaining their fields through writing, reviewing, editing, examining of new work. As Boud and Lee (2005) note, the pedagogy of peer learning in doctoral education involves the twin dynamics of being and becoming peers.

The excerpts discussed in this chapter illustrate exchanges among students as they negotiate these multiple dimensions of peer work. The selections have not been made to illustrate particular kinds of technical understandings about writing – rhetorical or grammatical – but rather to foreground the relational dimensions of the exchanges. We see clearly how writing groups facilitate exchange about writing construed as both text work and identity work (Kamler and Thomson 2006). Writing for the group – 'writing in' – is a mechanism for experimentation, in text and in dialogue over the text. At the same time, what is at stake is learning how to 'write out' for broader scholarly communities, positioning the unfolding dissertation text in ways that navigate and project a certain kind of writerly self.

References

Aitchison, C. (2003) Thesis Writing Circles, *Hong Kong Journal of Applied Linguistics*, 8(2): 97–115.

——(2009a) Research writing groups. In J. Higgs, D. Horsfall and S. Grace (Eds). *Writing qualitative research on practice*, Vol. 1, The Netherlands: Sense Publishers, pp. 253–63.

——(2009b) Writing groups for doctoral education, *Studies in Higher Education*, 34(8).

——(2010) Learning together to publish: writing group pedagogies for doctoral publishing. In C. Aitchison, B. Kamler and A. Lee (Eds). *Publishing pedagogies for the doctorate and beyond*. London: Routledge.

Aitchison, C., Kamler, B. and Lee, A. (2010) *Publishing pedagogies for the doctorate and beyond*. London: Routledge.

Aitchison, C. and Lee, A. (2006) Research writing: Problems and pedagogies, *Teaching in Higher Education*, 11(3): 265–78.

Boud, D. and Lee, A. (2005) Peer learning as pedagogic discourse for research education, *Studies in Higher Education*, 30(5): 501–15.

——(2009) *Changing practices of doctoral education*. London: Routledge.

Caffarella, R. S. and Barnett, B. G. (2000) Teaching doctoral students to become scholarly writers: The importance of giving and receiving critiques, *Studies in Higher Education*, 25: 39–54.

Grant, B. and Knowles, S. (2000) Flights of imagination: Academic women be(com)ing writers, *International Journal for Academic Development*, 5(1): 6–9.

Kamler, B. (2008) Rethinking doctoral publication practices: writing from and beyond the thesis, *Studies in Higher Education*, 33(3): 283–94.

Kamler, B. and Thomson, P. (2006) *Helping doctoral students write: Pedagogies for supervision*. Oxon: Routledge.

Larcombe, W., McCosker, A. and O'Loughlin, K. (2007) Supporting education PhD and DEd students to become confident academic writers: An evaluation of thesis writers' circles, *Journal of University Teaching and Learning Practice*, 4(1): 54–63.

Lee, A. and Aitchison, C. (2009) Writing for the doctorate and beyond. In D. Boud and A. Lee (Eds). *Changing Practices of Doctoral Education*. London: Routledge, 87–99.

Lee, A. and Boud, D. (2003) Writing groups, change and academic identity: Research development as local practice, *Studies in Higher Education*, 28(2): 187–200.

Maher, D., Seaton, L., McMullen, C., Fitzgerald, T., Otsuji, E. and Lee, A. (2008) 'Becoming and being writers': The experiences of doctoral students in writing groups, *Studies in Continuing Education*, 30(3): 263–75.

Murray, R. and Mackay, G. (1998) Supporting academic development in public output: Reflections and propositions, *International Journal for Academic Development*, 3(1): 54–63.

Murray, R. and Moore, S. (2006) *The Handbook of Academic Writing: A fresh approach*. Maidenhead: Open University Press.

Simon, R. (1992) The fear of theory. In *Teaching against the grain: texts for a pedagogy of possibility*. New York: Bergin and Garvey, 79–100.

22
Creating discursive and relational communities through an international doctoral student exchange

J. McLeod and M. Bloch

This chapter presents a case study of an international graduate student exchange with students from universities in Australia and the USA, convened by the two authors who are academic staff in Schools of Education: Julie then at Deakin University, Australia, and Marianne, [known as Mimi] at the University of Wisconsin-Madison, USA. We wanted to experiment with ways of conducting graduate education, and especially to see what might happen if we tried to teach together with our graduate masters and doctoral level students – across space and time zones. The exchange (conducted first in 2004 and then in 2006) was mediated through a combination of an online 15-week seminar that focused on discussion of readings and research that students read ahead of the seminar; occasional videoconferences and synchronous chat, and a 'face-to-face' research conference for students. The exchange was conceived as a valuable way for students to extend their research and doctoral studies through cross-national and comparative dialogue, and through the building of new kinds of doctoral communities that spanned time and space. It was imagined as a form of deliberate research training and induction into the culture of international networks and collaborations. And it was also imagined as a kind of learning and pedagogical adventure, embraced with enthusiasm and dedication by participants, and carried with it a sense of the unexpected and uncertain. Indeed, it has been the unexpected learnings, the unpredictable outcomes and 'lines of flight' arising from collisions and conjunctions of ideas and experiences that have provided some of the most powerful insights for participants in their reflections on their own research, and on pedagogies of doctoral learning.

The first time we collaborated on an exchange, in 2004, we devised a 15-week syllabus on the topic of 'Poststructuralist and feminist studies in education'. This course had some funding for technological support, a face-to-face conference at the University of Wisconsin-Madison for two days (travel support from Deakin for all students, lodging, food, technological support from University of Wisconsin). In 2006, we tried a second joint course, with no special funding available for technological assistance, or for a joint conference; this course was less of an exchange as it was primarily with University of Wisconsin-Madison students (there were two Deakin students who participated on occasions), with Julie contributing syllabus development, and online seminars whenever feasible. This second course focused on 'Poststructuralist, feminist, and postcolonial

270

studies in education'. Both the course in 2004 and in 2006 form the basis for our chapter, though most of what we report is from the more in-depth experiences in 2004 when students from Deakin and the University of Wisconsin participated actively as co-facilitators of the seminar in all virtual and face-to-face contexts.

The chapter first notes some of the broader educational context in which this international exchange developed, noting particularly the imperatives for and critiques of the internationalisation of education. Second, it documents the background to the exchange, outlining some of the features of the two participating universities. It then describes the structure of the programme, and the various components that helped build a sense of community, critique, and, on occasions, disconnections. Third, it discusses aspects of what we have described here as 'unexpected learnings', including key themes that emerged for students, and for staff. These are: time/space; embodiment; community; and doctoral learning. Finally, the chapter attempts to document a process and a model for developing other international doctoral collaborations, and to propose some new ways of thinking about doctoral learning and critical research communities that take advantage of new globally available, but locally contingent e-learning opportunities. We believe that these exchanges open new spaces for staff and students and for pedagogical innovation. The rapid circulation of knowledge through various discourse communities is allowing, or forcing, new ways to engage in pedagogical studies and relationships with scholars around the globe. We wondered whether advanced doctoral graduate students could be involved in such global discourse communities at an earlier moment. In part, then, our exchange was also an experiment to see if technology could support this idea, within a fairly structured exchange on theory and research in education.

Contemporary educational context

Internationalisation and higher education: market forces or global cultural exchange?

The current educational climate is marked by the expansion of educational markets and the twin imperatives to 'internationalise' and to embrace ICTs as a kind of technological 'fix' for challenges facing learning in higher education. As with many dimensions of contemporary life, higher education is embedded in, both part of and subject to, processes of globalisation (Beerkens 2003; Burbules and Torres 2000). The modern university is undergoing major changes, evident in 'the growing role of international markets and people exchange in education, coupled with the rise of global networks in information and communications' (Marginson 2000a: 98). This has been accompanied by increasing attention to the internationalisation of curriculum (Marginson 2000b; Otten 2003; Rizvi and Walsh 1998), and claims that it can assist in enhancing understandings of cultural diversity. Harman (2004) argues that given the economic benefits that derive from the import of international students and the export of education, there should be greater attention to the genuine internationalisation of curriculum, and to fostering exchanges between staff and students. Yet such calls for internationalisation typically remain located 'within a discourse of economic necessity' (Rizvi and Walsh 1998: 9) whereby recognising cultural diversity is too often reduced to a technical requirement to improve market positioning and economic ends, or to a characteristic valuable for human capital formation (higher education), and the job market. Rizvi and Walsh (1998) propose that

271

'curriculum and cultural difference ... [need] to be reconsidered in a more dynamic, relational way, rather than in purely instrumental terms' (ibid.). This case study is offered as one example of how teachers and students can work creatively and respectfully, albeit on a small-scale, to generate a productive and 'relational' intervention in the field of internationalisation and online learning, one that rests on notions of community rather than markets and on the value of opening up uncertain, and possibly risky, pedagogical spaces.

Although the USA, Canada, European Union and Australia have benefited from many students coming for higher education, these trends are shifting, given new regional affiliations, perceptions of greater opportunities, and desires to draw on less Westernised knowledge. The movement to recognise what is often termed indigenous knowledge, and to decolonise research and notions of science and knowledge, has also led to offering coursework within 'other' countries, delivering credits and degrees over the internet, or developing entire branches of universities online (rather than importing students and staff to 'centres' of Western learning (*The New York Times* 2008). Such moves toward a more indigenous form of higher education and alternative notions of research and training (e.g. Mutua and Swadener 2004; Smith 1999; Denzin *et al.* 2008) might also lead to more diversified knowledge systems. As universities contemplate the ways to globalise/internationalise, diversify what knowledge counts, and whose knowledge counts, the development of more diverse spaces for research and learning are emerging. These debates and factors – people exchange in education, internationalisation and curriculum, ICT, and new knowledge spaces – form one part of the wider backdrop in which our exchange developed, as we hoped to help ourselves and our students to think and do research from more global/local perspectives.

The two universities involved were enthusiastic and supportive of this initiative. On the one hand, such support can be interpreted as symptomatic of the sector push for markets and internationalisation, but on the other hand, it allowed for innovation in learning and cross-cultural collaboration. Students who participated in the exchange did not pay any additional university fees (beyond those they would normally pay to take a course) – there was no immediate 'market' or commercial gain, though the exchange very likely contributed to strengthening links between the two institutions. A primary motivating goal for all participants was to learn across and with national differences, to encounter different traditions of graduate education. It was not market-driven, its focus on 'differences' was not subordinated to economic ends, and it was designed as a collaborative exchange, where the 'host' country was neither one institution/country nor the other: the point of reference for 'difference' was constantly shifting. The exchange itself was made possible by the use of ICT, and ongoing reflection on the kind of learning and interactions this created (or inhibited) was a key feature of our learning experiences. As Joris *et al.* (2003: 94) suggest, 'ICT will be one of the most important vehicles for the internationalization processes, away from home and at home, and when you will stay at home, you will never be alone'.

A case study of an international graduate student exchange

Background

The 2004 exchange had its genesis during a period of sabbatical that Julie McLeod undertook at the University of Wisconsin-Madison in 2001. While there, she participated in several graduate student reading groups and seminars, and in informal discussions with Mimi and other colleagues they began to formulate the possibility of linking Deakin education graduate students with Madison students. Staff at the University of Wisconsin-Madison had been previously involved in doctoral student exchanges with a university in Sweden and had experiences they could draw upon, particularly in the early stages of development and gaining formal approval and endorsement.

In the first iteration (in 2004), the collaboration was imagined as a kind of online reading group, lasting about six weeks, with students reading in some common areas of interest, posting messages online to a dedicated discussion space, culminating perhaps in some writing and publications from the participating students. We hoped, but it seemed an unlikely fantasy, that we could arrange (let alone obtain funding) to incorporate a face-to-face meeting of the students. We were, however, able to secure funding, (see Acknowledgements) and in the end conducted a 15-week seminar, and associated con-ference, writing and reading group activities. We approached the possibility of an exchange with a great deal of enthusiasm, having enjoyed our research conversations, and were keen to develop ways of deepening and extending our collaborations. This relational aspect of the exchange proved to be a crucial element in its success. The existing connections, established during a period of working closely together, provided a sustaining and personally meaningful rationale for the exchange. It was not then an exchange that emerged strategically (as a response to institutional mission statements on internationalisation) or abstractly, or from a desire to improve educational markets. It was an exchange that had its beginnings in actual, embodied, day-to-day connections. Such embodied and interpersonal relations tend to be obscured in many discussions about and programmes for online learning, yet from our experience, they are vitally important, crucial in getting through the day-to-day difficult work of establishing and maintaining a collaborative partnership, given geographical distance, time, and university cultural dif-ferences. Indeed, one of the themes explored throughout the exchange was the blurri-ness of the virtual/actual, embodied/online binaries. Remembering and anticipating meetings, enjoying friendships and new levels and forms of graduate communities – all these filtered through our online worlds.

The two universities

There are significant differences in the structure and organisation of doctoral education in Australia and the USA, as well as differences in the history and learning cultures of the two participating universities. The University of Wisconsin system is a large state or public university system, comprising 13 four-year campuses, 13 two-year campuses, and a state-wide UW-Extension (adult education programme). UW-Madison is one of two doctoral universities in the UW System, and was a 'land-grant' university founded in 1848. It is located in Wisconsin's capital, Madison (population 203,000) and has a total enrolment of 40,858 undergraduate and graduate students. (The population of the state of Wisconsin is 5,400,000 and the population of the state of Victoria, where Deakin is located, is 4,822,000.) UW-Madison is the oldest and largest campus in the UW system, and probably the most well-known, with a prestigious and highly regarded tradition of graduate educa-tion. The doctoral programmes attract students from across the USA and internationally. The group of Madison students participating in this exchange comprised students from Taiwan, Chile, Korea, Turkey, as well as students living elsewhere in the USA who had moved specifically to Madison to enrol in the Curriculum and Instruction programmes;

during the 2006 seminar, one student from Chile, another from Korea, and another who was in Turkey doing her dissertation, participated in the seminar for a second time (the student from Turkey was online synchronously with us from midnight to 3 a.m. her time) because of its content, and the value attached to the learning they received, and the collaborative atmosphere.

At the University of Wisconsin-Madison, the primary mode of instruction is on campus, face-to-face classes, and in contrast to graduate programmes in Australia, doctoral students at UW-Madison, as elsewhere in the USA, undertake a substantial programme of coursework (over a two to three year period) before commencing their dissertation. In contrast, Australian doctoral education follows the British model, and a PhD comprises the equivalent of three years of full-time research for a dissertation: there is no structured programme of mandatory coursework as in the USA, instead, as in the British system, the research training is organised through individual meetings and consultations with a supervisor and sometimes other teaching staff.

Deakin University was established in the mid-1970s as a 'New University', located in a large regional city, Geelong, about a one-hour drive from the state capital of Melbourne (population 3,500,000) and it had a specific mission to provide off-campus or distance education. Australian universities, until quite recently, have been entirely public or state institutions, and there is not the tradition of private universities that exists in the USA. Deakin is now a multi-campus university, with two city campuses and three regional campuses, with overall enrolments of approximately 32,000 award students (combining on- and off-campus students). It continues to be a leading provider of distance education, and has been at the forefront in developing flexible delivery of education and online learning.

The Faculty of Education at Deakin has one of the largest programmes of graduate study in education in Australia, with the great majority of these students enrolled off-campus, undertaking their studies with either distance education materials for coursework at the masters level; or at the doctoral level participating in a range of supervisory practices that have evolved to cater for 'supervision at a distance' – including online research discussions and skill-based seminars on research strategies, email, teleconference and telephone, face-to-face meetings where and when possible, and residential summer and winter schools. But for most of the time, and for most of the students, doctoral students are not on campus. In addition, the majority of doctoral students are enrolled part-time, often combining full-time work, or family responsibilities with study. In contrast, at UW-Madison, the more common doctoral student experience is full-time, on-campus, and a full programme of face-to-face coursework instruction preceding a dissertation.

From this summary, a number of important differences between the two participating universities are evident. In many respects, the students were all part of a globalised knowledge economy, had some common ground in certain traditions of theory and research, and were all on the doctoral journey, yet there were also significant differences in academic traditions and styles of doctoral learning. Deakin students, for example, were already familiar with the demands and genre of online learning and virtual discussion spaces; whereas for UW-Madison students this was less familiar. Conversely, UW students were accustomed to having a rich and lively on-campus community of fellow graduate students, whereas for Deakin students, this was not the norm. While three of the participating Deakin students were on-campus students, they were not part of a larger graduate community because there were so few other on-campus students. One of the Deakin students participated from New Zealand, another from a county town in another state (New South Wales). Indeed, when we all went to Madison (Wisconsin), it was only the second time that the Deakin group had all been physically (rather than virtually) together. Recognising and working with such differences in expectation and experience became an important element of the exchange.

Structure of the programme

A number of parallel structures were in place to cater for the different requirements of students at the two universities. The UW-Madison students enrolled in the seminar as a graduate level credit course. Deakin students, however, because there is no requirement for formal coursework, participated in the exchange in a 'voluntary' capacity, viewing it as an enriching and extended reading programme. In order to make the volume of readings manageable for Deakin students, while also ensuring that Madison students fulfilled their formal course requirements, we divided the weekly readings into one 'core' reading per week, which all students read, with further reading for Madison students to pursue and for Deakin students to follow-up, if they wished then or subsequently. The Madison group scheduled their class in the early evening so that, with the different time zones, there would be opportunities to talk to them in real time via video and online chat (Madison students in the late evening, and Deakin students in the morning). At Deakin there was a group of seven to eight students, combining full- and part-time, and on- and off-campus students, who participated in online discussions and readings, and a smaller group of four who were able to visit Madison.[1]

There were four main modes of electronic communication:

1. *Web-board seminar: poststructuralist and feminist studies of education.* This online seminar provided the 'spine' for the exchange, with the online site combining a dedicated discussion site, functions for synchronous chat, readings available as PDF files, and the capacity to upload documents, visuals, photographs and video clips; this could be done by both staff and students. We began with informal introductions, photographs and some tentative messages. Everyone was encouraged to post comments on readings on the web-board and engage in discussion about our readings, making links to previous comments. Sometimes people posted summaries of critical issues for their research as they emerged in response to the readings. When students were a little uncertain, especially in the beginning, Mimi and Julie shared responsibility for trying to initiate and sustain online conversations and connections. There was also video-streaming of a presentation by a visiting professor to the UW from the University of Helsinki, Elina Lehelma.

2. *Paired email exchanges.* In order to assist with creating connections, we suggested where possible some cross-university student pairs. These were selected on the basis of shared research interests. Students then engaged in one-to-one email discussion of their work and shared readings outside the set syllabus.

3. *Synchronous chat.* On a number of prearranged occasions and also spontaneously if we happened to be online at the web-board during the UW-Madison class-time, students and staff from the two universities were able to engage in synchronous dialogue via the web-board. Students reported finding this a fascinating if somewhat bizarre experience. UW-Madison students were typically located in their regular Tuesday evening class with one computer, Mimi Bloch and various staff members, and on one occasion a visiting scholar, Elina Lehelma, from the University

275

of Helsinki. Deakin students were simultaneously at their computers trans-nationally (primarily Australia and New Zealand), from the hills outside coastal Byron Bay in NSW, to New Zealand, from Deakin Geelong or Burwood to at home in inner-urban Melbourne. We had 20-word snatches of communication about our week's reading, or Elina's paper, about feminist ethnography or about poststructuralist theory. Everyone 'talked' at once and, as students reported, synapses were buzzing as our thoughts flew into dialogue boxes across our com-puter screens. It was exhilarating but also very difficult and challenging to maintain the thread of the conversation and to convey a complex idea quickly in 20 words or less (there was a maximum limit per 'turn' of about 100 characters).

4. *Videoconferencing.* We had three videoconferences; these were set-up in a special seminar room with high-quality video capability, and technical assistance. Despite this support, sound and picture across space/time was sometimes stilted, sometimes ineffective as we talked as though we were in two different classes that were 'just meeting'. The focus of the videoconferences was planned beforehand on the web-board, with students prepared with commentary on readings, key texts selected and so forth. These conferences lasted for one hour, and usually we would agree on one or two papers to read closely, someone would be nominated to prepare a written response and start the discussion, just as you would do in a face-to-face tutorial. It was very exciting to engage in this real time conversation, despite the newness of relationships; it gave us a sense of who our fellow students were, and despite the frustrations of the technology and sound and visuals not quite syn-chronising, we developed a more immediate and in a sense even intimate con-nection with our 'virtual' class mates. And once the videoconference was finished, both the Deakin and the Madison group would remain talking for another hour or so, stimulated by the conversations, wanting to extend the connections, and pursuing what we came to call our 'lines of flight' that emerged in and out of this hybridised form of learning and research.

The videoconference experience, along with the synchronous chat, underlined for us some of the ambiguities of online learning, a pedagogy that tends to pre-suppose disembodied learners operating somewhere out in the ether, as if bodies do not matter. For the Deakin participants at least, the online experiences, and the associated videoconferences and online chats, all served to break down this view of ICT and learning, and to unsettle the easy contrast between embodied and disembodied, virtual/real. We illustrate this point with two brief examples.

There and not there

During our second planned synchronous chat, the Deakin students were scattered across different sites – their kitchen, their home office, their work office in New Zealand, and so on. It was mid-morning, coffee-drinking time. The Madison students were at Mimi Bloch's house having a 'potluck' reception for a visiting scholar, drinking wine, relaxing and ready to chat as a group. The conversations came fast and snappy: one student from Deakin kept losing her connection to the web-board, and felt left out, others felt under confident in this new space; Julie was trying to 'talk' students onto web-board via email, and also participate in the online chat. Deakin students and staff all felt emotionally and physically exhausted after the experience, whereas in Madison, the conversation with the visiting scholar continued, and the dinnertime food made the event very social for the

Madison group. While in Madison, there was little recognition of having 'excluded' our own class members from a social and convivial event; for the Deakin students, the virtual encounter produced intense, visceral responses, making us think again of the ways in which this form of learning and dialogue is embodied, enticingly inviting the imagination of a certain kind of community, while simultaneously underscoring the distance. The separation of space and time as well as doctoral 'cultures' seemed real and almost overwhelming. The course, at this moment, seemed to be separate – two groups, not at all one.

A second example. The videoconferencing also underlined, perhaps most strikingly, the blurriness between actual and virtual. The Madison class was running, together at their regular weekly meeting; the Deakin students joined them for a session, sitting in a less familiar technologically set-up room, with technicians on hand. We saw our colleagues on the screen; we were in the classroom at Madison, yet not; we were there, yet absent, we were images and sounds, and we were friends laughing together as we struggled with new ideas, literally trying to find the right words and forms of communication. These themes of embodied/disembodied, creating new communities, and traversing time/space were also on our minds as we approached our long anticipated face-to-face meeting in Madison.

A face-to-face meeting and conference

Four students from Deakin (and Julie) were able to visit UW-Madison during the week of 17–25 April 2004, where we held in an 'International Graduate Research conference on Feminist Theory and Educational Research' (from a strategic point of view, participation in such a conference could be an important addition to a doctoral student curriculum vitae). Each of the students from both Madison and Deakin who participated in the online seminar presented a research paper that arose from their research interests and drew on readings and reflections from the seminar. In order to encourage engaged feedback, the papers were circulated to each other via the web-board during the week we were at Madison. In addition, Deakin students met with Education faculty members and graduate students whose interests intersected with their studies of gender, cultural/social differentiation, and ethnographic, critical, and poststructural/postcolonial research. As one of the students wrote:

> We were eager participants in this international exchange program, which obviously went beyond the formal presentation of conference papers and encompassed immersion in the life of a dynamic, vibrant, very beautiful research university on the shores of Lake Mendota (in Madison). We toured the vast campus on foot and by bus, browsed and bought too much in the bookshops, sampled the local restaurants and wine and discussed the development of longer-term collaborative projects related to our mutual interests.

Through the informal face-to-face meetings in Madison, and the serious work of presenting at an international research conference, the students from Deakin and from UW-Madison joined into one community – at least for a while. The enthusiasm of finally meeting, having non-rushed time to present their work, the ideas that had been discussed virtually for three months previously, was exciting and challenging. Julie and Mimi, as well as others who were aware of the experience on both campuses, found this to be an almost crucial part of the seminar; it cemented what we had been trying to accomplish, erased frustrations of bad technological connections, poor communication of ideas, non-shared work, with the formation of a community of shared experiences.

Unexpected learning and research

The seminar readings and discussions contributed in different and relatively direct ways to each of the participant's own research projects and agendas. The Deakin and Madison participants all spoke of it at the time, and, subsequently, as an enriching personal and academic experience, one that enhanced their doctoral research journey and also informed how their dissertations developed. These are positive and desirable, if not especially surprising, outcomes. But here we want to briefly mention what we have called 'unexpected learnings'. These emerged from the intersection of the pedagogical experience of online learning, the relational dimension of the exchange, and the ideas, concepts and arguments raised in the seminar. In this collision of ideas and experiences, we have identified four themes that capture our over riding sense of the exchange, and in different ways, echo through participants' individual research projects. These themes are: time/space; embodiment; community; and doctoral learning.

We have noted above some of the ways in which themes of embodiment reverberated throughout the exchange. The opportunity to extend a sense of connection and collaboration between the two convenors first sustained the exchange and fuelled a desire to foster different kinds of doctoral communities – with attempts to construct online communities, to create a community of students and friends at Deakin and Madison, to anticipate, and then to try to work and interact together during our face-to-face meeting. Yet these themes of community and embodiment surfaced in other more complex and interactive ways; where aspects of experience of the exchange seemed to resonate with the ideas and analysis being developed in student research projects. Sue Snelgrove (2004) was researching the practices of inclusive education in relation to children with intellectual disabilities, and the possibilities of friendships between them and students without disabilities. Issues of embodiment (talk of disease, deficiency and looking different) are important motifs in discussions about inclusion; and the possibility of a community of friends, for making friends with children who are not intellectually disabled, is held out as a promise of inclusion. For Sue, themes of community and embodiment were both part of our and her experience of the exchange, but were also echoing in her own research. Reflecting on the movement between these different layers and forms of meaning became a significant feature of discussions during and after the exchange, complicating, troubling, yet deepening, our collective and individual learning. Exploring, struggling with and making such unexpected connections helped us to think anew about how online communities and new forms of doctoral pedagogy.

We have struggled, too, to find the words and metaphors to capture these layers of connections. In other work, (McLeod and Bloch 2004; Snelgrove 2004; Kamp 2004) we describe how, prompted by the writing of the French philosophers Giles Delueze and Felix Guattari (1988) (whose work we read as part of the seminar), we began exploring their metaphors of the 'rhizome' and of 'lines of flight'. These concepts offer ways of capturing the unexpected, unpredictable and multiple lines of thought and connections that can arise from the collision of events, ideas and experiences. The point to be emphasised here, however, is not whether one has found the 'right theory' to explain this process. Rather, the point is to convey the layers and linkages, the non-linear connections between the experience of online doctoral learning, the forging of new learning communities across time/space, the exploration of research projects and the simultaneously critical, reflexive and open embrace of new learning possibilities.

Concluding remarks

A substantial body of research exists on higher education and online learning, including evaluations of programmes, studies of the capabilities of the technology, its potential as a vehicle for learning that transcends space/time, allowing for links across national and regional boundaries (e.g. Zhao 2003; Whatley and Bell 2003). Numerous initiatives have sought to supplement and enhance doctoral teaching through incorporating online components, and this is widely seen as having particular benefits for distance and off-shore students because of its capacity to foster connections and to offer opportunities for engagement when none might have been affordable or available otherwise (Wisker *et al.* 2003; Feast and Anderson 2003; Evans *et al.* 2004). In many such initiatives, the introduction of online learning is intended to enhance the learning experience of students but is not always or explicitly linked to fostering comparative perspectives or creating communities. There is also surprisingly little discussion of the interpersonal dimensions of these learning encounters and communities.

This chapter has described the rationale and journey of an online international doctoral student exchange where creating discursive and relational communities was a central motivation. It has outlined aspects of the procedure and process that could be developed and adapted for comparable initiatives. Our experience highlighted some of the benefits of international collaboration, and the challenge of working intensively with a range of learning technologies. We have also tried to capture the intersection of relational, international, virtual and actual/embodied dimensions of the exchange. Similarly, contingency and uncertainty characterised much of the pedagogy, arising from colliding differences in time, space, research and national cultures, and while animated by a desire to forge new kinds of relational and discursive communities, how this unfolded was unpredictable and sometimes risky. The promise of online learning can be overstated, and its ambiguities, uncertainties and even frustrations understated. For us, though, it opened up a space for re-imaging doctoral pedagogy and doctoral learning. As the critiques of market-driven reforms show, there are many powerful and ethical reasons for pausing in the race to capture educational markets and to internationalise the curriculum. The exchange discussed here, although developed in the context of such economic and educational changes, offers an illustration of how an international student exchange might be otherwise; and of other kinds of scholarly benefits and unexpected learnings that it might generate.

Acknowledgements

We warmly acknowledge the students from the University of Wisconsin-Madison and Deakin University who enthusiastically participated; especially from Deakin, Annelies Kamp, Kirsten Hutchison, Sue Snelgrove and Sarah Culican for ongoing and stimulating discussions about the exchange and the ideas it generated, and, from Madison, especially Alejandro Azocar, Koeun Kim, Sabiha Bilgi, Devorah Kennedy, and Dar Weyenberg.

For travel funding for students, Julie thanks the Faculty (now School) of Education, Deakin University, and the invaluable assistance of Heather Davis, then working at the Research and Doctoral Studies Office; Mimi thanks the Department of Curriculum and Instruction, and the International Committee, School of Education, University of Wisconsin-Madison, USA for providing funding for this project, technology support, lodging, food and conference venue in 2004.

Notes

1 The following outline draws on a summary report of the exchange, prepared by one of the participating Deakin students, Kirsten Hutchison, who also attended the research conference in Madison.

References

Beerkens, E. (2003) Globalisation and Higher Education Research, *Journal of Studies in International Education*, 7 (2): 128–48.

Burbules, N. and Torres, C. A. (Eds) (2000) *Globalization and Education: Critical Perspectives*. New York: Routledge.

Deleuze, G and Guattari, F. (1988) *A Thousand Plateaus; Capitalism and Schizophrenia*. London: Athlone Press.

Denzin, N., Lincoln, Y., and Smith, L. T. (2008) *Handbook of Critical and Indigenous Methodologies*. New York: Sage.

Evans, T. Hickey, C. and Davis, H. *Research issues arising from doctoral education at a distance*. Paper presented at conference on Research in Distance Education, November 2004.

Feast, V. and Anderson, J. (2003) A case study of online support for international students in a doctoral program, *International Education Journal*, 4 (2): 78–88.

Harman, G. (2004) New directions in internationalizing higher education: Australia's development as an exporter of higher education services, *Higher Education Policy*, 17: 101–20.

Joris, M, van den Berg, C. and van Ryssen, S. (2003) Home, but not alone: Information and communication technology and internationalisation at home, *Journal of Studies in International Education*, 7 (1): 94–107.

Kamp, A. *The disembodied apprentice: Reflections on a doctoral exchange*. Paper presented at the annual conference of the Australian Association for Research in Education, University of Melbourne, November/December 2004.

Marginson, S. (2000a) The enterprise university in Australia, *Leading & Managing*, 6(2): 98–112.

——(2000b) Rethinking academic work in the global era, *Journal of Higher Education, Policy and Management*, 22: 23–35.

McLeod, J. and Bloch, M. *Pedagogical 'Lines of Flight': reflections on and from an international doctoral student exchange*. Paper presented at the annual conference of the Australian Association for Research in Education, University of Melbourne, November/December 2004.

Mutua, K. and Swadener, B. B. (2004) *Decolonizing Research in Cross-cultural Contexts: Critical Personal Narratives*. Albany, NY: State University of New York Press.

Otten, M. (2003) Intercultural learning and diversity in higher education, *Journal of Studies in International Education*, 7(1): 12–26.

Rizvi, F. and Walsh, L. (1998) Difference, globalization and the internationalization of the curriculum, *Australian Universities Review*, 2: 7–11.

Smith, L. T. (1999) *Decolonizing methodologies: Research and Indigenous Peoples*. London: Zed Press.

Snelgrove, S. *Maple syrup and meat pies: Rhizomatic wandering between Deakin and the University of Wisconsin-Madison as engagement with the other*. Paper presented at the annual conference of the Australian Association for Research in Education, University of Melbourne, November/December 2004.

The New York Times (2008). Online. (Available at www.nytimes.com/2008/02/10/education/10global. html?_r=3&oref=slogin&oref=slogin Accessed 10 February 2008).

Whatley, J. and Bell, F. (2003) Discussion across borders: Benefits for collaborative learning, *Education Media International*, 40(1/2): 139–52.

Wisker, G, Waller, S, Richter, U, Robinson, G, Trafford, V, Wicks, K, and Warne, M. *On nurturing hedgehogs: Developments online for distance and offshore supervision*. Proceedings of the HERDSA conference, July 2003.

Zhao, F. (2003) Enhancing the quality of online higher education through measurement, *Quality Assurance in Education*, 11(4): 214–21.

23
The relationship between doctoral students' approach to research and experiences of their research environment

K. Trigwell

Research has shown that undergraduate students' approaches to learning are broadly related to their perceptions of their learning environment and to the quality of their outcomes of learning (Prosser and Trigwell 1999). The question addressed in this chapter is whether a similar relationship is found for doctoral students in their research environment. In other words, are the approaches doctoral students take to their research related to their perceptions of their research environment? This relationship was the focus of a study carried out with graduate students at the University of Oxford to address the question of student perceptions of the research environment and its relationship to their approaches to research.

The postgraduate research experience questionnaire

The Course Experience Questionnaire (CEQ) that is used to monitor coursework students' perceptions of their learning environment (Ramsden 1991) has proved to be unsuitable for graduate research students. This led to the development of the Postgraduate Research Experience Questionnaire (PREQ) in Australia (Marsh *et al.* 2002). PREQ is used to investigate students' perceptions of the infrastructure support of the environment in which they are studying, of the intellectual climate in which they are conducting their research, and of supervision. An item on overall satisfaction with the quality of their research context is also included along with the extent to which students consider that they have acquired key research skills (Ramsden *et al.* 2003). Some of the research relevant to the inclusion of these variables in the design of the questionnaire is summarised in the following sections.

Infrastructure support

Students' perceptions of their infrastructure support refers to the extent to which students feel that they had access to resources (physical, financial and procedural), both in their department and in the whole institution, that would support their research. The PREQ study found that there were disciplinary differences in students' perceptions of their infrastructure support, with students in the arts, humanities and social sciences experiencing less access to resources than students in the sciences. In the UK, chemistry students perceived their infrastructure as more supportive than education students. At the University of Oxford, students in the arts, humanities and social sciences were more likely to rate their academic conditions as poor than students within sciences, medicine and education. These findings are unsurprising given the differences in the ways in which research degrees in different disciplines are structured. The important question, from the perspective of this chapter, is the impact this has on the quality of students' overall experience and how it relates to research approach. Due to the differences across disciplines, the effect of access to a supportive infrastructure was examined within two broad disciplinary areas (science and arts) as well as for all disciplines combined.

Intellectual climate of research

Students' perceptions of the intellectual climate in which they are studying refers to the opportunities available for social contact with other students, the extent to which they felt they were integrated into the departmental community, the opportunities to become involved in a broader research culture, the extent to which students perceived that there was a stimulating research ambience and their perceptions of the quality of the seminar programme that was provided for them.

Students in the humanities and social sciences have been found to have significantly lower scores on this scale than students in the sciences. In the USA, sociology students were less likely than students in chemistry, civil engineering and microbiology to see their departments as community-orientated. Similarly in the UK, Chiang (2003) found that chemistry students were more likely than education students to perceive the research environment as effective in terms of staff approachability, student–staff interaction and the research culture. Chiang argues that this is due to the 'teamwork research training structure' in Chemistry, in which research students and their supervisors work on the same projects, whereas education has an 'individualist research training structure', where students and supervisors work on separate problems. Although there is clearly variation, the chemistry and education outcomes reflect the position of the sciences and arts respectively.

At the University of Oxford, some evidence was found for students' dissatisfaction with the intellectual climate, with 32 per cent of respondents experiencing their academic contact with senior members as poor, and 22 per cent describing their academic contact with other graduates as poor. This dissatisfaction appeared to be unrelated to discipline or other factors.

Supervision

The PREQ items on the supervision scale focus on students' perceptions of the availability (and meeting frequency) of supervision, their perceptions of the support, guidance and feedback provided by their supervisors, including guidance relating to the literature review. Use in Australia of the PREQ on students' experiences of supervision shows students from humanities and social sciences feeling more supported than students from sciences and engineering.

It is also clear from examining the wider literature in this area, that students in different disciplines have very different experiences of research supervision. However, the differences are not the same, or even in the same direction as those found using the PREQ. Broadly stated, as noted above, these differences are that students within the natural sciences, particularly in experimental disciplines,[1] tend to be part of a research group in which they have a clear role and in which they work alongside other researchers on related topics. They tend to be more involved in group discussions and group publications. However, they tended to be assigned the research problems that they were to address in their doctorates. Those within the social sciences tend to report feeling socially isolated, as there tend to be fewer of them and they were often not involved in conferences and colloquia. They also report being intellectually isolated as they are treated as individual scholars with responsibility for their own projects. For social science students, this can make the supervisory relationship even more central to their doctoral experience.

Disciplinary differences have also been picked up within the University of Oxford. It was found that students within sciences and medicine had more day-to-day contact with their supervisors and expected more discussion with their supervisors than students within the humanities and social sciences. However, the amount of contact was seen as 'about right' by over 70 per cent of the students within each discipline.

Within the supervisory relationship, a tension has been highlighted between the extent to which students should be given autonomy in deciding their own work and the extent to which they should be guided by their supervisors. Such tensions are clearly related to the disciplinary differences outlined above and to the stage that the student has reached in their doctoral research. However, there is the potential for conflict if student and supervisor have different views of how this tension should be balanced. One area of particular conflict appears to be around the degree of support in learning how to conduct research that students expect to receive from their supervisors, with students' satisfaction with the level of support they receive in this area being related to their satisfaction with the supervision generally.

Skills development

The doctorate is now seen in the UK as a period of training for future researchers, and part of that training involves the development of a range of skills. The objective is to produce professionally trained researchers who are able to undertake any research project in their general discipline area having completed the skills training. The literature describes the key skills students expect to acquire during the PhD experience as an academic (such as methodological skills, how to produce scholarly writing or more particularly literature reviews, or personal/social skills). The more personal skills such as growing confidence and autonomy are given as positive outcomes of the research experience. There is also some mention of the skills that future non-academic employers would like postgraduates to work on, such as team-work, project management and communication skills.

The PREQ scale relating to skills development in Australia asks about the students' problem solving skills, written work, analytic skills, work planning and tackling unfamiliar problems. Students who completed the PREQ in 2000 reported a high level of satisfaction with their own development of research skills. According to Holdaway (1996), quoted by Bazeley (1999), the acquisition of knowledge and skills is only a secondary focus in postgraduate studies in Australia, as opposed to the American model.

In the UK, the Roberts Report led to a statement by the Research Councils, that doctoral research students funded by the research councils would be expected to develop transferable skills in seven broad areas during their research training. these areas are: research skills and techniques; research environment; research management; personal effectiveness; communication skills; networking and team-working; and career management.

The variation in students' responses to their experience of these four areas of their research context is now routinely used to monitor and improve the students' research environment. Information of this form is collected nationally and annually in Australia, using the PREQ. With these data, institutions are able to benchmark their research departments with similar departments in other institutions.

Approaches to research

There has been very little research into variation in the approaches to research adopted by postgraduate research students. Parallels with the coursework learning experience would suggest that approaches to research are likely to be focused more on the students' personal search for meaning (equivalent to a coursework deep approach to learning) than on attempts to satisfy an external assessor such as a supervisor or examiner (equivalent to a coursework surface approach). The research suggests that some research students may take a more holistic and integrated approach to their research, seeing it as part of an integrated whole, whereas others are more likely to see their research as being about developing techniques and about what it is that external others, such as supervisors, see as being important.

The hypothesised differences described above, and their implications, have been tested in the studies used to address the question raised in this chapter. What is clear from these studies is that there is variation in how doctoral research students approach (and conceive) their research, and that there are relations between the way students approach their research and their experience of key areas of their research environment. What this means, in terms of understanding the doctoral research experience, is presented in the concluding sections of the chapter.

The Oxford case study

This section now turns to a case study at a UK university. In order to investigate the relationship between research environment and students' approaches to research, an approach to research scale was developed (Trigwell and Ashwin 2005) and a research approach and experience questionnaire mailed to a sample of graduate students across the University of Oxford selected from a total of 3,855 eligible postgraduate research students who were in the student database in May 2005. The sample of one in five, was stratified by department, status (DPhil or Probationary Research Student (PRS)), college and gender. This gave a sample size of 756. A total of 626 students (82.8 per cent) returned the questionnaire. The proportions of the constituencies in the response set closely match those in the full sample and therefore in the whole university. The questionnaire (see Appendix A23.1) was developed from existing PREQ items, modified through a university-wide consultation process, and included the new Approaches to Research scale aimed at describing the extent to which students think and act like researchers. It contains seven items, such as: 'It is important to me that my research is well integrated with existing knowledge and topics in the field'. The new scale items are shown in the final section of Appendix A23.1.

Student responses show that the majority see their research as being more about contributing to the 'big picture', integrating and discussing ideas within and outside the project, that it is worthwhile research and it is something they have control over. This majority have a more integrated or *holistic* approach than other students who did not experience their research as being integrated with the wider field, or as part of a larger endeavour. They adopted more of an atomistic approach, and found that the reason 99 per cent of students decided to go to graduate school was a desire for knowledge. The results found in this study suggest that what is considered as knowledge, and how it is attained, varies widely within this University of Oxford group.

The study made use of the Approach to Research scale and perceptions of the environment scales in the same questionnaire to address the question: Do students whose research thinking and approach is more holistic have a different perception of their research environment than those with a more atomistic view? If the results suggest that they do, might this relationship provide a means to improve the research context for students, supervisors and administrators?

In addition to the Approach to Research scale, the other questionnaire scales used in the study are briefly described below. The items making up each scale, and the extent of the internal consistency of these items (scale reliability, alpha) are given in Appendix A23.1. Additional items making up scales on awareness of the assessment and college support are not included in the analysis presented in this chapter, but some individual (non-scale) items on overall satisfaction have been included (Appendix A23.1).

- *Supervision*. The Supervision Scale contains five items that address issues such as availability of the supervisor, feedback, literature and topic area guidance and the students' perceptions of the efforts made by supervisors to meet their needs. It has been designed to accommodate various forms of supervision, including sole and group supervision.
- *Skills development*. An item on each of the seven broad skills areas identified by the UK Research Councils (research skills and techniques; research environment; research management; personal effectiveness; communication skills; networking and team-working; and career management) makes up this scale. It forms a coherent set with a scale reliability above 0.7.
- *Departmental intellectual climate*. The ten items in this scale address the extent to which students experience support in areas such as opportunities in their department for social and academic engagement, working environments and a feeling of belonging to a departmental academic community.
- *General infrastructure support*. Six different broad topic areas are drawn together under this heading, such as library facilities, university administration, admissions and enrolments and complaints handling procedures. The extent of commonality between the items is low, but for this analysis the six items are combined to form a scale.
- *Departmental infrastructure support*. This scale contains six items on students' perceptions of their access to necessary equipment, technical support, working space, finance and the effectiveness of departmental administration.

Relations between research approach and the research context

Table 23.1 contains correlation co-efficients of relations between Approach to Research scale scores and perception of research environment scale scores. It shows that the students who describe a more holistic approach to research (higher scores on Approach to Research scale) perceive a more supportive departmental intellectual climate, a more supportive general infrastructure, and a supportive supervisory arrangement (correlation co-efficients (whole sample) of 0.27, 0.26 and 0.30 respectively). A similar result is found when the discipline areas are aggregated into the broad areas of arts and sciences (Table 23.1, arts and sciences columns) with the sciences also showing significant correlations with departmental infrastructure.

The Approaches to Research scale also shows moderate relations with indicators of outcomes of research. Table 23.2 shows the correlations between students' self-rating of the quality of their research (Questionnaire item 70), skills development and with their descriptions of their satisfaction with three areas of the research context (Appendix A23.1: Items 37, 38 and 39).

When students experience their research more holistically, they have a higher self-rating of the quality of their research, they are more satisfied with the quality of their supervision and with their research experience overall, and they report significant development in their research skills.

The correlations presented above are between individual variables, for example between approach to research and skills development. As students' experience of the research context is likely to be the experience of many of these variables simultaneously, the relations between groups of variables were investigated using cluster analyses. The results presented in Tables 23.3–5 indicate that systematic and logical relations for all the variables are found for the whole sample (Table 23.3) and the arts and sciences (Tables 23.4 and 23.5) populations.

Table 23.1 Analysis of relations (correlations) between approach to research and perceptions of the research environment (for scale information, see Appendix 1)

Perceptions of environment	Approach to Research		
	Whole sample	Arts	Sciences
Departmental Intellectual Climate Scale	**0.27**	**0.30**	**0.37**
Departmental Infrastructure Scale	0.09	0.12	**0.30**
General Infrastructure Scale	**0.26**	**0.24**	**0.32**
Supervision Scale	**0.30**	**0.30**	**0.37**

N = 618–626 (whole) 315 (Arts) 298 (Sciences); numbers in bold are statistically significant (p<0.05)

Table 23.2 Analysis of relations (correlation co-efficients) between approach to research and outcomes of the research approach

Outcomes of research	Approach to Research		
	Whole sample	Arts	Sciences
Self-rating (item 70)	**0.46**	**0.46**	**0.46**
Satisfaction with services	0.15	**0.21**	**0.28**
Satisfaction with supervision	**0.24**	**0.22**	**0.33**
Satisfaction with research generally	**0.41**	**0.43**	**0.50**
Skills Development Scale	**0.44**	**0.44**	**0.54**

N = 626 (whole) 315 (Arts) 298 (Sciences); numbers in bold are statistically significant (p<0.05)

The cluster analysis results are similar for each of the arts and sciences groups and the overall sample. In all three groupings, the differences between the two clusters (1 and 2) on the mean z-score, for each of the seven variables, is statistically significant (e.g. for departmental intellectual climate in Table 23.3, the difference between the mean z-scores of 0.72 for cluster 1 and -0.37 for cluster 2 is statistically significant). Although this difference is significant (and because of it), it is the resulting patterns of relations found within any one cluster that are of interest. In all three cases they are both logical and systematic. So, for example, in cluster 1 for the whole group (Table 23.3) the students in this cluster (n=212) who report experiencing a more supportive intellectual climate (mean z-score=0.72, are the same students who report experiencing a more supportive departmental and general infrastructure, more supportive supervision, describe adopting a

Table 23.3 Cluster analysis of perceptions of research environment, approach to research and outcomes variables (whole sample, n=623) (mean z-scores and s.d.)

	Cluster 1	Cluster 2
Variables	N = 212	N = 411
Departmental Intellectual Climate	0.72 (0.72)	−0.37 (0.92)
Departmental Infrastructure	0.76 (0.67)	−0.40 (0.91)
General Infrastructure	0.76 (0.71)	−0.40 (0.90)
Supervision	0.69 (0.62)	−0.36 (0.97)
Approach to Research	0.68 (0.80)	−0.35 (0.91)
Overall satisfaction	0.74 (0.58)	−0.38 (0.96)
Skills Development	0.71 (0.68)	−0.37 (0.94)

Table 23.4 Cluster analysis of perceptions of research environment, approach to research and outcomes variables (Arts, n=305) (mean z-scores and s.d.)

	Cluster 1	Cluster 2
Variables	N = 153	N = 152
Departmental Intellectual Climate	0.47 (0.81)	−0.47 (0.95)
Departmental Infrastructure	0.46 (0.83)	−0.47 (0.94)
General Infrastructure	0.63 (0.70)	−0.63 (0.86)
Supervision	0.49 (0.70)	−0.49 (10.02)
Approach to Research	0.56 (0.78)	−0.56 (0.89)
Overall satisfaction	0.60 (0.57)	−0.62 (0.94)
Skills Development	0.50 (0.76)	−0.51 (0.95)

Table 23.5 Cluster analysis of perceptions of research environment, approach to research and outcomes variables (Sciences, n=293) (mean z-scores and s.d.)

	Cluster 1	Cluster 2
Variables	N = 152	N = 141
Departmental Intellectual Climate	0.55 (0.73)	−0.59 (0.92)
Departmental Infrastructure	0.59 (0.66)	−0.65 (0.90)
General Infrastructure	0.48 (0.78)	−0.53 (0.95)
Supervision	0.61 (0.62)	−0.67 (0.90)
Approach to Research	0.41 (0.88)	−0.44 (0.94)
Overall satisfaction	0.56 (0.61)	−0.57 (0.96)
Skills Development	0.46 (0.76)	−0.50 (1.00)

more holistic approach to their research, have a higher satisfaction rating and feel that they are making more progress in their development of research skills. As a group, the students in cluster 2 have lower mean scores on all of these variables.

Implications of relations between research approach and experience of research environment

Most doctoral students at the research-led university (Oxford) that was the focus of this study see their research as being more about contributing to the research 'big picture', integrating and discussing ideas within and outside the project. They also see their research as being worthwhile, and as something they have some control over. This can be described as an integrated or *holistic* approach to research. For these students research is about how to approach open-ended questions, how to find new ways of working when the familiar ones don't work, and how to think not simply of answers, but also of new questions. It is likely to be the approach preferred by doctoral supervisors and by host departments, yet it is not the approach described by all students. Some students in the same context report a more atomistic approach where their focus is on their project as being more of an end in itself, where the emphasis is on developing techniques and what it is that is seen to be important to external others, such as supervisors. For this reason they are more likely to say they do not have sufficient control over the direction of their research and that it is less worthwhile. They adopt more of an isolationist stance, even in the science areas, in which it is not so important to them that ideas fit together and into the broader research field. These students are more likely to be learning to do than to be learning to be creative and learning to think.

When this variation is related to variation in perceptions of the research context, it is found that students who experience their research in the more holistic way, have a higher self-rating of the quality of their research, they feel that they are making more progress in their development of research skills, they are more satisfied with the quality of their supervision and with their overall research experience, and describe more supportive research environments.

The complexity of the relations described above, and the lack of any evidence of directional causality in the research means that any conclusions related to actions must be tentative. However, the fact that there are relations of the sort described above does suggest possible interventions that, without such relations, would not otherwise be worth trying.

Most doctoral programmes do not explicitly address, with students, their conceptions of, and approaches to research. Even if supervisors or departments are aware that there is variation in how students conceive and approach research, the 'appropriate path' is usually left to the student to find. The evidence presented here suggests that discussion of such topics may lead to students adopting the more desirable holistic approaches to research, just as helping coursework students become aware of the variation in approach to learning helps them adopt more meaningful approaches.

Doctoral students who do experience supportive research environments are more likely to be more satisfied with the quality of their research experience and complete in a shorter time (Trigwell and Ashwin 2005). This has led to the adoption of intervention processes to change (enhance) students' perceptions of their research environment, particularly their departmental intellectual climate, general infrastructure support and supervision arrangements. Given the relationships described in this chapter, the development of more holistic approaches to research may also assist in changing perceptions of the research context, and in the development of key research skills.

Notes

1 It should be noted that in theoretical scientific fields students may experience isolation (for example, see mathematics doctoral students in New Zealand).

References

Bazeley, P. (1999). Continuing research by PhD graduates. *Higher Education Quarterly*, 53(4), 333–52.

Chiang, I. (2003). Learning experiences of doctoral students in UK universities. *Internaional Journal of Sociology and Social Policy*, 23(1/2), 4–32.

Holdaway, E., Debois, C., and Winchester, I. (1995). Supervision of Graduate Students. *The Canadian Journal of Higher Education*, 25(3), 1–29.

Marsh, H., Rowe, K. and Martin, A. (2002) Phd Students' evaluations of research supervisors, *Journal of Higher Education*, 73(33): 13–34.

Prosser, M. and Trigwell, K. (1999) *Understanding Learning and Teaching: The Experience in Higher Education*. Buckingham: SRHE and Open University Press

Ramsden, P. (1991) A performance indicator of teaching quality in higher education: The Course Experience Questionnaire. *Studies in Higher Education*, 16, 129–50.

Ramsden, P., Conrad, L., Ginns, P., and Prosser, M. (2003, August). *Students' and Supervisors' Experiences of the Context for Postgraduate Study*. Paper presented at the 10th Conference of the European Association for Research into Learning and Instruction, Padua.

Appendix

Table A23.1 Questionnaire items, scales and scale reliabilities (response 1 = strongly disagree, 5 = strongly agree), R = reverse scored

Supervision (response range 1–5) (alpha=0.86) (Arts 0.85; Sci 0.86)
5. My supervisor(s) make(s) a real effort to understand difficulties I face
13. Research supervision is available when I need it
18. I am given good guidance in topic selection and refinement
22. My research supervision provides me with helpful feedback on my progress
26. I have received good guidance in my literature search

Skill Development (response range 1–5) (alpha=0.76) (Arts 0.76; Sci 0.79)
4. I have developed an awareness of the wider research community in my field
7. My postgraduate research studies have helped me to develop a range of communication skills
9. My postgraduate research studies have helped to develop my awareness of what I need to manage my own career progression
11. As a result of my research, I have developed the ability to work collaboratively with other researchers
14. My research has sharpened my analytical skills
17. As a result of my postgraduate research studies, I feel confident about managing a research project
30. As a result of my research, I have developed the ability to learn independently

Departmental Intellectual Climate (response range 1–5) (alpha=0.88) (Arts 0.88; Sci 0.87)
3. The department/faculty provides opportunities for social contact with other postgraduate students

(continued on the next page)

Table A23.1 (continued)

8.   I feel integrated into the research community in the department/faculty
15.   The department/faculty provides opportunities for me to become involved in the broader research culture
16.   I feel that other postgraduate students in my department/faculty are supportive
20.   I tend to feel isolated within this department/faculty (reversed)
23.   Interaction with other postgraduate students is actively encouraged in my department
24.   A good seminar programme for postgraduate students is provided
25.   The research ambience in the department stimulates my work
29.   I feel that this department provides a supportive working environment
31.   I feel respected as a fellow researcher within my department/faculty

General Infrastructure (response range 1–5) (alpha=0.59) (Arts 0.62; Sci 0.53)

1.   The library facilities at Oxford support my research
10.   I have access to a common room or a similar type of meeting place
27.   I manage to find conditions for studying which allow me to get on with my work easily
33.   The university administration is effective in supporting my research
34.   I was satisfied with the admission and enrolment processes
36.   Complaints handling procedures are clear to me

Departmental Infrastructure (response range 1–5) (alpha=0.72) (Arts 0.68; Sci 0.67)

2.   I have access to a suitable working space
6.   I am able to organize good access to necessary equipment
12.   I have good access to the technical support I need
19.   I have good access to computing facilities and services in my department
28.   There is appropriate financial support for research activities in the department
32.   The department administration is effective in supporting my research

Overall Satisfaction (response range 1–5)

37.   Overall, I am satisfied with the quality of the services and facilities
38.   Overall, I am satisfied with the quality of my research supervision
39.   Overall, I am satisfied with the quality of my research experience

Table A23.2 Questionnaire items, scales and scale reliabilities

Approach to Research (response range 1-5) (alpha=0.68) (Arts 0.67; Sci 0.70)

49.   I see my research as contributing in some way to 'big picture' issues
50.   I usually try to discuss with others new ideas I have in my research
53.   When I'm working on a research topic, I try to see in my own mind how all the ideas fit together
54.   Ideas that arise in my research often set me off on chains of thought of my own
57.   Often I find myself wondering whether the work I am doing here is really worthwhile (R)
58.   It is important to me that my research is well integrated with existing knowledge and topics in the field
59.   I feel as if I do not have sufficient control over the direction of my research (R)

24

Educating the doctoral student

Don't forget the teaching

T. Harland

On the fringe of the current debate over how best to educate doctoral students are concerns about how we prepare our future academics. At present we seem to do half the job because research education is still the principle vehicle for training teachers in higher education (Harris 1996). We all know this to be true but it is surprising how uncontentious the idea is. Just try it in another context and see how it works because doctors are trained in medicine, solicitors in law and so on. Learning one trade in order to practise in another does not make much sense except, apparently, in higher education where we have PhD students trained as researchers who then take up posts as university lecturers and become teachers. Because the modern university lecturer is simultaneously involved in the production and dissemination of knowledge, an education for doctoral students in both may be necessary for epistemological reasons as well as preventing later distortions of academic practice. Knowledge creation separated from the broader knowledge project changes the nature of the relationship and is likely to constrain intellectual development (see Beck and Young 2005), and a discrete education in research creates strong boundaries between research and teaching that may take many years to overcome.

Yet the situation higher education finds itself in is complex because many postgraduate students do teach when they are learning about research and consequently bring some experience to their lectureship. There has also been much effort over the past decade or so to support the professional development of new academics in their teaching role. Parts of these programmes have filtered down to the stage of postgraduate study although most initiatives tend to be limited in what they can provide.

The recent additions and changes to the traditional three-year doctorate do not help the case for teaching much as they are driven largely by economic and political rather than epistemological and professional development concerns (Barnacle 2005; Craswell 2007). Arguments for change and improvement tend to follow a similar pattern. First, more students wish to do a PhD and many will choose careers outside of research or academia. Second, the world is changing and uncertain and so educated people need to be flexible and innovative if they are to respond to this. These changes have required new forms of political control over the PhD to ensure that it fits within current neo-liberal free market ideological aspirations and the focus is on highly trained 'knowledge workers' for the 'knowledge economy'. Governments and their representative agencies now manage many aspects of the PhD such as completion times, quality assurance and even which topics should receive funding. To meet this agenda universities have to be more flexible, make sure the PhD is fit for purpose and be prepared to respond to different stakeholders that include employers and the nation (Park 2007). Park (2007: 8) defines benefits for the nation as 'enhanced creativity and innovation, and the development of a skilled workforce and of the intellectual capital and knowledge transfer, which drives the knowledge economy and are engines of the growth of cultural capital'.

Of course, such ideas about what the 'nation' wants are reasonable yet they dominate debate about doctoral study and because of this there is a danger that other voices are silenced. For example, there is relatively little interest in reforming postgraduate study in terms of teaching or recognising it as an authentic apprentice route into academia. Teaching gets an honourable mention in most commissioned reports on doctoral study and many universities now have tutor training programmes that recognise the postgraduate contribution to teaching (e.g. Hopwood and Stocks 2008). But little more is done. Even the more integrated Preparing Future Faculty schemes of North America (Richlin 1995) are limited and have not gained the wide support that might have been expected.

The employability argument also needs re-examining because the major employer of doctoral students is still academia, with nearly half of UK PhD students pursuing an academic career (UK GRAD 2004), and in the USA, more than half take up posts in universities and colleges (Boyer Commission 1998). So does doctoral study meet higher education's own professional needs? It seems reasonable to expect that all new academics should have a level of competence in both teaching and research before they take up their first post, and in this chapter I will try to make a case for educating postgraduates in this way, provide some examples in which learning about research and learning about teaching benefit the doctoral student, and show that for those wishing to make a career in academia we can provide a full and authentic learning experience through an apprentice–academic pathway.

The doctoral student as teacher

Many postgraduate students teach during doctoral study and even though this tends to be in a teaching assistant role and often limited in both time and scope, their experiences provide some insight into how this work impacts on learning, teaching and research.

To begin, it is worth restating that teaching in many universities would not be sustainable without the help of postgraduate teachers (Holt 1999). At my own university it has been estimated that 43 per cent of postgraduate students teach and that 50 per cent of these spend between six and 10 hours per week on teaching and 21 per cent more than 11 hours per week (Harland and Plangger 2004). These teachers may not have the vast knowledge of the more experienced lecturer but they can be up to date in certain areas and also offer something different for students. For example, their contribution includes a distinct understanding of student learning needs because they are typically closer in age and experience to the learner, providing support through informal mentoring and getting round hierarchical barriers that can exist between students and academic staff (Harland and Plangger 2004).

Postgraduate student-teachers feel disadvantaged by a shortage of disciplinary knowledge probably because declarative forms of knowledge dominate thinking about educational purposes. Other conceptions are less common, for example, the idea of teaching as 'making learning possible' rather than 'passing on expert knowledge'. In the first conception, the real worth of the educational experience for the learner comes from understanding the processes of how thinking comes about.

It is not only the 'results' of enquiry – the facts and theories – that the university should teach. Rather, the very object of enquiry should be to find out how thought can do better (Anderson 1993: 59).

This idea is remarkably similar to the underlying epistemology of research education, yet learning about research and teaching are still seen as different, partly because of the instrumental views that are commonly held about what teaching is. Doctoral students need a much deeper understanding of the purposes of their teaching as they acquire new skills and knowledge (Muzaka 2009). They may also need to accommodate the idea that although research and teaching are separate organisational features of higher education, the boundaries between them will blur depending on various role constraints and the orientation of the academic at a particular time. The example of the research seminar may illustrate this point. When a seminar is 'given' it is not usual to think of this as an act of teaching peers and knowledge is typically presented in a traditional, authoritative and didactic way. When the same knowledge is taken to undergraduate students (probably in a revised form) it becomes 'teaching' and may then even interfere with research. However, if the academic's purpose was to develop new thinking in both situations, then the differences between the seminar and class might diminish. In a case study that examined the experiences of novice postgraduate teachers it was found that boundaries between academic activities were not always clearly understood (Harland and Plangger 2004). In the extract in Box 24.1 June, who has just completed her PhD, reflects on her teaching.

June clearly values both research and teaching and as she comes to terms with the complexity of academic practice, she reflects on her own learning and how research and teaching come together. Other students from the same study saw the opportunity to teach as providing a 'refuge from research' because it created a safe space in which to try out research ideas and rehearse arguments, and teaching also opened up the possibility for developing relationships as part of a wider community without the pressures and competitiveness that characterise research cultures. Yet teaching as 'telling' and a teacher-centred view of practice was typical for this novice group and such narrow conceptions will limit educational opportunities for the learner and there is further risk if such ideas are taken uncritically into academic life.

It was also surprising how quickly this group of postgraduate teachers adopted the norms and values of the academic profession, and the 'academic as researcher' was clearly inspirational. This powerful image is likely to be re-enforced over time because the logic of teaching for the doctoral student reflects a deficit model (Craswell 2007; Shulman *et al.* 2006). Any time away from research study subtracts from the research experience and this situation mirrors how some experienced academics feel about teaching and its relation to research in higher education. Teaching is seen to *interfere* with research and postgraduates need *permission* to spend time on any activities other than research.

Many small-scale initiatives support postgraduate students as teachers to address some of these concerns about learning to teach and professional academic formation (Lueddeke 1997; Smith and Bath 2004; Park 2004; Hopwood and Stocks 2008). However, it is likely that the majority of these programmes are limited in scope and seen by students as something separate or additional to their research commitments. Although teaching experience positions the doctoral student in a different form of professional education

Box 24.1.

June: …the pressure for tutors to teach sometimes outweighs their own research. It does in an incredible amount. You can't tutor and do research at the same time. I think. And that's a sorry state for the culture of research actually. [ ] And I would have to say that last year I was senior tutor for the 100 level course in the second semester and in the first semester for the 200 and 300 level courses. I didn't have time for my own research. I didn't have time to maintain a sort of postgraduate environment under those conditions.

Interviewer: Why did you continue teaching?

June: Because it's — that's a really good question. Part of the professional development of being a PhD student is to also have the opportunity to teach and administer. And do administration work, so that is part of the professional development of a PhD student, which is as important as the research. You know, to get up the CV, the profile, to get teaching experience and that's why I did it. Because it was suggested to me that this is a good way to get experience. And it was a good experience. [ ] Very stressing time, but a wonderful opportunity. And that actually fed into my research.

Interviewer: How?

June: … having to teach these texts gave me the opportunity to learn at a phenomenal rate. Rather than just reading and writing about them. It's about communicating with the students, these complex ideas and having to understand them before you can relay them to the students. So teaching is very much part of my own learning plan for research. Teaching in my own paper this year was very much – very much feeding into my own research because like trying out these ideas, seeing how the students respond and you know reacting to that – those very real responses. So no, incredibly, incredibly valuable teaching experience. I must not forget that. I mean when I think about the bad side of things.

Interviewer: Were you teaching or researching there?

June: It's interesting isn't it? Research is about talking with peers. Isn't it? If I'm at a conference I'm talking to my peers about my research and we're talking at a particular level. Whereas teaching is, that power dynamic. 'One is the teacher' and 'one is the taught'.

(Pearson 1996), at present we do not fully understand the impact of this. Furthermore, when a future academic is set on the path of teacher-as-learner during doctoral study we still know little of the impacts of this on later professional life.

The doctoral student as academic apprentice

In the late 1990s the Carnegie Foundation proposed that all doctoral students should be educated in both research and teaching as apprentice academics (Boyer Commission 1998) and similar arguments have been made by Barrington (1999) and Austin (2002). There is some evidence that PhD supervisors do view their students as apprentices

(Muzaka 2009), but the term seems to be used loosely. In a genuine apprenticeship, new skills and knowledge are acquired in authentic situations of practice where expertise is used to guide the learner as they integrate the different dimensions of practice over time. It is, therefore, a social practice, often done side by side with a more experienced practitioner. Such a condition exists for the research dimension of doctoral study but not typically for teaching, at either postgraduate level or when the new academic is in post. If we take the extreme case, a new lecturer without any teaching experience can start to teach and then spend their whole career without any form of teacher-education. It is staggering to think how private teaching can be and the idea of the self-taught teacher must raise concerns about impact on student learning experiences.

If PhD supervisors educated their students in both research and teaching they could claim that they were providing an apprenticeship, although the student might also risk becoming encultured into a narrow set of expectations if the supervisor does not have the expertise to provide this education. However, such an objection would diminish over time as each generation of academics gained more experience in both teaching and in helping others to learn about it. In the modern apprenticeship it is also quite usual for the learner to be exposed to different teachers (e.g. learning on the job and learning from day release at college) and there is a strong case for arguing that the supervisor and student can be supported within a wider academic community and draw on others' experiences. This is often the case for research education, for example, the student may attend a graduate school or research methods course, and the principle of accessing appropriate expertise may be important for learning about teaching in any full apprentice-academic pathway.

One such initiative that could claim to provide an authentic apprenticeship experience is the Postgraduate Certificate in Higher Education at the University of Sheffield, UK, which began in 1996. This initiative is described more fully elsewhere (Harland 2001; Harland and Scaife in press) but, in brief, doctoral students from any discipline who intend to embark on an academic career can take a two-year part-time qualification in university teaching, which is integrated within their research programme. The concept explicitly supports the development of the academic as both researcher and teacher and after three years, students graduate with two degree awards, a postgraduate certificate in teaching and a PhD.

The PCHE uses a multi-disciplinary approach to learning and students join a new group outside their department whose members have a common interest in becoming academics. There are practical benefits as they learn about teaching through researching their practice and, as dual researchers in two distinct fields (their subject and the pedagogy of their subject); they enhance their skills as effective writers, problem solvers and critical thinkers (see Boyer Commission 1998). Yet the development of students as both teachers and researchers during the PCHE has been more profound than might be expected. New relationships reduce feelings of isolation common to new researchers and different discourses emerge that are not accessible to students in their home departments, mainly because of the dominant academic research culture of the university and power differences between the student, their supervisors and other academic staff. In the PCHE students find a spiritual home in a peer community whose members recognise the importance of each others' commitment to both teaching and research. In addition, because the programme takes a constructivist perspective, learning becomes recognised as a central component of teaching that begins to connect the processes of teaching and researching. The idea is that learning to teach and learning to research are similar activities, that enquiry binds everything and that no 'transfer of learning' is necessary because the whole of the student's practice becomes integrated; as they teach they are learners, as they research they are learners. In addition, the reflexive nature of the PCHE ensures that students understand they are creating knowledge as they learn about teaching by studying the world that they are experiencing (Harland and Scaife in press).

The main objections to the PCHE apprenticeship have largely stemmed from compliance concerns where supervisors have been worried about late completion of PhD theses and the financial penalties that this can incur. Yet the data gathered each year since 1996 have shown that postgraduates can do both the PCHE and a doctorate within the allotted timeframe and this mounting evidence may serve to alleviate such fears in the future (Harland and Scaife in press). One research supervisor commented:

> The time spent on this course, which has been substantial, has actually given him space to think about research. Working towards a very different qualification from the PhD has become help rather than a hindrance. Thus the PhD and PCHE work well alongside each other.
>
> (Harland 2001: 273)

Muzaka (2009) points out that the PCHE has selective entry and only serves a limited number of potential doctoral students who wish to become academics. However, it does provide a working model of an authentic apprenticeship.

Conclusion

The debate on doctoral education is mainly concerned with how higher education is changing to meet the needs of the world of work. In my argument, I am attempting to capture what Craswell (2007: 378) terms the 'employability debate' by suggesting that the higher education sector should also make the experience of doctoral study more relevant for those who wish to work within its own institutions. This idea has not received as much attention as it deserves, despite the fact that higher education is still the major employer of doctoral students.

There are initiatives to help postgraduates as teachers and the graduate schools of the USA, UK and Australia sometimes organise teaching support (Poole and Spear 1997) and alternative routes to obtaining a PhD may have an elective skills component that can include learning about teaching (New Route PhD 2009). Postgraduates on traditional three-year doctorates may also get access to professional development support in order to enhance their skills in teaching, and universities typically provide this in the general form of tutor training workshops (e.g. Smith and Bath 2004). Without this bare minimum of provision, novice student teachers are clearly at risk and we also need to keep in mind that many postgraduate students will not experience *any* teaching before they become lecturers. For example, 57 per cent at the University of Otago (Harland and Plangger 2004) and about 33 per cent at the University of Oxford (Hopwood and Stocks 2008) complete their doctoral studies in this way.

Through apprenticeship we can help future university lecturers acquire a critical rationale for their teaching; this would radically alter higher education as successive generations of academics offered higher levels of expertise in both teaching and research at the start of their careers. Lecturers would no longer be typecast as expert researchers and accidental teachers. However, the influential Carnegie Foundation made this suggestion 12 years ago and there has been little reported uptake of the idea. The traditional doctorate has resisted serious challenge (Park 2005; Boud and Tennant 2006) and over many years academia has provided a standard model of the professional research scholar and distributed it throughout the system (Anderson 1993: 7). It is difficult to see how this will change. Inertia might be partly explained by the fact that no institution, professional body or government agency seems to be responsible for doctoral study (Park 2007), and therefore no one appears to have a mandate for change. The present award is clearly highly valued by the powerful research intensive universities and these institutions set the standard for academic norms that others seek to imitate (Marginson and Considine 2000). Teaching is also a private space that the academy finds difficult to breach and Manathunga (2005) argues that supervision can be seen in a similar way.

Supervisors might do well to question their role in relation to supporting PhD students as teachers, in terms of mentoring them when they are teaching assistants, preparing them as future academics and working out how teaching can benefit doctoral research. Boud and Tennant (2006) suggest that cultural change for new forms of doctoral education will not come from outside but from supervisors who are prepared to build communities with shared goals, rather than structural imposition of new ways of working.

The concept of the apprentice-academic has a clear logic for the contemporary university lecturer. The traditional three-year doctoral research programme may have once been adequate to prepare lecturers when higher education was the province of a few elite members of society, but since the worldwide neoliberal reform of higher education that gathered pace in the 1980s and 1990s, we now have a changed academy. Student demographics provide huge challenges for the university lecturer who is now required to teach larger classes, a broader range of abilities and students from different backgrounds. Teaching is no longer an amateur business and if we want to educate *all* students (Elton 2000) we need a highly skilled teaching workforce to do this. Doctoral students themselves understand that there is a moral obligation to provide undergraduates with trained, knowledgeable teachers (Hopwood and Stocks 2008) and undergraduates are beginning to demand this as they have been recast as paying customers with their lecturers as service providers.

Even though a model for an authentic apprenticeship is available, this is still very much on the periphery of higher education and it might not be convincing enough for the academic community to consider seriously, even though the postgraduates from the Sheffield initiative go on to work in academia and there is evidence that their experience enhances research, teaching and professional practice. Finally, we often seem to forget that research supervision is also a form of teaching and many of the present doctoral students will soon be part of the new generation of supervisors who in turn will need to teach their own doctoral students. Will they be educating researchers or future academics? How will the PCHE apprentices approach this?

References

Anderson, C.W. (1993) *Prescribing the life of the mind. An essay on the purposes of the university, the aims of liberal education, the competence of citizens, and the cultivation of practical reason.* Madison, WI: The University of Wisconsin Press.

Austin, A. E. (2002) Preparing the next generation of faculty. Graduate school as socialization to the academic career, *Journal of Higher Education*, 73(1): 94–122.

Barnacle, R. (2005) Research education ontologies: exploring doctoral becoming, *Higher Education Research and Development*, 24(2): 179–88.

Barrington, E. *Catching Academic Staff at the Start: Professional Development for University Tutors*. Paper presented at Higher Education Research and Development Society of Australasia Annual Conference, Melbourne, July 1999. Online. (Available www.herdsa.org.au/wp-content/uploads/conference/1999/pdf/Barring.PDF Accessed 26 May 2009).

Beck, J. and Young, M. F. D. (2005) The assault on the professions and the restructuring of academic and professional identities: a Bernsteinian analysis, *British Journal of Sociology of Education*, 26(2): 183–97.

Boud, D. and Tennant, M. (2006) Putting doctoral education to work: challenges to academic practice, *Higher Education Research and Development*, 25(3): 293–306.

Boyer Commission (1998) *The Boyer Commission on Educating Undergraduates in the Research University. Reinventing Undergraduate Education: A Blueprint for America's Research Universities*. New York: Stoney Brook.

Craswell, G. (2007) Deconstructing the skills training debate in doctoral education, *Higher Education Research and Development*, 26(4): 377–91.

Elton, L. (2000) Turning academics into teachers: a discourse of love, *Teaching in Higher Education*, 5(2): 257–60.

Harland, T. (2001) Pre-service teacher education for university lecturers. The academic apprentice, *Journal of Education for Teaching: International Research and Pedagogy*, 27(3): 269–76.

Harland, T. and Plangger, G. (2004) The postgraduate chameleon: changing roles in doctoral education, *Active Learning in Higher Education*, 5(1): 73–86.

Harland, T and Scaife, J. A. (in press) Academic apprenticeship. In T. Kerry (Ed.) *Meeting the Challenges of Change in Postgraduate Education*. London: Continuum.

Harris, M. (1996) *Review of postgraduate education*. London: Higher Education Funding Council for England.

Holt, S. (1999) *Preparing postgraduates to teach in higher education*. Coventry: Council for Graduate Education.

Hopwood, N. and Stocks, C. (2008) Teaching development for doctoral students: what can we learn from activity theory?, *International Journal of Academic Development*, 13(3): 187–98.

Lueddeke, G. R. (1997) Training postgraduates for teaching: considerations for programme planning and development, *Teaching in Higher Education*, 2(2): 141–51.

Manathunga, C. (2005) The development of research supervision: turning the light on a private space, *International Journal for Academic Development*, 10(1): 17–30.

Marginson, S. and Considine, M. (2000) *The enterprise university. Power, governance and reinvention in Australia*. Cambridge: Cambridge University Press.

Muzaka, V. (2009) The niche of graduate teaching assistants (GTA's): perceptions and reflections, *Teaching in Higher Education*, 14(1): 1–12.

NewRoute PhD (2009). Online. (Available at www.newroutephd.ac.uk/ Accessed 26 May 2009).

Park, C. (2004) The graduate teaching assistant (GTA), lessons from North American experience, *Teaching in Higher Education*, 9(3): 349–61.

——(2005) New variant PhD: the changing nature of the doctorate in the UK, *Journal of Higher Education Policy and Management*, 27(2): 189–207.

——(2007) *Redefining the doctorate*. York: Higher Education Academy.

Pearson, M. (1996) Professionalising PhD education to enhance the quality of the student experience, *Higher Education*, 32: 303–20.

Poole, M. E. and Spear, R. H. (1997) Policy issues in postgraduate education: An Australian perspective. In R. G. Burgess (Ed.). *Beyond the first degree. Graduate education, lifelong learning and careers*. Buckingham: The Society for Research in Higher Education and Open University Press.

Richlin, L. (1995) Preparing the faculty of the future to teach. In W. A. Wright (Ed.). *Teaching improvement practices*. Bolton: Anker Publishing Company Inc.

Shulman, L. S., Golde, C. M., Bueschel, A. C. and Garabedian, K. J. (2006) Reclaiming education's doctorates: a critique and a proposal, *Educational Researcher*, April: 25–32.

Smith, C. and Bath, D. (2004) Evaluation of a university-wide strategy providing staff development for tutors: effectiveness, relevance and local impact, *Mentoring and Tutoring*, 12(1): 107–22.

UK GRAD (2004) *What do PhD's do? A regional analysis*. Cambridge: UK GRAD.

Index

Abbott, A. 222
about this book: acknowledgements 5–6; ambitions and understandings 4–5; becoming a researcher 2; organisation 3–4; purpose of 1–3
abstract spaces of disciplines 185, 187, 189–90
academic activities, boundaries between 294–95
academic apprentices, doctoral students as 295–96, 297–98
academic competence 294
academic conventionality 222–23
academic literacies 154–55; problems with 139
academic writing: appropriateness in, issue of 154–55; assumptions about 155; culling and maiming written work 64; doctoral writing, talking about 43–44; narrative writing, developments in 247–48; reflective writing by multilingual students 138–39; writing as enquiry method 83–84; see also doctoral writing groups
Acker, S. 177
Acker, S. et al. 39
Adams, Douglas 240
advisory relationships 144
Agunga, R. and Belcher, D. 143
Aims and Ambitions for Lifelong Learning (Cologne Charter) 22
Aitchison, C. 262, 264, 266, 268
Aitchison, C. and Lee, A. 260, 266, 267, 268
Aitchison, C. et al. 260
Alguire, P.C. 115
ambivalence 100–101, 102
Anderson, C.W. 294, 298
Anderson, N. and Henderson, M. 82
Andrews, D. and Edwards, C. 19, 20, 34
Annaud, Jean-Jacques 241
Antes, T. 62

anxiety, experience in doctoral process of 209, 210, 213
Appadurai, A. 161, 162, 198
Arnot, M. 249
Aronowitz, S. and Giroux, H. 15
Asera, Rose 118
Aspin, D.N. 22
Aspland, T. 152
assessment: burden of 264; criteria for, issue of 151; doctoral assessment, formalisation of 251; forms of 173; observation and 39; politics of 42; problematic assessments 85; quality assessment 40
Atkinson, D. 155
audiences 80; and explanations, matching of 216
Audran, Marîd 243n18
Auster, Paul 240, 244n22
Austin, A.E. 296
Australia: doctoral education in 10, 12; doctoral education in, relocation of 220–22; House of Representatives Standing Committee on Industry, Science and Innovation 67–68, 71
authenticity: authentic professional learning 77–78; and truth, questions of 233–34
authority: challenges to, inability to mount 43, 107; modes of power and 63; and power of teacher 102; supervisor as knowing authority 91, 93, 102, 267

Bachelard, G. 190
Bakhtin, M. 78
Ball, S. 5, 41
Banks, J. 197
Barnacle, R. 292
Barnacle, R. and Dall'Alba, G. 20
Barnacle, R. and Usher, R. 72
Barnett, R. 16, 18, 23

Wissler, Rod 84

Wodak, R. 264

A Woman's Guide to Doctoral Studies (Leonard, D.) 254

women, motherhood and role of 250–51

Woolf, Virginia 191, 192

work and study, integration of 136

working relationships 88, 133–34

workplace studies 39

The World is Flat (Friedman, T.) 164

Wright, I. and Lodwick, R. 177

Wright, T. and Cochrane, R. 125

writing: as enquiry method 83–84; narrative writing, developments in 247–48; research on, doctoral education and 154–55; written work of part-time doctoral students 134–35; *see also* academic writing

Wu, S. 152

Yates, L. 3, 11

Yuval-Davis, Nira 201

Zadja, J. *et al.* 201

Zhao, F. 279

Zizek, Slavoj 235, 236, 237

DATE DUE

WITHDRAWN

GAYLORD   PRINTED IN U.S.A.

LB 2372 .E3 R683 2010

The Routledge doctoral supervisor's companion